What People Are Saying About the Better Communications™ Reader-Centered Writing Approach

We won the largest switch sale in AT&T's history as a result of your recommendations.
—Bob Clark, President, Pacific West, Lucent Technologies, Inc. (formerly AT&T)

This customer-focused writing style may be the missing link in our quality improvement process.
—Chuck Ray, V.P., Xerox Corporation

If people would write to me in the Better Communications style, I could cut my reading time by 50%.
—Tom Wagner, V.P., Ford Motor Company

Our customers noticed the difference immediately. They asked who had helped us improve our proposals. Now they're working with Better Communications, too.
—Gary Collier, Manager, EDS Corporation

Time is money. Cutting writing time by 50% more than pays for the course.
—Steve Hochman, Product Marketing Engineer, Intel

The time spent in this course was an excellent long-term investment.
—Pamela Rogal, V.P., Fidelity Investments

You are changing Xerox culture.
—Pat Dugan, Practice Manager, Xerox Corporation

The Six Steps to Reader-Centered Writing™ immediately improved my writing skills. I am now able to create a document in a fraction of the time I used to spend.
—Judd Andres, Manager, Bristol-Meyers Squibb

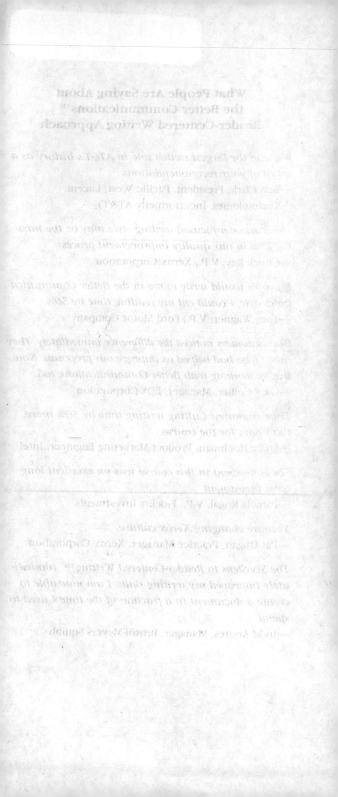

What People Are Saying About the Better Communications™ Reader-Centered Writing Approach

"Ranks as the largest single sale in AT&T's history as a result of your recommendations."
— Bob Clark, President, Pacific West Lucent
   Technologies, Inc. (formerly AT&T)

"Reader-centered writing may may be the most ... This is the only quality improvement process ..."
— Buck Ray, V.P., Xerox approach

"I could not wait for one of the Better Communications ... Now I could cut my reading time by 50%."
— Tom Wagner, V.P., Ford Motor Company

"Customers notice the difference immediately. They ... now had helped us change our programs. Now it's ... working with Better Communications and ..."
— ... Collier, Manager, EDS Corporation

"More effective ... writing than by 50% more ... than I got for the course."
— Steve Bechmann, Product Marketing Engineer, Intel

"... excellent an excellent long ..."
— Pamela Royal, V.P., Fidelity Investments

"You are changing Xerox culture."
— Pat Hogan, Practice Manager, Xerox Corporation

"The Six Steps to Reader-Centered Writing™ is amazingly ... able to structure my writing skills. I am now able to create a document in a fraction of the time I used to spend."
— Linda Andres, Manager, Bristol-Myers Squibb

Vest-Pocket Guide to BUSINESS WRITING

The Instant-Answer Source for Today's Business Writer

by **Deborah Dumaine** and the Better Communications Team, the authors of the best-selling **WRITE TO THE TOP**™

PRENTICE HALL
Paramus, New Jersey 07652

Library of Congress Cataloging-in-Publication Data

Dumaine, Deborah.
  Vest-pocket guide to business writing : Deborah Dumaine.
    p. cm.
  Includes index.
    ISBN 0-13-440348-7 (pbk.), 0-13-614264-8 (pbk.),
  0-13-440355-X (lexotone)
    1. Business writing—Handbooks, manuals, etc.
  2. Commercial correspondence—Handbooks, manuals,
  etc. 3. English language—Business English—Handbooks,
  manuals, etc. I. Title.
  HF5718.3.D846   1996   96-559
  808′.06665—dc20   CIP

Printed in the United States of America

10 9 8 7 6 5   (P)

10 9 8 7 6 5 4 3 2 (P)

10 9 8 7 6 5 4 3 2 (L)

ISBN 0-13-440348-7 (P)
ISBN 0-13-614264-8 (P)
ISBN 0-13-440355-X (L)

PRENTICE HALL
Paramus, NJ 07652

A Simon & Schuster Company

On the World Wide Web at http://www.phdirect.com

Prentice-Hall International (UK) Limited, *London*
Prentice-Hall of Australia Pty. Limited, *Sydney*
Prentice-Hall Canada Inc., *Toronto*
Prentice-Hall Hispanoamericana, S.A., *Mexico*
Prentice-Hall of India Private Limited, *New Delhi*
Prentice-Hall of Japan, Inc., *Tokyo*
Simon & Schuster Asia Pte. Ltd., *Singapore*
Editora Prentice-Hall do Brasil, Ltda., *Rio de Janeiro*

**Dedicated to Better Communications'
customers, who have proven that strategic
writing gives them a measurable advantage**

Special thanks to our customers, from whom we learn as much as we teach.

Amgen, Inc.
AT&T
Baxter Healthcare Corporation
Bell Atlantic
Biogen, Inc.
Boston Gas Company
Colonial Investment Services, Inc.
Dana Corporation
Digital Equipment Corporation
Dun & Bradstreet
Eastman Kodak
EDS Corporation
Federal Reserve Banks
Fidelity Investments
The First National Bank of Boston
Ford Motor Company
Genentech, Inc.
General Motors Corporation
Genzyme Corporation
The Gillette Company
GTE Corporation
Hewlett-Packard Company
Hewitt Associates
Hoechst Celanese Corporation
Jaguar Cars North America
Massachusetts Institute of Technology
MCA, Inc.
MCI Telecommunications Corporation
Medco Containment Services, Inc.
Millipore Corporation
New York State Government
Panhandle Eastern Corporation
Parker Brothers
Polaroid Corporation
Rhone-Poulenc Rorer
The Royal Bank of Canada
Tambrands, Inc.
United States Department of Transportation
UNUM Life Insurance Company of America
Warner-Lambert Company
Xerox Corporation

About Better Communications™ Inc.

A leading document consulting and training company since 1978

The Better Communications team updates the writing skills of more than 5,000 corporate people each year. Through its *Write to the Top*™ **Workshops** and **Document Consulting**, the company is redefining corporate writing. Clients like Xerox—The Document Company—say Better Communications is changing their culture by transforming *their* documents.

Documents that command customers' attention

Better Communications' clients consistently see that *their* customers prefer *Write to the Top* documents—and reach for them ahead of others competing for attention. These powerful new documents result from following the process outlined in this book: The Six Steps to Reader-Centered Writing™

Measurable productivity results

Better Communications is proud of its graduates' success:

- Over 70% of graduates estimate cutting writing time 30% to 50%.
- Readers estimate a 50% time savings—*Write to the Top* documents communicate twice as fast.

Better Communications offers

- **In-house Writing Workshops**, including:

sales	e-mail
customer service	technical
ISO/QS documentation	financial
train the trainer	basic/grammar

- **Document Consulting**—writing/editing solutions and assessment
- **Public Seminars**

How are companies benefiting?

- **Revenues increase** because documents sell products and ideas more effectively.
- **Costs decrease** because documents are immediately transformed from productivity drains to quantifiable productivity enhancers.
- **Customers receive greater value** because daily documents confirm a company's quality commitment.

**Please let us know
your response to this book.**

Better Communications Inc.
1666 Massachusetts Avenue
Lexington, Massachusetts 02173
Phone: 617.862.3800   Fax: 617.862.8383
e-mail: workshops@bettercom.com
World Wide Web:
http://www.bettercom.com/bettercom

Table of Contents

Acknowledgments

Since 1978, our team of writing consultants has helped develop the skills of over 30,000 corporate people. In this book, we've gathered practical document strategies from many worlds: sales, technical, finance, manufacturing, and more.

The breakthroughs our customers have made are all shared with you here: proposal tactics that have won major business for the Fortune 500, customer letters that have turned around irritated customers, internal memos that have driven productive action.

Many members of the Better Communications team contributed at different times.

- Thanks first to Kathy Smith, who put in countless difficult hours writing and researching the entries on editing, mechanics, and grammar. She worked patiently to make sure that every rule was clarified for the business writer. She assembled the core of writing fundamentals that support this book and any strategic document.

- Barbara Blanchard, former leader of Better Communications' instructional development, shared her advice on writing for publication and helped enormously as a conceptual editor. Her boundless energy kept the project alive when other priorities pressed.

- Larissa Hordynsky is one of the most impeccable wordsmiths I know. She could always find one more edit to improve the manuscript, no matter how many eyes had approved it. She is one of those rare writers who can work at both the highest and most minute levels with equal ease.

- Caroline Sutton, an author in her own right, wrote many entries and offered thoughtful advice and research on advanced writing issues. She was always patient in offering an opinion about book decisions day or night.

- Sandra Mitchell took over the complexities of the final advanced formatting. In the process her editorial advice proved invaluable as well.

- Sandra Boncek, an emerging writer and Better Communications' curriculum administrator, added many valuable entries, such as *project planning charts* and *electronic mail*.

- Marya Danihel was one of our key editors. As a top Better Communications instructor, she found many ways to insert her wisdom into this reference tool.

Special entry writers

Barbara Blanchard	Mark Hochman
Peter Gerler	Larissa Hordynsky
Dianne Palter Gill	Linda Mitchell
Patricia Hamilton	Sandra Simpson

Graphs and charts experts

Marianne Robberts, Professor of IS at Bentley College, writer

Joe Kelley, Government Finance Officers Association, editor

Mark Hochman of Rath and Strong, editor

Readers

Jane Evanson
Patricia Hamilton
Marlene Johnson

The support team: proofing and manuscript preparation

Geri Blitzman	Amy Robillard
Johannah Davies	Helen Ryan
Jessica Forbes	

Donors of Model Documents for inspiration

Roger and Sally Demler
Mark Hochman
Michael Wolfe

Heroes

Deborah Daw, Vice President of Better Communications, for bringing the message of strategic writing to the world and for relentless process improvement at headquarters.

Barbara Blanchard and Larissa Hordynsky, for believing in this project in the face of countless challenges.

General supporters

Don Nepveu	Jon Holmes
Dennis Chambers	Donna Denison
the Better Communications staff	

How this book can help you

Since 1978 Better Communications Inc. of Boston has been training thousands of business people each year to write with greater clarity and impact. In scores of Fortune 1000 companies, Better Communications offers strategic advice on documents from reports to e-mail to proposals.

Four kinds of help

The *Vest Pocket Guide to Technical Writing* supports you in four key ways:

First, it offers a quality writing process designed specifically for anyone in business who writes—no matter how technical the document.

Better Communications has developed the Six-Steps to Reader-Centered Writing™ based on what the *reader* needs to know. The process breaks down any writing job into separate steps so that you can concentrate on one step at a time.

Second, the book contains clear instructions for writing a wide range of business and technical documents:

- strategies for writing attention-getting e-mail
- how to organize a formal report
- guidance on writing winning proposals
- sample formats and charts

Third, this book is a rich compendium of English grammar, usage, and syntax. From its workshops in diverse industries, Better Communications has pinpointed the most common problems people encounter in business writing and the errors they make most frequently.

This book helps you recognize those problems and understand clearly how to correct them.

Fourth, the book contains an appendix of model documents inspired by some of the most prominent corporations nationwide. You'll find over 20 examples of proposals, letters, and memos. By studying these, you'll see how our recommendations and guidelines can be put into action for best results.

How to find the information you need

The entries in this book are organized alphabetically so that you can easily turn to the help you require. Therefore, all entries—whether about document types, planning strategy, grammar, or punctuation—are easy to locate.

In addition, all entries are followed by a "See also..." section that leads you to further reading in this book on a particular topic.

The book contains a full index that will help you quickly find the information you need.

How to use this book to best advantage

First, read the Six Steps to Reader-Centered Writing™ either in preview form following or in depth in their separate entries (throughout the book) so that you understand this easy-to-follow process. Then consult the book again at any point in your writing.

It can help you overcome writer's block, choose a strategy for creating a persuasive document, decide on the most effective format for highlighting your ideas, and edit for impact. Since most of the book is devoted to tactics for editing a document, keep it by your desk for easy reference when questions of correctness arise.

Why are the Six Steps to Reader-Centered Writing™ invaluable?

Documents drive action—action that can create personal success. Skillful writing will advance you and your company. Writing is difficult if we don't have a process to follow.

Many of us get stuck and frustrated because we haven't understood our readers' needs correctly, or we have started editing before truly focusing our content. It is only logical, then, to divide the process into tasks that, taken one at a time, are easier to handle. The steps and their entry titles follow:

1. Analyze your audience and define your purpose (**readers, analyzing**)

2. Use a Start-up Strategy (**getting started with a Start-up Strategy**)

3. Group information under headlines (**grouping ideas**)

4. Sequence your ideas (**organizing information**)

5. Write the first draft (**draft writing**)

6. Edit for clarity, conciseness, and accuracy (**editing your draft**)

Using the Six Steps, thousands of graduates of Better Communications' workshops attest that they are reducing their writing time by 30% to 50%.

Equally significant: every day readers worldwide are choosing to pay attention to documents prepared with the Six Steps over competing documents because this method is built around the reader's needs and point of view. Those readers are cutting their reading time by half because information is presented succinctly and organized logically.

Following is a fuller explanation of the Six-Steps to Reader-Centered Writing™. Expanded versions appear in the text body, and references to the Six Steps are found in many entries throughout the book, wherever relevant.

Introduction to the Six Steps to Reader-Centered Writing™

Following is a brief summary of the Six-Step entries in the body of this book. Turn to them for greater depth and examples.

Step 1: Analyze your readers and define your purpose

The biggest error in business writing occurs when writers fail to consider their readers' needs. What could be difficult about asking yourself who your readers are and what they need? Yet business people we see daily skip this easy step and immediately lose their direction.

A brief but thoughtful picture of your reader is vital for communicating powerfully and clearly. As you bring your readers into focus, you will also be defining the tone and scope of your writing.

We have designed a Focus Sheet™ to help business and technical writers pinpoint their purpose and understand their readers' needs. We urge you to fill one out before you do any writing. It is the core of our writing process.

Focus Sheet

Step 1

Answer these questions as the first step in any writing task.

☞ Be sure to use these items for short documents.

1. Purpose:

☞ A. Why am I writing this? _____

☞ B. What do I want the reader to do? _____

2. Audience:

A. Who is my reader? Do I have more than one? _____

B. What is the reader's role? _____

C. What does the reader know about the subject? _____

D. How will the reader react? _____

E. What's in it for the reader? Why should the reader read this or agree with it? _____

F. How will the reader use this document? _____

G. Whom should I include in this mailing? _____

3. Bottom Line:

☞ If the reader were to forget everything else, what one key point do I want remembered? _____

4. Strategy:

A. Should *I* be writing this? At *this* time? Would a phone call or meeting be more effective?

B. Should I send this at all? Am I too late? Too early?

C. Is someone else communicating the same information? Should I check with that person?

D. Is my method of transmission the best? Should I be using e-mail, fax, or traditional mail?

The Focus Sheet has four components:

PURPOSE

Your task in business writing is usually to inspire an action or to convince someone to agree with you. If you begin by defining your purpose, you'll be able to make all the parts of your document work together to achieve it. Define your purpose with an action verb, such as "to persuade."

AUDIENCE

By thinking carefully about your readers, you will determine

- how much they need to know
- how technical you should be
- what tone—formal or friendly—you should use
- how they are likely to react and, consequently, how persuasive you need to be.

BOTTOM LINE

Define the most essential point you wish to convey and place it strategically in your document.

STRATEGY

Consider the best form for your communication—fax, e-mail, memo, letter, formal report—and the timing. These are critical elements to the success of your document. Perhaps you shouldn't be writing at all: the Focus Sheet will help you decide.

(See also **readers, analyzing**.)

Step 2: Use a Start-up Strategy

For a lot of people, getting started is the hardest part of writing. The blank page or computer screen can be forbidding, especially with a dead-line fast approaching.

This book offers a variety of strategies to help you generate and communicate ideas. By using these methods, you will have the substance of your report or letter in front of you before you even begin to draft. With good planning, you won't ever have to face that blank screen again.

LOOK BACK AT YOUR FOCUS SHEET

Your Focus Sheet will keep you on target and remind you about the quantity and quality of information your readers need.

SELECT THE START-UP STRATEGY THAT WORKS FOR YOU AND YOUR TASK

Some of the following strategies are more appropriate for long documents, others work better for letters and e-mail. Experiment to find out which ones work best and feel most comfortable for you.

TRADITIONAL OR LIST OUTLINE

A traditional outline is an organized list that highlights important ideas and subordinates less important ones. It allows you to group related ideas, and see their sequence and hierarchy of importance.

Many writers create a traditional outline with letters and Roman and Arabic numerals. Others prefer a decimal system that uses a progression of numbers and decimal points.

An informal list outline may be all you need. This is a casual list of key ideas that may appear in random sequence. A list outline may result from various start-up strategies, like questioning, free writing, or simply jotting down your principal points on index cards.

You can keep track of your main ideas by listing them; seeing them together will make it easier for you to move on to Steps 3 and 4—grouping and sequencing information.

QUESTIONING

Questioning is a strategy that can sharply focus your writing by putting you in your reader's place.

- First, assume the role of your reader. Imagine the questions your reader might have, and list them.

- Second, reassume your role as writer. Try having an imaginary conversation with your reader in which you answer all the questions on your list. Discuss each question as fully as possible. You can edit later and pull out the most essential information.

Then turn your questions and answers into a list or traditional outline.

BRAINSTORM OUTLINE

The brainstorm outline is a free-form, nonlinear map of ideas developed by Tony Buzan. It's a good way to write down a lot of ideas and decide how they relate to each other. If you are overwhelmed by the complexity of your topic and the dizzying number of ideas you have about it, try a Brainstorm Outline.

Define your purpose and place it at the heart of your outline, starting with the word *to*: for example, "To propose purchase of a new network." Then, on lines extending in any direction from the center, write down your ideas. Make less important ideas branch from more important ones.

The free association that this outline allows you is excellent preparation for thoughtful writing like problem-solving memos. There is plenty of room to add ideas, and you can see at a glance what the main issues are.

The computer is an ideal outlining tool because it allows you to manipulate ideas easily.

- Try the questioning technique to focus your main points. The questions become headlines; your responses are subheads.

- If you prefer a brainstorm outline, it, too, can be transferred to the screen. Circle clusters of related issues and transfer the information to your computer in the form of a traditional or list outline.

(See also **getting started with a Start-up Strategy**, **outlines**.)

Step 3: Group information under headlines

Now that you've generated ideas for your document, you need to cluster them into related groups. This process requires two steps:

1. define the categories
2. decide which information goes in which categories

Clarifying and labeling your information now will save a lot of time and aggravation later, when you sit down to draft.

Although you may write on a wide range of topics, you'll find that some broad generic categories prove useful again and again for grouping information. Some typical categories for organizing business documents include:

- purpose
- request for action
- recommendations
- explanation of a process
- deadlines
- suggested next steps

FROM START-UP STRATEGY TO GROUPING IDEAS

If you used a traditional outline, you've already defined key topics and placed subordinate ones underneath. Step 3 is well under way.

If you generated ideas using the questioning technique, reread all the questions and decide which ones are related. Concentrate only on grouping; you can determine the most effective sequence later.

If you used a brainstorm outline, you have already done some grouping because related ideas branch from main ideas. Now study your outline again. Do some main branches belong together? If so, circle them.

HEADLINES COMMUNICATE YOUR CORE IDEAS

After grouping your ideas, you are ready to create your main headlines. These are the short phrases that act like titles and divide your document into logical sections. Headlines help busy readers find just the information they need.

Good headlines

- are informative
- indicate a change in topic
- emphasize actions or decisions
- match the content of the paragraph that follows

Usually it's better to use a longer, more specific headline instead of a general one. For example, instead of "Problem," you might write "Budget considerations in converting to the new technology."

HEADLINE LEVELS HELP READERS NAVIGATE LONG DOCUMENTS

If you're writing a report with many sections and subdivisions, your headline levels, or hierarchy, should reflect the outline of the report and show the relative importance of ideas. Decide on a headline hierarchy before you begin to write. Use font style, size, and character formatting to define the different levels.

(See also **grouping ideas**, **headline levels**, **headlines**.)

Step 4: Sequence your ideas

KEEP YOUR READERS IN MIND

Perhaps the most difficult and most important element in writing is organizing, or sequencing, information. As you choose a method of organization, review your Focus Sheet™. Answering the following questions will help you organize your document.

- Who are your readers?
- What do they already know about your topic?
- What do you need to tell them?
- Do you need to convince them?

CHOOSE A METHOD OF DEVELOPMENT

Unless you are following fixed company guidelines, you have many options in how you sequence your document. A number of organizational formats, or methods of development, follow.

MOST IMPORTANT TO LEAST IMPORTANT

This method works best for the majority of writing projects. Consider how much time and interest in your subject your reader has. Using the most important to least important sequence lets you take advantage of the reader's high attention near the beginning of the document to get across your key points.

THE BAD NEWS SANDWICH

If you have something to say that your reader doesn't particularly want to hear—loosely described as "bad news"—you'll need to put it in a "sandwich" to make it more palatable.

If the bad news is the filling, then what's the bread? If possible, some positive news. Always try to begin tactfully and end on a positive, action-oriented note.

CHRONOLOGY

Some documents require a chronological method of development, where events are listed in the order in which they happened. However, even when using a chronological sequence, you may need to emphasize important information.

Imagine your reader asking, "What's the bottom line?" Highlight important points by stating them first and then providing details.

PROCESS

Some documents explain a process that requires a particular order. Typically you'll find this type of organization in manuals and work procedures. Complete and accurate sequencing of steps or parts is crucial.

ORGANIZATION IN SPACE

For trip reports, descriptions of inventions, sales research reports, and some other kinds of documents, a spatial organization may be the most logical. You invite your readers to journey with you from Point A to Point B and so on, whether it's from one geographical location to another or from one part of a mechanism to another.

GENERAL TO SPECIFIC OR SPECIFIC TO GENERAL

In this method of development you lead with a general statement and follow with examples and support statements; or start with the specifics and expand to explain an overall idea.

This method is tricky because there are no fixed rules governing which sequence to use. Your Focus Sheet™ will help you decide: your readers' prior knowledge of your topic is a key factor here.

COMPARISON/CONTRAST

Sometimes the best way to convey information is by comparing and contrasting it to something else. Try this in some sections of feasibility reports, proposals, and research results.

When you compare two objects or ideas, you reveal what they have in common; when you contrast, you focus on their differences. This technique is especially useful if your readers aren't familiar with your topic or product.

ANALYSIS

When you analyze, you put your subject under a microscope and examine every part. If you miss anything, someone could use that overlooked fact to discredit your analysis. Worse, your incomplete analysis of a situation could lead to an erroneous business decision.

If you analyze material in technical reports, annual reports, economic forecasts, or financial analyses, you need sharp focus and a mind for details.

FOLLOW THESE ORGANIZING GUIDELINES

1. Put important, "bottom-line" information first in a short document or in each section of a report. This position will give your key message the emphasis you want.

2. Group similar or related ideas so readers don't have to search for them.

3. In most business and technical writing, put conclusions or decisions first. Then give supporting facts and reasons. Subordinate details and background.

4. If your report is long, restate important ideas at the end as well as at the beginning. Your conclusion should re-emphasize key information, too. Most readers still look for the "bottom line" at the end of the document.

5. Let your purpose and type of information determine your method of development. You may combine several to achieve the best possible organization for your document.

(See also **organizing information**.)

Organize your writing time

As you follow the Six Steps to Reader-Centered Writing™, you may be worried that all this preparation is only adding to the time you spend on your document. Writers who use this process, however, find quite the opposite. Good planning will reduce your actual writing and editing time by a lot more than the hours you spent in preparation.

Let's see how your time spent planning, writing, and editing compares with the experiences of professional writers. Complete the left-hand column of the chart below, then compare it with the information on the right.

	You	Professional writer
Planning (Steps 1-4)	_____%	50%
Drafting (Step 5)	_____%	20%
Editing (Step 6)	_____%	30%

Using the Six Steps will naturally help you change your emphasis from undisciplined drafting to planning and editing.

You have just completed the planning part of the writing process. Now you're ready to sail through your first draft.

Step 5: Write the first draft

In this step you implement your planning stages. Begin writing *without editing*. Your first draft is nearly always an unpolished version. Expect it to be rough in sentence structure, spelling, grammar, and punctuation.

Start to write anywhere that's easy for you, not necessarily at the beginning. Try starting with a headline, then write a paragraph. Don't worry about how graceful or correct your sentences are. Just get your thoughts down, following the plan or outline you've developed in the first four steps.

Remember: don't get it right, get it written! Stop periodically to read over what you've written and to compare it to your outline. When you've finished your first draft, it's time to edit.

(See also **draft writing**.)

Step 6: Edit for clarity, conciseness, and accuracy

Drafting is a creative process which gives form and substance to your thoughts; editing is an analytic process in which you critique and refine what you've written.

Since these functions are very different, don't slow yourself down by editing before you've finished drafting. If you do, you're likely to get stuck somewhere in the middle. It's better to have the entire draft completed before you begin editing sentences.

Editing covers virtually all aspects of writing. As you edit, you will:

- analyze whether you've written what you intended to express

- fine tune your sentence structure

- make sure your grammar, punctuation, and spelling are correct.

Since there are so many elements to consider, Better Communications has created the "Be Your Own Editor" Checklist, which lists editing steps in a logical progression from major issues to the smallest details.

The "Be Your Own Editor" Checklist
Step 6

☞ *Be sure to check these items for short documents.*

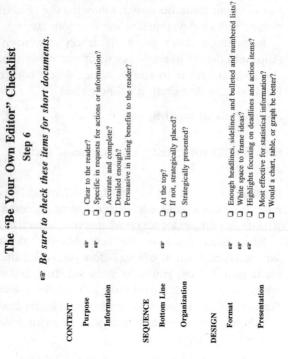

CONTENT

Purpose
- ☞ ☐ Clear to the reader?
- ☞ ☐ Specific in requests for actions or information?

Information
- ☐ Accurate and complete?
- ☐ Detailed enough?
- ☐ Persuasive in listing benefits to the reader?

SEQUENCE

Bottom Line
- ☐ At the top?
- ☐ If not, strategically placed?

Organization
- ☐ Strategically presented?

DESIGN

Format
- ☞ ☐ Enough headlines, sidelines, and bulleted and numbered lists?
- ☞ ☐ White space to frame ideas?
- ☞ ☐ Highlights focusing on deadlines and action items?

Presentation
- ☐ Most effective for statistical information?
- ☐ Would a chart, table, or graph be better?

Personalize this checklist with your specific writing problems.

STRUCTURE

Paragraphs
- ☐ Begin with a topic sentence?
- ☐ Focus on one topic?
- ☐ Use transitions to connect ideas?
- ☐ Stay within 5-6 lines in length?

Sentences
- ☐ Varied in structure and length?
- ☐ Streamlined to 15-20 words?

TONE/STYLE

Words
- ☐ Simple, specific, and straightforward?
- ☐ Free of affectation and gobbledygook?
- ☐ Acronyms explained and terminology familiar to readers?
- ☐ Headlines worded for impact?

Style
- ☐ Personable, upbeat, and direct?
- ☐ Appropriate for the audience?
- ☐ Active voice?
- ☐ Positive approach?
- ☐ The *you* attitude?

FINAL PROOF
- ☐ Are grammar, punctuation and spelling correct?
- ☐ Did you run the spellcheck program?
- ☐ Should someone else review it?
- ☐ If this is a repeat mailing, did you highlight new information?

<u>DON'T TRY TO ACCOMPLISH ALL EDITING STEPS IN ONE READING</u>

Let the format of the checklist guide you.

1. Pay attention to content first. Is your information accurate and complete?

2. Next, consider sequence and structure. Reread to make sure your ideas are organized logically and sequenced for maximum impact.

3. Finally, read with an eye for detail—grammar, punctuation, and spelling.

(See also **editing your draft**, **proofreading**.)

Why should you use the Six Steps?

The Six Steps offer a systematic writing process that will guide you through any document, no matter how complex. They have worked for thousands of participants in Better Communications workshops, and they will work for you.

Take the time to understand and practice the Six Steps, and you'll more than make up that time when you tackle future writing projects.

For more information see the handbook for Better Communications workshops, Deborah Dumaine's *Write to the Top: Writing for Corporate Success*, Random House, 1989.

How to Find the Six-Steps to Reader-Centered Writing™ in This Book

Step	Book entry
1. Analyze your readers and define your purpose	• readers, analyzing
2. Use a Start-Up Strategy	• getting started with a Start-up Strategy • outlining
3. Group information under headlines	• grouping ideas • headlines • headline levels
4. Sequence your ideas	• organizing information
5. Write the first draft	• draft, writing a
6. Edit for clarity, conciseness, and accuracy	• clear writing • editing your draft • proofreading • tone

A

absolute words: they defy comparison

Absolute words can't logically be compared to anything since they are already superlatives. You can't write *deader* or *most unique*. Here are some common absolute words.

round	unique	exact	perfect	inferior
complete	always	correct	indispensable	obvious
final	vertical	dead	libelous	permanent

Some acceptable ways to compare

Sometimes you may want to show degrees of these qualities, especially in technical writing when you must be as accurate and precise as possible.

instead of: Genetic's proposal is the *most complete* of the three.

write: Genetic's proposal is the *most nearly complete* of the three.

instead of: Marketing gave us the *most exact* figures to date on the new system's sales.

write: Marketing gave us the *most accurate* [or *up-to-date*] figures on the new system's sales.

Always use modifiers sparingly with absolute words.

A special case

Of all the absolute words, *unique* is the one that should always be used alone, without other comparisons.

> Putting the day-care center in the largest first-floor conference room would surely be a *unique* [not *most unique*] use of that space.

(See also **comparative degree, comparisons**.)

abstract and concrete words

Words that name specific actions and things are usually **concrete**; we can often perceive them through the five senses. *Concrete* derives from the Latin word meaning "grown together." Certain abstract qualities like *communication* and *breakthrough* come together and are embodied in the concrete word *fax machine*.

Note that although concrete, *fax machine* is still fairly general. A *Xerox Model 1210 Fax* is both concrete and specific.

Abstract words refer to ideas, qualities, and characteristics. *Abstract* comes from a Latin word that means "taken away." We can talk about ideas or characteristics, like *innovation* or *strategy,* without referring to anything concrete, like *fax machine*.

In other words, we can disassociate certain qualities or concepts from actual objects. Since we usually don't have a precise mental image for an abstract word, it can have different meanings for different people. For this reason you may need to define abstract words with concrete words.

abstract:	What this department needs is *more cooperation*.
concrete:	What this department needs is a *weekly meeting between the managers and the service reps*.

Compare the two lists following.

abstract:	*concrete:*
dedication	overtime on Fridays
power	chief executive officer
chaos	power outage during the second shift
conformity	white shirts and navy suits
information	two-page memo

Should you use an abstract or a concrete word?

One class of words is not categorically better than another. Certain purposes require the use of abstract words; others can be handled better with concrete words. However, in any writing you do, beware of too many abstract words.

> Single-leader groups perform more effectively initially because they are easier to form and more efficient to lead. They protect against bad financial results in terms of performance risk because the leader really does know best.

Such passages are vague and tedious to read. Concrete words help your readers visualize a situation by supplying specific and useful information.

> When we appoint experienced leaders to head teams, they have the authority to form the team and make decisions quickly. They can use their experience from previous lending groups to make informed decisions about lines of credit.

Abstract and concrete words work well together

Often abstract words and concrete words complement each other. A typical case: introduce your overall general idea, then substantiate it with concrete and specific words.

> To stay afloat in the 21st century our company needs to reduce *overhead* [abstract] and take advantage of *technological advances* [abstract]. To start, we will *close our office* [concrete] in Atlanta.
> Next, we will purchase *new networking software* [concrete] for our employees in our home office. Then we will establish a *virtual group of designers* [concrete] upon whom we can call as needed.

EXPLAINING AN ABSTRACT IDEA WITH A CONCRETE EXAMPLE

If you wanted to illustrate an abstract concept like *supply and demand*, you might use a concrete example like the following, which describes the rental of commercial property.

> When supply is low, prices are high. Therefore, when space is limited in a desirable area, rental prices are high. When supply is high, however, prices go down. If there are many vacancies and

few businesses wanting to rent, the property owner will lower the cost in order to rent the space.

Readers can visualize renting a property more easily than they can the concept of supply and demand; however, through the specific example they come to understand the abstract term.

Degrees of abstraction

Sometimes words are abstract/general or concrete/specific in relation to other words. For example, *computer* is concrete but more general than *Macintosh. Power Mac 5200/75 LC* is even more specific. The following list demonstrates a progression from abstract to increasingly concrete and specific:

- nourishment
- food
- meat
- beef
- hamburger
- Big Mac

(See also **nouns, word choice**.)

---

abstracts

An **abstract** is a 100-250 word statement that presents the main points of a report. Place it right after the title page or table of contents.

On the basis of the abstract—a self-contained unit capable of standing on its own—busy readers will decide whether to read the report itself, and if so, which sections to study.

Similarly, since abstracts are stored and readily available on computerized databases, researchers use abstracts to decide whether to read a particular report or article. Some useful CD-ROM products containing abstracts are

- ABI/INFORM, which draws on about 800 English-language journals in areas of business
- Wilson Business Abstracts
- WilsonDisc: BPI, an on-line version of *Business Periodicals Index*.

How is an abstract different from an executive summary?

Different format: an abstract is one paragraph, though sometimes a very long one. An executive summary is formatted with headings, distinct sections, and white space in between. It looks like the rest of your document. It is usually longer than an abstract.

Different uses: both provide an overview of your document and both can stand alone. However, an executive summary is considered part of the document; an abstract is frequently stored on CD-ROM products separate from the document.

Due to this difference, you're likely to use an executive summary for proposals, feasibility studies, and some kinds of reports. An abstract is more appropriate for scholarly articles and research reports.

What kind of abstract should you write?

People in the business and technical world commonly refer to two types of abstracts: descriptive and informative. A descriptive abstract concisely describes the contents of a report. It lists the subjects included, without drawing conclusions or making recommendations.

An informative abstract, like a summary, actually summarizes the information in the report; it explains the problem, scope, and method of a study as well as significant results and recommendations.

Some companies specify a particular type of abstract; others allow some latitude in presentation. Check your company guidelines first. If you are unsure, write an informative abstract.

How to write a descriptive abstract

Since a descriptive abstract is basically a list of what is in your report, a good way to begin writing one is to state the contents of each chapter or section. Don't omit any sections of the report. For example:

> Chapter 1 describes the production of glow-in-the-dark substances; Chapter 2 defines and illustrates purposes for these substances; Chapter 3 analyzes marketing difficulties, . . .

To keep your readers interested use strong verbs like *argues, compares, illustrates,* and *concludes* rather than *covers.*

Next, streamline and polish your sentences to be as precise and accurate as possible. You may not need to keep the identifying *Chapter 1, Chapter 2,* but merely present the information as in the following descriptive abstract.

> This report studies the effect transatlantic flying has on sleep for the 48-hour period following the flight. The study divided 2 groups of 5 people each according to age: 30-39 and 40-49.
>
> Individuals' sleep times were recorded following an east-west flight, then a west-east flight at least three months later. The report discusses the effects the flights have on sleep for the people within each group and between the groups.

A descriptive abstract is brief, no more than 100 words. It's essential, therefore, to include strong descriptive detail in every sentence.

You may use abbreviations and acronyms only if you are sure your readers will recognize them. If you are in doubt, write them out.

How to write an informative abstract

An informative abstract is a highly condensed version of your report. It includes

- a problem statement, which defines the reason for the project or report
- important findings, which may include results, recommendations, conclusions, and implications.

Longer than a descriptive abstract, an informative abstract is 200-250 words, or 10-20 percent of the length of the report. Find out what length your company dictates and use the maximum.

You want to provide as much information as your readers need, so give your abstract some serious thought.

To begin writing an informative abstract, scan the entire report, pinpointing main ideas. In a good report you will find all the key ideas in headlines, topic sentences, and concluding paragraphs. Underline them if you're working from a paper copy. Copy and paste them into another document if you're working on-line.

Your abstract outline should match the outline you developed during Steps 1 through 4 of the Six Steps to Reader-Centered Writing™.

Next, review the information you have assembled. Check it against the entire document to make sure you haven't omitted essential information. Then rewrite, making your ideas as compact as possible.

After editing your draft for grammar and punctuation, check it against the original to be sure all statistics and names are correct.

Here is an example of an informative abstract:

This report studies the effects transatlantic flying has on sleep for the 48-hour period following the flight. The study divided 2 groups of 5 people each according to age: 30-39 and 40-49. Individuals' sleep times were recorded following an east-west flight, and then a west-east flight at least three months later.

The report discusses the effects the flights have on sleep for the people within each group and between the groups. Results are that sleep times are nearly identical for east-west and west-east flights in each group. The 30-39 age group slept an average of 12.4 hours in the 48 hours following each flight.

Four of five people in this group reported a resumption of normal sleep patterns at the end of forty-eight hours. The 40-49 age group slept an average of 10.9 hours. Only one individual reported the resumption of normal sleep patterns at the end of 48 hours. The older age group either required less sleep or was unable to sleep as long as the younger group. People in the 40-49 age group should expect to take longer than 48 hours to return to normal sleep patterns.

This long paragraph is an exception to the rule of keeping paragraphs to five or six lines on 8 1/2" × 11" pages.

Be sure to include key words

As you review your report to write an abstract, look for key words that identify your particular topic. It's important to use these words in your abstract because researchers will look for them in an on-line data search.

If you omit identifying words in your abstract, your report may well be overlooked.

(See also **executive summaries, Introduction to the Six Steps, professional articles, reports**.)

---

acronyms and initialisms

Acronyms are abbreviations made up of the first (or the first two or three) letters of several words. They replace longer terms with simpler ones. You pronounce acronyms as words and usually omit periods.

random access memory	RAM
National Organization for Women	NOW
local area network	LAN
modulator and demodulator	modem

Write most acronyms in capital letters without periods. If they have become common nouns, some people write them in lowercase letters.

When you write the first letter of each word in a multiword term, you've created an **initialism**. Pronounce each letter separately.

end of month	e.o.m.
cash on delivery	c.o.d. or COD
ante meridiem	a.m. or AM
standing room only	SRO

Initialisms can be either upper or lowercase letters. It's fine to drop the periods after uppercase letters *(CEO)* if this doesn't cause confusion. Do include periods after lowercase letters *(a.k.a.)*.

A few tips on using acronyms and initialisms

1. In technical and business writing, people who work together or share specialties—for example, electrical engineers or software technicians—understand common abbreviations and initialisms.

   As with all abbreviations, be careful to explain acronyms and initialisms to readers outside specific groups. Write the complete term first with the shortened form in parentheses following.

   At the end of *fiscal year (FY)* 1989, we showed a loss of 1.1 million. By the end of FY1990, our profits were 1.7 million.

2. To form the plural of acronyms and initialisms with periods, add an *'s*.

   c.o.d.'s   r.p.m.'s   Ph.D's

   To form the plural of acronyms and initialisms without periods, just add an *s*.

   POs   RNs   CRTs

3. If you find yourself using the same multiword term once or more in each paragraph, it's probably a good idea to switch to acronyms or initialisms. However, try to limit your acronyms to phrases you use at least three times.

The total number of acronyms in a short document should be three. In a long document, you may need to use many acronyms and introduce them throughout the text. In this case, try limiting yourself to three acronyms per section of the document.

Consider including a glossary in which you list all the acronyms and their full names.

(See also **apostrophes**.)

active voice/passive voice

Voice describes who is performing the action in a sentence. In the **active voice**, the subject performs the action. In the **passive voice**, someone or something is acted upon. You should use the active voice most of the time, but be aware that the passive voice has its place also.

Three basic elements make up most sentences:

1. the *subject* or actor—the person or thing doing the action

2. the *verb*—the action

3. the *object* or receiver—the person or thing receiving the action or being acted upon.

The order of these elements in an *active voice* sentence is

actor	*action*	*receiver*
The president	approved	the proposal.

The order of these elements in a *passive voice* sentence is

receiver	*action*	*actor*
The proposal	was approved	by the president.

Notice that the passive sentence uses the helping verb *was*, a form of the verb *to be*. All passive voice sentences will have a form of this verb.

FORMS OF THE VERB *TO BE*

is	was	has been
are	were	had been
is being	was being	
are being	were being	

Why is active voice usually better than passive?

1. The active voice has these advantages over the passive. It is

   - livelier
   - more dynamic
   - friendlier
   - more straightforward
   - more forceful
   - generally shorter.

2. The active voice is easier to listen to and read. Look at these active voice sentences:

   > NCSA has produced useful software for the scientific community.
   >
   > We will hold a meeting to decide this issue.
   >
   > Many Usenet sites do not receive the alternative collection of newsgroups.

   Here are the same sentences in the passive voice. As you read them, notice what happens to the force of the sentences and accountability for the action.

   > Useful software for the scientific community has been produced by NCSA.
   >
   > A meeting will be held to decide this issue.
   >
   > The alternative collection of newsgroups is not received by many Usenet sites.

   These statements are decidedly weaker and their tone is distant because no one is taking direct action. Instead, things are being acted upon. In the middle sentence, the actor is absent altogether, and readers don't know who is holding the meeting.

3. Technical writing tends to use jargon and complicated information that can make reading difficult. Use the active voice so your readers

understand your meaning exactly. Make your sentences as concise and direct as possible.

instead of: The tying mechanism operation *is timed* to synchronize with the plunger movement. [passive]

write: *Time* the operation of the tying mechanism to synchronize with the plunger movement. [active]

4. Use the active voice even when the subject, or actor, is not human.

instead of: The NEMIS function can be copied with the OSE. [passive]

write: OSE can copy the NEMIS function. [active]

Despite its frequent use, the passive voice is no more authoritative or professional than the active voice. The passive can sound evasive, wordy, and ineffectual if it's not necessary. But sometimes it is.

When is it acceptable to use the passive?

1. Use the passive when the actor is not significant.

    The lab samples *are refrigerated* each night.

2. Use the passive voice when you don't know who is performing the action.

    The intake valve *was not properly closed* at the end of the second shift.

    However, use the active voice for tighter writing that doesn't call attention to this lack of knowledge.

write: There *was* an improperly closed intake valve at the end of the second shift.

or: *They found* an improperly closed intake valve at the end of the second shift.

3. Use the passive when you want to be tactful and avoid saying who performed the action.

Though the plant *had been inspected*, several violations *were not reported*.

4. Use the passive when the person or thing that receives the action is more important than the one doing the action.

The layout of strips and landings *can be used* for the life of this stand of trees, thus reducing future operation costs.

5. Use the passive when you need to make a smooth connection between sentences, sometimes by repeating a key word.

The bale chamber may not accept *wet hay* easily. *Wet hay can be baled*, but the baler will operate under excessive strain. [An active voice version of the second sentence, *You may be able to bale wet hay*. . ., may be more direct, but the passive version connects better with the first sentence.]

Avoiding the passive

Don't use the passive instead of writing *I, me, we*, or *us*. These first person pronouns are perfectly appropriate in business writing and sound better than ambiguous passive sentences like this:

It has been determined that the rehabilitation project *should be started* by the end of the month.

Who determined it? Who is supposed to start the project? Include the actors whenever you can by using the active voice. Change the sentence—

write: The evaluation committee determined that Dr. Knowles' group should start the rehabilitation project by the end of the month.

or: The determination was that the rehabilitation project should start by the end of the month. [when you don't want to name names]

How to change passive to active voice

If the action of the sentence uses a form of the verb *to be*, and if the actor is not doing the action, then the sentence is passive.

1. Change the verb to a different one that is active.

   instead of: Fifteen aircraft accidents *were caused* by air turbulence last year, according to the Federal Aviation Administration.

   write: The Federal Aviation Administration *attributed* 15 aircraft accidents to air turbulence last year.

2. Turn the sentence or clause around by putting the person or thing doing the action in front of the verb.

   instead of: These results *are described* further in Appendix II.

   write: Appendix II further *describes* these results.

3. Rewrite your sentences entirely by rethinking them.

   instead of: New sensitivity factors *have been calculated* and stored in the network. They *are located* in the RSF directory under the label S287V.

   write: The newly calculated sensitivity factors *are* now in the RSF directory under the label S287V.

A matter of emphasis

The choice of either active or passive voice is often a matter of emphasis. The first word or words in a sentence usually carry more weight than do the last. So if you want the emphasis on the person or thing doing the action, use the active voice.

Jim Stanley *won* this month's sales award.

Putting this sentence in the passive—*This month's sales award was won by Jim Stanley*—makes the person who won it seem secondary to the sales award.

On the other hand, if you want to stress the receiver of the action or avoid mentioning the actor, use the passive.

> Three disks *were destroyed* in the office over the weekend.

Here the important thing is that three disks were destroyed. This sentence avoids accountability either because the actor is not known or because the writer is diplomatically not saying who did it. To put this sentence in the active voice, you'd have to create an actor.

> *The carpet cleaner* destroyed three disks in the office over the weekend.

Now the emphasis is on *who*, not *what*.

Can you switch voices?

Yes, but not in the same sentence. Within a paragraph, a switch might be necessary if you are using the passive voice to avoid naming names.

| *instead of:* | Once this report has been written, you should distribute it. |
| *write:* | Once you have written this report, you should distribute it. |

If you must use the passive, maintain the same voice by writing:

> Once this report has been written, it should be distributed.

(See also **verbs**.)

---

adjectives

Adjectives are descriptive words that modify nouns, pronouns or other adjectives. They answer the questions: how much or how many? which one? what kind? Adjectives clarify your meaning by describing and limiting. They usually come before nouns.

> Use the *dir* command to list the *updated* contents of *these three* directories.

> *Last* year we replaced *our old printing* machinery with *state-of-the-art electronic* equipment.

These are some of the endings that adjectives can have:

-ful	grateful, plentiful, boastful
-able, -ible	reliable, manageable, sensible, visible
-y	scary, thirty, cloudy
-ive	decisive, passive, constructive
-ous	nervous, conscientious, humorous
-ary	secondary, visionary, contrary

Some adjectives follow verbs like *is, be, look, feel, sound, taste,* and *seem* that don't show action but link a subject with an adjective.

> The production department is *happy* with the new equipment.
> The new computers are much *faster* than our older ones.
> That just doesn't sound *right.*
> Your layout looks *good* to me.

Modifiers that follow verbs

If the word that follows the verb describes the subject (*happy* describes department), use the adjective form rather than the adverb form (*happily*) of the word.

The following words are adjectives when they modify nouns:

words that demonstrate	*this, that, these, those*
words that show possession	*his, hers, theirs, ours, my, its*

question words	*which, what, whose*
numbers	*eight, fifteen, seventy-nine*
indefinite words	*none, some, any, all, few, several*

This proposal is the most comprehensive of all.

Beverly told us that *her* proposal will be ready tomorrow.

Whose proposal is the best?

We had to reject *several* proposals because they arrived after the deadline.

Comparing

When you compare two things, add *-er* to the adjective or put *more* or *less* before it:

| wider | hotter | faster |
| more confident | less pleasing | more suitable |

Upgrading the system will mean *faster* data retrieval.

I think Ibrahim Sandali is the *more suitable* of the two applicants.

When you compare more than two things, add *-est* to the adjective or put *most* or *least* before it:

| widest | easiest | fastest |
| least careful | most desirable | most impressive |

Appendix IV describes the *easiest* way to retrieve data.

Please discard the *least impressive* resumes from the stack.

Some adjectives are irregular in their comparisons:

bad	worse	worst
many	more	most
little	less	least

Most data-retrieval systems are not as cost effective as this one.

This is the *worst* resume of the lot.

The company is allocating *less* money for entertainment expenses this year.

Nouns as adjectives

Especially in technical writing, nouns are sometimes used as adjectives.

The *performance* data in table 3 show how the new design compares to the old one.

The T-31 *platform* scale is the most cost-efficient model for our needs.

Sometimes a string of nouns used as adjectives can be confusing.

Jenny worked all weekend on the *needs analysis proposal* strategy.

In this situation, to clarify what you mean, use a hyphen to join adjectives that can act as one word.

Jenny worked all weekend on the *needs-analysis proposal* strategy.

A caution about adjectives

It's easy to overuse adjectives, so you should question the need for them in your writing. Try not to use trite or general adjectives (*fine, nice, interesting, good*). If you decide you need an adjective, find one that's precise for your meaning.

(See also **absolute words, articles, commas, comparisons, hyphens, modifiers, possessive case**.)

---

adverbs

Adverbs modify verbs, adjectives, or other adverbs. They answer the questions: when? where? how? in what manner? to what extent?

Adverbs often comment on the action of a verb.

> Please read the enclosed manuscript *slowly* and check *carefully* for errors.

Adverbs further define adjectives.

> We are pleased to announce that there are *nearly* 50 new parking spaces on the top floor of the garage.

Adverbs can describe or limit other adverbs.

> Our department uses the new database *more* frequently than any other department.

Use adverbs when you want to be more precise about your meaning in describing an action or a state of being.

Types of adverbs

1. Many adverbs end in *-ly*.

   > thoughtfully   hourly   entirely   orderly

   > We need to hire an assistant to check our experiments *hourly* . [*Hourly* tells how often the action of the verb *check* occurs.]

   But be aware that some words that end in *-ly* are actually adjectives.

   > friendly   costly   lively   earthly

   > This year the company has chosen a *lively* Mexican band for the Christmas party. [*Lively* describes the band.]

2. Some adverbs of time, place, and degree don't end in *-ly*.

time:	now, then, often, seldom
place:	here, out, backwards, under
degree:	somewhat, much, less

3. A conjunctive adverb joins two independent clauses.

   > The consultant advised against purchasing new computers; *however,* our equipment is definitely outdated.

Note that the conjunctive adverb is preceded by a semicolon and followed by a comma and an independent clause.

A conjunctive adverb can also act as a connector between two sentences. In this case it clarifies the relationship between the sentences.

> The publicity department lost nine employees this year and is months behind schedule. *Nevertheless,* the department will begin marketing your product in June.

Here the conjunctive adverb introduces the sentence and is followed by a comma.

The most common conjunctive adverbs are

also	otherwise
besides	so
consequently	still
furthermore	then
hence	thus
nevertheless	

4. Adverbs that ask questions include:

how? why? where? when?

> *Why* don't we transfer the new group to the main office downtown?

Comparing adverbs

Like adjectives, adverbs use *-er* or *more* or *less* to compare two things.

sooner	closer	harder
more directly	more quickly	less successfully

> The new sales group worked *harder* than ever to meet this month's quota.

> They met this month's quota *more quickly* than expected.

To compare more than two things, use the ending *-est* or put *most* or *least* before the adverb.

farthest	nearest	latest
most often	least happily	most promptly

Of all our workers, Benny Thomas lives the *farthest* from the construction site.

We tried out several bicycle messenger services and found that yours delivers the *most promptly*.

Irregular comparisons include:

well	better	best
little	less	least
much	more	most

The equipment will run *better* after servicing.

Position in the sentence

The general rule is to put adverbs as close as possible to the words they modify. Pay special attention to words like *only, almost, ever*, and *merely*. If the modifier is in the wrong place, the sentence can have a different meaning than you intended.

We *only* could hire two new representatives. [Only *we* could hire them.]

We could *only* hire two new representatives. [We could hire them, but not train them.]

We could hire *only* two new representatives. [Not three or four.]

(See also **comparisons, modifiers**.)

---

ambiguity

Avoid **ambiguity**—muddled or unclear meanings—when you write. Be as clear and precise as you can.

What, exactly, does this sentence mean?

When Julian sent the e-mail to Dave about the missing files, he was quite angry.

Who was angry, Julian or Dave? The writer leaves you guessing because the pronoun *he* could refer to either person. To clear up the confusion, you could write the sentence this way:

Dave was quite angry when he got Julian's e-mail about the missing files [if it was Dave who was angry].

Ambiguity often occurs when pronouns and their antecedents don't agree.

instead of:	The lab found a contaminated sample in Batch 8. Should we discard it? [Discard what: the sample or the batch?]
write:	Should we discard the contaminated sample the lab found in Batch 8?

Three causes of ambiguity

1. Vague pronouns that follow more than one idea or statement

instead of:	The engineers are investigating the best site for the bridge. Once they decide, another group will look into purchasing the land for the approaches to the bridge. *This* will add extra time and cost to an already expensive highway project. [Which information does *this* refer to?]
write:	The engineers are investigating the best site for the bridge. ~~Once~~ they decide, another group will look into purchasing the land for the approaches to the bridge. *These two projects* will add extra time and cost to an already expensive highway project.

2. Incomplete comparisons

instead of:	I have visited my nephew less frequently than my siblings. [less frequently than I have visited my siblings?]
write:	I have visited my nephew less frequently than my siblings *have*.

3. Modifiers in the wrong place

instead of:	Steve found the original report filed in the backup folder that we thought was lost. [Did they think the backup folder was lost?]
write:	Steve found the original report *that we thought was lost* in the backup folder.
instead of:	The committee will *only* select three finalists for this position. [Select but not decide upon?]
write:	The committee will select *only* three finalists for this position.
instead of:	Turning the corner quickly, *the bookcase* was knocked over by Chris. [Did the bookcase turn the corner? *Turning the corner quickly* is a dangling modifier.]
write:	Turning the corner quickly, *Chris* knocked over the bookcase.

The opposite of *ambiguity* is *clarity*.

(See also **dangling modifiers, misplaced modifiers**.)

---

analogy

Think of an **analogy** as a comparison between two things, often familiar and unfamiliar. Analogies help explain your meaning.

> The proposed highway would be the main artery through the city. [A highway is compared to an artery because both suggest connections, routes, and carrying things from one place to another.]

> Sky-diving feels like the drop in a roller coaster.

> The writer's work is similar to the sculptor's: both begin with rough material that they shape and reshape into a finished piece, discovering its form as they work.

Make sure the relationships between the things compared in your analogy clarify your meaning instead of confusing it.

Good analogies can be persuasive for readers. Technical writers can use them to bridge gaps between what their readers already know and particular facts or theories presented.

> In some materials, the spin of the electron around the nucleus causes a magnetic movement that is aligned with the axis of spin.
> Compare this spin to the alignment of the earth's magnetic field between the north and south poles.
> [The atomic-level magnetic field being explained is compared to the earth's magnetic field. This comparison helps readers understand.]

A *faulty analogy* sometimes results when two things are presented as similar just because they have one or more characteristics in common.

It would be *false analogy* to suggest that the United States will fall like the Roman Empire fell because, like Rome, the United States spends large amounts of national income on the military.

Many other facts that might make the comparison suspect are not considered here.

annual reports

An **annual report** is a financial record of a company's performance over the past year. Public companies use annual reports to keep their shareholders, employees, and other interested parties informed about important developments at the company.

For public companies an annual report is required by law. Most companies hire experts to write their annual reports since these documents are so highly visible.

What's in an annual report?

A summary of finances and operations, as well as forecasts for the coming year, make up the bulk of an annual report. It highlights and analyzes a company's strengths and developmental needs. It may also offer growth plans and solutions to problems the company faces.

Presentation in these reports varies from elaborate to spare, but most combine required financial information with sections that show the company in its best light. The tone—from conservative to conversational—will usually fit the image the company wants to convey.

There are five major sections in most annual reports.

1. <u>Financial summary</u>: an overview of sales and earnings, often including the percent of change over about a three-year period. This section is the most widely read part of the report.

2. <u>Statement to stockholders</u>: a letter or formal statement that comments on the year's performance, discusses plans and new directions, and explains any shortcomings.

3. <u>Articles on the company's operations</u>: a presentation of new products, developments, or operations, such as sales trends, comparisons with the competition, organizational changes, labor relations discussions, and social responsibilities.

4. <u>Financial statement</u>: a detailed document that is often last in the report or packaged as a separate booklet.

5. <u>Board of directors and company officers list</u>: a list of names and other corporate affiliations, sometimes with photographs.

Most readers skim an annual report rather than read every word, so use illustrations, photographs, charts, and graphs throughout to catch your reader's eye. A good annual report makes generous use of graphics and photographs with captions that contain key messages.

apostrophes

The **apostrophe** (') is a mark of punctuation that may indicate possession, plural, or the omission of some letters. Though many rules govern its use, the apostrophe is not difficult to use correctly.

Apostrophes that show possession

1. To form the possessive of a noun that does not end in *-s,* use an *'s.* (This rule also applies to words that are plural but don't end in *-s,* such as *women.*)

    This *program's* main advantage is its ease of use.

    We have rescheduled the night *attendant's* shift for 4 p.m. to midnight.

    Jim has taken paternity leave after each of his *children's* births.

    We found *someone's* briefcase in the conference room.

2. Singular nouns that end in *-s* may take either an apostrophe alone or an *'s* after the final *-s.* If you add a syllable when you say the word in the possessive, then you should add an *'s.* Don't add an *'s* if the extra syllable makes the word hard to pronounce.

    Workforce diversity will be the subject of the *president's* next newsletter article.

    The judge charged the jury to consider each *witness's* testimony equally.

    Los Angeles' [not *Los Angeles's*] smog problem is a real deterrent.

    Never put the apostrophe within a word that ends in *-s.*

    Jane Jones' request [not *Jane Jone's* request]

3. An apostrophe alone forms the possessive of plural nouns that end in *-s.*

Our *suppliers'* overlapping delivery schedules are causing problems at the loading dock.

Three *weeks'* vacation is a very generous benefit.

4. To show joint possession, the last noun takes the apostrophe or *'s.*

The project manager decided to implement *Bill and Eileen's* idea. [They had one idea together].

5. To show individual possession, give each noun an apostrophe or *'s.*

Besset's and McKay's products [each one's separate products] are the ones we're considering.

6. Don't use the apostrophe with the possessive pronouns *yours, hers, his, its, ours, whose,* and *theirs.*

It's [contraction for it is] a good thing the company has enough money left in *its* [possessive pronoun] budget to pay for these unexpected roof repairs.

The choice to locate the plant in Denver was *hers.*

7. Always use a possessive word in front of a verb ending in *-ing* that's used as a noun (gerund).

Tim's working late was the reason inventory was completed on time.

Do you remember *our deciding* to move the meeting to 4 p.m.?

Apostrophes that make plurals

If you want to show the plural of numerals, letters, or words used as words, you may use either an *'s* or an *-s* alone. The trend is to drop the apostrophe unless doing so will cause confusion.

For example, if the apostrophe is omitted from *do's* and *don'ts,* the word *do's* could be confused with the disk operating system acronym *DOS.* Be consistent and make sure the word is understandable.

If you are making handwritten corrections, make sure your *2's* don't look like *Q's.* [or *2s* and *Qs*]

Hannah used three *but's* [or *buts*] in her first sentence.

Our Huntington plant has been in operation since the late *1970's*.

The company hired four *Ph.D.'s* last year.

Apostrophes that show omission

1. The apostrophe is necessary in contractions to show omitted letters.

   Please put in a service call—we just *can't* get the copier to work today.

   A personal day *doesn't* count as part of your vacation time.

   The reception will begin at three *o'clock*.

   Using contractions can help create an informal tone in your writing. If you want a formal tone, avoid contractions.

   We *won't* be contacting you until *we've* finished our evaluation.

   We *will not* be contacting you until *we have* finished our evaluation.

2. Put an apostrophe in place of omitted figures in numbers.

   The end of *'87* was a turning point for our company.

Apostrophe as symbol

The apostrophe is also a symbol for measurement in feet.

The new loading dock will be 20' by 14' when it's finished.

(See also **acronyms and initialisms, contractions, possessive case, punctuation**.)

---

appendix

A separate reference section at the end of a business or technical report or document is called an

appendix (plural *appendixes;* also *appendices*). This added section is sometimes also called an *attachment* or *annex.*

An appendix will help your reader by organizing pages of data or explanations that would otherwise interrupt and slow down your text.

What's in an appendix?

The kinds of information that typically appear in appendixes include

- numerical data including tables or research statistics
- case studies
- document excerpts that support the text
- photographs
- computations
- letters and memos
- detailed analyses
- parts lists
- background information
- charts or tables.

Whenever possible, integrate a chart or table into the body of the report and put the backup figures in the appendix.

Don't create an appendix from miscellaneous bits of information that you just couldn't fit anywhere else.

How to set up an appendix

Be sure to put only one kind of information in each appendix. Don't include a parts list and pages of computations in the same one. Give each appendix either a number or letter and a title. (If you have only one appendix, give it a title but not a letter or number.)

Appendix B: Costs of Dredging Equipment [one of three appendixes]

Costs of Dredging Equipment [only one appendix]

Remember to refer your readers to the appendix in the body of the text. Make the references informative and not too short.

instead of: (see Appendix D)

write: See Appendix D (Non-FDA
Approved Cancer Treatments) for
further analysis of laetrile use.

Arrange the appendixes at the end of your report in the order that you mention them in the text. Include them in the Table of Contents by number, title, and beginning page number.

Why include an appendix?

Your readers are busy people who want to read a concise report that gives conclusions and recommendations up front. Separate the main information your readers need to know from the subordinate. Put the subordinate material in an appendix that your readers can consult as needed.

Ask yourself if the information you want to put in the appendix would help your readers interpret your report. If it would, then include the appendix.

(See also **reports**.)

appositives

A word or group of words placed next to a noun that further identifies the noun is called an **appositive**. It functions in the sentence the same way the noun it identifies does.

Mark Windham, *spokesman for the Wisconsin
Department of Natural Resources,* will address the
symposium about recreational facilities improvement. [Notice that the appositive, *spokesman for
the Wisconsin Department of Natural Resources,* is
set off by commas because it is nonrestrictive, or not

essential to the meaning of the sentence. The appositive in this case provides *additional* information.]

The book *Write to the Top* is the most useful how-to book on business writing I've ever read. [In this sentence, the appositive, *Write to the Top*, is not set off by commas because it is essential to the meaning of the sentence. Without it, we wouldn't know which book the writer means.]

(See also **commas, dashes, restrictive and non-restrictive elements**.)

---

area charts

Area charts look like line charts that are added or stacked, displaying changes in a data set over time, but they emphasize the area between the lines. Individual values are downplayed while the magnitude of change is stressed.

Computer-generated charts include an area graph which is really a line graph, with the area below the line shaded. These area charts are displayed as individual areas under each line drawn.

Though the display can be two dimensional or three dimensional, there is no advantage to using the three dimensional display as far as communicating your message goes.

(See also **charts or graphs, line charts, tables**.)

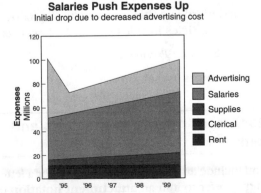

Salaries Push Expenses Up
Initial drop due to decreased advertising cost

articles

The three **articles** in the English language—*a, an,* and *the*—make the words they modify limited and more precise. Articles are adjectives.

A and *an* are indefinite in what they indicate.

> We are planning to hire *a* new contractor next month. [does not specify a particular contractor]

> There might be *an* opening in marketing this year. [does not specify what particular opening]

The is definite in what it indicates.

> We will hire *the* new contractor next month. [indicates that we will hire a particular contractor]

Choose either *a* or *an* according to the beginning sound of the word that follows, not the beginning letter.

A is correct in front of a consonant sound (*a* terminal, *a* hung jury, *a* personal perspective, *a* USAir flight). *An* is correct in front of a vowel sound (*an* optical scanner, *an* opinion, *an* AFL-CIO meeting).

Never leave out articles to be concise—even in technical writing. Your text will be choppy and difficult to read.

instead of:	Turn shut-off valve to "off" position before beginning test.
write:	Turn *the* shut-off valve to *the* "off" position before beginning *a* test.

If the first word in a title is an article, capitalize it. Otherwise, articles in titles should be lowercase.

> *The Making of a President*

(See also **nouns**.)

attachment notations in letters and memos

If you include an attachment to a memo or a letter, you may refer to it in an **attachment notation** on the line below the reference notation. (The reference notation is usually the typist's and sometimes the author's initials placed two lines below the final line of text.) If you have more than one attachment, put the number in parentheses after the word "Attachments."

.... *this is the last line of the memo.*

jlr [reference notation]
Attachments (3)

Use a staple or a paper clip to keep the memo and its attachments together.

Use the word *enclosure* only if you are putting a separate item in an envelope.

(See also **letters, memorandums**.)

attention line in letters

The **attention line** has the name of the person or department to whose attention you are addressing your letter. Use an attention line only if the inside address doesn't have an individual's or department's name.

Type the attention line two lines under the address, aligned with the left margin. Although some writers omit the colon after "Attention," it's still best to include the colon in most business writing.

Regis Movers, Inc.
38 Grand Avenue
Colorado Springs, CO 80000

Attention: Henry Talbot

(See also **letters**.)

B

bad news letters and memos

Nobody wants to receive bad news. But if you must deliver it, you can help the reader understand your point of view, and perhaps even align with you.

Deliver the good news first

How do you make bad news most palatable? Present the good news first—something that gives the reader a reason to read further. On reaching the bad news, your reader will want to continue, for your larger message brings a benefit.

Try to find the silver lining. Lead up to a controversial announcement or recommendation by demonstrating the need for it.

Begin by using a specific example to describe a problem—and then show how implementing your idea can prevent the situation from happening again. For example, you wouldn't ask to exceed your software budget unless you knew that doing so would save you money and avert system breakdowns.

In writing a layoff notice, you can offer the employee a letter of reference and perhaps an interview you've arranged at another firm.

End with more good news

After you've written the bad news, add the finishing touch—an upbeat closing that helps the reader accept the unpleasant reality. Let the laid-off employee know, for example, how hard you lobbied to keep her on as the firm suffered hard times, and how much everyone appreciates her valuable contributions.

By "sandwiching" the bad news between two pieces of good news, you make the bad news easier to digest.

good news:	We've found a team system that will cut our production costs by 30% a month.
bad news:	We need $250,000 now for training and implementation.
good news:	By starting now, we can offset the purchase price of our new industrial lasers and save $1,250,000 over the next five years.

What if there is no good news?

If you truly can't find a positive fact, at least offer a positive tone. Start with a personal or friendly note before going to the hard issues.

End with supportive statements offering to help if possible. At a minimum, show that you understand how the bad news will affect the reader and that you care. Sending bad news is never easy, but these strategies can make it easier.

(See also **good news letters and memos**, **letters**, **memorandums**, **organizing information**.)

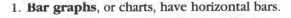

bar and column charts

Bar charts have bars that represent data values. The bars allow your reader to compare growth rates, product performance, or year-end profits across time.

1. **Bar graphs**, or charts, have horizontal bars.

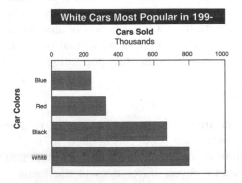

2. **Column graphs**, also called histograms, have vertical bars.

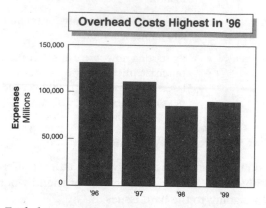

Each bar or column represents a unit of a distinct set, usually sequenced. The units may be

- months: January, February, March . . .
- continuous years: 1997, 1998, 1999 . . .
- eras: 1980-1989, 1990-1999 . . .
- values: 100, 200, 300 . . .

Column charts are useful for showing frequency distributions. Each column represents the number of units in a category. The whole chart shows the amount of variation and the distribution pattern.

Column chart or bar chart?

Your data will determine whether to use vertical or horizontal bars. Vertical columns tend to emphasize change over time, while horizontal bars are better suited for items at a fixed period of time. They are also useful when there is no natural order in the variables, such as comparing populations of cities.

Cautions

1. Data that generate only one or two large columns are better described in text. The number of columns should be sufficient to visually reveal differences in the totals. Too

many columns prevent individual labeling and make it difficult to see the values. Use a column chart when

- there is sufficient space to fully distinguish each column
- the trend of the columns is the message.

2. When the values are equal, the columns are all the same height and the graph does not reflect changes over time. Express this as text instead.

3. When using columns to present a range of data, do not use overlapping values in columns, for example: *100-250, 200-400, 350-500*. Also avoid values that are not uniformly spaced: *Monday, Wednesday, Thursday*.

Multiple variables

One chart can compare quantities of different items. Compare multiple values across time by placing several columns at each interval.

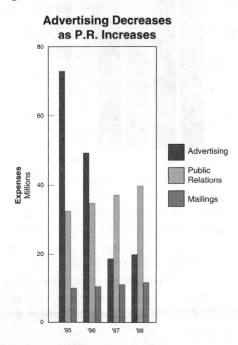

- Display two, three, or, infrequently, four significant variables for each unit.
- Make sure each column is clear and identifiable. More than four variables blur the information and make labeling impossible. Even three columns are sometimes confusing to the eye.

Stacked columns

Column charts may be subdivided into sections, each representing a subpart of the whole column.

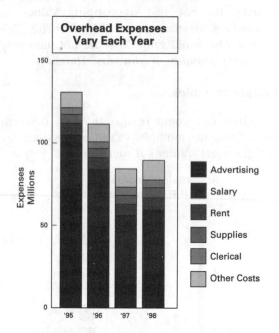

- Sections must be consistent across all the columns. If annual expenses are subdivided into rent, advertising, and salaries, then each column must contain the same set of subdivisions. If all subdivisions are not relevant for each column, don't use stacked columns.
- The total of the subparts must constitute all of the column. There can be no unaccounted-for space on a column, though *Other* is a valid category.

Three-dimensional charts

Think carefully before displaying columns as three-dimensional solids. Although it is tempting to do so for effect or variety, it will make the values more difficult to read, as in the following chart. This is such a serious problem that it is best to avoid three dimensions in almost any chart.

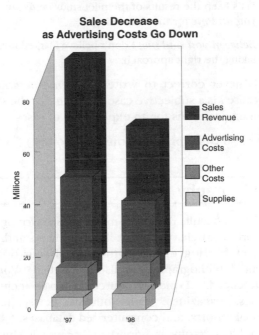

Here are two tips if you absolutely must use a three-dimensional chart:

1. The arrangement of the columns is critical. The smallest values must appear in front or they will be lost behind the larger column.

2. The order of the columns cannot vary; the first data set must remain first across time. If the height of the values varies significantly from year to year, a high-value front column may obstruct other columns. In this case use two-dimensional multiple variable columns.

(See also **charts or graphs**, **tables**.)

between you and me

Between you and me is a prepositional phrase consisting of the preposition *between* and the pronouns *you* and *me*. Because *you and me* follow a preposition, you must use the objective case of the pronouns.

> Let's keep the results of the pilot study *between you and me* for the time being.

> *Between you and me*, I don't believe Marketing is taking the right approach.

It is never correct to write *between you and I* because *I* is a subjective case pronoun. See the section on pronouns for an explanation of cases.

(See also **case**, **prepositions**, **pronouns**.)

bibliography

If you consult resource materials in writing a report or article, you must list them in a standard list, or **bibliography**, at the end of your document. A bibliography can also be entitled "Works Referenced." Typical resource materials include books, magazines, trade journals, newspapers, annual reports, and computerized databases.

A bibliography is important because it shows readers the source of your ideas and helps them find more information if they need it. If you consult only one or two books or articles, you have the option of using footnotes rather than a separate bibliography—but always give credit to your sources.

Include in your bibliography all materials that you cite in your text as well as other resources you consulted. The materials in a bibliography must be listed alphabetically by the author's last name or by the first word in the title if an author is not credited.

See **documenting sources** for more detail on how to write bibliographic entries.

Here is an excerpt from a typical bibliography:

Bednar, A. and W. H. Levie. "Attitude-Change Principles." Eds. Fleming and Levie, *Instructional Message Design: Principles from the Behavioral and Cognitive Sciences.* 2nd ed. Englewood Cliffs, NJ: Educational Technology Publications, 1993.

Geber, B. "Managing Diversity." TRAINING Magazine, July 1990.

Jamieson, D. and J. O'Mara. *Managing Workforce 2000: Gaining the Diversity Advantage.* San Francisco: Jossey Bass Inc., 1991.

Also use a standard bibliographic format for any list of books or articles, such as recommended readings or new publications.

(See also **documenting sources**, **reports**, **research**.)

blind courtesy copy notations

Blind courtesy copy notations show the distribution of a letter or memo without your correspondent's knowing about it. Put the notation on internal copies of the letter only—never on the original that the addressee will receive. Write *bcc* with or without a colon following.

bcc	C.J. Taylor	*or:*		bcc:	C.J. Taylor
	B. Gupta				B. Gupta

Put this notation flush left below the enclosure notation or, if none, below the reference initials or the writer's name. Double space between name, reference initials, and copy notations.

(See also **letters**.)

borders: how to add visual appeal

Borders in a report or document can frame your text for visual impact. Many techniques produce borders:

- a box around either the entire text or selected portions of text
- a line of asterisks or bullets between sections of text
- white space

Use borders to organize your document visually and give emphasis where you want it. Consult the **Model Documents Appendix** for examples of borders.

(See also **editing your draft**, **footers**, **headers**, **headlines**, **letters**.)

---

box charts

Box charts or box plots are used to graph distributions, showing how many items fall into a series of progressive numerical ranges. They are essentially scatter charts with significant clumps of data boxed for emphasis.

After you plot the data as points, group the points that need highlighting together inside a box. When grouping the data, make one variable—that is, the value represented on the x-axis—independent. The other variable—represented on the y-axis—is dependent.

First look at the scatter chart before the boxes are added.

**More Education Yields
Higher Income**

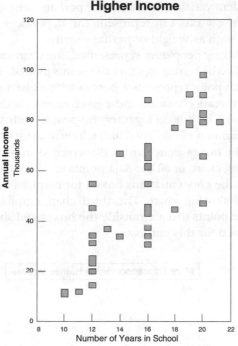

In box chart 2, unimportant stray data points are removed, leaving the clusters or clumps of data points boxed to tell the story.

More Education Yields Higher Income

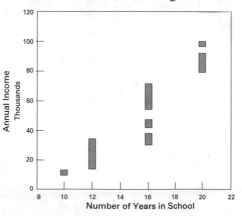

For example, the x-axis can represent an independent variable such as age or perhaps time units; and the y-axis can represent the dependent variable such as weight or perhaps salary.

If many people are represented, the chart can be clarified by boxing together the points plotted. Thus, if each point represents a person with a given number of years education and a given salary, clarify the message by boxing together the people with a certain amount of education and within a salary range.

The boxes alone can be displayed as in the preceding chart, or all the data points can be included with the concentrations boxed for emphasis, as in the following chart. The third chart emphasizes those points that are outside the boxes and should be used for this purpose.

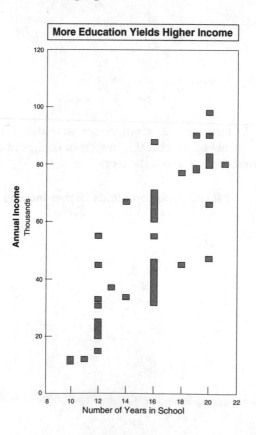

About box charts

- Box charts typically include a caption or message, for example:

   More education yields higher income

   In June most sales were in the $5,000 to $10,000 range

   The majority of shipments were delivered in one-to-two days

- Box charts are a special case of the box and whisker, or high-low-close-open chart, where only the group is significant, not the highest and lowest values within the group.

- Box charts are good for showing outlying data points and data "clumping."

- Box charts do not display all data points, only a summary of the data.

- Box charts can compare chosen percentiles effectively. Since you select how to box the data, you can choose to highlight those percentiles which will support your text.

- Whenever you make a scatter chart, ask yourself if you should take it a step further into a box chart for greatest clarity.

(See also **charts or graphs**, **high-low-close-open charts**, **scatter charts**, **tables**.)

C

capital letters

Capital letters (also called uppercase letters) focus attention on such words as proper nouns, main words in titles, and the first words of sentences. Capital letters help writers communicate clearly by clarifying the meanings of some words that might otherwise be confusing.

may/May   rose/Rose   afghan/Afghan

"Capitalizing" means writing only the first letter of a word, not the entire word, with a capital letter. "All caps" means putting the entire word (or acronym or abbreviation) in capital letters.

Proper nouns and adjectives

In general, capitalize proper nouns: the names of particular persons, places, months, holidays, trade names, historic events, organizations, departments, and titles.

Henry Ford	Hewlett Packard
Chanukah	Senator Jones
Fritos	Battle of Bunker Hill
Peace Corps	Tuesday, May 28
Outer Banks	Starfleet Academy

Common nouns are general, or generic, and don't need to be capitalized.

an engineer   the night shift   winter   hotel

Capitalize some *adjectives* that come from proper nouns.

Newtonian physics   Puritan ancestors   Japanese
                                           auto industry

Many other adjectives that come from proper nouns aren't capitalized.

congressional   french fries   india ink   oriental

As a general rule, capitalize adjectives that come from proper nouns only if the original meaning is retained. You will find variations in different dictionaries and style guides. Use your best judgment—and be consistent.

Capitalization rules

1. <u>PEOPLE'S NAMES AND TITLES</u>

   a. Capitalize personal names.

      Oksana Baiul   Bill Gates   Margaret Meade

      Capitalize the prefix in a proper name if it stands alone; otherwise, write it in lowercase.

Van Vogt	Mrs. van Vogt
La Poudre	James la Poudre

   b. Capitalize titles with personal names.

      Mr. Norman Oates   Ambassador Likert
      Queen Elizabeth

      Write titles in lowercase if no proper name follows.

      Pat Kowalski, *mayor* of the city, spoke at the rally. [but *Mayor Pat Kowalski*]

      Capitalize job titles when you write them with personal names.

      Vice President of Marketing Bill Wexel is out of town till Tuesday. [but: The *vice president of marketing* is out of town till Tuesday.]

      The policy of some companies, however, is to capitalize job titles when jobs are announced or otherwise mentioned with special emphasis.

      The position of *Junior Accountant* is open to new applicants.

Every *Division Manager* must attend the meeting in Houston.

Refer to your company's style guide, and be consistent.

2.   <u>ETHNIC GROUPS, NATIONALITIES, AND LANGUAGES</u>

a.   Capitalize the names of ethnic groups, nationalities, and languages.

Native American   Afrikaner   Bosnian
Mandarin Chinese

Write the names of economic and social groups in lowercase.

middle class   urban subculture   white-collar jobs

3.   <u>PLACES AND DIRECTIONS</u>

a.   Capitalize the names of particular streets, cities, buildings, parks, counties, rivers, states, oceans, mountains, geographical divisions, and the like.

Cincinnati	Dumas Avenue
Sears Tower	Appalachian Mountains
Madison County	Southern Hemisphere
Strait of Gibraltar	Yukon River
Boston Common	Quebec

Capitalize *city* and *state* only when they're part of a name.

Oklahoma City	Washington State
the city of Syracuse	the state of Maryland
a city worker	an employee of the state

b.   Do not capitalize geographic features and compass directions unless they refer to specific regions.

Many of the *streets* in this area, such as *Barney Way* and *Beetle Street,* weren't paved till after World War II.

We opened an office on the *West Coast* last year.

Our California sales reps must make two trips *East* every year.

We always hold our January meeting in the *South*.

To get to the Springfield office, go *north* on I-81 to Exit 3.

The words *northern, southern, eastern,* and *western* are capitalized if they are part of an established place name. Also capitalize these words if they refer to people or cultures. But when these words refer to a general region or its climate or geography, write them in lowercase.

Western civilization	Westerners
western landscape	westerly winds
northern California	Northern Ireland

c. The words *sun, moon,* and *earth* are capitalized only in context with other heavenly bodies. Never capitalize *earth* when it follows *the*.

The first three planets from the *Sun* are Mercury, Venus, and *Earth*.

Where on *earth* did you find the missing file?

The *sun* is so bright on that side of the building that it faded the shades.

What will be the effect of global warming on the *earth's* atmosphere?

d. Don't capitalize *the* unless it's part of an official place name or title.

the Hague   *The Wall Street Journal*

4.   <u>SEASONS, HOLIDAYS, AND EVENTS</u>

a. Seasons of the year should be written in lowercase, unless they are capitalized by another rule.

The exceptionally hard *winter* caused a lot of structural damage that we fixed in the *spring*.

but:

Enclosed is a copy of our *Spring* Training Catalogue.

b. Don't capitalize the names of centuries or decades.

the music of the *nineties*
the *twentieth* century

c. Capitalize the names of holidays.

Independence Day   Christmas
Fourth of July   Rosh Hashanah

d. Capitalize the names of historical events and cultural ages.

Battle of Bull Run   Age of Enlightenment
Second World War   Roaring Twenties

5. ORGANIZATIONS, INSTITUTIONS, AND LAWS

a. Capitalize the names of organizations, institutions, buildings, companies, associations, societies, conventions, clubs, independent committees, and the like. Use the style of the organization as it appears in its own written communications.

Penn Central Transportation Company
Empire State Building
American Association of Retired Persons
Oberlin College
Grolier Society
World Science Fiction Convention
Girl Scouts
Democratic National Committee

Generally capitalize internal departments within a company.

Board of Directors
Research and Development
Marketing

but:

our *marketing* people

Kinds of organizations aren't capitalized if they're not part of an official name.

Starting next month, we will hold our *club* meetings at the Community Center because the Rotary Club wants its space back.

Our *advertising department* hired three new copywriters last year.

b. Words such as *federal, government, commonwealth,* and *union* are written in lowercase unless they're part of an official name.

federal laws on flying

Federal Aviation Association

Union of Soviet Socialist Republics

Commonwealth of Independent States

Please contact the *Commonwealth* of Virginia for further information.

The citizens of the *commonwealth* wish to preserve its natural beauty.

Our offices have moved to *Government Center* in Boston.

c. Capitalize the titles of laws, acts, bills, programs, and the like.

Sherman Antitrust Act   the Fifth Amendment
Social Security Administration   the Hawkins Bill

but:

public *acts*, propose an *amendment, social security benefits*

6.   <u>TITLES</u>

a. Capitalize the first word and all the main words of books, articles, reports, and other documents.

> The Secret Life of Machines
> "Eating at the Office on $2 a Day"
> "Trade Show Exhibits: Choosing a Space"
> Annual Report 1991
> "Caring for Your House Plants"

b. Capitalize articles (*a, an, the*), conjunctions (*and, but*), and prepositions (*to, on, over, during*) only if they begin a title or have more than four letters.

> "*The* Best Program *for* This Environment"
> "Mind *over* Matter"
> Report *on* Maternity *and* Paternity Leave
> "Increasing Profits *During a* Recession"

c. If a preposition is part of a verb, capitalize it.

> "Setting *Up* the Conference Room"
> "Getting *Down* to the Business of Writing"
> "How to Log *On* to the System"

d. Generally capitalize each word in a hyphenated compound, except for articles, short prepositions, and connecting words.

> "*State-of-the-Art* Laser Photography"

> "*Twenty-Five* Ways to Save Energy in Your Office"

> The Cool Comfort of *Cotton-Lined* Clothing

7. BEGINNING WORDS IN SENTENCES

a. Always capitalize the first word of a sentence or an expression used as a sentence.

> *How* much time did you spend drafting the proposal?

> *Self*-confidence soared as the final day of training approached.

> *The* end.

b. Capitalize the first word in a quoted sentence.

His e-mail said, "*You* all deserve Friday afternoon off since this project is ahead of deadline."

c. Capitalizing after a colon is optional if the words can stand alone as a sentence. Many writers no longer capitalize a sentence after a colon. Whichever style you choose, be consistent.

Let me tell you this much: *We* couldn't have finished this project without your input.

There are two important requirements for this job: *every* applicant must be computer literate and a graduate of customer-service training.

If the thought after the colon explains the thought in the first part of the sentence, a lowercase letter should follow the colon.

I never should have left the house today without an umbrella: *it* always rains on Wednesdays.

d. A complete sentence inside dashes, parentheses, or brackets takes a lowercase initial letter if the enclosed material is part of the main sentence.

We plan to introduce new items to increase our sales—*sales* last year dropped 7 percent.

We plan to introduce new items to increase our sales (*sales* last year dropped 7 percent).

If the enclosed words are a complete sentence but the enclosure lies outside any sentence, capitalize the first letter.

We plan to introduce new items to increase sales. (*Our* sales last year dropped 7 percent.)

8. <u>BEGINNING WORDS IN LISTS</u>

Capitalize the first word in bulleted lists of items only if the item is a complete sentence or begins with a proper noun. If you capitalize one item by this rule, capitalize all to be consistent.

Before we decide, we must consider

- product costs
- salaries
- plant maintenance.

By the end of the month, we must pay

- FICA
- State tax
- Federal tax.

This section explains how to

- take personal days
- report sick days
- schedule vacations.

but:

This section answers the following questions:

- How many personal days can you take?
- How do you report sick days?
- What is the procedure for scheduling vacations?

9.   <u>LETTER SALUTATIONS AND CLOSINGS</u>

Capitalize the first word of salutations and closings of letters.

Dear Dr. Barker: Cordially,

10.   <u>ABBREVIATIONS</u>

In general, capitalize abbreviations when the words they represent are capitalized.

UNH	University of New Hampshire
FBI	Federal Bureau of Investigation
R.N.	Registered Nurse
ZIP	Zone Improvement Plan

11. <u>HYPHENATED WORDS</u>

In a hyphenated compound, capitalize only the proper nouns and adjectives.

The new offices are in *neo-Gothic* style.

Enclosed is our latest catalogue, which includes *pre-Columbian* pottery.

We now offer translation services for our *non-English-speaking* clients.

Our *follow-up* training takes place three months after the workshop.

Use your dictionary

If you aren't sure whether to capitalize, check a good dictionary or the style book your organization uses.

(See also **acronyms and initialisms**, **headlines**, **lists**, **nouns**, **titles**.)

---

case

Case refers to the relationship a noun or pronoun has to other words in a sentence. The three main cases in English grammar are the *subjective*, the *objective*, and the *possessive*. The form of a noun changes only in the possessive case. Pronouns may change for all three cases.

Subjective or nominative case

Words that name the topic of a clause are in the subjective or nominative case.

MAIN USES OF THE SUBJECTIVE CASE

1. The subject of a verb. The subject performs the action of the sentence. It answers the question *who?* or *what?* and normally precedes the verb.

   E-mail has revolutionized business communication. [noun subject]

   He finished the proposal yesterday. [pronoun subject]

2. The complement of a linking verb. A linking verb such as *to be*, *become*, *seem*, or *appear* expresses no action—it links the subject of the sentence to its complement, a word or phrase that completes the meaning of the subject. Like the subject, the complement must be in the subjective case.

   She became our *treasurer* last year. [Noun subjective complement. *Treasurer* is subjective because it complements the subject, *she*.]

   The first one to qualify was *he*. [Pronoun subjective complement. *He* indicates who qualified. It is subjective because it complements the subject, *the first one to qualify*.]

3. A comparison after *than* and *as*. The noun or pronoun is the subject of the missing clause.

   Tony is a better writer than *Monica* [is].

   Tony is a better writer than *she* [is].

   The temporaries we hired did the job as completely as *we* [would have].

Objective or accusative case

Words in the objective or accusative case are direct or indirect objects. They receive the action of the verb.

MAIN USES OF THE OBJECTIVE CASE

1. The direct object of a verb. The direct object answers the question *who?* or *what?* and normally follows the verb.

   We need a new *printer* for the fourth floor. [*Printer*, a noun, is the direct object of the verb *need*.]

   My supervisor wants *me* at the meeting. [*Me*, an objective-case pronoun, is the direct object of the verb *wants*.]

2. The indirect object of a verb. The indirect object answers the question *to* or *for what?* or *for whom?* and follows the verb.

   Yesterday we sent [to] the *client* a proposal. [*Client*, a noun, is the indirect object of the verb *sent*. *Proposal* is the direct object.]

   Mark bought [for] *us* tickets to the game. [*Us*, an objective-case pronoun, is the indirect object of the noun *bought*. *Tickets* is the direct object.]

3. The object of an infinitive. The infinitive is the form of the verb that follows *to*—*to improve*, *to sell*.

   Let's try to prevent this *situation* from happening again. [*Situation* is the noun object of the infinitive *to prevent*.]

   I encourage you to tell *him* about the problem. [*Him* is the pronoun object of the infinitive *to tell*.]

4. The object of a gerund. A gerund is a verb that ends in *-ing* and acts as a noun.

   Moving *pianos* is a hard way to make a living. [*Pianos* is the object of the gerund *moving*.]

   Susan thinks that promoting *him* would be beneficial to the department. [*Him* is the object of the gerund *promoting*.]

5. The object of a preposition.

   Use Command-N to move to the next *message*. [noun object of a preposition]

Jerry finally went on a sales call with *her*. [pronoun object of a preposition]

Possessive case

The possessive case shows ownership. Most nouns form the possessive case by adding an apostrophe or *'s*.

POSSESSIVE NOUNS

Our *lawyer's* advice is to secure a copyright. [singular possessive noun]

Three *days'* research is more than enough for this project. [plural possessive noun]

The roof leaks in the *men's* gym. [plural possessive noun]

Peter's and Ivanna's ideas are the best ones we've heard. [two singular possessive nouns—different ideas of two people]

POSSESSIVE PRONOUNS

Possessive pronouns do not use apostrophes. The common possessive pronouns are *mine, ours, yours, his, hers, its, theirs*.

Is this diskette *yours* or *mine*? [singular possessive pronouns]

We had to admit that the idea was *theirs*. [plural possessive pronoun]

Do not confuse possessive pronouns and possessive adjectives. Possessive adjectives cannot stand for nouns or pronouns because they require a following noun.

Would you like a copy of the report? I sent Jack *his* yesterday. [singular possessive pronoun]

I sent Jack *his* copy of the report yesterday. [singular possessive adjective modifying *copy*]

(See also **apostrophes**, **nouns**, **objects**, **possessive case**, **pronouns**.)

---

charts or graphs—an overview

Charts are visual representations of numeric data. They allow comparison of values, show the relationship between values, and display trends over time. A table (or spreadsheet) is the first step to any chart.

Most charts today are computer generated. Business charts are usually created through spreadsheet applications, such as Excel or Lotus 1-2-3.

These applications produce many types of charts based on data you enter into a spreadsheet—it's easy to display the data in different formats to see what kind of chart works best for your data.

One benefit of a computer-generated chart is its dynamic nature. When the data in the spreadsheet change, the change is immediately reflected in the graph. This makes spreadsheet packages especially useful for running scenarios and projections.

A well-designed chart focuses your readers' attention on your message. Charts are powerful tools for transmitting information, but designing your chart requires clear vision and skill to get the message across.

Decide the chart's message *first*, before including it in a report. Use charts to study the data and learn what the message might be. Look back at your Focus Sheet to be sure you're on track.

Why use a chart?

- Save your readers' time. A chart delivers a message effectively, without extraneous facts.
- Direct your readers' attention to information you consider important.

- Explain statistical relationships more clearly than words would.

- Capture your readers' attention. Your readers are more likely to study and remember a well-done chart than a paragraph, no matter how elegantly written.

- Illustrate nonvisual concepts visually. For example, use a scatter chart to show a correlation between two variables.

Types of charts

Following is a list of charts typically used in business. Particulars about each chart type appear in their separate alphabetical entries throughout the book.

area	map
bar or column	organizational
box	pictograms
flowcharts	pie or circle
high-low-close-open (HLCO)	process control
logarithmic	radar
line	scatter

Hybrid charts

Another type of chart is a **hybrid**, or combination, chart. A hybrid chart combines two or more traditional chart types. In a single chart, a line can show the increase in sales or growth, while columns display profit. Both forms of data can be imposed on an area chart.

Include a third chart only if it adds significant information. Remember that when it comes to graphs, more is less and less is more.

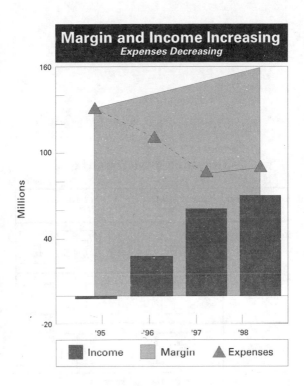

Which chart should you choose?

The biggest challenge of using charts is choosing the one that will best convey your message. With a computer it's easy to try several different charts for your data. Seeing the various charts can often help you choose. The best chart will represent the data in the most reader-friendly way.

The following matrix can also help you determine which chart is best suited to your needs.

Graphing Advice Matrix

If your message is about . . .	your 1st choice might be . . .		your 2nd choice might be . . .		
Parts of a whole					
Time series	Many data points		Few data points	Many data points	
Comparisons or display with no natural order					
Comparisons between two or more variables	Few data points		Many data points	High low series	
A cause and effect relationship			XY with trend line		

Graphing Advice Matrix

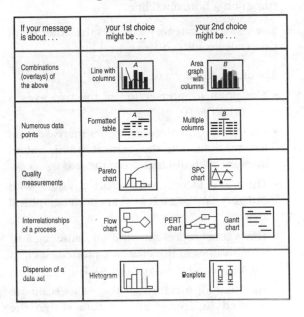

If your message is about . . .	your 1st choice might be . . .	your 2nd choice might be . . .
Combinations (overlays) of the above	Line with columns	Area graph with columns
Numerous data points	Formatted table	Multiple columns
Quality measurements	Pareto chart	SPC chart
Interrelationships of a process	Flow chart	PERT chart / Gantt chart
Dispersion of a data set	Histogram	Boxplots

Chart components

If you need a brief review of the elements of charts, skim the following sections.

X AND Y AXES

Charts that compare two sets of data, such as time and sales results, have two axes:

1. The x-axis, or category axis, has one set of data (time) on a horizontal line.

2. The y-axis, or category axis, has the other set of data (sales results) on a vertical line.

   About the x and y axes:

   • The point of intersection of the two axes is the origin or (0, 0).

   • On the horizontal x-axis, values increase from left to right. On the vertical y-axis, values increase with distance from the x-axis.

   • The x-axis identifies the charted values with category labels, such as years or geographical area.

   • The y-axis represents the measure against which values in the chart are plotted, such as dollars, quantity, or amount sold.

   • The units of measure on the y-axis scale are adjusted to display all the data within the bounds of the chart (for example, units, thousands, millions).

FIGURES

When you establish reference numbers for your graphics, count your charts as Figures (Fig. 1, Fig. 2, and so on). Each consecutive figure number is displayed at the bottom of a chart. If the figure has a caption, put the figure number to the left of the **caption.**

GRIDS

Grids are the horizontal and vertical lines parallel to chart axes on which data points are plotted. The lines are spaced evenly, and numerical scales appear on each axis. You can plot precise data on grids.

Grid lines should be light and thin so the graph's data lines will be the focus. If you write labels or numbers on the grids, delete the grid beneath the labels for easier reading. If the chart looks cluttered, consider eliminating or reducing the number of grid lines.

KEY

A key is a set of instructions for interpreting or translating symbols in a chart, map, or illustration. For example, the key for a map usually indicates the number of miles per inch.

LEGEND

A legend is an explanatory list of the symbols on a map or chart. The legend tells the reader what each color, pattern, and marker means. Include a legend if there is any risk of confusion on the part of your reader. Make your legend specific.

instead of:	Green represents Data 1
write:	Green represents Income

REFERENCE INFORMATION

Since charts generally contain summary data only, you must direct the reader to the source from which you derived the summary. A reference line can cite the reference from which the data was obtained or can refer to an appendix that contains the full set of data.

SCALE

A scale is a system of measurement used for a chart. The scale is formed by dividing the axis into equal parts and labeling each part to correspond to the values needed to show the chart's data.

TICK MARKS

Tick marks label the intervals along the x- and y-axes. Label tick marks to show the value of each interval.

TITLES AND CAPTIONS

A title is a statement that summarizes the meaning of your charts, figures, and tables, above them.

Captions are explanatory comments that you may add to your charts. The caption is the text below the chart that can add more to explain your message. Charts should speak for themselves; use as few words as possible on your charts.

Chart design guidelines

Keep these pointers in mind as you design your chart.

- Do not add a chart to fill space or look pretty. A chart should give information that is easier to see graphically than to read as text.
- Are you trying to include more than one message in a chart? Don't: you will only confuse your readers.
- Do the data support the message? If the message is "sales have continuously increased over the past ten years," do not display a line that goes up and down.
- Charts are not interchangeable; they are designed to display specific types of information. Select your chart type carefully.

- Your readers must be able to grasp information instantly from the chart. If your message is not reflected in the title and supported by the chart, it will not succeed.

- Label all lines and axes that are not self-evident.

- Is the scale on the graph consistent? Do not rely on the reader to convert the values or make adjustments for scale variations. Set the scale to fit the space and remain consistent.

- Do not include more data than readers can comprehend at a glance. A cluttered look will cause readers to skip the chart.

- If your chart is good, you should not need to present the same information at length in the text. Use the space for interpretation, not for restating the same message in words.

The "Be Your Own Chart Editor" Checklist

Use the following checklist to edit your charts.

❏ Is there a clear and concise message on the chart?

❏ Have you decided where to place the chart?

❏ Are all charts mentioned in the text?

❏ Have you selected the best chart for the data and message?

❏ Is the reader familiar with the chart type?

❏ Have you titled, referenced, and dated the chart?

❏ Is the time period of the data clear?

❏ Have you added the appropriate emphasis?

❏ Do you have maximum message and minimum ink?

(See also **area charts**, **bar or column charts**, **box charts**, **diagrams**, **figures**, **flowcharts**, **high-low-close-open charts**, **line charts**, **map charts**, **numeric data**, **pictograms**, **pie or circle charts**, **process control charts**, **radar charts**, **scatter charts**, **tables**.)

---

clear writing

Your purpose in writing is to give your readers information and ideas. To achieve this goal, your writing must be clear. Follow these guidelines to **clear writing**:

- Organize your document for readability. Put the "bottom line" or key message at the beginning, so your readers will immediately know what they are reading and why. Sequence your ideas logically and label them clearly with headlines.

- Write short paragraphs. Each one should contain a topic sentence and one key idea. Use transitions between paragraphs to help the flow of ideas.

- Make sure your sentences are well structured and coherent. Streamline them: use as few words as possible to convey your message. Remember that variety in sentence structure will maintain your readers' interest.

- Use words that are precise and suitable for your audience. Don't use technical terms and jargon for nontechnical readers.

- Create a visual design that breaks up your text with white space and helps your readers navigate your document.

The best way to achieve clarity and coherence is to follow the Six Steps to Reader-Centered Writing™.

Unclear writing

Here is an excerpt from a U.S. government request for proposal (RFP).

> SOL N00000-95-X-0000 POC Contract Specialist, Tom Bergeron (999) 999-9999. Contracting Officer, Susan Jablonski. Technical Contact, Dr. Damian Wolfe. Broad Agency Announcement (BAA). The Naval Command, Control and Ocean Surveillance Center (NCCOSC), RDT&E Division (NRaD) is seeking proposals (technical and cost) with innovative approaches for a research and development effort primarily to support the Advanced Research Projects Agency's (ARPA) Hyperspectral Mine Detection (HMD) Program.
>
> Consideration may be given to proposals to use this same technology for other applications. Uncleared land mines pose a significant challenge to the achievement of key U.S. military and foreign policy objectives. They inhibit the safe movement of soldiers and repatriation of refugees . . . Advanced technology offers the promise of enabling more effective assistance to be offered to afflicted areas and thereby reducing the human suffering which now results from uncleared minefields.
>
> The objective of the HMD program is to investigate, develop, and demonstrate a hyperspectral infrared technology . . .

Consider the following questions:

1. Where is the bottom line—the objective of the RFP? How much background information did you have to wade through before you found it?

2. Would breaking this passage up into headlined paragraphs help you read it?

3. How would you streamline such passages as *offers the promise of enabling more effective assistance*?

4. Did the acronyms improve the readability of this RFP?

For examples of clear writing, turn to any of the model documents in the appendix of this book.

How to edit for clarity

To improve the clarity of your writing, pay attention to these issues as you edit:

- paragraph length
- sentence length
- sentence variety
- number of subordinate clauses
- transitions
- streamlining
- word choice
- pace

PARAGRAPH LENGTH

The more difficult the material, the shorter the paragraphs should be. Short paragraphs make a page look more understandable even before the reader pays attention to individual sentences. In general, paragraphs shouldn't be more than six lines long if pages are 8 1/2″ × 11″.

SENTENCE LENGTH AND VARIETY

Sentences that are heavy with technical details are easier to read if they're short. Try not to exceed 20 words in length.

instead of:	A unique feature of this circuit is the low headroom design of the high-gain amplifier, which produces a precision 3.0 V output from an input voltage as low as 4.5 V, or 2.5 V from a 4.0 V input.
write:	A unique feature of this circuit is the low headroom design of the high-gain amplifier. It produces a precision 3.0 V output from an input voltage as low as 4.5 V, and 2.5 V from a 4.0 V input.

Vary your sentences. Too many short, choppy sentences can be as hard to read as overlong ones, for all the ideas may seem equally important. Combine short sentences for readability.

instead of: We called the limousine service to the airport. Five of us wanted to use it. We were all going to the trade show in Houston.

write: Since five of us were going to the trade show in Houston, we called the limousine service to the airport.

Make complex ideas or a series of thoughts easier to understand by putting them in shorter, easier-to-read sentences.

instead of: First you consider how children learn and then incorporate those principles into how they use interactive software, especially in a math program, which makes use of both text and numbers in an attempt to interest children in real-life problems.

write: Consider how children learn, then incorporate those principles into interactive software design. Math programs, in particular, should use both text and numbers to interest children in real-life problems.

SUBORDINATION

Put your important points in independent clauses and the subordinate points in dependent clauses and phrases. Sentences with subordinate elements create variety, too—just don't make them too long.

instead of: A unique feature of this circuit is the low headroom design of the high-gain amplifier. It produces a precision output.

write: A unique feature of this circuit is the
                low headroom design of the high-
                gain amplifier, *which produces a
                precision output*.

TRANSITIONS

Transition words help the material flow by guiding
readers from one thought to another. Contrasts
and similarities are clearer when transitions are
clear.

instead of: A unique feature of this circuit is
                the low headroom design of the
                high-gain amplifier. It produces a
                precision 3.0 V output from an
                input voltage as low as 4.5 V. It also
                produces a 2.5 V output from a 4.0
                V input.

write: A unique feature of this circuit is the
                low headroom design of the high-
                gain amplifier. *For example*, it is
                capable of producing a precision 3.0
                V output from an input voltage as
                low as 4.5 V. It can also produce 2.5
                V output from a 4.0 V input.

STREAMLINING

Eliminate unnecessary words to make your message clear.

instead of: Advanced technology offers the
                promise of enabling more effective
                assistance to be offered to afflicted
                areas and thereby reducing the
                human suffering which now results
                from uncleared minefields.

write: Advanced technology offers a
                promise: to reduce the human suffer-
                ing that is the result of uncleared
                minefields.

WORD CHOICE

If you use language that is simple, clear, and straightforward, your readers won't be slowed by complicated or unknown vocabulary. Define new or difficult terms. Don't use jargon or acronyms unless they are necessary to understanding the document.

PACE

If you pack sentences with too much information, you will overwhelm your readers. But if you draw your ideas out with wordy sentences that weaken your main points, your pace will be too slow; and you will lose your readers' interest.

The following examples show a hasty and unclear passage, a slow and wordy passage, and a suggested rewrite.

too fast: Small dealers face a lot of competition from megadealers although small dealers can hold their own if they have loyal customers, who are like friends, coming back again and again. Don't forget it's the customer who *really* signs the dealer's paychecks!

too slow: Small dealers usually have many problems when they try to compete with the bigger dealers, often referred to as megadealers.

However, small dealers can take charge of their businesses and hold their own in a cutthroat market if their customers are loyal—if they return over and over again for more business because they like the way they're treated.

When the dealer treats customers like old friends who deserve to be treated well, those customers will indeed come back again. Remember, it's the repeat customer who has the

> power to keep small dealers in business and who also has the power to, in effect, sign their paychecks.

write: Small dealers face a lot of competition from megadealers. However, small dealers can hold their own if they have developed customer loyalty. When the dealer treats customers like friends, they will come back again and again.

Remember, it's the customer who *really* signs the dealer's paychecks!

(See also **headlines**, **Introduction to the Six Steps**, **readability**, **sentences**, **streamlining**, **transitions**, **unity**, **word choice**.)

---

cliches

A **cliche** is any trite, hackneyed phrase that was originally imaginative and meaningful. The word "cliché" means "stereotype" in French. In English, cliche is usually written without an accent mark over the *e*.

Cliches come easily in both speaking and writing because they're so familiar. Beware of them, however: language lovers frown on them as unoriginal and dull. Cliches may also be both imprecise and wordy.

Cliches are like television commercials. They may be amusing at first; but after you've seen them a dozen times, they become simply irritating.

Here are a few cliches and better expressions for them.

Cliche:	*Better:*
days are numbered	will end shortly
face the music	face the consequences
throw a monkey wrench into	complicate
once in a blue moon	rarely; almost never

In rare cases, a cliche will serve better than a more wordy route around it.

> We are sure you will agree, once you have seen our presentation on the impact of color charts, that *a picture is worth a thousand words*.

If an expression doesn't stand out in a sentence as a cliche, but instead fits the context, then it's probably acceptable to use it.

How can you tell if an expression is a cliche?

If you think of one word and a familiar phrase occurs to you, that phrase is probably a cliche. For instance, if you think "smart," then immediately "as a whip," that phrase is a cliche to avoid in writing.

How many people actually think of the sharp crack of a whip when they read "smart as a whip"? It is an outdated expression that has lost its original meaning.

If you ask your colleagues to complete an expression and they use the same words you thought of, that expression is probably a cliche. For instance, if you say "by leaps," and your coworker adds "and bounds," you can be sure that expression is too stale to be meaningful.

This paragraph has a few cliches.

> We *have on the table* a proposal to purchase two trucks to start our delivery service. As we await the *green light* from our parent company, we will *not close any doors* to other enterprises that might give our profits a *shot in the arm* this year.

The same paragraph is stronger—and much more concise—without the cliches.

> We *are considering* a proposal to purchase two trucks to start our delivery service. As we await a *decision* from our parent company, we will *look for* other enterprises that might *boost* our profits this year.

Colorful language is a form of word play everyone enjoys, but only if it adds meaning to your writing.

(See also **word choice**.)

closing a document

How you **close a document** is just as important as how you open it. In fact, the introduction and the conclusion are the most critical sections in conveying your message. Many readers focus on the introduction and the conclusion and merely skim what goes in between.

Use an action-oriented headline

You usually want to leave your reader with one main idea or request. To make that information more emphatic and more visible, place it under an eye-catching headline. Try

- Action requested
- Deadline
- Suggested next steps.

Remember your purpose in writing

Before you write a conclusion, take a final look at your Focus Sheet™ to make sure your document serves the purpose you intended. The conclusion is a good place to restate your main goal.

You may want to close with a prediction.

If we delay in developing a new digital filter, we risk losing out on a growing and potentially lucrative market. Increasing the R&D budget by 7 percent should enable us to develop such a product within four months.

Or you may ask a provocative question that gets the reader thinking about your ideas.

I believe our telemarketing techniques are inefficient and outdated. Can we afford to continue using our slow and outdated system in the face of our second-quarter losses?

Think clearly about the overriding purpose of the document and then decide whether your conclusion should summarize information, request an action, make a recommendation or prediction, or reach a judgment. A personal touch in closing leaves a friendly feeling and invites further business.

Concluding a letter, memo, or e-mail message

In correspondence use your conclusion to say thank you, offer help, or request action by a certain date. The main rule is to exit quickly and gracefully. Don't repeat information unless it adds emphasis to your final point.

To avoid using cliches, think about how you would say goodbye to this reader face to face. Chances are you wouldn't say, "Do not hesitate to contact me" or "Should you have any further questions . . ."

Don't write anything you wouldn't say. In other words, make your ending personable and, if appropriate, friendly.

Here are some endings you might try:

I'm available to answer your questions at extension 824.

Please let me know if you need more information.

Since the vice president has asked me to respond by May 10, I'd appreciate receiving the information from you by May 1.

Thank you again for your inquiry. I will call you next Wednesday to ask if I can answer any further questions.

(See also **electronic mail**, **getting started**, **letters**, **memorandums**.)

colons

A **colon** (:) is a mark of punctuation that tells readers that a list or related thought follows.

With clauses and phrases

You may put a colon between two independent clauses, or between an independent clause and a phrase, if the second clause or phrase explains the first.

> I remember the experience I got at the real estate company: it prepared me well for the sales work I'm in now. [two independent clauses]

The colon makes the second thought more important than the first.

> He believed only one thing ruined his dry cleaning business: the new mall across the highway. [independent clause and explanatory phrase]

With lists

LISTS WITHIN SENTENCES

A colon can introduce a list within a sentence.

> There are four basic ways to connect to the Internet: an e-mail gateway, terminal access, a UUCP connection, and MacTCP access. [commas between short items]

> The Lowell Road site is the best choice for four reasons: (1) proximity to I89; (2) immediate availability; (3) reasonable rent; and (4) capability for expansion. [semicolons between enumerated items]

> This company offers some unusual benefits: for example, aerobics classes, paternity leave, and subsidized parking. [colon before, not after, introductory words *for example*]

Never put a colon between a verb or preposition and its object.

> *instead of:*   The three doors that serve as emergency exits are: the basement, the south side, and the third floor fire escape. [colon between a verb and its objects]

write:	The three doors that serve as emergency exits are the basement, the south side, and the third floor fire escape.
instead of:	During summer vacations, we may have to assign you to: accounts receivable or transportation. [colon between a preposition and its objects]
write:	During summer vacations, we may have to assign you to accounts receivable or transportation.

VERTICAL LISTS

A colon can introduce a vertical list.

The Lowell Road site is the best choice for four reasons:

1. proximity to I89
2. immediate availability
3. reasonable rent
4. capability for expansion

If the listed items are sentences, punctuate each as a complete thought, with a capital letter and a period. If the listed items complete the introductory sentence, a period is helpful.

Omit the colon in a vertical list when:

1. The last word introducing the list is a verb.

   The three doors that serve as emergency exits are

   1. the basement
   2. the south side
   3. the third floor fire escape.

2. The last word introducing the list is a preposition.

   Please check the emergency exits between

   • the second and third floors
   • the computer room and the back hallway
   • the cafeteria and the parking lot.

3. The list items finish the sentence.

> The proposal will be ready when
>
> • Derek inserts the graphics
> • Hannah proofreads the Appendix
> • Frank writes a cover letter.

With quotes

A colon can introduce a direct quote. Capitalize the first word of the quote if it's capitalized in the quoted material.

> Author Zora Neale Hurston says: "Research is formalized curiosity."

Always put a colon outside quotation marks.

> Here is one thing we can do with this anonymous "accusation": ignore it.

Omit punctuation before an indirect question or quote.

instead of: Our problem is: delegating the work without fragmenting the project.

write: Our problem is delegating the work without fragmenting the project.

With expressions of time and proportion

Use a colon to separate hours from minutes.

> 11:45 a.m.   3:00

Use a colon in expressions of proportion. The colon stands for *to*.

> 4:1   9:2

With references

Use a colon to separate volumes from pages.

> See *Technical Book Review Index* 9:121

Use a colon to separate titles from subtitles.

> *Sleep: Tracking the Elusive Sandman*

With salutations

Use a colon after the salutation in a business letter.

Dear Ms. Amato: Dear Manager:

(See also **capital letters**, **lists**, **punctuation**.)

---

color: the latest strategy for reaching readers

More and more organizations are using the power of **color** in advertising, sales presentations, overhead transparencies, reports, and letters. They are exploiting color to excite an audience, attract attention, and sell their product. Although businesses have been doing this for years, color is more prevalent today because it's more affordable.

Color monitors and color printers have become standard equipment in most offices, and software programs offer a tempting assortment of colorful graphics.

Limit yourself to two colors in a business document

With color at your fingertips, it's easy to overdo it. Bear in mind that color in business documents should enhance communication, not just decorate.

It should unify your report or otherwise further your purpose, not bombard your readers with so many color sensations that the serious message of your document is lost.

Use your Focus Sheet™ to analyze color needs

To decide whether color would benefit a piece of writing, you must first consider the purpose of your document and your readers.

Look at your Focus Sheet. Do you need an especially strong approach? Will your document be
your readers' first exposure to your business? If so,
what message do you wish to convey?

Your organization's corporate identity may dictate color guidelines. Be sure to familiarize yourself
with these before proceeding.

With the purpose of your document in mind,
consider how color could further your goals. Color
will

- unify a document
- highlight key ideas
- convey a mood
- code information
- enhance readability
- make your document stand out from the
  competition's.

The clearer you are about the purpose of your
document, the easier it will be for you to decide
your color objectives.

Where to use color

A common place to use color is in section titles,
headlines, and subheads. Like using a different
font, adding color helps differentiate between sections of your document. Highlight key points using
colored bullets. Outline boxes, charts, and graphs
in color so they stand out from the text.

You may be considering a color instead of black
for the body text. Tests indicate that comprehension increases as text color approaches black.

If you do decide to use color, be sure the contrast is strong between text and background. Light
text on a light background seems to shrink back,
while dark text on a light background leaps out at
you.

Decide the color of your largest text areas first,
then select colors for progressively smaller areas.
Give your document a balanced look by using

stronger colors in the smaller areas, paler colors in the larger ones. Aim for simplicity and unity with a consistent use of color throughout.

Some important terms

If you plan to work with a graphic designer or simply need to discuss color with your art department, it's helpful to know some color vocabulary. Here are the terms that will help you describe qualities of color:

1. *Hue* means color.
2. *Saturation* is the degree of purity of a given hue; royal blue is highly saturated, grayish-blue is not.
3. *Tint* is the result of adding white to a hue.
4. *Shade* is the result of adding black to a hue.
5. *Color temperature* means how warm or cool a color appears. Warm colors are red, orange, yellow, and brown; cool colors are blue, green, and violet.
6. *Color scheme* is the selection of particular hues, tints, shades, and temperatures.

Color connotations: which should you use?

The more you work with colors, the more familiar you'll become with the results they can produce.

A high-contrast color scheme, for instance, will enhance visibility and heighten the impact of your message. A monochromatic color scheme unifies, while a warm one lends a strong and vital tone to your work.

Different colors evoke different sensations and emotions. The following are some typical ways we respond to individual colors. Remember, these responses are culturally based. The color scheme you select for an American audience may have a very different impact on readers in China.

- *red*: active, powerful, striking; in business may suggest debt
- *pink*: sweet and playful; softens the impact of red
- *orange*: festive, fun, bright
- *yellow*: sunny, cheerful, lively
- *green*: natural, healthy, fresh
- *purple*: sophisticated, regal, mysterious
- *blue*: calm, reliable; the darker the more conservative; in business suggests fiscal reliability
- *brown*: earthy, secure, useful
- *white*: clean, honest, pure
- *gray*: important and authoritative
- *black*: sophisticated

Color tips

1. Bright colors like orange or red are good for highlighting key ideas. Vivid red creates excitement and suggests action. Use brown for less important items.

2. Gray and yellow are good background colors—bright colors contrast well with them.

3. Neutral grays lend a high-tech look. Use a bright color for highlight.

4. Muted hues on a buff, ivory, or gray background create a natural appearance.

You have many options in your use of color. If the selection process seems overwhelming, learn by analyzing the documents you read.

How would you feel about getting a bright red and yellow proposal? Think about the image a company presents with deep purple headings on thick, gray paper. Your own observations will guide you when it's time to make decisions yourself.

For more advice on using color, contact the Xerox Corporation directly. They sell software to help you make color choices and equipment to create and copy color documents.

(See also **getting started**, **graphics**, **illustrations**, **visual design**.)

---

commas

A **comma** (,) is a mark of punctuation that groups information, making sentences readable and understandable. In general, commas either *set off* elements of a sentence that interrupt the main thought, or *separate* elements from each other to make their relationships clear.

With independent clauses

An independent clause can stand alone as a sentence. Commas separate two independent clauses that are joined by conjunctions, such as *and, or, but, for, nor, yet*, and *so*.

> Anne needs to leave work at 4:00 today, for she has a dentist's appointment.

> Our e-mail connection is down, so I am faxing you the information you requested.

Always put the commas before the conjunction.

instead of: There are dozens of editing commands *but,* you need to know only a few to get started.

write: There are dozens of editing commands*, but* you need to know only a few to get started. [comma before the conjunction *but*]

You may omit the comma if the independent clauses are each only three or four words long, but it's always correct to put the comma in.

> The door was locked and the window was open.

or:

> The door was locked, and the window was open.

With introductory elements

INTRODUCTORY PHRASES AND CLAUSES

Always use a comma after a long introductory phrase or clause. Most writers define long as four to six words.

When Bill accepts the job, he'll take us all out to celebrate. [introductory dependent clause]

During the accident investigation, the police found that the suspect dealt in stolen appliances. [introductory phrase]

Three of our trucks were out of commission at one time. *When we looked at the garage invoices,* we realized the problem was the manufacturer's fault in each case. [The dependent clause *When we looked at the garage invoices* introduces the independent clause in the second half of the sentence.]

Phrases and clauses beginning with *if* always take a comma, regardless of their length.

If necessary, call me.

INTRODUCTORY WORDS

Put a comma after introductory emphasis words, such as *yes* and *no.*

No, the books you ordered haven't arrived yet.

If you begin a sentence with a name in direct address, follow the name with a comma.

Vivian, it was a pleasure to meet you yesterday.

It is optional to put a comma after transitional words and short phrases—such as adverbs, adverb phrases, and prepositional phrases—that introduce sentences. (Remember that if the phrase or clause has four or more words, you should always follow it with a comma.)

Therefore, the supplies you need won't arrive till June 6.

At first, we couldn't believe we won the contract.

As a rule, the cafeteria closes by 2:00.

Put a comma after the introduction to a direct quote.

Colleen said, "This proposal should go out today."

But if you are not quoting directly, write it this way:

Colleen said this proposal should go out today.

With nonessential interruptions

Some phrases and clauses that interrupt a sentence are necessary to its meaning, but some are not.

If a clause, phrase, appositive that identifies the noun it follows, or transitional word is not essential to the meaning of the sentence, set it off with commas. Your readers will then know that the information between the commas is optional or extra.

Our newest salesman, *who came from our biggest competitor,* sold the most term life policies last month. [clause]

This picture, *according to the graphics department,* is too big for the scanner. [phrase]

The two technicians, *laboring hard in the lab,* managed to finalize the results by the deadline. [phrase]

Krista, *an excellent editor,* has offered to review the final report. [appositive]

Mike warned us, *however,* that the system will be down from 6:30 to 7:00 p.m. [transitional word]

If you address someone directly, put commas around the name.

Thank you again, *Vivian,* for meeting with me yesterday.

With items in a series

When three or more nouns, verbs, phrases, or clauses occur in a series, and the last one has *and, or,* or *nor* in front of it, use serial commas. Put a comma after each item, but omit it after the last item in the series.

It's good to know as much about *grammar, usage, and punctuation* as you can. [nouns; no comma after *punctuation*]

The vice president for Latin America *loved* the presentation, *rejected* the corporate logo change, and *stayed* until 9 p.m. discussing options with our marketing director. [verbs]

You can make an appointment for *early morning, just after lunch, or after business hours.* [phrases]

The president announced that *John is the new product manager, Lisa is transferring to design, and Margaret will retire in August.* [clauses]

If you omit any commas in a series, the sentence may be confusing or may not have the meaning you intended.

confusing: The new teams are Maria and Kurt, Dolores and Pat and Peter and Fran.

clear: The new teams are Maria and Kurt, Dolores and Pat, and Peter and Fran.

With adjectives in a series

Use commas to separate a series of three or more adjectives. Don't put a comma between the last adjective and the noun.

He has a reputation as an *efficient, hard-working, caring* supervisor.

He has a reputation as an *efficient, hard-working, and caring* supervisor.

He has a reputation as an *efficient and caring* supervisor. [No comma between *efficient* and *caring* because they are joined by *and*.]

Also use a comma for two adjectives that are not joined by *and*.

For a *quick and easy* way to add color to your graphics, see Section 5. [No comma between *quick* and *easy* because they are joined by *and*.]

For a *quick, easy* way to add color to your graphics, see Section 5. [Comma between *quick* and *easy* because the *and* has been removed.]

To determine if you need a comma between adjectives, put *and* between them.

The Golden Gate is a *graceful suspension* bridge. [You wouldn't say *graceful and suspension bridge*, so you don't need a comma.]

Bart always has a *calm, businesslike, congenial* manner. [You could say *calm and businesslike and congenial manner*, so the commas are correct.]

For clarity

Try to rewrite a sentence that has the same word twice in a row, rather than using a comma to prevent confusion.

instead of: All this memo is, is a request for increased funding.

write: This memo is a request for increased funding.

Use a comma to replace an omitted verb.

Natalie requested a lamp for her office; Tom, a bookcase. [omitted verb: *requested*]

Urban Bank will occupy the first floor; Beeman Sales, Inc., the second and third floors; and The Grand Corporation, the top floor. [omitted verb: *will occupy*]

Use a comma to prevent confusion in a sentence where the grouping of words may otherwise be unclear.

Immediately before, the board gave a surprise directive to close the Ewing plant. [Use a comma even though *immediately before* is a short introductory phrase. Otherwise your audience may read *immediately before the board* as a single phrase and not understand your sentence.]

Consuelo left him, confident that he understood the procedure. [*Consuelo* was confident.]

Consuelo left him confident that he understood the procedure. [*He* was confident.]

Put a comma between the elements of an expression with two or more parts that are similarly structured and equally balanced.

The more I see of his work, the more I like it.

Put a comma between two contrasting thoughts.

We're using PCs, not Macs.

You got the e-mail from Julie, didn't you?

Separate two unrelated numbers with a comma.

In 1995, 37 vendors submitted proposals.

With names, addresses, dates, and numbers

DIRECT ADDRESS

If you address someone directly, put commas around the name.

Thank you again, *Vivian*, for meeting with me yesterday.

If you begin a sentence with a name in direct address, follow the name with a comma.

Vivian, it was a pleasure to meet you yesterday.

SALUTATIONS AND CLOSINGS

Put a comma after the salutation in a friendly or informal letter or e-mail, and after a complimentary closing.

Dear Bobbie,   Cordially,

TITLES AND DEGREES

Put a comma between a name and title or degree.

Roger Halberstein, Executive Director   Edith Wyatt, Ph.D.

GEOGRAPHICAL NAMES AND ADDRESSES

When geographical and country names are within a sentence, put commas between the elements. Separate geographical or political subdivisions from larger units and set the entire location within commas.

> We have to call *Vancouver, British Columbia, Canada*, to order these materials.

> We chose *St. Louis, Missouri, U.S.A.*, for our new branch office.

> The on-site training will be in *Rutland, Vermont,* next month.

> He commutes from *Englewood, New Jersey,* to *Mamaroneck, New York,* every day.

Put commas between the parts of an address that's written on one line.

> Jamie McNeely, 84 Overton Road, Fairfield, OH 45014

DATES

When you write a date within a sentence, put commas after the day. Commas after the year are optional, depending on sentence structure.

> I remember *June 12, 1991,* for that was the day my book was published. [*but* don't use commas if the date is in this order: *12 June 1988*]

Don't put a comma between just the month and year.

> The office subscription to *Fortune* began with the *July 1995* issue.

With other punctuation

SEMICOLONS

Put a comma after such conjunctions as *however, therefore, moreover, furthermore, consequently,* and *nevertheless* when they introduce an independent clause. Always precede these conjunctions by a semicolon when they join two independent clauses.

> The color printer is down for the afternoon; *consequently,* we'll have to print the graphics tomorrow.

If the items in a series or list already have commas, separate these items with semicolons.

> These are the people who will serve on the ad hoc committee: Elizabeth Marrett, Public Affairs Director; Mark Friedman, Human Resources Director, who also wrote the article on workforce diversity; and Salim Malek, Engineer.

To avoid the preceding punctuation problem, you could display the information in a bulleted list. In that case, don't put semicolons after each item. Putting a period after the last item in the list is optional.

> These are the people who will serve on the ad hoc committee:
>
> * Elizabeth Marrett, Public Affairs Director
> * Mark Friedman, Human Resources Director, who also wrote the article on workforce diversity
> * Salim Malek, Engineer

QUOTATION MARKS

Always put a comma inside quotation marks, even when they enclose a complete sentence.

> Now that I've read your article, "Scanning the Future," I understand why you want to be on the planning committee.

> "Our strength is our people," the president said.

PARENTHESES AND BRACKETS

Always put a comma outside parentheses and brackets.

> Matt left a message on your voice mail (he called about 2 o'clock), but he couldn't wait for you.

END PUNCTUATION

Don't use a comma with end punctuation (period, exclamation mark, question mark) except with abbreviations that end with periods.

instead of: "Have you put together those figures yet?," she asked.

write: "Have you put together those figures yet?" she asked. [no comma after question mark]

Wingspan, *Inc.,* will meet all your teleconferencing requirements.

Unnecessary commas

Most pauses in sentences require commas, but not all. Beware of situations that tempt you to use commas incorrectly.

SUBJECT—VERB—OBJECT

Don't put a comma between a subject and verb or a verb and object, even if the sentence is long.

instead of: Monitoring the progress in the plant's assembly time, will not divert us from our goal of closing inefficient plants.

write: Monitoring the progress in the plant's assembly time will not divert us from our goal of closing inefficient plants.

instead of: He is looking for another word processor and says, he'll use a temp if he must.

write: He is looking for another word processor and says he'll use a temp if he must.

Dependent clauses

If a dependent clause follows the main clause and begins with a transitional word like *because, since,* and *after,* omit the comma unless there is a possibility of confusion.

> We are against investing in the stock you recommend because we anticipate a cash flow problem in the next quarter. [no comma before *because*.]

> We haven't invested in the stock you recommended yet, because we anticipate a cash flow problem in the next quarter. [comma before *because* to separate it from *yet*]

Comma splice

A comma splice occurs when two independent clauses are separated by only a comma. The comma is too weak to hold the sentence together.

> The regional managers have the information, the salespeople need it right away. [Two independent clauses separated by a comma.]

Here are a few ways to correct a comma splice:

1. Put a semicolon between the two clauses.

   > The regional managers have the information; the salespeople need it right away.

2. Put a semicolon and a transitional word (such as *however* or *therefore*) between the two clauses. Always follow the transitional word with a comma.

   > The regional managers have the information; however, the salespeople need it right away.

3. Put a conjunction—*and, but, or, nor, for, yet, so*—after the comma.

   > The regional managers have the information, *but* the salespeople need it right away.

The difference between the examples in 2 and 3 is mainly stylistic. The semicolon with *how-*

ever is more formal and indicates a stronger pause between the clauses. The comma with *but* is less formal and reads more smoothly.

4. Make one clause dependent on the other.

   If the regional managers have the information, the salespeople need it right away.

5. Make two sentences.

   The regional managers have the information. The salespeople need it right away. [These particular thoughts, however, sound choppy as two sentences.]

(See also **appositives**, **conjunctions**, **punctuation**, **semicolons**, **transitions**.)

comparative degree

The **comparative degree** of an adjective or adverb is more than the positive degree but less than the superlative degree.

	positive	*comparative*	*superlative*
adjective:	fast	*faster*	fastest
	good	*better*	best
	bad	*worse*	worst
adverb:	little	*less*	least
	well	*better*	best

The comparative degree compares two words or ideas in quality or manner. The superlative degree compares three; be careful not to use it to compare two things.

instead of:	Of the two new interns, Franco is *the best*.
write:	Of the two new interns, Franco is *better*.
correct:	Of the three new interns, Franco is *the best*.

How to use the comparative

Use the ending -er to form the comparative degree of most one-syllable and some two-syllable words.

There are currently two computers in the shipping room. We need to replace the *older* one.

Of the two reels, this one has the *newer* clips.

The conference had *fewer* participants this year than last.

This version of the program is a lot *better* than the previous one.

Many words use *more* to form the comparative degree.

I think medium blue is a *more pleasing* color than orange for the new conference center chairs.

This manual is *more useful* than the one from the manufacturer.

Some words can use either -er or *more* to form the comparative degree.

Stan thinks it's *more likely* that the new line will show a profit.

Stan thinks it's *likelier* that the new line will show a profit.

(See also **absolute words**, **adjectives**, **adverbs**, **comparisons**.)

---

comparisons

When you make a **comparison**, you show how two things are similar or dissimilar.

The following rules govern comparisons.

1. Make sure you compare the same kinds of items or concepts.

   instead of: These *results* are much clearer than last week's *samples*.

   write: These *results* are much clearer than the *results* from last week's samples.

2. Make comparisons complete and clear.

   instead of: The new offices are closer to the manufacturing plant *than the warehouse*. [closer to the plant or the warehouse?]

   write: The new offices are closer to the manufacturing plant *than the warehouse is*.

   or: The new offices are closer to my office *than they are to the warehouse*.

3. Make comparisons logical.

   instead of: Martha doesn't appreciate the newsletter as much as Helen. [as much as she appreciates Helen?]

   write: Martha doesn't appreciate the newsletter as much as Helen *does*.

4. For clarity in a compound comparison, use the words *as . . . as* or *as . . . as . . . than* to complete the comparison, or complete the first comparison before the second.

   The new printer is *as* fast *as*, if not faster *than*, the old one.

   instead of: This is *one of the best, if not the best,* proposals we ever wrote.

   write: This is *one of the best* proposals we ever wrote, *if not the best*.

(See also **absolute words**, **adjectives**, **adverbs**, **analogy**, **comparative degree**.)

---

concise vs. wordy writing

Conciseness and **wordiness** are opposites. Conciseness, from the Latin word *concisus*, means "to cut off." During the editing process, cut off wordiness—in other words, streamline.

Your goal is to present as much information as you can in the fewest possible words. Your readers are busy people: they shouldn't have to cut through the excess verbiage themselves to figure out your meaning.

You are guilty of wordiness if you use more words than you need, repeat yourself unnecessarily, and obscure your message.

instead of: Until such time as there is a revised company policy on unpaid vacation, please submit an application to your supervisor within a time frame of several weeks before you want to schedule unpaid vacation.

write: Until we revise unpaid vacation policy, please apply to your supervisor several weeks before you want to take unpaid time off.

Techniques for concise writing

Wordy prose can bore or confuse your reader. A concise writer makes every word count. Here are some techniques to help you write more concisely.

USE THE ACTIVE VOICE

Use the active voice rather than the passive. Make the subject perform the action of the sentence.

instead of: Wordiness should be eliminated by careful writers. [Passive: the subject, *Wordiness,* is acted upon.]

write: Careful writers eliminate wordiness. [Active: the subject, *writers,* performs the action.]

USE SIMPLER LANGUAGE

Avoid wordy, overly formal, or outdated phrases.

instead of:	Due to the fact that our cans and bottles are picked up once every weekend, please make it part of your regular routinized practice to transport your empty containers to the aluminum and glass salvaging bin in the proximity of our food concession by Friday each week.
write:	Since our recycle pick-up is on the weekend, please drop off your empty cans and bottles in the bin outside the cafeteria by Friday.

Rewriting such phrases as *due to the fact that*, *part of your regular routinized practice*, *to transport*, *in the proximity of*, and *food concession* results in a much more readable sentence.

Revise your sentences to eliminate the *it . . . that* construction, which is wordy and often uses the passive voice.

instead of:	I just heard that *it* has been decided *that* the revised deadline is May 5.
write:	I just heard that the revised deadline is May 5.
instead of:	It has been determined *that* the new system will be tested at Brand Data, Inc. [passive]
write:	Marketing decided to test the new system at Brand Data, Inc. [active]

Notice how the active sentences are shorter, more direct, and more precise in their meaning.

BE POSITIVE

Write a positive version of your statement rather than a negative one.

instead of:	When the green light does not appear, don't attempt to operate the copier.

write: Operate the copier only when the
                  green light is on.

ELIMINATE REDUNDANCY

1. Don't repeat yourself unnecessarily: simplify
   phrases that use several words where one will
   do.

   instead of: We will hold an *advance planning*
                   meeting, *brief in duration*, to *con-*
                   solidate together the work assigned
                   to Nancy's committee before they
                   continue on.

   write: We will *meet briefly* to *consolidate*
                   Nancy's committee work before the
                   group *continues.*

instead of:	*write:*
enclosed herewith	enclosed
at this point in time	now
at an early date	soon
first and foremost	first
draw to a close	end
for the reason that	because
in the event that	should
in the proximity of	near, about
involve the necessity of	require
period of time	period
revise downward	lower
subsequent to	after, following
with the exception of	except
absolutely complete	complete
circle around	circle
surround on all sides	surround
hidden pitfall	pitfall
mutual cooperation	cooperation
advance prediction	prediction
total of ten	ten
completely unique	unique
young juvenile	juvenile, youth
past history	history
empty cavity	cavity

personal opinion   opinion
visible to the eye   visible
specific example   example
fresh beginning   beginning

2. Redundancy can also result when a modifier or prepositional phrase repeats an idea contained in the modified word (*past history, visible to the eye*).

3. Watch out for explanatory phrases or clauses: instead of clarifying your meaning, they may simply be redundant.

> This overnight mail package, *which will be delivered in the morning,* contains the latest version of the interactive program I am developing. [eliminate the italicized clause]

4. Some words that intensify and qualify are so overused that they sound weak. Eliminate them: they add nothing to your writing.

instead of: Alex made it *perfectly* clear that he thinks we are *quite* capable of completing this *very* long process ourselves.

write: Alex made it clear that he thinks we are capable of completing this long process ourselves.

STREAMLINE YOUR MODIFIERS

Streamline modifiers to the fewest words possible; put them close to the words they modify.

instead of: Our business venture made us a great deal of money, *so it was successful.*

write: Our *successful* business venture made us a great deal of money.

instead of: The people *who were hired last week* must attend a meeting *which will cover building safety.*

write: The *newly hired* staff must attend a
                        building safety meeting.

DELETE THOSE EXPLETIVES

Beginning a sentence with an expletive (a pronoun
without an antecedent) is indirect and adds no
meaning.

instead of: *There are* three other commands in
                        the file menu.

write: The file menu has three other com-
                        mands.

A final hint

Don't worry about wordiness until you're ready to
revise and edit your draft. Beware of cutting so
much that your readers have difficulty figuring out
what you mean.

(See also **active voice/passive voice**, **clear writing**, **redundancy**, **streamlining**.)

conjunctions

Conjunctions, or joining words, connect other
words or groups of words and show their relationship to one another. The three kinds of conjunctions function differently in sentences. They may
be

1. coordinating
2. paired or correlative
3. subordinating.

Coordinating conjunctions

Coordinating conjunctions connect two elements
that have equal functions in the sentence. The
common coordinating conjunctions are

for, and, nor, but, or, yet, so

You can remember these conjunctions easily by the first letter of each, which spell out the acronym FANBOYS.

When a coordinating conjunction joins two independent clauses, you always put a comma before the conjunction.

We all appreciate vacations *and* holidays. [joins two objects]

Would you prefer to edit *or* to proofread? [joins two infinitives]

Shin said he sent the materials Friday, *but* I haven't received them yet. [joins two independent clauses]

CONJUNCTIVE ADVERBS

A few adverbs act as coordinating conjunctions when they come in the middle of a sentence and join two independent clauses. They are called *conjunctive adverbs*. The most common ones are

however	certainly
therefore	on the other hand
consequently	at first
thus	accordingly
moreover	instead
for example	otherwise

Beginning a sentence with a conjunctive adverb is now acceptable in business and technical writing. This is not yet correct in more formal academic writing.

However, we intend to review all the proposals before we make a decision.

Paired (or correlative) conjunctions

Paired conjunctions have a coordinating job in a sentence and join parts of equal rank. The most frequent pairs are

both . . . and
either . . . or
neither . . . nor
not only . . . but also

Specify *both* height *and* width. [joins direct objects]

Frank should take his vacation *either* in July *or* in November. [joins prepositional phrases]

Not only did Mireille learn the new computer program, *but* she *also* used it to update the audit procedure. [joins independent clauses]

Subordinating conjunctions

Subordinating conjunctions join two elements that are not equal, usually an independent with a dependent clause. The subordinating conjunction introduces the dependent, or subordinate, clause. The most common subordinating conjunctions are

after	when
because	where
since	while
unless	as
although	that
before	

The subordinating conjunction tells your reader what the relationship is between the two elements in the sentence.

When we tried to run the program, the system crashed. [time]

We're doing it this way *because* the client requested it. [cause]

Unless you're in good physical shape, don't sign up for the ropes course. [condition]

Although the manual method is more time consuming, it works much better than the automatic. [contrast]

Put a comma after the dependent clause when it comes at the beginning of the sentence. No comma is necessary when the dependent clause comes last.

Unless you're in good physical shape, don't sign up for the ropes course.

Don't sign up for the ropes course unless you're in good physical shape.

A final note

Although conjunctions are little words, they are important to the logic of a sentence because they connect ideas.

(See also **adverbs**, **commas**, **sentences**.)

contractions

A **contraction** is an abbreviation that joins two words with an apostrophe where a letter or letters are left out.

do not	don't	could not	couldn't
let us	let's	she will	she'll
I have	I've	you are	you're

Don't confuse contractions with possessive pronouns, which show ownership. Possessive pronouns never have apostrophes.

possessive pronoun	*contraction*	
its	it's	(it is/it has)
his	he's	(he is/he has)
their	they're	(they are)
your	you're	(you are)
whose	who's	(who is/has)

Contractions create an informal, often conversational tone in writing. They aren't usually appropriate in formal reports and technical writing.

(See also **apostrophes**, **tone**.)

copyright

Copyright gives the author or originator of a publication legal ownership. The copyright holder holds the exclusive right to the publication, production, and sale of rights to the published work.

U.S. federal law allows a copyright holder to prevent unauthorized use of an original work, either published or unpublished. No one else can copy or distribute the work without obtaining the copyright holder's permission. There is usually a permission fee, too.

Work-for-hire

If you create something under a work-for-hire agreement, the person or company that commissioned the work owns the copyright. Work-for-hire can be done by an employee of a company, or it can be commissioned separately for a specific assignment.

How long does a copyright last?

The copyright law protects both published and unpublished works for the life of the author plus 50 years. If a work has more than one author, the copyright lasts for the life of the last survivor plus 50 years.

If you use a pseudonym or create a work anonymously, copyright protection lasts 100 years after the creation of the work or 75 years after publication, whichever is shorter. This same period of time applies to works created under a work-for-hire agreement.

When the copyright period is over, the work passes into the public domain. Anyone can then reproduce and use it without obtaining permission or paying a fee.

Registering for a copyright

Your work is protected whether or not you register it with the Copyright Office or publish a notice of copyright in the work. The advantage to registering a work is that it simplifies making a claim of infringement against the copyright.

An official copyright notice is the symbol © or the word "Copyright"; the year of first publication; and the name of the copyright owner or owners.

© 1991 by Edmond Garrett   *or*
Copyright 1991 by Green Street Press

Fair use

If you wish to use copyrighted material in a document, be sure to give credit in footnotes or endnotes, acknowledgments, or right in the text.

You may need to obtain permission and pay a fee to use the material; however, copyright law allows for fair use, or limited use of material free of charge in some cases.

How do you know whether to obtain permission? There is no specific number of lines or words that may be used without permission; authors and publishers vary widely on the limits of fair use. It's therefore best to check in all cases.

Generally, academic presses are freer with copyrighted material, especially when used by other academics; commercial presses are the most restrictive.

When you want to use copyrighted material, consider these criteria, which Congress outlined in 1992 to protect authors:

- the purpose of the use; whether it is for commercial or nonprofit educational purposes
- the nature of the copyrighted work
- the amount and content of the portion used
- the effect of the use upon the market for the copyrighted work

Some accepted purposes for fair use are teaching, news reporting, and research, but recent rulings have put limits on even these uses. A teacher, for example, may not photocopy a whole chapter from a book without paying royalties.

You may use U.S. government publications freely because they are not copyrighted.

For copyright applications or detailed information about copyright law, contact:

Copyright Office
Library of Congress
Washington, DC 20559
202.707.9100

(See also **documenting sources**, **plagiarism**, **professional articles**, **quotations**, **research**.)

---

cover letters for resumes

Focus on the company—not on yourself

The main objective of a **cover letter** is to show a potential employer that your skills are an excellent match for the position to be filled.

Rather than starting out with background information about yourself, concentrate on the target company and explain why you're interested in it. Then highlight your skills that would be most useful in the position advertised.

Use your letter to tailor your resume to the job. Pull out three key skills or experiences from your resume that show your suitability for the position. Put them in a bulleted list.

For example, experience with desktop publishing might be a big advantage in the new position, yet it might appear at the end of your resume under computer experience. Highlight that skill in your letter.

Avoid stiff language

Formal language is dull to read and doesn't convey anything unique about you. Your readers will not find you unique as they read sentences like these:

Enclosed please find my resume and letters of recommendation.

I am writing with regard to your position, which was listed in *The Globe & Mail*.

Let your own voice come through in your letter. Imagine that you are carrying on a conversation with your prospective employer in person. You can be polite and quietly assertive without being formal.

Does your personality come across?

Try to show your reader something about who you are by using a few adjectives, like "energetic" or "team player." Give an example of business experience that shows something about your character.

It's difficult to describe your own personality; but if you do it well, it may prove the best way to stand out from other candidates.

Be careful not to oversell yourself. If you make a bold statement like "I'm perfect for the job," be sure you fill all the requirements. If your employer finds a reason why you're not fully qualified, you'll lose all credibility. It's best to strike a balance between self-confidence and quiet assurance.

(See also **letters**, **opening letters and memos**, **Model Documents Appendix**.)

---

cultural bias

In all business writing you do, it's essential to be tactful. If you insult your reader by suggesting any sort of **cultural bias**—even inadvertently—your document may not even be read. People today are more sensitive to racial and gender issues than ever.

Try to avoid mistakes due to lack of awareness.

Choose the correct terms

Over the past 10 or 20 years some cultural groups have changed the name by which they wish to be identified. Many find the old names derogatory or degrading. Keep abreast of acceptable terminology. Some examples follow:

instead of:	*write:*
black	African American
Indian	native American
oriental	Asian

Of course you should also avoid all slang designations, such as "Japs" or "Canucks," even in the most casual settings.

Avoid stereotypes

It's easy to lapse into cultural stereotypes, often without realizing it. Just as you should avoid sweeping statements based on sexual stereotypes, be equally attuned to cultural ones.

Even if the statement isn't particularly negative, it can be misinterpreted, and there are always exceptions to broad generalizations. Avoid such statements as:

Japanese are quiet and polite.

The Irish are hot-tempered.

Southerners are slow.

Youth culture

Unlike other cultures, American culture today fails to look up to older people as a source of knowledge, wisdom, and experience. Rather, youth is glamorized.

When you write, you may have no idea about the ages of your readers. Avoid being critical of anyone on the basis of age—you may inadvertently insult a senior executive.

(See also **sexist language**.)

D

dangling modifiers

A **dangling modifier** is a phrase or clause that doesn't logically refer to, or modify, another word in the sentence. Often such troublesome modifiers come at the beginning of a sentence. They often include verbs that end in *-ing* or *-ed*.

The typical error that occurs: the noun or pronoun immediately following the opening phrase does not represent the person or thing described in that phrase.

instead of:	Confused by the legal jargon, the contract had to be explained to me. [Was the contract confused?]
write:	Confused by the legal jargon, *I* had the contract explained to me. [Supplying the subject *I* gives *Confused* something to modify logically.]
instead of:	Knowing the warehouse door was locked, the delivery was taken to the front office. [How could a delivery know anything?]
write:	Knowing the warehouse door was locked, the *driver* took the delivery to the front office. [Adding the doer *driver* solves the problem.]

A simple change from passive to active voice in the main clause will often solve the problem. In the correction of the preceding example, the main clause is in the active voice with the subject, *driver*, performing the action, *took*. The modifier, *Knowing,* now modifies a noun, *driver*, and makes sense.

How to test for a dangling modifier

The modifying clause must always refer to the next noun or pronoun in the sentence. If you suspect a dangling modifier, try this test, which works with most constructions. Insert the modifying phrase after the subject of the main clause and see if it makes sense there. If it doesn't, you have a dangler.

Note the dangling modifier in this sentence:

Investing in stocks and bonds, profits rose.

Rearrange the sentence with the modifying phrase after the subject of the main clause.

Profits, *investing in stocks and bonds*, rose.

Now you can see that *profits* don't do the investing: *investing* requires a subject. Rewrite the sentence with a subject.

After *they* invested in stocks and bonds, profits rose.

Ways to correct dangling modifiers

1. Add a noun or pronoun for the word or phrase to modify, and change the main clause from passive to active voice.

instead of:	After working so hard on the proposal, a break is *well deserved*.
write:	After working so hard on the proposal, *you deserve* a break.
instead of:	To receive your rebate, the coupon *must be mailed* within 30 days of purchase.
write:	To receive your rebate, *you must mail* the coupon within 30 days of purchase.
or:	To receive your rebate, *please mail* the coupon within 30 days of purchase. [*You* is understood in this imperative sentence.]

2. Make the modifying phrase into a clause with a clear subject.

instead of: *Adding columns*, the table becomes too complex.

write: The table will be too complex *if you add columns*.

instead of: *If ordered* by December 1, you will receive an additional discount.

write: *If you order* by December 1, you will receive an additional discount.

Some special cases

A few *-ing* words, such as *concerning, pending, judging,* and *considering,* are often used as prepositions. When they are, these words don't have to refer to anything in the sentence.

Considering the costs, we have decided not to build the annex this year.

(See also **dangling participles**, **infinitive phrases**, **misplaced modifiers**, **participles**, **prepositions**, **sentences**, **"you" understood**.)

---

danglIng participles

A participle is a verb that ends with *-ing* and is used as an adjective. A **dangling participle** is a type of dangling modifier that doesn't logically refer to any word in the sentence.

instead of: Moving the equipment, the scanner was damaged. [The participle *Moving* modifies the subject *scanner* in the main clause. Because a scanner can't move equipment, the participle *moving* is dangling.]

write: Moving the equipment, the painters damaged the scanner. [Now the participle has something to modify that's logical—*painters*.]

or: Moving the equipment damaged the
              scanner. [Rewrite the sentence if
              you don't want to blame the painters
              directly.]

(See also **dangling modifiers**, **participles**.)

---

dashes

The **dash** (—) is a mark of punctuation that sets off
a break in thought or an explanation. A dash most
often replaces a colon or parentheses and is a
stronger mark than either of these because it adds
emphasis. A dash can also replace a semicolon.

Capitalize the first word after a dash only if the
word is a proper noun.

How to type a dash

A dash is longer than a hyphen. Most word-processing programs have a dash character. On a typewriter (or if you have no dash on your word
processor), make a dash by typing two hyphens—
no spaces before or after them.

Three main jobs of dashes

1. To link beginning or ending thoughts of a sentence. In this case, the dash replaces the more
   formal colon.

   Breaking ground before winter—that was Graber
   Construction's aim.

   Of all the logos Jane proposed for our shop,
   there was only one we all liked—the infinity
   sign.

2. To enclose related material that's not part of the
   main idea of the sentence.

   Ask Gary Littleton—I believe he's the buyer—to
   order a special cartridge.

> By using this inventory system—and it's available
> at this price only till July—you can save at least
> ten percent at your Baltimore plant alone.

You could use parentheses instead of dashes in
these two examples, but dashes make the
enclosed material more emphatic.

3. To separate a sharp interruption in thought
from the rest of the sentence.

> The proposal will be ready by Thursday—or do
> you want it by Wednesday?

A final hint

The dash can give your writing variety and infor-
mality. Be careful not to overuse it—it can make
your writing seem disorganized or too casual.
Some people refer to the dash as the "cowboy" of
punctuation marks because it adds a casual yet
powerful tone.

(See also **colons**, **emphasis**, **parentheses**,
punctuation, **restrictive and nonrestrictive
elements**.)

---

dates

In most business writing, a **date** includes the
month, day, and year, with a comma between the
numbers.

> March 16, 1999

Rules for writing dates

1. A comma after the year is optional when you
write a date within a sentence.

> June 2, 1999, was the day I received my degree.
> June 2, 1999 was the day I received my degree.

However, use a comma after the year if the phrase or clause requires it.

> *Since I received my degree on June 2, 1999,* I've been working here. [Always put a comma after an introductory clause.]

2. Don't use a comma if you write only the month and year.

> The April 1999 election of Joyce Markowitz as union leader was a surprise to her opponents.

3. The military system uses day-month-year order. Don't use commas unless the sentence requires them.

> 31 December 1999
>
> After the birth of our third child on 2 December 1999, we moved to the base in Alabama. [comma after an introductory phrase of four or more words]

4. Write the day with an ordinal suffix *(2nd)* or spell it out *(second)* if it comes *before* the month.

> Alicia will be on vacation from the *3rd* of September through the *9th*. [These suffixes are an informal style that may not be appropriate in all situations.]
>
> Alicia will be on vacation from the *third* of September through the *ninth*.

5. If the day comes *after* the month, write the day in numbers.

> Payment is due on April *3*. [not April *3rd*]

6. Use the month-day-year form *6/29/99* only on forms or for informal letters or memos. This numerical form is not appropriate for business letters or formal reports.

7. Some very formal documents, such as engraved invitations, spell out all the words of the date.

> November ninth, nineteen hundred and ninety-nine
>
> the ninth of November, one thousand nine hundred and ninety-nine

Writing the century

Write the century as a noun without a hyphen.

> The technology in this office must date back to the *nineteenth century*.

Write the century as an adjective with a hyphen.

> *Twentieth-century* technology has made extraordinary progress.

Dates in meeting announcements

The following information might appear in a memo or informal letter:

Date:	Friday, June 3, 1995
Time:	9:30 a.m.
Place:	My office
Note:	Bring your copy of the budget

(See also **commas, numbers**.)

---

definitions

As an expert in a field, you must give **definitions** —explicit statements of meaning—of specialized terms when you write to people outside your area of expertise. A definition will limit technical terms to your intended use of them.

Using your Focus Sheet™, think carefully about who your readers are and what help they'll need to understand any jargon in your letters and documents.

There are several ways to give a definition that are especially useful in business and technical writing.

1. Use a signal word

A signal word alerts readers that a definition is coming. Some commonly used signal words are *or, that is, for example,* and *such as.*

Be especially accurate in filing the transmittals, *or* records of the pages we forwarded to production.

2. Describe an opposite

One way of defining something is to describe its opposite.

Unlike a stream-fed pond, this one is a kettle pond that formed from a trough in a glacier.

3. Use punctuation

Some marks of *punctuation* show that a definition follows or is separate from the rest of the sentence. The usual marks are colons, dashes, and commas.

The plant manager explained what sludge is: the solid by-product of sewage treatment processes. [colon]

The plant manager explained what sludge is— the solid by-product of sewage treatment processes. [dash]

The plant manager explained that sludge—the solid by-product of sewage treatment processes —poses a disposal problem. [set off by dashes]

The plant manager explained that sludge, the solid by-product of sewage treatment processes, poses a disposal problem. [set off by commas]

Deciding which punctuation to use is mostly a matter of style. A dash, however, usually indicates a stronger break in thought than other punctuation marks.

4. Provide an explanation

You can always give an *explanation* that defines a term. The other three methods, however, are usually more elegant.

The plant manager discussed sludge. *This material is a solid by-product of sewage treatment processes.*

Other ways to define

1. By example:

   The *Boston Red Sox* and the *Montreal Expos* are baseball teams.

2. By explaining what something does:

   The transmittal gives us a record of which pages we forward to production.

3. By describing properties:

   A smoke detector is a battery-powered device attached to the ceiling. An alarm sounds when the detector comes in contact with smoke.

4. By explaining purpose:

   The calculator is an instrument for computing numbers.

5. By giving the cause:

   Sludge is the solid material produced by sewage treatment processes.

6. By stipulating the meaning in a certain context:

   By "delete" I mean "remove from the report but save on the spreadsheet."

Styles of definition

FORMAL

In a formal definition, you categorize a term, then explain how it differs from other items in the same category.

   A bulletin is a brief public notice, usually issued from an authoritative source.

INFORMAL

In an informal definition, you give a synonym for the word you are defining and explain it in familiar terms.

A prototype is an original model used for a manufacturing pattern.

An abstract term, such as "lean production," may need a few sentences or a paragraph of explanation. This is an extended definition—a lengthy explanation that includes many qualities of the term. Most extended definitions include examples.

Tips for defining

1. Be sure that your definition is clearer than the term you're defining. Use familiar words. Don't repeat the term itself in the definition.

   instead of: A business writing book explains business writing.

   write: A business writing book explains how to write strategic communications that move others to action.

2. Don't use the words "is where" or "is when" in your definition; they cloud your meaning. Give the definition directly.

   instead of: A database *is when* you have a group of related records arranged for ease and speed of retrieval.

   write: A database *is a* group of related records arranged for ease and speed of retrieval.

3. Try to tell what something *is* rather than what it *is not*. Be positive in your definition.

   instead of: A personal computer *is not* as large as a mainframe computer.

   write: A personal computer *is a* small computer usually designed for desktop use.

4. You may put the word you're defining in italics or quotation marks to emphasize it. After the first mention of the term, leave out italics or quotation marks. If you can't italicize, quotation marks are preferred to underlining.

> A *database* is a group of related records arranged for ease and speed of retrieval. In this office we use three databases: product, sales, and client.

(See also **ambiguity**; **organizing information**; **readers, analyzing**; **word choice**.)

---

dependent clauses

A **clause** is a group of words that has a subject and a verb. A sentence can have one or more clauses, depending on its structure.

A **dependent clause**, also called a subordinate clause, has a subject and a verb but can't stand alone as a sentence. Dependent clauses need independent clauses to complete their meanings. In the following examples, the dependent clauses are in italics.

> *After the new inventory program had been in place for two weeks,* everyone knew how to use it.

> Use this program *if you want to access services from the system.*

Dependent clauses can be introduced by conjunctions or prepositions such as *after, because, unless, before, which, while,* and *that,* among others.

The role of dependent clauses

Dependent clauses make meanings more precise. They define relationships of time (*after*), cause (*because*) or condition (*if, unless*) between ideas.

Dependent clauses also show the subordination of one idea to another.

The power plant, *which is located in Dracut County,* provides power for Biltmore County as well. [The location is a subordinate idea.]

If two people are on vacation at the same time, we'll have to hire a temp. [The condition of two people on vacation is a subordinate idea.]

Comma rules for dependent clauses

1. The general rule is that a comma follows the dependent clause when it begins the sentence and contains at least four words.

   After the new inventory program had been in place for two weeks, everyone knew how to use it.

2. Do not use a comma before a dependent clause if it comes at the end of the sentence.

   Use this program *if you want to access services from the system.*

3. If a dependent clause in the middle of a sentence is nonrestrictive, or unnecessary to the meaning of the sentence, it is set off by commas.

   The new loading dock, *which is twice the size of the old one,* can now accommodate all our deliveries.

(See also **appositives**, **commas**, **conjunctions**, **independent clauses**, **restrictive and nonrestrictive elements**, **subordination**.)

---

description

Description is the use of selected details to create a picture in readers' minds. In technical and business writing, description helps readers visualize an object or process and understand how it works.

An oil spill boom acts as a mechanical barrier to obstruct surface water and oil, while allowing subsurface water to pass. An upper barrier of polyurethane, polyethylene, foam, or compressed air covered with plastic reaches above the water and is supported by a float. Below this tubular float hangs a "skirt" made of plastic, rubber, canvas, or plywood, which blocks the oil.

When you write a technical description, give specific details that will help your reader create a mental picture of the object you are describing.

Take your time, and don't assume that your readers have prior knowledge of the mechanism or process. Otherwise you may leave out a crucial step in a procedure.

Physical description of a mechanism

When you describe a mechanism, include these characteristics of the whole item and its component parts:

- purpose
- size
- shape
- position
- color
- texture

PARTS OF THE DESCRIPTION

1. Begin with an overview of the mechanism that describes its purpose, how it works, and its main parts.

2. Then describe each part and explain, in more detail, how it works within the larger mechanism. Include shape, dimension, material, and significant physical details. Choose a logical progression for the parts of the description:

   - from top to bottom *or*
   - in the sequence you would use to operate the mechanism

3. Conclude with a brief summary that emphasizes how the parts work together.

TIPS FOR WRITING DESCRIPTIONS

1. Compare the parts you describe to familiar objects to help your readers visualize the item. This technique is especially useful if your readers are not technical experts.

   The device for buttering corn on the cob is a little box the size and shape of a stick of butter. *Think of it as a large, rectangular tube of lip balm.* You push the butter down from the top and rub the open bottom of the device along the ear of corn.

2. You can be imaginative in technical descriptions as long as you create an accurate and understandable picture of what you're describing.

   An automatic screwdriver makes driving screws faster and easier for you. Why? First, when you use a traditional screwdriver, after every turn you make, you must remove the screwdriver bit from the screw head, turn your hand back, reset the screwdriver bit in the screw, and then turn the screw one more turn.

   You might find it difficult to reset the screwdriver in the screw head's new position. And the continual resetting of the bit significantly increases the chance that you will strip the slot in the screw head, making your job much more difficult, if not impossible.

   With an automatic screwdriver, you never have to lift the bit away from its secure position on the screw head; to tighten the screw, you twist your wrist clockwise as you would with a conventional screwdriver. But then, without lifting the screwdriver bit from the screw, you twist your hand back counterclockwise to prepare for the next tightening motion.

   To loosen the screw, you reverse the motions. As a result, you speed your job, use far less effort, and reduce the chance of stripping the screw head.

   How does the automatic screwdriver work? The automatic screwdriver, like a conventional screwdriver, contains a solid metal rod with a bit on the end. But it differs because the solid rod rotates inside a metal tube that is attached to the handle you twist to turn the screw.

You can connect the outside tube and the inside rod with a sliding piece of metal, called a pawl. You slide the pawl to connect the outside tube to the inside rod so you can apply torque to tightening or loosening the screw.

When you put torque on the outer tube, the tube and the rod rotate together, and you transmit the torque to the screw. Then when you turn your hand back for the next twist, the pawl slides out of place, disconnecting the outer tube and inner rod, so the outside tube can rotate past the inside rod that remains in place on the screw head.

As a result, you can twist your hand without turning the screw in an undesired direction.

3. Using your Focus Sheet™, pinpoint what your readers need to know about the object you're describing. You can use specialized language for an audience of experts.

For a lay audience, you may have to define specialized terms and write longer explanations. For a mixed audience, include a glossary.

4. Ask yourself what the purpose of your description is.

   • Do you want your readers to visualize how a new product looks?

   • Do you want them to buy the item?

   • Do you want them to understand how internal parts fit together?

   Tailor your language to your purpose. Always keep your readers in mind.

5. If appropriate, include illustrations or drawings with the text of your description. They will help, especially if the mechanism is too complex to describe in words.

   Use photographs to show how an item looks. Cutaway and exploded-view diagrams are invaluable for internal details. Illustrations make objects easier to visualize and understand.

Describing a process

You can describe a process by giving instructions for carrying it out. You may also explain the reasons for instituting a process in the first place. Give a step-by-step description, in the correct order. Don't give your readers more—or less—information than they need.

If there are lots of parts to your process description, try jotting them first on Post-it™ Notes. This technique works particularly well if you are on the shop floor taking notes. Then, once you have recorded all the steps, arrange your Post-it Notes in the correct sequence.

MAKE YOUR SENTENCES IMPERATIVE

When you explain procedures, use imperative sentences with *you* understood to be the subject.

> [*You*] Enter your security code, wait for the green recognition light, and open the door.

Feel free to use the word *you* if you need it.

USE THE ACTIVE VOICE

In describing a process, use the active rather than the passive voice. It makes your explanation more direct, less wordy, and easier to understand.

instead of: The air supply *is controlled* by the green knob on the left. [passive voice]

write: The green knob on the left *controls* the air supply. [active voice]

PARTS OF THE DESCRIPTION

1. Start with an overall description of the process and its purpose.

2. Provide a detailed, step-by-step description. Use a chronological method of development and identify all the parts involved. Include illustrations for clarity.

3. Summarize how the steps work together.

Describing a place

You may need to describe a place to explain

- the location of proposed construction or of an accident
- property boundaries
- travel directions.

Before you write, choose a physical point from which to "view" the location. "Look" at it and describe it from that point of view only. If you change the point of view, let your readers know. In the paragraph that follows, the point of view is from the air above.

> An aerial map shows the eight-acre office park site bounded by the river on the south and I33 on the north. To the west is the property line of Wilson Electronics, and to the east is the township conservation area. In the northwest corner of the property is a 60,000 square-foot pond.
>
> A one-lane access road parallels the highway and enters the property in the northeast corner.

As with all descriptions, check scrupulously for accuracy.

(See also **active voice/passive voice**; **illustrations**; **Model Documents Appendix**; **point of view**; **procedures**; **readers, analyzing**; **"you" understood**.)

---

desktop publishing

Nothing has altered the process of document preparation so much as **desktop publishing**

(DTP). It is, quite literally, publishing professional-looking newsletters, brochures, manuals, business cards, even books—from the top of your desk.

Working from your computer, you can control document production from start to finish. Furthermore, if you use a laser printer that produces high-quality, camera-ready copy, you may even be able to avoid sending your copy elsewhere to be printed.

Eliminate typesetting

DTP significantly streamlines the publishing process, both in time and in cost. First of all, since text can be set into its final form right in the initiator's computer, the middle step—typesetting—is unnecessary.

What used to be a multistep process that took weeks of back-and-forth handling between printers, typesetters, editors, and publishers can now be done in a fraction of the time, and at a fraction of the cost.

Considering the cost of typesetting, post-typesetting proofreading, and transfer of text between vendors at every stage of the process, any DTP equipment a corporation invests in pays for itself many times over.

Keep it standard

An important point: don't use too much variety in design when working in DTP programs. Choose no more than two standard fonts and type sizes. Anything more will look too cluttered. See the **visual design** entry for an example of font misuse.

Although your options for visual presentation are endless, remember that you must reflect your organization's identity. If your company has a style guide, follow it.

(See also **font**, **page design**, **style guides**, **visual design**.)

diagrams

Diagrams reduce complexity by displaying the relationship between objects graphically. A schematic diagram displays the relationships between parts, as in an electrical wiring diagram.

Diagrams also illustrate the flow of events.

- A data flow diagram shows the logical sequence of relationships and activities of an information system.

- A flowchart diagram illustrates the path from the starting point to the end point of a process or decision.

(See also **charts or graphs**, **figures**, **flowcharts**, **illustrations**, **tables**.)

directions, giving

When you **give directions**, generally use the imperative sentences that begin with a verb. This construction is more direct and less ambiguous than a passive-voice verb.

| *instead of:* | This schematic *should be completed* by Friday [passive]. |
| *write:* | Please *complete* this schematic by Friday [imperative]. |

(See also **active voice/passive voice**, **procedures**, **sentences**, **verbs**, **"you" understood**.)

distribution lists

For e-mail

Many e-mail writers fail to edit their distribution lists when they send repeated messages. As a result, countless readers waste time reading information that does not apply to them. Companies could save hundreds of hours if writers would update their distribution lists regularly.

For letters and memos

The distribution list generally appears at the top of a memorandum and at the bottom of a letter.

Keep in mind that when too many people receive a copy of a document, its effectiveness may be lost. Readers may think that, if the subject applies to everyone, it can't be very important. Where distribution lists are concerned, shorter is better.

documentation

Documentation is any printed information that accompanies computer software and manufactured goods. The purpose of documentation is to

- explain how to operate a program or a piece of equipment
- present in careful detail how the program or equipment was designed.

There are two types of documentation.

1. Technical, such as software documentation, is written by a technical writer for a technical audience.
2. User documentation is designed for a nontechnical audience. An example of user documentation—your word-processing manual—is probably sitting right next to your computer.

(See also **manuals**, **procedures**.)

documenting sources

When you **document sources**, you give credit to the sources you used in writing reports, articles, or other documents. There are three reasons for accurately documenting sources:

1. to let readers know where you found material you didn't write, thereby avoiding plagiarism

2. to make it easy for readers to do further research on the subject

3. to give authority and credibility to your document

You might use material from books, articles, reference manuals, and even correspondence. Your style of documentation should be consistent. For documentation format, consult a style manual for your industry.

What must you document?

There are four kinds of information you must document in notes:

1. any material that is not common knowledge to your audience; for example, statistics on domestic versus foreign car sales in a given year

2. a speculative idea in a book or article; for example, a suggestion that the merger of two government contractors is more politically than financially motivated

3. a paraphrase of someone else's ideas; for example, a summary, in your own words, of what a CEO said at a shareholders' meeting

4. direct quotations, either written or spoken

If you're not sure whether or not to document a specific item of information, be conservative and include the source.

Reference notes

Provide sources and explanations for specific information in reference notes. There are four types of reference notes: footnotes, endnotes, parenthetical documentation, and content notes.

FOOTNOTES

A footnote appears at the bottom of the page that has the referenced material. Calculating page and footnote length used to be a difficult task, but now your word-processing software will do it for you.

Indicate footnotes in the text with superscript numbers, placed after final punctuation.

"Coherence means linking sentences and ideas with transitional words."[3]

Your word processor will number footnotes correspondingly and place them at the bottom of the page. You must type the author's name, title of the publication, publisher, date of publication, and page number of the reference.

[3] Deborah Dumaine. *Write to the Top: Writing for Corporate Success.* New York: Random House, 1989, p.58.

Remember that footnotes can make your document look formidable and scholarly to some readers. If you do use footnotes, limit their number as much as possible.

ENDNOTES

Endnotes appear in a list on a separate page at the end of the document or at the end of each report chapter. Footnotes and endnotes both contain the same information.

GENERAL ORDER IN FOOTNOTES AND ENDNOTES

Style manuals vary, but this order of information is common to most note styles:

1. author's or editor's name (in first name-last name order)
2. title
3. place of publication
4. publisher or name of publication

5. publication date
6. page number

To document a film or videotape, use the following order:

1. title
2. director
3. distributor
4. year
5. writers, performers, or producers, if the information is relevant

PARENTHETICAL DOCUMENTATION

Parenthetical documentation is the Modern Language Association of America (MLA) style, detailed in the *MLA Handbook for Writers of Research Papers*. (See the full reference on this manual later in this entry.)

This style does not use numbers, but rather gives the author's last name and page number in parentheses in the text.

". . . which causes the emission to be toxic"
(Jameson, 113-115).

Notice there is a comma after the author's name and no *p.* to indicate *page*. This parenthetical citation directs readers to the corresponding bibliographic entry at the end of the document.

EXPLANATORY OR CONTENT NOTES

When you want to give information that might distract from the flow of your text, use explanatory or content notes. You can put these either at the bottom of the page or in a list at the end of the chapter or document.

Content notes are not citations of sources, but additional explanations or analyses. If such information is frequent or lengthy—more than two or three lines—consider putting it in an appendix.

Example:

> To insert multiple columns into your document, first divide it into sections. Use the Section Break command from the Insert Menu. Then choose Section from the Format Menu. Type the number of columns in the Number Box.*
>
> Use the Spacing Box to adjust the space between columns.
>
>
> *If you are formatting only two or three columns, you may use the columns button on the ribbon.

USING BOTH CITATIONS AND CONTENT NOTES

If your document is heavily referenced, you may want to separate notes of substance from simple citations. Put content notes into footnotes or endnotes indicated by symbols, such as * or §. You can then use numbered notes for the citations.

Bibliographies

A bibliography is an alphabetical list of sources that usually appears at the end of a report or document. Bibliographies can also be general lists of references independent of a report. Like footnotes and endnotes, their details vary with different styles, but the general order of information is

1. author's or editor's name (in last name-first name order)

2. title

3. place of publication

4. publisher or name of publication

5. publication date

Jameson, Derrick. *Cleaning Up the Environment*. New York: Random House, 1991.

Style manuals

Many organizations publish their own style manuals that give detailed formats for documenting sources. Follow the style manual that your company uses, or find one designed for your field. Here are some good sources to consult:

The Chicago Manual of Style, 14th ed. Chicago: University of Chicago Press, 1993.

Dodd, Janet S., ed. *The ACS Style Guide: A Manual for Authors and Editors*. Washington, D.C.: American Chemical Society, 1986.

Gibaldi, Joseph, and Walter S. Achtert. *MLA Handbook for Writers of Research Papers*. 3rd ed. New York: Modern Language Association of America, 1988.

U.S. Government Printing Office. *A Manual of Style*. New York: Gramercy, 1986.

Webster's Standard American Style Manual. Springfield, MA: Merriam-Webster, 1985.

(See also **bibliography**, **copyright**, **plagiarism**, **research**, **style guides**.)

---

double negatives

In a **double negative**, two negatives (like *not* or *no*) appear in the same phrase or sentence.

instead of: Carl *won't* be taking *no* phone calls tomorrow.

write: Carl *won't* be taking *any* phone calls tomorrow.

The second negative may be meant to emphasize the first. Actually, such a construction sounds awkward and confusing. Double negatives are incorrect.

Double negative traps

1. A double negative can be an incorrect word, such as *irregardless*. The prefix *ir-* and the suffix *-less* are both negative. Always write *regardless*.

2. The words *scarcely, barely,* and *hardly* are negative and should not be used with another negative.

   instead of: I *won't hardly* be able to finish this by next week.

   write: I'll *hardly* be able to finish this by next week.

3. Putting a negative with another word that has a negative-sounding prefix is not incorrect grammatically. However, such constructions can be confusing unless you mean to be imprecise.

   We were *not unhappy* when the project was canceled. [Our feelings were somewhere between happy and unhappy.]

---

draft writing: Step 5 to Reader-Centered Writing

Writing a draft is Step 5 to Reader-Centered Writing. Follow the plan you developed in Steps 1 through 4. Keep your Focus Sheet™ as well as your outline before you, be it in traditional, brainstorm, or list form. Now begin to write—*without editing*.

Expect your first draft to be a rough, unpolished version of your final document. You'll worry about sentence structure, word choice, spelling, grammar, and punctuation during Step 6, **editing your draft**.

Begin to write anywhere that's easy for you—it doesn't necessarily have to be at the beginning. Choose one of your headline categories from Step 3, **organizing information**, and start there. Write the headline, then a paragraph.

Again, don't worry about how elegant, or even correct, your sentences are. Just get your thoughts down, following the plan you developed in the first four steps of the writing process.

Refer to your Focus Sheet now and then to remind yourself of your purpose in writing and your reader's needs.

Remember the goal of Step 5: Don't get it right, get it written!

Writing paragraphs

Under each headline you've generated, write as many paragraphs as you need to explain your point. Follow these guidelines:

1. Each paragraph should contain one main idea.

2. Begin with a topic sentence or headline. Your "bottom line," or key message, will usually be your first sentence. You may occasionally want to vary this pattern and create anticipation by placing your key idea later in the paragraph.

   Don't overdo this technique, however—busy readers prefer the bottom line on top.

   > The Huron Water Filter System includes a water-saving device for each faucet in your home.

3. Use transition words and phrases and a judicious amount of repetition to keep the ideas flowing smoothly.

   > Maurice is checking the inventory. *Meanwhile*, I'll call the distributor.

4. Make nontechnical paragraphs five to six lines long; technical paragraphs three to four lines long.

Drafting guidelines

1. Use headlines to organize sections of information. In Step 6, you can create a headline hierarchy, or levels of headline subordination.

2. Write without attention to correctness or any editing concerns.

3. Try writing with a time limit. Fill a page as quickly as you can, but instead of free associating as you did during free writing in Step 2, use your plan or outline. If this method makes you anxious, however, don't use it.

4. Stop after a while. Reread what you've written, consult your Focus Sheet, and make sure your writing reflects your true purpose. Don't resume working on the project immediately.

5. When you return to writing, reread again to recover the last thought you had.

6. Try dictating your draft, but don't send it unedited.

Once you've finished your first draft, it's time to edit. Before you begin this very different function, however, take a break. You'll be able to clear your mind, improve your objectivity, and approach your material as if someone else had written it.

Step back and ask yourself, "What, exactly, does this document communicate?"

(See also **editing your draft**, **headline levels**, **headlines**, **Introduction to the Six Steps**, **paragraphs**, **transitions**.)

E

editing your draft: Step 6 to Reader-Centered Writing

After you've completed Step 5 of the writing process and produced your first draft, you're ready for Step 6: **editing**.

Remember: drafting is a creative process that gives form and substance to your ideas; editing is an analytical process that critiques and refines what you've written.

Since these functions are so different, you should not edit until you've finished drafting. Resist the impulse, or you'll get stuck somewhere in between drafting and editing. Postpone editing until you have your whole document before you.

Use the "Be Your Own Editor" Checklist

Editing is an essential process in all the writing you do. It covers virtually all aspects of writing craft, including:

- analyzing whether you've expressed what you intended
- measuring the readability of your writing
- making sure you have met your readers' needs
- eliminating sexist language
- fine-tuning your sentence structure
- correcting grammar, punctuation, and spelling

Since there are so many elements to consider, Better Communications™ has developed the *"Be Your Own Editor" Checklist*, which follows. It lists editing elements in a logical progression from the broadest issues to the smallest details.

The "Be Your Own Editor" Checklist

Step 6

☞ *Be sure to check these items for short documents.*

CONTENT

Purpose ❧❧
- ☐ Clear to the reader?
- ☐ Specific in requests for actions or information?

Information
- ☐ Accurate and complete?
- ☐ Detailed enough?
- ☐ Persuasive in listing benefits to the reader?

SEQUENCE

Bottom Line ❧
- ☐ At the top?
- ☐ If not, strategically placed?

Organization
- ☐ Strategically presented?

DESIGN

Format ❧❧❧
- ☐ Enough headlines, sidelines, and bulleted and numbered lists?
- ☐ White space to frame ideas?
- ☐ Highlighted deadlines and action items?

Presentation
- ☐ Most effective for statistical information?
- ☐ Would a chart, table, or graph be better?

STRUCTURE

Paragraphs
- ☐ Headlines worded for impact?
- ☐ Begin with a topic sentence?
- ☐ Focus on one topic?
- ☐ Use transitions to connect ideas?
- ☐ Stay within 5-6 lines in length?

Sentences
- ☐ Varied in structure and length?
- ☐ Streamlined to 15-20 words?

TONE/STYLE

Words
- ☐ Simple, specific, and straightforward?
- ☐ Free of affectation and gobbledygook?
- ☐ Acronyms explained and terminology familiar to readers?

Style
- ☐ Personable, upbeat, and direct?
- ☐ Appropriate for the audience?
- ☐ Active voice?
- ☐ Positive approach?
- ☐ The you attitude?

FINAL PROOF

- ☐ Are grammar, punctuation, and spelling correct?
- ☐ Did you run the spellcheck program?
- ☐ Should someone else review it?
- ☐ If this is a repeat mailing, did you highlight new information?

Personalize this checklist with your specific writing problems.

_____
_____
_____
_____
_____
_____
_____
_____

Check the writing of your team members

You can also use the checklist to evaluate documents you assign to others. When a team member submits a report or proposal to you, go down the checklist and consider content, sequence, and design, as well as the fine points of grammar and punctuation. If the document needs revision, circle the problem area on your checklist. Return both document and checklist to the writer.

This supportive approach encourages learning and helps writers improve. They won't be left with the feeling that they've been peremptorily corrected. On the contrary: they will learn a valuable lesson by editing themselves—and you will save valuable time.

Personalize your checklist

You can tailor your checklist to your own needs. The more writing you do, the more aware you will become of specific, recurring problems. Add them to your checklist so that you can focus on them.

Professional writers have internalized most or all of the elements on the checklist. They know the many steps involved in the editing process without referring to an outside source. As you use the checklist repeatedly, you will learn to do this too.

The more carefully you edit your document, the closer you'll come to saying exactly what you mean. Consider editing as a favor to your readers.

(See also **clear writing**; **draft writing**; **Introduction to the Six Steps**; **readability**; **sexist language**; **writing as a team**.)

---

e.g./i.e.

The Latin phrase *exempli gratia*, meaning "for example," is often abbreviated *e.g.* Use this abbreviation mainly in notes and other informal writing if you need to save space. In general, though, *e.g.* is a poor substitute for *for example*.

instead of: Our new delivery routes, *e.g.,* from Cincinnati to Covington, required adding another truck to our fleet.

write: Our new delivery routes, *for example*, from Cincinnati to Covington, required adding another truck to our fleet.

The Latin phrase *id est*, meaning "that is," is often abbreviated *i.e.* Unlike *for example*, *i.e.* offers a complete clarification of the term(s) preceding it, not just an instance of it. Use this abbreviation sparingly in informal writing.

instead of: Ayisha used three types of visual aids in her presentation, *i.e.,* video, large charts and diagrams, and actual samples of the products.

write: Ayisha used three types of visual aids in her presentation, *that is*, video, large charts and diagrams, and actual samples of the products.

better: Ayisha used three types of visual aids in her presentation: video, large charts and diagrams, and actual samples of the products. [Use a colon instead.]

A note of caution

The abbreviations *e.g.* and *i.e.* are not interchangeable. A common error is using *i.e.* when you mean *e.g.* Don't confuse your readers. Avoid these—and other Latin expressions—altogether when you write.

electronic mail: how to guarantee your message is read

Electronic mail, or e-mail, has rapidly become a preferred medium of communication for both business and personal use. It's fast and efficient, reducing telephone calls and paper waste; it works weekends, nights, and holidays; and it zips across time zones with the push of a button.

Written communication has never been faster.

What makes e-mail unique?

E-mail is not simply a faster way of writing to someone—it has its own needs and conventions. But because of e-mail's on-line ease, senders may be tempted to disregard proper writing procedure.

Usually, however, you need to plan an e-mail message just as thoroughly as you would a conventional memo.

Consult the Six Steps to Reader-Centered Writing and memorandums entries for general memo-writing guidelines. This entry focuses specifically on e-mail conventions.

A REPLACEMENT FOR BOTH WRITTEN AND ORAL COMMUNICATION

E-mail fulfills more functions than sending a memo electronically. It also replaces face-to-face, as well as voice-to-voice, communication. Today, rather than phoning coworkers or walking over to their cubicle, you often send an e-mail instead.

A major advantage of e-mail over oral communication: you can think before you respond. In an emotional or heated situation, you have the time to cool off and compose both yourself and your reply.

USING SMILEYS

Replacing meetings or phone calls with e-mail is an efficient means of communication only if you succeed in conveying the facial expressions, body language, and voice inflections of an actual conversation.

In informal, internal e-mail, *smileys* may replace such physical and verbal cues. A smiley is a string of keyboard characters that draws an expressive little face. To read the following examples, tilt your head to the left:

:-)	I'm smiling.
:-D	I'm laughing.
;-)	I'm winking.
:-(	I'm frowning.
(:-\	I'm sad; I have bad news.
%-(	I'm confused; I've been staring at the screen too long.
:-[	I'm fed up; I'm disgusted.
8-O	I'm amazed.
:-X	My lips are sealed.

Put your smiley at the end of the sentence.

> At this morning's meeting, Stan didn't seem very concerned that our profits were down last quarter. 8-O

> I just spent two hours deciphering D&G's latest technical memo. %-(

If your readers are unfamiliar with smileys, make sure you explain them the first time you use them. Otherwise, they'll look like careless typing.

Why is the subject line so important?

Just as memos should have only one subject, e-mail messages should follow the same rule. Your reader will have trouble filing a document for later reference if it contains more than one topic.

Be concise. Use as few words as possible, since most computers won't display more than 25 or 30 characters (about 5 or 6 words) in the subject-line field.

Your choice of words for your subject line sets the tone for your message. It helps your readers decide whether they'll read your message now—or never.

How concise can you be? Spare your readers time: send a message that's only a subject line!

> Sales mtg change: 7/13 at 3 pm

Don't leave your reader unclear about your message. Use

1. action words that capture your readers' attention

2. abbreviations of common words (like *mtg* for *meeting*) to fit as much as possible into your subject line

3. key words that

   • convey the nature of your message to readers as soon as they look in their e-mail in-boxes

   • make message filing and retrieval as easy as possible.

instead of: System maintenance scheduled for 12/6

write: System shutdown 12/6, 4-6 pm

Which message would you definitely read?

It's just an e-mail–why bother editing it?

Pressing "send" on an e-mail message is tantamount to putting your signature beneath your words.

Would you sign your name to a document that was poorly thought out and carelessly written? That is exactly what you are doing if your e-mail message is sketchy, disorganized, or ungrammatical.

Every extra moment your readers spend trying to figure out your message wastes their valuable time. They probably won't even bother to read the next message you send them.

If your message is unclear, your reader will end up e-mailing or calling you back for clarification. Your e-mail is no longer saving time.

How to emphasize words and phrases

Since you can't italicize, underline, or bold in many e-mail systems, use these conventions for emphasis:

   • Set off a word or phrase with asterisks or underscores. For added emphasis, you may capitalize a word or two.

Always edit your e-mails.

In contrast to the first half year, profits were
_UP_ again last quarter.

- Avoid typing in all capital letters. This is seen
  as shouting and offends readers. Capitalize
  an occasional word only.

Should you use abbreviations and acronyms?

By all means—if you are certain your readers will
understand them. But do not save keystrokes at the
expense of clarity.

Remember, too, that an international audience
may not understand such shortcuts. Also, your
business correspondents in other countries may
expect more formal communication, even in an
electronic medium.

ABBREVIATIONS

The following abbreviations are so familiar that
they probably don't require definition:

acct	mgr
contrib	mtg
co.	nat'l, internat'l
conf	admin
info	wk

E-MAIL SHORTHAND

Acronym-like abbreviations are a popular way to
shorten frequently-used comments. Most consist
of the first letters of each word in the phrase:

ASAP	as soon as possible
BCNU	Be seeing you.
FWIW	for what it's worth
HHOJ	Ha ha, only joking!
IMO	in my opinion
IMHO	in my humble opinion

JIC	just in case
OIC	Oh, I see!
OTOH	on the other hand
POV	point of view
TIA	Thanks in advance.
TNSTAAFL	There's no such thing as a free lunch.

Acronyms and abbreviations are especially useful in subject lines.

> Call me before the mtg for my POV.

Don't overuse acronyms and abbreviations–they will make your message difficult to read. The same rule applies to smileys and emphasis.

> JIC, I'll send the info to Eugenie *B4* the mtg. DON'T WORRY—I won't tell her the source. :-X   IMHO, we'll have to pay *big $$$* for this.   :-(TNSTAAFL!!! BCNU.

E-mail etiquette

1. <u>Don't assume that people read your messages the moment they receive them</u>. Give readers time to respond before following up.

   For immediate action—an unexpected meeting this afternoon—use the phone. For convenience, use e-mail. And remember: if you want your e-mail read, use a specific, action-packed subject line.

2. <u>Know when to stop e-mailing and pick up the phone</u>. When a message generates a string of four or more replies, it's time for a phone call or meeting.

   Do you have a question that will evoke a follow-up question depending on the response? Call rather than e-mailing. Otherwise your reader will have to answer multiple messages. Always consider your reader's convenience before your own.

3. <u>Don't break the link</u>. When responding to a complex e-mail, especially when several cor-

respondents are involved, don't start a new e-mail message. Instead, use the "reply" function, which will attach your e-mail to the original message.

That way, even after several rounds, readers will be able to follow the link between the original message and multiple replies from several readers.

4. Forwarding: when should you rewrite the subject line? If you are forwarding a message to new readers who are unaware of your topic, strongly consider changing the subject line to orient these new readers. You risk being ignored if readers ask, "Why on Earth was this sent to me?"

5. Don't flame. Sending an e-mail message when you're irritated is always risky. If someone's actions or words have upset you, your impulse might be to fire off a nasty message then and there: a practice commonly known as *flaming*.

Remember this guideline: if you wouldn't say it to the person's face, don't send it.

Likewise, don't respond to flames. You'll just encourage the sender and get caught up in a flame war. If you can't disregard the flame—it's from your manager or a client—respond politely to any requests for action and ignore the rest of the message.

6. Respect your reader's time. Keep your words short and to the point. If you like to think on-screen, don't send your message before editing your thoughts. No one has time to waste deciphering what you're trying to say.

What's your "bottom line," or key point? Don't press "send" until your main message is in your subject line.

| *instead of:* | Conference info |
| *write:* | Great conference: Let's go! |

Which subject line would you rather see in your e-mail list? The second example has only two more words, but you've already saved the reader time.

7. <u>Check your distribution list before sending an e-mail</u>. Prevent your messages from being ignored—be sure your recipients need your information.

No one likes to receive e-mail that's annoying or useless. Many people now have what's known as a *bozo filter*—at the recipient's request, all messages from selected senders are filtered out before they even arrive in the intended in-box.

8. <u>Target your readers according to message importance—to them, not you</u>. Use the "to" field for readers who have action items to complete; use the "cc" field for those who need the information but don't have to act upon it.

If your system doesn't permit you to flag urgent messages, design your own flags. Some companies now prioritize e-mail messages from 1 to 3, with 1 indicating an urgent message. Others use code letters like FYI: (for your information), A: (action needed), or U: (urgent).

Obviously, these systems won't work unless the whole company—or at least your e-mail distribution list—agrees to use them.

9. <u>Keep your e-mail short</u>. In those cases when you can't, include a table of contents or summary up front. It will give your readers a preview of what you're sending.

A better solution: if your message is too long for e-mail (more than three or four screens), you probably have the option of attaching a word-processing document to the message.

10. <u>Activate the quote feature</u>. Reply to an e-mail by quoting the relevant part of the sender's message rather than the whole thing. That way, your reader doesn't have to scroll

through several screens to find your response.

Each line of quoted text automatically appears with > (an angle bracket); lines without brackets are your response to the quoted material:

>To summarize, we think it would be better to>roll out the SD1050 in>March instead of February. A single month's postponement would>give us the time we need to fine tune the advertising campaign.

Good idea—tell Jake I agree completely. :-)

11. <u>Sign your e-mail</u>. To make it clear to your reader who sent the message, enter your name, title, and department at the end. The automatic "from" line might show just an abbreviated name or number.

    Especially on the Internet, include your e-mail address—it can be hard to find in the string of characters that make up the transmission information.

12. <u>Don't use jargon unless you're sure your reader will understand it</u>. Jargon refers to industry-specific words and acronyms that may be foreign to the average reader.

    Every company and industry has its own jargon. If there's even the slightest doubt that your reader may not understand your jargon, don't include it.

13. <u>Spell check your e-mail</u>. Experts say that, for every grammar mistake in an e-mail message, there is an average of three spelling mistakes.

    When your readers have to break their concentration to decipher a word because you didn't bother to spell check, you look sloppy, if not illiterate. Worse, they may decide simply to stop reading.

    Here's an example of a concise, effective message—or it would have been if the sender had used her spellchecker!

From: Gretchen Deere

To: John Dimitriades

Subject: Next sales mtg: our goals

Date: Monday, February 8, 19— 4:23PM

One of ur goals for thte meeting is to decied onn the new customers we need: for example, Financial, Technical, SAles. If this item is not on the agneda, please see me. Or better: may I see hte agenda? Tx.

If your e-mail system doesn't have a spellchecker, proofread carefully. Alternatively, type out the message in your word processing program, spell check it, and cut and paste it into an e-mail message.

14. <u>Observe "netiquette."</u> Internet etiquette follows the general rules outlined above. If you have access to the Internet, you may want to join a news group: a forum where people with a common interest exchange e-mail messages on a specific topic.

To learn the conventions that a particular news group observes:

- Spend a few days *lurking*, or logging on to the newsgroup without actually participating. Make sure the news group is relevant to your interests and learn what behavior is acceptable.

- Look for an FAQ (frequently asked questions) section or message, and read it. It will describe the purpose of the newsgroup, the conventions it observes, and guidelines for posting messages.

E-mail abuse

As in all correspondence, do not use e-mail to transmit material that is vulgar, obscene, or sexually harassing. In addition to these basic rules, never

- use someone else's name and password to send a message

- send "junk e-mail": mass-mailing advertisements.

Some final tips

These ideas will help you make the most of e-mail technology:

- Use e-mail to brainstorm. Try an idea out on a distribution list and build on each other's responses for inspiration.
- Use e-mail to automate paperwork. On-line forms are an efficient way to eliminate the endless circulation of multiple paper copies.
- Use e-mail to save paper. Don't print messages unnecessarily. Read them on screen and, if you need to, save them in electronic, rather than a physical, filing system.

E-mail is a powerful, extremely accessible communication tool, so make it work for you. Writing action-oriented e-mail is a critical skill that will help you get results—and reach more people faster than ever before.

(See also **concise vs. wordy writing, grouping ideas, Six Steps to Reader-Centered Writing, memorandums, streamlining, subject lines, Model Documents Appendix**.)

electronic publishing

Every published document follows a specific process: not just planning, writing, and editing, but also updating and storage.

Because of the many steps involved in each stage, publishing demands a logical process with a steady progression. Until now this process, particularly for book-length publications, has been anything but efficient.

Electronic publishing has revolutionized document production. Now you no longer have to send camera-ready artwork or laser-printed originals to an offset printer or copy shop, arrange for documents to be scanned elsewhere, then assemble everything for binding and collating.

The all-in-one machine

An electronic printer—like the Docutech from Xerox Corporation—has the capability to completely automate the production needs of desktop publishing. It has facilities for memory scanning, electronic cutting and pasting, duplex copying, automatic signature generating, and binding.

You don't have to sequence the steps yourself: all these jobs can run concurrently.

Document quality is higher than ever because every copy is first generation. There's no need to worry about crooked copies or smudged originals—everything is saved electronically.

Any document, be it a manual, newsletter, or book, can be accessed, printed, bound, and distributed in a fraction of the time it used to take.

Benefits of electronic publication

An electronic publisher will

- prepare one job while another is printing, reducing lead time dramatically

- repaginate and automatically generate tables of contents and indexes for any job

- accept many types of software to handle all kinds of programs

- reduce reliance on offset printing without sacrificing quality

- customize or tailor books, collections of diverse materials, and anything else you want to publish.

Printing on demand

Best of all, electronic publishers print on demand. This is an important breakthrough economically. You no longer have to print large quantities to get the best price. Since the documents are all saved on the network server, they can be printed whenever you ask, in whatever quantity you need.

Cash and inventory are no longer tied up with a printer or publisher.

It's also far easier to update and edit documents: no more waiting for six months or a year for the next edition. Your new, updated document, whether it's a book or a brochure, will be available to you in a fraction of the time it used to take.

---

emphasis

Emphasis means giving importance or force to selected parts of your writing. When you speak, you use facial expressions, voice, and gestures to emphasize what you say. When you write, you also have many ways of making one point stand out over another.

Adjectives and adverbs

The most obvious way to add emphasis to your writing is with adjectives and adverbs.

This is a very good proposal—in fact, it's *outstanding*. [adjective]

I know an *amazingly* talented designer who would be perfect for this project. [adverb]

Emphasis through position

1. Put important ideas either first or last in a sentence.

instead of:	Tadpoles, through metamorphosis, turn into frogs.
write:	Tadpoles turn into frogs through metamorphosis. [The more important main clause should come first.]
instead of:	Pierre and Marie Curie succeeded in isolating radon after many years of difficult and unrewarding work.
write:	After many years of difficult and unrewarding work, Pierre and Marie Curie succeeded in isolating radon. [The beginning of the sentence emphasizes the complexity of the work.]

2. The first and last sentences in a paragraph are the most emphatic. Details and explanations belong in the middle or in appendixes.

> *Begin with a topic sentence.* The topic sentence helps you—and your readers—get to the point immediately. Your readers are busy people: they don't have time to plow through a poorly organized paragraph. Even when they do, if you don't have a clear and concisely stated topic sentence, they might miss your point completely.

Use a one-sentence paragraph occasionally to isolate an important point and make it stronger.

> Remember: the deadline for proposal submission is October 15.

3. Vary the types and lengths of sentences. Following a long sentence with a short one, for instance, creates an emphatic punch.

> Though Anthony Bastino is a recent college graduate, he shows promise with his experience as a camp counselor, editor of the student newspaper, and member of the rowing team. *Let's hire him.*

Take a sentence with two equal clauses and make one idea subordinate to emphasize the other one.

instead of: These smoke detectors are the most reliable on the market, and they come in a variety of decorator colors.

write: These smoke detectors, which come in a variety of decorator colors, are the most reliable on the market.

4. Put ideas in descending order of importance. The strongest points come first.

> Melissa Edelman designs our advertising materials, supervises the graphics staff, proofreads the copy, and serves on the redecorating committee.

Visual techniques for emphasis

1. How you space and arrange information on a page can set off the important points.
   - Use headlines.
   - Leave extra spaces between lines to isolate a meeting date and time.
   - Center an announcement in the middle of the page.
   - Make a bulleted list.
   - Use italics, boldface, capital letters, and underlining—sparingly.

2. Put headlines above key paragraphs. Headlines will draw readers' eyes where you want them.

3. Include visual aids to group information and set it apart. Whenever possible, use charts, diagrams, photographs, drawings, and other graphics to illustrate and summarize information.

Other techniques for emphasis

1. The active voice is stronger and, therefore, more emphatic than the passive.

> *instead of:*   Our department *was thanked* by the client for all the hard work. [passive voice]
>
> *write:*   The client *thanked* our department for all the hard work. [active voice]

2. Direct address emphasizes the person you're addressing.

> Thank you, *Terry*, for taking the time to meet with me last week.

3. The dash and the exclamation point are two marks of punctuation that create emphasis.

> No one told Matt to reorganize the database—he volunteered.
>
> You have only one day left to take advantage of our opening sale!

4. Repeat important words or ideas to emphasize them.

> It's not enough for *managers* to be *good* at planning, organization, and administration. Skilled *managers* are also *good* with people.

Effective use of emphasis will help you control how readers see and understand what you write. Help your audience identify, remember, and act on the important points in your document.

(See also **active voice/passive voice**, **headlines**, **sentences**, **visual aids**.)

---

endnotes

Notes that show documentation for sources and are listed on a separate page at the end of a report are called **endnotes**. They are the same as footnotes except for their position in the document. Footnotes appear at the bottom of the page.

(See also **documenting sources**, **footnotes**.)

---

envelopes

Business **envelopes** of all sizes should have the recipient's full address and your return address on the front.

The addressee

Use the person's or company's full name and address. Make this address exactly the same as your correspondent's letterhead stationery and your inside address.

Don't abbreviate any words unless the addressee abbreviates them. You may, however, abbreviate the state according to U.S. Postal Service abbreviations.

Start the address about two inches down on a standard business envelope, roughly centered right to left on the envelope. For window envelopes, be sure to position the inside address so it appears in the window.

The sender

If you aren't using an envelope with a preprinted return address, type the sender's full name and address in the upper-left corner.

Special notations

Mailing notations go under the stamp in the upper-right corner. They include CERTIFIED MAIL, SPECIAL DELIVERY, and REGISTERED.

Other notations, such as CONFIDENTIAL or PLEASE FORWARD, go either under the return address or above the main address.

A sample envelope

```
Gregory Sadowsky, Esq.
9 Arlington Place                              (stamp)
Cambridge, MA 02139
                                           REGISTERED

CONFIDENTIAL

                    Ms. Agnes Korosi
                    Seattle Seafood Distributors
                    4778 Hawks Drive
                    Seattle, WA 93345
```

Folding letters

Fold a letter in thirds to fit standard business envelopes.

1. Fold the bottom third up first, then the top third down. Don't fold the bottom third over the top third.
2. Put the edge you folded second into the envelope first.

For smaller envelopes, fold the letter in half and then in thirds.

(See also **letters**.)

---

etc.

We abbreviate the Latin phrase *et cetera* as *etc.*, meaning "and other things."

With *such as, for example, and*

1. If you introduce a series with *such as* or *for example*, don't end with *etc.* These phrases imply that you've selected only a few items of many. Since *etc.* also suggests that you could list more, it is redundant.

2. Don't use *and* with *etc.*

instead of:	Simplify list management with *such* functions *as* data organization, data display, *and* summary report generation, *etc.*
write:	Simplify list management with the following functions: data organization, data display, summary report generation, *etc.*
better:	Simplify list management with *such* functions *as* data organization, data display, *and* summary report generation.
or:	Simplify list management with *such* functions *as*

- data organization
- data display
- summary report generation.

Strong endings

Avoid using *etc.* altogether because it's weak and suggests you can't think of anything else to add to your list. For more effective writing, describe what you mean.

instead of:	We now have the facilities to repair VCR's, CD players, microwave ovens, *etc.*
write:	We now have the facilities to repair VCR's, CD players, microwave ovens, *and other small appliances.*

Punctuation

Use a comma before *etc.* If you must put *etc.* in the middle of a sentence, put commas before and after it.

We now have the facilities to repair VCR's, CD players, microwave ovens, *etc.,* on site.

---

exclamation points

The **exclamation point** (!) is a mark of punctuation that most often expresses surprise. You may also use it to make bold assertions, show excitement, express disbelief, and convey other strong or sudden feelings.

> I can't believe Margaret wrote that whole report in a week!

> Amazing!

> How wonderful!

> I know Herman asked you to send the tape to Topeka!

Technical writing is objective, so the exclamation point is usually inappropriate. It can, however, add emphasis in advertising copy.

Just four days to go till liquidation!

Hurry! Hurry! Hurry! These Chesapeake lounge chairs are going fast!

With quotation marks

Exclamation points can go inside or outside quotation marks, depending on the meaning of the sentence.

> I posted the message, "Please: no food or drink in the lab!" on the door.

> Congratulations—we hear your presentation was rated "the most interesting in the whole of Knoxville"!

A final hint

It's easy to overuse exclamation points. Avoid them in most writing and let your words convey your feeling. Limit yourself to one exclamation point per letter.

(See also **emphasis**, **punctuation**, **word choice**.)

executive summaries

The first section of a report or other long document is often the **executive summary**. It should present a concise and accurate summation for senior-level readers who won't be reading the entire report.

An executive summary usually includes

- a brief statement of purpose

- results and conclusions

- recommendations

- background, such as problems addressed and methods used

- review of pertinent data readers may need to understand conclusions.

An executive summary does not necessarily include all the sections of the entire report, just the more important ones. Present the sections you do include in the same sequence as in the report itself.

Guidelines for writing an executive summary

1 Write the whole report first, then begin the executive summary.

2. Be sure you know all the main ideas you want to include, from observations to recommendations.

3. Include your points in the order you present them in the report.

4. Reduce the report's key paragraphs to simple, direct statements. Leave out supporting statements.

5. Don't include table or figure references from the report unless they convey your core message better than a paragraph can.

6. Don't add information you haven't put in the report.

7. Make sure that the summary can stand by itself, separate from the report.

8. Keep an executive summary to two, maximum three, pages in length. In no case should the summary be longer than 10 percent of the total document.

9. Put the executive summary right after the table of contents or list of figures.

Differences between executive summaries and abstracts

- Scientific or research documents, rather than management reports, have abstracts.

- An executive summary is usually longer than an abstract.

- Unlike an abstract, an executive summary is considered part of the report—even though its contents can stand alone.

- An abstract is often published separately from the document it summarizes. Many abstracts are available through on-line and CD-ROM search services.

- Writers often submit abstracts to publishers before acceptance of their report or article.

(See also **abstracts**, **Model Documents Appendix**, **reports**.)

F

fax

A reproduction of a letter or other document transmitted electronically is called a **fax**. The word "fax" is a short version of "facsimile," which means "exact copy." You might send proposals, price quotes, invoices, lists, and other urgently needed information by fax.

Do not fax confidential information because many people may have access to the receiving fax machine.

Fax cover notes

Fax cover notes or transmission sheets tend to be less formal than business letters. Here are some tips for writing cover notes.

- If you write the cover note by hand, it may get more attention than a typed one would. (Type the cover note, however, if it's more than a paragraph long.)

- Be careful not to be so casual in cover notes as to appear careless.

- Indicate how many pages follow so recipients can make sure they received the whole document.

- If your company has its own cover sheet, use it.

Reader-centered faxes

- Headline next steps, deadlines, actions requested, and other important information, just as you would in any memo or letter.

- Use numbers or letters in the body of your fax for easy reference in a follow-up telephone conference.

A caution about faxing

Faxing can encourage bad writing because of the pressure to send a draft quickly. Get a little distance from your letter or document after you write it. Make sure it says what you want to say, and always take time to edit and proofread what you send.

Stamp or write "draft" on faxes which must be sent in a hurry.

(See also **electronic mail**, **memorandums**.)

---

figures

Illustrations, which include charts, graphics, diagrams, photographs, and drawings, are often called **figures** when integrated into text. Number your figures sequentially and mention them so readers can match text with illustrations. Refer to each figure by its number.

Fig. 3 illustrates the monthly increase in sales from 1995 to 1997.

Number figures independently from tables, and include a list of both figures and tables in your table of contents.

(See also **charts or graphs**, **diagrams**, **illustrations**, **tables**.)

---

flowcharts

Flowcharts are schematic diagrams that show relationships. They can depict the path of a process from the first step to the last. Through the use of symbols like rectangles, diamonds, lines, and ovals, a flowchart displays the logical relationships between events or system components.

Use flowcharts to illustrate:

- program descriptions
- proposals
- specifications
- computer systems design.

Your readers will be able to trace a process such as decision-making from start to finish.

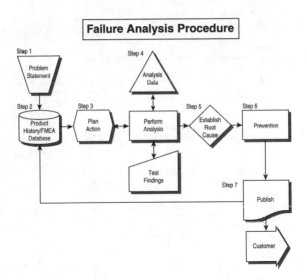

Flowchart symbols have standard interpretations. To be sure that you use the symbols correctly, review the list of standard symbols that follows.

Symbols for Flow Charts

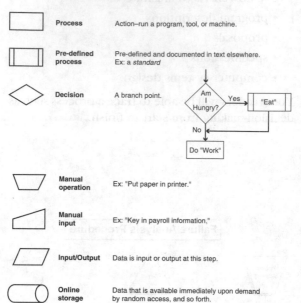

	Process	Action–run a program, tool, or machine.
	Pre-defined process	Pre-defined and documented in text elsewhere. Ex: a *standard*
	Decision	A branch point.
	Manual operation	Ex: "Put paper in printer."
	Manual input	Ex: "Key in payroll information."
	Input/Output	Data is input or output at this step.
	Online storage	Data that is available immediately upon demand by random access, and so forth.

Symbol	Name	Description
	Document	A paper record–used for input or output, perhaps.
	Display	Action–put this information up on a screen.
	Entrance or Exit Connectors	
	Terminal interruption	Query operator.
	Comment	An aside, not part of the flow.
	Preparation	Requires validation that the preparation or pre-process has been performed.
	Start or end	Beginning or end of flow diagram.

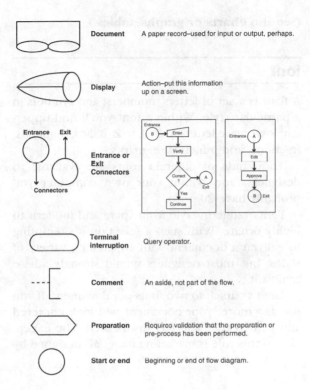

(See also **charts or graphs**, **tables**.)

---

font

A **font** is a set of letters, numbers, and symbols in a particular style. Within a font you'll find upper- and lowercase letters from A to Z, italics, numerals, fractions, and punctuation marks.

Thousands of different fonts are available to designers, and within your own computer you probably have 20 or so.

Fonts range in style from spare and modern to highly ornate. With such a selection it's tempting to enliven a document with an exciting variety of styles, but most designers would strongly advise against it.

Limit yourself to two fonts per document. If you use any more, your document will look cluttered and your reader will feel disoriented. The exception to this rule is marketing materials designed by experts.

Serif or sans serif?

The font you select can give a formal, technical, tra- ditional, or old-fashioned appearance to your writ- ing. One of the distinctions is serif or sans serif type.

Serif refers to the small projections at the end of each stroke in a letter. Serif type, though not cur- sive, looks somewhat more connected than a sans serif font (*sans* being French for *without*), which looks open and clean.

Generally, a sans serif type like Helvetica looks more technical than a serif font such as Times. Many people find serif type easier to read, but sans serif works well for headlines. For tables and other figures where words and numbers are small, sans serif is a good choice.

Choosing a font size

Fonts come in different sizes. They are measured by a unit called a *point*, which is 1/72 inch high. Most business documents that you receive in the mail are set in 10 to 12 point. Eleven is an excellent all-purpose size. Smaller than 10 is difficult for some people to read.

Sometimes examples and quotations printed as extracts in a text appear in a slightly smaller font.

This font is called Times. The font size is 10 point.

This font is called Helvetica. The font size is 12 point.

This font is called Palatino italic. The font size is 14 point.

A final note

The font you choose helps convey your message. If you mix several styles, your ideas will appear dissimilar and disjointed.

(See also **graphics**, **headlines**, **italics**, **visual design**.)

---

footers

A **footer** is the line of information or the graphic along the bottom of each page of a document. The footer may include the date and page number. Sometimes the name of the publication or the chapter is also in the footer.

(See also **format**, **headers**.)

footnotes

Footnotes explain sources you used in writing a report or document. A footnote is written in a standard format at the bottom of the page on which the cited material appears. A superscript number follows the material in the text and refers the reader to a corresponding footnote.

Footnotes are the same as endnotes except for their position in the document. Endnotes appear on a separate page after the main body of the text; footnotes appear at the bottom of the page itself.

Explanatory footnotes

Sometimes you need to explain a point further, but the explanation would interrupt the flow of the text. In such cases, include the additional information in an *explanatory footnote*. You may put these notes at the bottom of the page or in a list of endnotes.

(See also **bibliography**, **documenting sources**, **endnotes**, **reports**.)

format

Format refers to the design and sequence of information in a letter, report, or document. Many kinds of writing, such as general business letters and formal reports, have standard formats. Your company probably uses its own formats for letters, proposals, and reports.

Using predesigned formats for such frequently used documents as credit analyses and audit reports can greatly improve both your writing speed and your audience's reading speed and comprehension.

Design

A format design should present information to readers visually, in the most easy-to-read and understandable way possible. Consider these elements on the page:

- margins
- white space
- paragraph length
- type size and style
- headlines
- graphics

Make the page visually pleasing. Draw your readers' eyes to the most important information. Remember that most readers will scan your letter or report, so essential information should be easy for them to find.

Sequence of information

Many formats dictate a certain sequence for arranging information. Business letters begin with an inside address and end with copy notations. Formal reports begin with a title page and end with a bibliography, appendix, or glossary.

When you choose a format sequence, use a standard one or a variation that keeps the information as simple as possible. Your readers won't necessarily read every word, so put the information they need most in accessible form.

Word processing formats

Most word-processing software has some built-in formats, such as standard margins and tabs. You can use predesigned templates and style sheets or set up your own formats for headlines, tables, and other designs you frequently use.

(See also **headlines**, **letters**, **memorandums**, **reports**, **style sheets for word processors**, **templates for word processors**, **visual design**.)

G

gender

The word for sexual reference in grammar is **gender**. The three genders in English are *feminine*, *masculine*, and *neuter*. Only pronoun forms change with gender.

he/him/his [masculine]
she/her/hers [feminine]
it/its [neuter]

Sometimes gender depends on the sex of the word.

grandmother [feminine]
husband [masculine]
keyboard [neuter]

Many words could be either masculine or feminine. These are called *common gender* words.

programmer   employee   manager   writer
everyone   somebody

Agreement in gender

A pronoun must agree with the word it refers to (its *antecedent*) in gender.

The new *department supervisor* will be moving into *her* office next week.

The *clothing factory* will close *its* doors in August.

The *director* asked me to find out about upgrading *his* computer.

SOLVING THE *HE* OR *SHE* PROBLEM

1. With singular common gender words, you must decide which pronoun to use. The choices are a masculine or feminine pronoun, both, or changing all related words to the plural.

Avoid using the masculine *he* because it excludes women. The construction *he or she* is cumbersome, so you should use it sparingly. The preferred choice is changing the noun and the pronoun to the plural whenever possible.

instead of: Each new *voter* should bring *his* voter registration card to the table on the left.

write: All new *voters* should bring *their* voter registration cards to the table on the left.

instead of: We want to thank every *participant* in the seminar for *his or her* involvement.

write: We want to thank all seminar *participants* for *their* involvement.

2. If all the people are of one sex, use a gender-specific pronoun.

Each employee who uses the women's locker room should bring *her* own lock.

Everyone on the men's softball team played *his* best, despite the rain.

3. You may want to eliminate the pronouns altogether to avoid agreement problems in gender.

instead of: Every technician must complete *his or her* lab report by Friday.

write: Every technician must complete *a* lab report by Friday.

Avoid gender-specific words

Whenever you can, avoid using words that refer to one gender but could include both.

instead of:	*write:*
mankind	people, humans
chairman	chairperson, chair
fireman	firefighter
mailman	letter carrier

instead of:	This report needs editing. The jargon will be incomprehensible to the *layman*.
write:	This report needs editing. The jargon will be incomprehensible to the *lay reader*.
instead of:	This presentation needs editing. The jargon will be incomprehensible to the *layman*.
write:	This presentation needs editing. The jargon will be incomprehensible to the *lay audience*.
instead of:	We don't have the *manpower* we need to finish the project by the new deadline. We estimate that it will take 75 *man hours* to complete.
write:	We don't have the *staffing* [or *labor*] we need to finish the project by the new deadline. We estimate that it will take 75 *work hours* [or *labor hours*] to complete.
instead of:	Next week we will conduct *man-in-the-street* interviews.
write:	Next week we will conduct *random street* interviews.

(See also **he**, **he/she**, **s/he**, **(s)he**; **pronouns**.)

---

generalizations

A **generalization** is an assumption that what is true in one or a few situations is true in all similar situations. Avoid making such statements. Watch out for words like *everyone* or *no one* combined with *never*, *always*, or *ever*.

instead of:	Please inform your service department that the equipment *never* works properly.
write:	Please inform your service department that the equipment has broken down for the third time this month.

instead of:	*No one* learned *anything* in the last training session.
write:	Few employees benefited from the last training session.

If you make unfounded generalizations, people might consider your opinion unreliable.

---

gerunds

A verb form that ends in *-ing* and functions as a noun is called a **gerund**. You use gerunds just as you would nouns—as subjects, objects, and complements.

> With this new service, *logging on* to the Internet is a much simpler procedure. [subject]

> Gwen proposed *postponing* the deadline to accommodate the new engineering schedule. [object of the verb]

> Jose's manager was happy with his *completing* the project ahead of schedule. [object of preposition]

> For me, happiness would be *completing* this project ahead of schedule. [complement]

Always put the possessive form of a noun or pronoun in front of a gerund.

> *Theresa's* working at night is interfering with *her* performing her daytime job.

Other *-ing* words

Words ending in *-ing* may also be participles, or verb forms used as adjectives.

> Installation of a new network three days before the project deadline is certainly a *complicating* factor.

> The *engineering* department will submit project specifications by next Friday.

Most verbs that end in *-ing* are ordinary verbs, not gerunds.

Nassim was *logging on* when the system crashed.

We are *postponing* the deadline to accommodate the new engineering schedule.

(See also **participles**, **verbs**.)

---

getting started with a Start-up Strategy: Step 2 to Reader-Centered Writing

For a lot of people, **getting started** is the hardest part of the writing process. The blank page or computer screen can be forbidding, especially with a deadline fast approaching.

Why is it so hard to start? You may feel your message isn't interesting enough, or you won't be able to convey it convincingly. You may expect your first draft to be perfect, so you get distracted by details like word choice before you've even formulated your ideas.

Maybe you do your best thinking while taking a shower, walking the dog, or driving to work. You will lose those great flashes of inspiration if you don't store them safely on paper, disk, or audiotape.

The strategies that follow are designed to help you generate and save ideas. If you use these techniques, you'll have the substance of your report or letter in front of you before you even begin to draft.

With good planning, you won't ever have to face the blank page or screen again. Getting started on your writing project will be a lot less painful.

Use the Focus Sheet™

Before using a Start-up Strategy, it is vital to analyze your readers by using the Focus Sheet described in the **readers**, **analyzing** entry. You must also determine your purpose for writing, again using the Focus Sheet.

If you use a Start-up Strategy without filling out the Focus Sheet first, you may end up by not giving your readers the quantity or quality of information they need.

The importance of research

If you're an expert on your topic and already have all the research or information necessary for your document, your first task is simply to jot down your main ideas using one of the Start-up Strategies.

If you don't have all the information yet, you may need to conduct research, analyze data, or discuss your ideas with colleagues or consultants. As you do so, record your findings carefully.

Seeing all your ideas together will help you make an informed judgment about what to include, what to leave out, and how to organize your material effectively. This information will supplement—but not replace—your Focus Sheet.

Choose the Start-up Strategy that works for you—and your task

The following are descriptions of some of Better Communications'™ favorite strategies for getting started:

- questioning
- the traditional outline
- the brainstorm outline
- free writing
- starting at your computer

Experiment and find the approach that works for you. Keep in mind, though, that a brief letter will not require a massive brainstorm outline: you may be wasting time. On the other hand, a detailed outline or data files on your computer will surely save you time in preparing a long report.

Questioning (for letters and memos)

The questioning technique is a strategy that can sharply focus your writing by putting you in your readers' shoes.

Questioning helps you focus on what your readers need to know. You began this process by filling out a Focus Sheet. Questioning allows you to get even more specific. It helps you define the information you'll need so that you won't have to interrupt your writing for more research or analysis.

FIRST, ASSUME THE ROLE OF YOUR READER

Imagine the questions your reader might have about your report, memo, or letter, and list them. Consider such issues as advantages, timing, costs, principal features, background, deadlines, and action steps.

SECOND, REASSUME YOUR ROLE AS WRITER

Have an imaginary conversation with your reader in which you address all the questions on your list. Answer each question as fully as possible. You can edit later and pull out the most essential information.

Suppose, for example, that you are drafting a memo announcing an off-site strategy session. What will your readers ask?

1. Where and when is the meeting?

2. What's on the agenda?

3. How must I prepare for the meeting?

4. Who will attend?

5. Is there a dress code?

6. Is transportation provided?

Be sure you can answer all your questions. Being prepared will spare you both the embarrassment of circulating a half-thought-out memo and the time wasted answering follow-up questions from your readers.

Traditional outline

Some people shy away from traditional outlining; others can't write a document without it. If you are able to picture a logical structure and sequence for your document at the outset, then this strategy is for you.

A traditional outline is an organized list that highlights important ideas and subordinates less important ones. It allows you to group related concepts and examine their sequence and hierarchy of importance.

You may write a traditional outline using either numbers and letters or a decimal system. Consult the **outlines** entry for more information.

To write a really useful outline, you need to generate ideas, group them, and sequence them.

For most people this is a difficult and frustrating task: you are, in essence, jumping ahead to complete Steps 3 and 4 to Reader-Centered Writing. If you can easily do this, however, you'll save time. If not, try a different Start-up Strategy.

Brainstorm outline (for longer memos and reports)

The brainstorm outline, a non-linear map of ideas, was originated by Tony Buzan, who named it "mind-mapping." It's a fast and free-form tool for writing down a lot of ideas, deciding whether or not they relate to each other, and determining which are of greater importance.

If you are overwhelmed by the complexity of your topic and the numerous ideas you have about it, try a brainstorm outline. It works for shorter documents too, like memos and e-mail messages.

How do you produce a brainstorm outline?

1. On a piece of plain white paper, at least 8 1/2 by 11 inches, draw a circle in the middle in

which you can fit about six words. Here you will write your purpose. It should begin with *to* and a verb such as *persuade, propose, explain*, or *analyze*.

In the sample outline in this entry, for example, the purpose stated in the circle reads: "To persuade my manager to purchase XYZ software."

2. Think of important ideas related to your subject. To start, draw a line from the circle, like the spoke of a wheel, and write your first idea or topic on the line. It might, for instance, be benefits, or background, or costs.

    Remember, this idea doesn't have to come first in your final document. You haven't yet decided on sequence.

3. If this idea inspires others related to it, draw branches from your first line and pencil in the new issues. If ideas occur to you that are entirely separate from the first, draw a new spoke right from the center. Let your mind race, keeping the momentum going.

    Continue to draw branches from the main spokes as you generate related ideas.

The free association that this outline allows you is excellent preparation for thoughtful writing like problem-solving memos. There is plenty of room for fresh ideas, and you can see at a glance what the main issues are. Your brainstorm outline will be most useful if you remember to

- keep ideas that are related on or near the same spoke
- let less important ideas stem from more important ones.

However, don't let choosing the correct spoke slow you down. It's better to put an idea in the wrong spot and keep on thinking. You will move ideas later, in Steps 3 and 4 to Reader-Centered Writing.

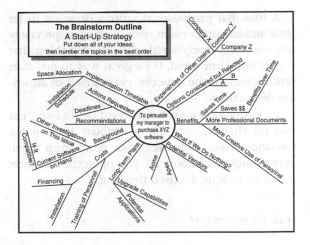

The Brainstorm Outline
A Start-Up Strategy
Put down all of your ideas;
then number the topics in the best order

HOW DO YOU USE YOUR BRAINSTORM OUTLINE TO WRITE
A REPORT?

With your outline before you, think about which
ideas go together. If you think a group of ideas
radiating from a stem should appear together in
your report, circle the whole area.

Your outline may be so complicated that circled
areas may overlap or related ideas be too far apart
to include in the same circle. If so, highlight related ideas in the same color.

At this point you may wish to refine your plan
by turning your brainstorm outline into an informal, or list, outline. Decide based upon how complex your brainstorm outline is.

If you're using your brainstorm outline for short
documents, you may already see your ideas clearly
displayed. How do you judge the most effective
sequence? You will do that in Step 4, **organizing
information.**

Free writing

Feeling blocked? Ill at ease before the critical eye
of your manager? Free writing may be the fastest
and most rewarding way out.

A tool that professional writers draw on to let their imaginations roam, free writing is precisely that—writing freely anything and everything that comes into your mind. It's a great way to just start writing and, in the process, rid yourself of annoying distractions.

By jotting down even irrelevant issues like, "get that oil change," or "buy a birthday present for Cassandra," you help free your mind from those very thoughts. In doing so, you open the channels for more serious, focused thinking.

How do you start?

The overriding principle in free writing is that there are no rules. Don't worry about grammar and syntax. Anxiety about these details is often what causes us to stumble and stop in mid-sentence.

Don't stop to reread or even answer the phone. The goal is to develop a rhythm and keep your thoughts—both relevant to your document and irrelevant—flowing onto the page. Write in sentences or fragments, whichever comes naturally to you.

The very act of writing limbers up your thinking processes like warm-up exercises before an aerobic workout. Keep at your free writing for a sustained period; by the time you've poured all your thoughts onto the page or screen, you'll undoubtedly have something substantial to work with.

From free writing to outline

With a number of full pages of writing in front of you, you'll probably feel calmer and more confident. Now take a different-colored pen and assume a more analytical role.

Read through your free writing and circle your most useful ideas, whether they're single words or whole passages. You may find that a framework for your document is starting to emerge.

Once your best ideas are clearly visible, transfer them to a traditional outline or brainstorm outline, or simply write down your key ideas on index cards. Later you can sequence and develop them further.

Starting at your computer

Most of us have become so comfortable and versatile at the computer that we write on-line, avoiding draft recopying and correction fluid. If we write on the computer, why not use it as a start-up tool too?

You can use word processing to get your ideas down quickly, produce outlines and sequence them, and generate and manage additional information. You may create files for different categories of data and add to them over time.

Whether you use a Start-up Strategy like questioning or quickly produce a free-writing draft, **a** computer will save you time.

Let's look back at several of the strategies already discussed in this entry to see how the computer can speed them up.

AUTOMATIC OUTLINING

You may shudder at the idea of writing a traditional outline if it resurrects memories of rigid documents laboriously produced and rigidly critiqued in grammar class. Computers have revolutionized outlining because they allow you to manipulate the sequence of your ideas so easily.

The outlining function of your word-processing program helps you reorganize your outline. It also allows you to see your outline in different forms.

For example, it can display all lines beginning with capital letters and conceal subordinate information in between. You can switch easily from an overview of the document to the smallest subtopic. Such a fresh perspective often triggers new ideas.

QUESTIONING AT THE COMPUTER

Type the questions you anticipate your reader will ask. They will become the main points of your document. Then answer each question fully: you'll already have a rough pre-draft.

Don't worry yet about the sequence of ideas. It will be easy to shift them around later. Use your questions as temporary headlines to label your information and make it easy to locate.

FOLLOWING UP ON YOUR BRAINSTORM OUTLINE

You may have made a detailed brainstorm outline or simply jotted down a web of ideas. Now circle clusters of related issues and transfer the information to your computer in the form of a traditional outline.

The sequence will probably still be somewhat random, but it will be easy to insert new ideas, details, data, steps, and events as they occur. At this point, the main objective is to get all your ideas onto the screen.

FREE SCREENING (TO OVERCOME WRITER'S BLOCK)

If you have trouble free writing because you can't help critiquing your every word the minute it appears on the page or screen, try this experiment. Simply turn down the contrast till your screen is black, then let your ideas flow.

You won't be slowed down by anxiety about grammar, spelling, and word choice because you can't see what you're writing!

When you've finished free writing, turn up the contrast and see what you've written. Even if the sequence is illogical, you'll probably have more ideas of substance than if you'd sat there paralyzed with self-criticism. It takes self-control to try this method, but it has saved many a blocked writer.

DATA FILES (FOR ORGANIZING LOTS OF INFORMATION)

As you know, your computer can help you store large amounts of information efficiently. Use separate files for different sections of your document and simply add data as you acquire it. Begin all file names in a similar way so that they will appear grouped together in your directory list.

Before drafting you may want to print a copy of each file so that you have all your information in front of you at once.

If you frequently write very complex documents, consider using a set of integrated programs. They allow you to transfer information easily between database, word processing, and spreadsheet functions.

(See also **Introduction to the Six Steps**; **outlines**; **readers**, **analyzing**; **research**.)

---

gobbledygook

Stuffy, pompous, wordy, or abstract writing is called **gobbledygook**. You will find it in government documents, official communications, business letters, memos, and technical writing. Gobbledygook can make writing nearly unintelligible.

> This office is in receipt of information which seems to indicate that Directive 402.1, alluded to in the attached copy of the employee newsletter, is not being implemented; therefore, to the fullest extent possible, supervisors are urged to post the attached notice (Directive 402.1 a) with a view to correcting what would appear to be a disregard of said Directive.

Writer William Safire reports, in his *An Anecdotal Dictionary of Catchwords, Slogans, and Political Usage*, that Texas Senator Maury Maverick first coined the word *gobbledygook*.

Some characteristics of gobbledygook

- unnecessary words: during the *course of the* week
- redundancy: *young* juveniles
- obscure terms: Report immediately any *williwaw* outside the company gates.
- nouns made into verbs: *incentivize, regulationed, to liaise*
- hedging: *It may seem* to require . . .
- abstract words: *actors in the situation*
- euphemisms: *hospital* instead of *repair shop*
- cliches: *beyond the shadow of a doubt*
- foreign words in English: The chaotic shipping room is the *bête noire* of the company.
- passive voice: *It was noted* that silicon nitrite *was used* as the base material.

Avoiding gobbledygook

1. Write, brief, clear, unambiguous sentences.

   instead of: At the warehouse, the task-time element involved rendered nonoperational the expectation of project completion within the originally designated time-frame.

   write: The project at the warehouse took so long that the staff couldn't finish it on time.

2. Avoid wordy phrases.

   instead of: Table 4.2 shows an example of a table which presents the varied excavation depths of sole-source aquifers at the proposed site.

   write: Table 4.2 shows the varied excavation depths of sole-source aquifers at the proposed site.

3. Replace overblown and affected language with simple words.

> *instead of:*   It would appear that we must request Kyoko's assistance in ascertaining what has transpired pursuant to our most recent communication.

> *write:*   Apparently we have to ask Kyoko to help us find out what happened after we sent our last fax.

4. Change passive voice to active whenever possible. Give accountability for actions.

> *instead of:*   The side slope construction technique and the width of the construction right-of-way *should be described* in this section of the report.

> *write:*   In this section of the report, *describe* the side-slope construction technique and the width of the construction right-of-way.

Appropriate jargon

Jargon may be a shorthand approach to communication when you're writing for an audience who knows your field. However, you should use only jargon that all your readers understand.

> If we use *boilerplate* for the chapter sections, the *B-heads* will all look the same. Are we including them in the *TOC*?

Technical jargon is appropriate for e-mail, user manuals, procedures, specifications, trade magazines—anything written for a technical audience.

If your readers don't know your subject well, use a minimum of jargon. Always explain terms as you use them.

What's wrong with gobbledygook?

If you're reluctant to say anything too bold or certain, you might end up writing gobbledygook to avoid being direct. If you try to impress your readers with high-sounding words, you risk gobbledygook. These are some impressions gobbledygook may give your readers:

- Your thinking sounds weak rather than sure.

- You sound confusing and unclear rather than impressive and authoritative.

- You may be hiding unpleasant news or ideas behind obscure language.

- You didn't keep your readers in mind and answer their questions.

- You didn't edit your writing.

A final hint

Read what you write aloud before you send it out. Would you want to receive it?

(See also **active voice/passive voice**, **cliches**, **concise vs. wordy writing**, **jargon**, **word choice**.)

---

good news letters and memos

Always try to present **good news** first in letters and memos, even if unpleasant news follows.

Make sure the tone of your good news letter is

- direct—don't talk around the subject
- kind, respectful, and courteous
- positive
- encouraging of goodwill in the future.

If good news is the main subject, use a most-important-to-least-important method of development and put the good news in the first paragraph.

(See also **bad news letters and memos**, **letters**, **memorandums**, **organizing information**.)

grammar

Grammar is the study of the rules governing the use of words: the structure of a language. We understand others when we write and speak because we agree on how words relate to each other. A point of usage or punctuation becomes a rule of grammar when most people accept and use it.

Studying grammar can help native speakers understand their language better and, therefore, communicate more effectively. For non-native speakers, studying grammar is an essential part of learning English.

What are the advantages of using good grammar?

When you are writing, you may have to make decisions about correct word choice, such as whether to use *her* or *she*.

Let's say you know that the pronoun object of a preposition must be in the objective case. You would then be able to write—or edit—your sentence to read: *The team selected John and* me (*not* I) *for promotion.*

When you use grammar rules correctly, your writing will appear educated, informed, and understandable to most readers.

Knowing grammar also gives you choices about the conventions of usage. You'll be able to construct different kinds of sentences so your writing isn't boring. You'll use clauses and phrases correctly and in different positions for varied emphasis.

Do grammar rules change?

Yes. Change comes slowly, but rules do change, usually by consensus. The majority of educated people may consistently use an alternative form or construction in speaking or writing.

Gradually, the formal rules taught in academia may change. Informal usage often changes long before formal rules do.

For example, a rule that some writers think may change is the one that governs agreement of pronouns and their antecedents:

When you have a singular noun of common gender (both masculine and feminine), you must use a singular pronoun to refer to it.

Formal: *Each* auditor should bring *his or her* own laptop to the meeting.

The *his or her* construction is correct, but cumbersome. Most grammarians suggest making the noun plural so you can use a plural pronoun that includes both genders.

Formal or informal: *Auditors* should bring *their* own laptop to the meeting.

The rule may eventually change to make using the plural pronoun with the singular noun correct. This plural/singular construction is already used routinely in e-mail messages and informal internal memos.

Each auditor should bring *their* own laptop to the meeting.

Don't write a sentence this way in formal documents because many people still consider it grammatically incorrect. That opinion, however, is less common every year.

graphics

Graphics is a broad term referring to many different elements that make up visual design. In business writing, the kind of graphics you are likely to encounter include drawings, flowcharts, photographs, maps, graphs, and organizational charts.

Increasingly, people in business have come to expect a strong visual element in any serious report. Give careful attention to this aspect of a document or presentation. Appropriate use of graphics can make almost any report more appealing and accessible.

A clear, uncluttered chart that your readers can absorb at a glance will save them time and effort. They won't have to labor through several paragraphs of number-filled text. Include eye-catching photographs of your product or a series of shots highlighting stages of development over time.

Graphics can lend a warm, friendly appearance to a document, but they must be functional as well as decorative.

Using your computer graphics

As you prepare a piece of writing and analyze its purpose, you should start visualizing a format. You may find that you can create an effective design with your own computer.

Many excellent software packages are available for generating charts, graphs, and illustrations, and overhead transparencies for presentations. With graphic software you'll enrich your writing and save yourself time in the end.

Clip art

Clip art refers to a collection of predrawn and computerized images. They are simple to use: just choose the picture you want and paste it—electronically, of course—into your document.

Clip art pictures for general business applications include people, buildings, computers, maps, and many other subjects. More specialized clip art packages contain newsletter art, cartoons, borders, and sports or nature images.

Virtually every industry or profession now has a clip art gallery tailored to its needs. Are you a real estate agent, an engineer, a lab technician, or a healthcare worker? A clip art package exists for you.

Using a graphic designer

"But what if I have no sense of visual design?" you may be asking. "What if I have absolutely no idea how to select effective graphics?" If this is the case, you may want to seek help from a graphic designer.

You may turn to a designer if

- you have to write a long report and don't have time to design it yourself;

- the kind of graphics you require aren't available in a computer program;

- you feel graphics could really enhance your project, but you're not quite sure how.

Before you contract with a designer, be sure to see some work samples. They will help you decide if the artist will be appropriate for your needs.

Using a graphic artist will definitely cost you more than doing the design yourself or in-house. If everything runs smoothly, it's probably money well spent. But if you aren't sure what you really want, the designer could wind up redoing the project several times—and that means time and money wasted.

Here are a few issues to consider before you meet with any graphic designer.

WHO ARE YOUR READERS?

The designer needs to know what the approach should be: formal? technical? upbeat? restrained? whimsical? The graphic style of your document should be compatible with the tone of the writing. Take your Focus Sheet™ with you and share your reader analysis with the designer.

WHAT KINDS OF GRAPHICS? HOW MUCH?

To estimate the time required for a project, a designer will ask you how many visual elements you want and how many different types. If you're an engineer, you may need schematic designs. If you're in the travel business, you may be working with color photographs.

Drawings are useful for illustrating step-by-step procedures, internal parts of a mechanism, and how parts fit together. Be as precise as possible as you describe your needs to a designer.

DO YOU NEED COLOR? ONE, TWO, OR FOUR?

Cost escalates as you add color. A black-and-white photograph is considered to be one color: black. A drawing can be in a single color; say, blue. Two-color art might be black and red.

The term *four-color* means full color. If you scan in a color photograph, for example, you'll need four colors. If you want to keep costs down, a designer can translate your color photograph to black and white or some other single color—but the contrasts in your original must be strong.

WHAT KIND OF PAPER?

Thick, coated paper is more expensive than the thin, uncoated variety. Analyze your needs and check your budget. If you want a really luxurious look, use 60- to 80-lb glossy paper. As a point of comparison, most copy machines use 20-lb paper.

WHAT'S THE SETUP ON THE PAGE?

Will the designer have the freedom to decide the width of the margins, the placement of the illustrations, the amount of text per page, and the column setup? Or are you limited by your internal style and corporate identity rules?

Be sure to discuss with your designer your headline, credit, caption, and legend needs. Once again, be specific about your requirements.

WHICH FONTS SET THE TONE?

Consider whether you want a modern, technical look or a more old-fashioned, conventional one. That will help your designer choose an appropriate font.

DO YOU NEED AN OUTER PACKAGE?

Talk with your designer about the overall appearance of your report. Should it be lavish? formal? technical? A cover is the first thing your reader will see. Be sure you convey the message you want.

WHAT'S YOUR DEADLINE?

Plan well in advance if you decide to work with a graphic designer. Rush jobs cost more and may not turn out as you want them. Give your designer as much time as possible. For a 32-page report, talk to your designer *two to three months* before your deadline.

A FINAL NOTE

If you are unclear about all the elements that go into designing a report, listen to the advice of your graphic designer. After all, there's a reason you hired an expert. Trusting in that expertise will help prevent endless, costly revisions.

(See also **font**, **illustrations**, **visual design**.)

grouping ideas: Step 3 to Reader-Centered Writing

Now that you've completed Step 2 of the writing process, getting started with a Start-up Strategy, you need to cluster your ideas into related groups. **Grouping information** is a two-step process:

1. define the categories
2. decide which ideas go in which categories

The categories may be obvious to you. On the other hand, defining them may require some thought. Be persistent—organizing your ideas now will save a lot of time and effort later when it's time to write your draft.

Common categories for business documents

Although you may write on a wide range of topics, you probably find that some broad generic categories prove useful again and again for grouping information.

For example, you may write a memo to complain about noisy working conditions or to suggest a new strategy for your sales force: two completely different ideas, but both require that you formulate a statement of purpose. That, then, is a category to think about as you organize material for any memo.

Other generic categories you are likely to use in business documents include:

proposal	request for action
announcement of a change	rationale for action
background information	observations
directions or procedure	scope of investigation
results of a study	analysis of findings
explanation of a process	evaluation
expression of thanks	implementation plan
conclusions	recommendations
description of a situation	explanation of cause
sequence of events	introduction of a new idea

From Start-up Strategy to categories

If you used a traditional outline as a Start-up Strategy in Step 2, you've already defined key topics and subordinate ideas. Step 3 is well under way.

If you generated ideas using questioning as a Start-up Strategy, reread all your questions and decide which ones are related. Number them 1A, 1B, 1C, 2A, and so on, or use a color code to show how they are related.

At this point concentrate only on grouping similar ideas; you will decide the most effective sequence during Step 4, **organizing information**. You can't sequence your ideas until you know what they are.

The brainstorm outline Start-up Strategy encourages some grouping right from the start since related ideas branch from main ideas.

As you analyze your brainstorm outline, look at the big picture. Do some main branches belong together? If so, circle them or group them with a color code. Then turn your diagram into a simple list outline with major categories highlighted.

From categories to headlines: help your readers see your message

Once you've grouped your information into categories, you will be able to see and understand the framework of your document. Share that information with your readers by supplying headlines that clearly state the contents of each category or section of your document.

First create rough category headlines, such as "Results of study," "Evaluation," or "Recommendations." In Step 6 to Reader-Centered Writing, **editing your draft**, you will fine-tune your headlines, making them more specific and more interesting for your reader.

For example, you might replace "Implementation" with "Importance of a quick decision." Or you may decide to use both the generic and the specific headline together: "Proposal: We need to hire a new financial analyst."

Remember, headlines label your information for easy assembly and sequencing. Until your information is categorized with labels, it's hard to see what you're trying to organize.

Word processing facilitates the task

Use your computer to help you organize information. Word processing makes it easy to shift groups of ideas so that you can see how they best fit together. Also, it's easy to add information under a particular heading as you do more research.

Automatic outlining lets you see your outline in different forms and helps you restructure it. If you've accumulated a lot of research under your main headlines, you'll especially appreciate the program's ability to extract the outline instantly.

Check periodically to see if the overall structure of information clusters is logical.

The end result of Step 3 is a list of grouped and subordinated ideas that you will organize, or sequence, during Step 4 to Reader-Centered Writing.

(See also **getting started**, **headlines**, **Introduction to the Six Steps**, **organizing information**.)

H

he, he/she, s/he, (s)he

The constructions *he/she, s/he,* and *(s)he* are artificial and awkward. They try to compensate for the English language's lack of a singular pronoun that indicates both sexes.

It's better not to use *he* to refer to both sexes because it excludes women. But you should try to avoid the *he/she* constructions because they are clumsy and difficult to read. Also don't write *his/her, him/her.*

How to avoid *he/she, s/he,* and *(s)he*

1. Rewrite the sentence with a plural pronoun.

   instead of: After the applicant has submitted an application, *he/she* (or *s/he* or *(s)he*) should wait for us to call.

   write: After *applicants have* submitted applications, *they* should wait for us to call. [Notice that the subject *applicants* and the verb *have* are also plural.]

2. Rewrite the sentence without the pronoun.

   Applicants should submit applications and wait for us to call.

Each, everyone, and *someone*

Be on the lookout for indefinite pronouns, such as *each, everyone,* and *someone.* If you use these singular pronouns in a document, you may trap yourself into using the *he/she* constructions later on.

   instead of: After someone has submitted an application, *he/she* (or *s/he* or *(s)he*) should wait for us to call.

or:	After someone has submitted an application, *they* should wait for us to call. [Incorrect: *someone* is singular; *they* is plural.]
write:	After *applicants have* submitted applications, *they* should wait for us to call. [Notice that the subject *applicants* and the verb *have* are also plural.]

In the occasional cases when you do use both pronouns, write *he or she*, *his or her*, or *him or her*. Avoid slashes and parentheses—they're more difficult to read.

One out of ten employees does not drive *his or her* own car to work. [*One* has to be singular.]

We do not discriminate on the basis of gender and encourage everyone to work up to *his or her* full potential. [*His or her* intentionally emphasizes both genders.]

(See also **gender**, **person**, **pronouns**, **sexist language**.)

headers

A **header** is the line of information or the graphic along the top of each page of a book or report. The header can include the section or chapter title and the page number.

The header on each page of this book contains

- the first reference word on the page on the left-hand pages
- the last reference word on the right-hand pages
- the page number.

(See also **footers**, **format**.)

headline levels: help your readers navigate long documents

If you're writing a report with many sections and subdivisions, your **headline levels**, or hierarchy, should reflect the outline of the report. The headline levels should reveal the importance of the ideas. For example, major ideas may be level 1; secondary ideas, level 2; and sub-ideas, level 3.

The size font that you use in your headlines should relate to the importance of ideas. You may further define your headline hierarchy by centering, capitalizing, bolding, or underlining.

Design your headline levels before you write

To save time and aggravation later, decide on a headline hierarchy before you begin to write. Usually three or four levels are enough. You don't want to confuse your readers with too much subordination.

Selecting and using a three- or four-tiered headline hierarchy at the beginning of your project will also help you with your table of contents later—especially if you use the table of contents compilation feature of your word-processing software.

What might have taken hours can now be accomplished in a matter of minutes.

Tips for setting up headline levels

1. Headlines on the same level all follow the same format. Consider

    - font style and format (such as boldface, italic, all caps, or underlining)

    - font size

    - position on the page (such as flush with the left margin, centered, or indented)

    - capitalization.

Here is an example of a three-level headline hierarchy:

Level 1:	**ACTION REQUESTED**
Level 2:	**Researching the database**
Level 3:	<u>Did you document your research?</u>
Level 1:	**PERSON TO CONTACT**
Level 2:	**Making the time**
Level 3:	<u>Did you keep a record of the transaction?</u>

2. If possible, all same-level headlines should also have parallel phrasing.

instead of:	*Let's consider three points and Contacting key people*
write:	*Three points to consider and Key people to contact*

3. You don't have to use the same number of levels in each section. The organization of your material will dictate how many levels you need.

4. In long or technical documents, consider using a numbering system to show relationships among headline levels. This system has many similarities to the formal outline.

Formal outline		*Numbering system*
I.	*(Level 1)*	1.
A.	*(Level 2)*	1.1
B.	*(Level 2)*	1.2
1.	*(Level 3)*	1.2.1
2.	*(Level 3)*	1.2.2
a.	*(Level 4)*	1.2.2.1
b.	*(Level 4)*	1.2.2.2
II.	*(Level 1)*	2.

(See also **font**, **headlines**, **organizing information**, **parallel structure**, **reports**, **underlining**, **visual design**.)

headlines: how to highlight your message

Headlines (or *headings* or *headers*) are the short phrases or sentences that act like titles and divide a letter or report into logical sections. Headlines organize your document for your readers and make your writing easier to read.

Some characteristics of good headlines

Most good headlines

- are brief
- are informative
- show where you've changed the topic or made a new category
- emphasize actions or decisions
- match content of the paragraph that follows
- guide the reader.

These are some effective generic headlines in business and technical writing:

Action requested	Person to contact
Action taken	Personnel affected
Next steps	Schedule
Deadline	Background
Problem	Recommendation
How to . . .	Conclusion

Usually it's better to use a longer, more specific headline instead of a general one. For example, instead of "Problem," you might write "Budget considerations in converting to CD-ROM." Decide how best to cue your reader to what follows.

Remember, the more information a headline gives, the better—unless your topic is controversial. In that case, use a neutral headline.

Can a headline ask a question?

Yes. A headline in the form of a question can be especially effective and eye-catching. Questions make readers think, and sometimes act. Consider these examples:

Are deadlines flexible?

Do you have suggestions for changes?

Why the delay?

How much time can you give?

Where should you send the data?

Another benefit of headlines

Many readers don't want or need to read a whole report or document. Good headlines will help these readers scan the report to find just the topic they need.

Headline format

- Capitalize only the first word in most headlines, except for proper nouns.

- Underline or boldface headlines to separate them clearly from the text.

- Line up headlines flush left.

- To make major headlines stand out, use all caps and center them.

- Don't use punctuation marks after headlines, except for question marks and occasional exclamation points. Avoid colons altogether—they're redundant.

(See also **format**, **headline levels**, **Introduction to the Six Steps**, **memorandums**, **Model Documents Appendix**, **reports**, **visual design**.)

high-low-close-open (HLCO) charts

Use **HLCO** charts to show both ranges (intervals) and data points (values). Data that fluctuate over a time interval, such as stocks, commodities, and currency rates, are best illustrated with an HLCO chart.

Whisker HLCO chart

The whisker chart consists of a set of vertical bars showing the high and low values, plus two markers, one on each vertical line. The left marker shows the starting or opening value and the right marker shows the ending or closing value.

You can use this chart to track daily stock prices and trading volume over a specified time period, perhaps a week.

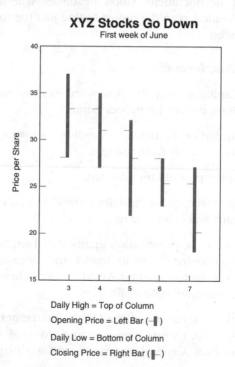

XYZ Stocks Go Down
First week of June

Daily High = Top of Column
Opening Price = Left Bar (─█)
Daily Low = Bottom of Column
Closing Price = Right Bar (█─)

In a typical situation such as the preceding chart, the x-axis represents time in days or weeks, and the y-axis represents values in dollars. The top of each bar is positioned on the chart to show the high value for the stock; the bottom shows the low value. The length of the line will vary. The horizontal markers crossing the vertical bars indicate the opening value on the left and the closing value on the right.

Consider including a column chart at the bottom, showing the volume of sales for the same time period.

Candlestick HLCO chart

A candlestick chart represents the same variables and is used in the same manner as a whisker chart. The difference is that the open and close values are represented as wide vertical bars rather than horizontal markers.

A white bar shows advance: the closing value is higher than the opening one. A solid bar shows decline: the closing value is lower than the opening one.

The vertical lines above and below the bars show highs and lows.

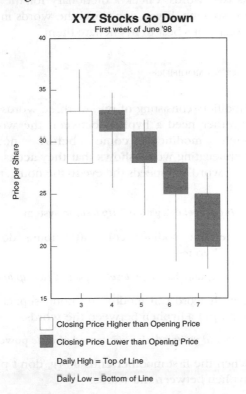

XYZ Stocks Go Down
First week of June '98

Price per Share

☐ Closing Price Higher than Opening Price

■ Closing Price Lower than Opening Price

Daily High = Top of Line

Daily Low = Bottom of Line

(See also **box charts**, **charts or graphs**, **tables**.)

---

hyphens

The **hyphen** (-) is a mark of punctuation that most often connects compound words. It also divides words at the end of a line, replaces the word *to*, clarifies long phrases, and has a few other uses.

Don't confuse hyphens with the longer dashes, which separate words instead of connecting them.

Hyphens that connect

Connected words are called compounds. Compound words can be adjectives, nouns, or verbs. They can appear hyphenated, as one word, or as two words. Check a dictionary for the preferred spelling. If you don't find the words in the dictionary, it's best to hyphenate them.

COMPOUND MODIFIERS

1. Modifiers consisting of two or three words put together need a hyphen between the words. Such modifiers come before nouns. Hyphenating words shows that they act as one long word and speeds the eye to the noun at the end.

     high-level delegation   *up-to-date* system

2. If the same modifiers come after nouns, do not use a hyphen.

     delegation that's *high level*   system that's *up to date*

3. If each word can modify the noun separately, don't put a hyphen between the words.

     an *old rolltop* desk   *decreased electric* power

4. When the first modifier ends in *-ly*, don't put a hyphen between the words.

concisely worded memo   *poorly* trained staff

5. Always hyphenate compounds that include an adjective and a participle, or verb form ending in *-ing* or *-ed*.

acid-catalyzed reaction   contract is *high-priced*
odd-sounding request

Though most compound adjectives are hyphenated, others are either one word or two separate words.

halfhearted try   *worldwide* distribution
sugar beet crop

COMPOUND NOUNS

Some compound nouns are one word, some have a space between the words, and some are hyphenated. Here are some hyphenated compound nouns.

know-how   secretary-treasurer   cross-reference
A-frame   follow-up   free-for-all

Some compound nouns aren't hyphenated.

backup   handbook   airmail   profit sharing

COMPOUND VERBS

Write compound verbs either with a hyphen or as one word. The choice usually depends on style or convention.

Here are some compound verbs written with hyphens.

off-load   spot-check   double-space   field-test

Here are some compound verbs written as one word.

downgrade   proofread   troubleshoot   pinpoint

Hyphens with numbers

1. Put a hyphen between compound numbers from twenty-one to ninety-nine.

thirty-eight   sixty-seven   eighty-one

Usually you should write these numbers as numerals. At the beginning of sentences, write them as words. Don't use hyphens when you write hundreds, thousands, or millions.

Three hundred forty-three
One thousand nine hundred seventy-six

2. Always hyphenate fractions.

one-fourth yard   *two-thirds* ownership
one-half tablespoon

3. If a compound begins with a number, put a hyphen between the two parts.

three-page letter   *30-amp* fuse
50-50 chance   *12-foot-long* board

Hyphen instead of *to*

A hyphen can take the place of *to* or *through* in word and numeral compounds.

New York-Vancouver flight   letters *A-G*   pp. *2-67*

Hyphens with prefixes and suffixes

In general, hyphens don't separate prefixes and suffixes from their root words. When they do, follow these rules.

1. Use a hyphen after a prefix to a capitalized word.

pre-Civil War   trans-Pacific   non-Catholic

2. A hyphen is optional when the prefix ends with the same first letter as the root word. However, unless the double letter is already standard spelling, most writers separate the letters for clarity.

de-escalate   reemploy   semi-industrial
re-educate   cooperate

3. Use a hyphen to avoid mistaking one word for another that's spelled the same.

   re-act the part   *react* to the news

   re-pose for the picture   a figure in *repose*

   re-sort the copies   a room at the *resort*

4. Use hyphens after *ex-* and *self-* when they are prefixes.

   ex-manager   self-evident

Series hyphen

In a series of modifiers that have the same second word, write the second word only at the end of the series. Put a hyphen and a space after each of the other modifiers.

   We are out of *quarter-* and half-inch plywood.

   The manager scheduled *two-*, *three-*, and five-day seminars in customer service.

   Do we have any *250-* or 300-mg samples?

Hyphens to show spelling

If you want to show how a word is spelled, put hyphens between the letters.

   e-n-u-n-c-i-a-t-e   v-a-r-i-a-t-i-o-n-s

Hyphens that change meaning

If you're not careful, a hyphen can change the meaning of your sentence. The following sentence can have two meanings, depending on where you put the hyphen.

   Should our company have a *new client-data base*?

   Should our company have a *new-client data base*?

In technical writing, be especially careful to use hyphens with two- and three-word unit modifiers for clarity.

instead of:	Refer to the *piloted control valve stem body* in the diagram.
write:	Refer to the *piloted-control valve-stem body* in the diagram.

Dividing words at the end of a line of print

Word hyphenation at the end of a line, also called syllabication, improves the appearance of your document. In justified text, hyphenation enhances readability by reducing the spaces between words.

Even if your text is not justified, hyphenating it will prevent an overly ragged right margin.

The hyphenation feature of your word-processing software will automatically apply the following rules.

1. Divide between syllables.

    respon-sibility   diction-ary

2. Divide after a prefix or before a suffix.

    re-duce   im-proper   friend-ly   study-ing

3. Divide between the parts of a compound word that you can write as one word.

    fire-proof   back-stop   breath-taking

    So your readers will know the hyphen is part of the word, avoid dividing hyphenated words at the hyphen.

instead of:	Pat submitted an all-encompassing proposal.
write:	Pat submitted an all-encompassing proposal.

4. Do not leave only one letter at the end of a line.

instead of:	a-mazing
write:	amaz-ing

5. Don't divide abbreviations, contractions, or one-syllable words. Also try not to divide proper and business names.

(See also **justification, numbers, punctuation.**)

I

idioms

Idioms are common phrases that don't follow the regular patterns of language. You usually can't determine the meanings of idioms from the meanings of their separate words.

What are you *up to*?

The manager expected his team to *carry out* the plans.

Carla was *waiting on* a customer when the accident happened.

Idioms are customary expressions that native speakers of a region usually have no trouble writing or understanding. Foreign speakers often have trouble with English idioms because there's no logic to them.

In English we say, "What time is it?" but a direct translation of the Spanish or French expression would be "What hour is it?" In the American South you may hear, "What do you say?" as a greeting, while in the North people say, "How do you do?"

Watch out for prepositions

Correct use of prepositions is often idiomatic. We say *adapt for a purpose*, but *adapt to a situation*. You *look up a telephone number*, but *look over a contract*. No logic explains these and many other idioms—they must simply be memorized.

Check a dictionary if you're not sure what the correct idiom is.

A caution about your international audience

If you know that some of your readers are not native English speakers, avoid idioms that might cause confusion. Remember that it's difficult to translate idioms from one language to another.

instead of: Ben *needs a hand* with this week's status report.

write: Ben *needs help* with this week's status report.

(See also **ambiguity**, **prepositions**.)

if clauses

Clauses that begin with *if* require a special type of verb to express the condition that something is unlikely, hypothetical, or untrue. A special form is necessary only for the verb *to be*. Use *were*, even for the first and third persons.

instead of: If I *was* you, I'd attend the conference.

write: If I *were* you, I'd attend the conference.

instead of: If the testing *was* complete, we'd be into phase three of the project by now.

write: If the testing *were* complete, we'd be into phase three of the project by now.

When the *if* clause expresses something that is true, possible, or likely, don't use the subjunctive.

> *If* Sophia tells us she *wasn't* able to schedule a meeting, we'll have to postpone our discussion.

(See also **verbs**.)

illustrations

Illustrations can give a long report an inviting appearance and break up weighty blocks of text. However, they shouldn't be used purely as ornamentation: illustrations in business and technical documents must convey information.

Sometimes they're the only way to allow a reader to visualize, for example, the intricate inner workings of a machine.

Many kinds of illustrations—tables, charts, and maps as well as drawings—save both the writer and reader time by presenting large amounts of complex information concisely. Often readers can target what they need at a glance.

When should you use an illustration?

Here are some specific instances where illustrations are invaluable.

- Drawings can demonstrate step-by-step instructions for operating or assembling equipment. The sequence should run from left to right or from top to bottom. Make sure each segment is labeled clearly.

- A cutaway drawing conveys details clearly and relates it to the whole. In a cutaway drawing a normally visible part is removed or cut away.

  For example, an airplane might be shown with the outside of the fuselage removed, to expose the interior seat layout. Or, a land mass may be cut away to show the geological layers.

Cutaway Drawing

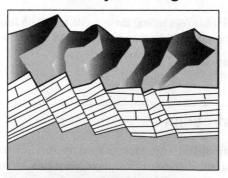

- An exploded view shows many parts in detail and demonstrates how they fit together.

   If you draw an assembled doorknob, for instance, you won't be able to show the small components that make up the spindle. When you spread them out across the paper, however, you can see each piece, both individually and in relation to the other components.

   Next is a view of a section of earth.

Exploded-View Drawing

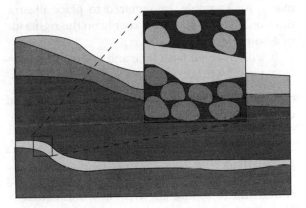

- A conventional drawing shows overall appearance and relative size of one object to another. For example, you might draw a human figure next to a piece of heavy equipment to convey the immense scale of the latter.

- Photographs are best for showing products and places. Color is far more expensive than black and white. Most graphic designers prefer to work with slides or negatives rather than prints.

Use informative captions

To help your readers understand the purpose of your illustrations, label them fully and clearly. Be specific. What information does your illustration present? Your readers should know by reading the caption of a graph precisely what it contains.

Integrating illustrations with text

It's important that your readers see clearly how your illustrations fit your text. Explain or refer to illustrations before they appear, so your readers will know what to look for.

If you are using many illustrations, number them for easy reference. Call them Fig. 1, Fig. 2, Fig. 3, along with the caption of the illustration.

Many organizations have specific guidelines for the positioning of illustrations in the text. You might, for example, be required to place illustrations only on the left and text only on the right side of a bound document.

It will save you both time and effort to familiarize yourself with company style before you begin.

(See also **charts or graphs**, **graphics**, **visual design**.)

---

indenting

Indenting is setting any type in from a margin. Many formats in business and technical writing use indenting.

Paragraphs

The first line of a paragraph in a book, article, or double-spaced document is often indented one tab stop (roughly equivalent to five spaces) from the left margin.

> To save time, three programmers are working on
>
> transactions that still need specifications and system-
>
> index locations. This work should be finished at the
>
> same time as the rest of the project.

The first lines of paragraphs are also indented in handwritten manuscripts.

In letters, memos, e-mail, and other single-spaced documents, the first line of a paragraph is usually not indented. The extra space between paragraphs serves the same purpose as indenting.

Aligning numbered and bulleted text

Numbered and bulleted lists look best if each line of text is indented and aligned on the left, leaving the numbers or bullets standing apart from the text in a vertical line. Each point is then easy to see. You may want to leave a line after your headline or opener.

We want a product that can provide us with

- user-level programs independent of communications protocols

- higher-level protocols independent of lower-level protocols

- systems-based protocols integrated with the OS file system.

Use a hanging indent to format numbered and bulleted lists. A hanging indent is just the opposite of a paragraph indent: the first line begins—*hangs*—to the left of the other lines in the paragraph.

Your word-processing software will allow you to set margins and indents. If you frequently use a certain type of indenting format, put it in your on-line style sheet.

Tables of contents and indexes

Indent tables of contents to show relationships between major and subordinate groups of information.

Indent subordinate index entries beneath the main entry.

Outlines

Outlines also use indenting to show how topics relate to each other.

I.   Introduction: How this study will help you

II.   Major findings of the study

    A.   Business challenges of the 21st century

    B.   Strategic resources and how to use them

        1. Capital

        2. Knowledge

        3. People

           a. Employees

           b. Consultants

    C.   The importance of good management

III.   Conclusions: Implications of the study

Quotations

Indent long quotations in a manuscript five spaces from both right and left margins. Write these quotations single-spaced and without quotation marks.

According to *Write to the Top*,

> Headlines illustrate the content of the paragraph that follows by converting general categories to more specific and informative words.
>
> The primary difference between categories and headlines is that headlines are used as a device in a written document, and they are often more specific. "Background" as a headline wouldn't be as helpful as "We've never had a policy on early retirement."

Writing quotations this way avoids the cumbersome problem of quotation marks within quotation marks. Compare the format above to:

". . . 'Background' as a headline wouldn't be as helpful as 'We've never had a policy on early retirement.'"

Emphasis

You can emphasize information such as an example by indenting it in a memo, letter, document, or book. Indenting can set off lists from the rest of the text and draw attention to important points.

For example, suppose you are drafting a memo announcing a new monthly department meeting. What are some of the questions your reader will ask?

1. What will be on the agenda?
2. How should I prepare for the meeting?
3. Am I *required* to go?
4. What if I can't make it?

Answer the questions you've generated and you're on your way.

Use indenting to give your pages visual appeal and clarity.

(See also **format, Introduction to the Six Steps, lists, paragraphs, quotations, style sheets for word processors**.)

---

independent clauses

A **clause** is a group of words that has a subject and a verb. A sentence can have one or more clauses, depending on its structure.

An **independent clause** is a group of words that contains a subject and a verb and expresses a complete thought. This type of clause can stand alone as a sentence.

The next reporting period will include results of these continuing studies. [This whole sentence is one independent clause.]

An independent clause often forms part of a complex sentence, which contains an independent and a dependent or subordinate clause. The dependent clause cannot stand alone as a sentence.

> Before you send out the proposal, *please make me a copy.* [This complex sentence is introduced by a subordinate clause. The independent clause is in italics.]

Compound sentences contain more than one independent clause.

> Please finish the proposal, make me a copy, and put it in the mail. [This sentence contains three independent clauses.]

(See also **commas**, **conjunctions**, **dependent clauses**, **semicolons**, **sentences**.)

infinitives: *to improve, to give, to retire*

The basic form of a verb without any endings is called an **infinitive**. The word *to* usually comes before the infinitive form: *to hire, to design, to construct.*

An infinitive can act as a noun, adjective, or adverb.

> Redesigning next year's top-of-the-line electric lawnmower caused us *to lose* [direct object—noun] market share.

> Our computer facilities department designed on-line forms for us *to use* [adjective].

> The month-to-date transactions were listed in the report *to avoid* [adverb] confusion.

Tense

Use infinitives in the present and the present perfect tenses.

> Please remember *to order* user manuals for the new employees. [present]

> *To have ordered* the user manuals, Pat would have needed your signature on the supply request. [present perfect]

Split infinitives

If you put a modifying word between *to* and the infinitive, you have split the infinitive. The best stylistic rule is to avoid splitting infinitives.

instead of: I advise you *to* most carefully *consider* Mario's offer.

write: I advise you *to consider* Mario's offer most carefully.

If a split infinitive sounds less awkward than keeping the infinitive intact, it's acceptable in informal writing.

instead of: Really *to appreciate* the benefits of last year's merger, you should look at our current profits.

write: *To* really *appreciate* the benefits of last year's merger, you should look at our current profits.

A split infinitive is considered a stylistic, not a grammatical, error.

(See also **tense**, **verbs**.)

---

infinitive phrases

An **infinitive phrase** is a group of words introduced by an infinitive. The phrase starts with *to* followed by a verb, plus all the words that are related to the infinitive or complete its meaning.

> The seminar leader's plan was *to teach designing, prototyping, and testing new products.*

Infinitive phrases are usually subjects, objects, and complements.

> *To schedule a weekly video conference* is our first goal. [subject]

> I need *to have a wider range of system configurations* if I'm going to meet the design standards. [direct object]

The company's aim is *to consolidate the property development accounts* by fiscal 19—. [complement of a linking verb]

Dangling infinitive phrases

Avoid creating a dangling modifier with an introductory infinitive phrase. Be sure the infinitive phrase applies to the subject of the main part of the sentence.

instead of: To finish the survey, 17 more
                 respondents need to be interviewed.
                 [Since *To finish the survey* doesn't
                 modify the subject *respondents*, you
                 have a dangling modifier.]

write: To finish the survey, we need to
                 interview 17 more respondents.
                 [Now *To finish the survey* modifies
                 the subject *we*.]

(See also **dangling modifiers**, **infinitives**, **phrases**.)

---

information, requests for (RFI)

Making a request for information

If you are called upon to request information from a potential vendor or business ally, consider first if you should write one document or two. Only the briefest **request for information (RFI)** should be a single document.

You may want to start with a friendly, possibly informal cover letter that briefly outlines your reasons for writing. Include the following information:

1. State clearly what you need and why you need it. If you are under time pressure to get the information, mention the deadline in a polite way: "I would appreciate a response by August 8 because . . ."

2. Be sure to mention where your readers should send a reply, although it isn't necessary to repeat letterhead content. "Please send the information to me at the above address" is sufficient. Be concise.

3. Mention how you are going to use the information, and assure confidentiality if appropriate.

4. Thank your readers in a polite, sincere way.

MAKE IT EASY FOR YOUR READERS TO REPLY

Then write your RFI in list form and attach it to your cover letter. Number your list and suggest, "Please respond by number."

Include a self-addressed stamped envelope, fax number, or e-mail address.

Consider sending a form for your readers to complete. This may save them writing time when they respond.

Responding to a request for information

Scan the RFI to be sure you're the person who should be answering it. If not, send it to the proper respondent immediately. It is a good idea to attach a handwritten note to your colleague explaining why you are forwarding it.

If you are asked to respond to an RFI addressed to someone else, always state that the request was forwarded to you because you are in the best position to provide the necessary information.

WHEN YOU CAN'T RESPOND IN 48 HOURS

It is good public relations to send a note, fax, or e-mail message acknowledging an RFI if you won't have time to respond to it immediately. In any case, be sure to respond within one week.

WʜAT STYLE SHOULD YOU USE IN AN RFI?

Read the letter carefully for clues to the writer's style, so that you can mirror it. You can often tell, by the way a letter is phrased, just how much detail is necessary. Look at the writer's title and vocabulary, especially technical language and jargon, as well as the request itself.

Don't overwhelm a nontechnical person with detail.

ALWAYS OFFER TO BE OF FURTHER HELP

Use natural language—avoid cliches.

instead of:	Do not hesitate to request further assistance in this matter.
write:	Please let me know if you need more help.

(See also **letters**, **lists**, **request for proposal**.)

---

interjections

A word or phrase that stands alone and expresses sudden or strong emotion is called an **interjection**. Interjections have no grammatical relationship to the rest of the sentence.

Congratulations! You have won the sales competition.

Many interjections use an exclamation point to show their intensity. Others are milder and require a comma only.

Yes, delivery is free as long as the promotion lasts.

Interjections have limited uses in business and technical writing because they usually express forceful feelings that are inappropriate or too informal. Such interjections as *wow! hey! look out! ugh!* and *sssh!* are never appropriate, except perhaps in advertising copy.

(See also **commas, exclamation points, parts of speech**.)

Internet

The **Internet** is a rapidly growing open information network of computer links. Like a vast net encircling the globe, it connects millions of computers in some 90 countries.

Many commercial, academic, and government institutions use the Internet to share information and collaborate with peers.

Research and development organizations as well as businesses specializing in collecting information are increasingly joining the system. So is the general public, through local access providers.

Use the Internet to advertise your services, send e-mail, post messages on electronic bulletin boards, conduct research using government, university, and business databases, make travel arrangements, chat electronically, and shop.

The World-Wide Web

The World-Wide Web, known as *WWW* or simply *the Web*, is a very large collection of interconnected documents stored in computers on the Internet. Any computer connected to the Internet may read and copy these documents.

To load a Web document, your computer must run a special program called a *Web browser*.

Web files contain *hypertext links*, or highlighted words and phrases that cross-reference separate but related documents. Click on the highlighted passage, and your computer will load the related document from another Internet location.

Hypertext links interconnect many thousands of documents in web-like fashion.

Hypertext links point to text, pictures, sounds, and even video footage. When documents contain links to information other than simple text and pictures, they are called *hypermedia*.

Some background on the Internet

The Internet originated from a network set up by the Defense Department in 1969. When the National Science Foundation developed its own network, the NSFnet, in 1986, it became the heart of the Internet.

Later, networks of the Department of Energy and the National Aeronautics and Space Administration also joined.

Overseeing the network's complex functions is the Internet Society, an international organization created in 1991. It coordinates operations among foreign countries, upholds standards, and helps introduce the Internet to technologically developing countries.

For further information contact the Society at

Internet Society
12020 Sunrise Valley Drive, Suite 270
Reston, VA 22091

http://ftp.isoc.org/home.html

The information superhighway

The Internet is an essential component of the information superhighway, a complex network of fiber-optic cables and digital switches.

In 1991 Albert Gore, then senator from Tennessee, coined the term "information superhighway" when he proposed a bill to back research on how to connect supercomputers.

The superhighway soon started growing at astounding rates, with phone, cable, and entertainment companies racing each other to upgrade equipment and provide new services.

introductions: getting off to a good start

The **introduction** to a long document like a report or proposal follows the executive summary. An introduction guides readers into the document by giving them the information they need to understand what follows.

General purpose and length of introductions

An introduction can explain the context for a document, how it originated, and its purpose. If necessary, briefly mention related documents or special facts about the project.

Beware of long introductions if your readers are already familiar with your material—it's a sure way to lose their attention.

In short reports or letters, a headlined paragraph may be enough of an introduction.

When to write an introduction

You shouldn't write the introduction until you know everything that's in your document. The best advice: write the introduction last, when you have a full understanding of your project.

(See also **letters, opening letters and memos, professional articles, proposals, reports.**)

irregular verbs

Irregular verbs form the past tense in nonstandard ways. They do not follow rules and must be memorized. Here are the infinitive, past tense, and past participle of the most common irregular verbs.

(See also **participles, verbs**.)

Irregular Verbs

Infinitive	Past	Past participle
be (I am)	was	been
become	became	become
begin	began	begun
bite	bit	bitten
blow	blew	blown
break	broke	broken
bring	brought	brought
build	built	built
buy	bought	bought
catch	caught	caught
choose	chose	chosen
come	came	come
cost	cost	cost
cut	cut	cut
do	did	done
draw	drew	drawn
drink	drank	drunk
drive	drove	driven
eat	ate	eaten
fall	fell	fallen

Infinitive	Past	Past participle
lead	led	led
leave	left	left
lend	lent	lent
let	let	let
light	lit, lighted	lit, lighted
lose	lost	lost
make	made	made
mean	meant	meant
meet	met	met
put	put	put
quit	quit	quit
read	read	read
ride	rode	ridden
ring	rang	rung
run	ran	run
say	said	said
see	saw	seen
sell	sold	sold
send	sent	sent
set	set	set

feed	fed	fed
feel	felt	felt
fight	fought	fought
find	found	found
fit	fit	fit
fly	flew	flown
forget	forgot	forgotten
forgive	forgave	forgiven
freeze	froze	frozen
get	got	gotten
give	gave	given
go	went	gone
grow	grew	grown
hang (clothes)	hung	hung
hang (people)	hanged	hanged
have	had	had
hear	heard	heard
hide	hid	hidden
hit	hit	hit
hold	held	held
hurt	hurt	hurt
input	input, inputted	input, inputted
keep	kept	kept
know	knew	known

sew	sewed	sewed, sewn
shake	shook	shaken
shrink	shrank	shrunk
sing	sang	sung
sit	sat	sat
sleep	slept	slept
speak	spoke	spoken
spend	spent	spent
stand	stood	stood
steal	stole	stolen
sweep	swept	swept
swim	swam	swum
take	took	taken
teach	taught	taught
tell	told	told
think	thought	thought
throw	threw	thrown
understand	understood	understood
wake	woke	woken
wear	wore	worn
win	won	won
wind	wound	wound
write	wrote	written

it

It is a pronoun that should have an antecedent (a word that it refers back to) in most uses.

We took our *proposal* to the company representatives, and they received *it* with enthusiasm. [*Proposal* is the antecedent for *it*.]

When *it* doesn't have an antecedent, the pronoun is called an *expletive*. Expletives can lead to unclear writing because they often don't fill a useful purpose in the sentence. In formal writing, omit this useless pronoun and rewrite the sentence without it.

instead of: When stocks drop dramatically, *it* is difficult to maintain confidence in the market.

write: When stocks drop dramatically, investors can lose confidence in the market.

Rewriting the sentence usually means finding a more specific subject. This change can add life to your writing since pronouns without antecedents can make your writing dull.

Acceptable expletives

In informal writing, such as letters to people you know well, memos, and e-mail, *it* as an expletive—a pronoun without an antecedent—is perfectly acceptable. The *it* in the following sentences does not refer to any other word.

It was a tough week, but worth the effort. You did a wonderful job.

We missed the deadline; *it*'s too late to do anything now.

(See also **pronoun reference**.)

italics

Italics refers to a distinctive style of slanted typeface *that looks like this*. An <u>underline</u> serves the same purpose: when your equipment does not allow you to italicize, the underline tells a printer to set the type in italics. Italics separates emphasized words from plain type.

Italics in titles

Italicize the titles of full-length works published in any medium, such as newspapers, books, magazines, pamphlets, films, and television programs. Names of works of art are also italicized.

> *The Chicago Sun Times*
> *Housing Options for the Elderly*
> *The Perpetual Enterprise Machine*
> *The MacNeil/Lehrer Newshour*
> *Fortune*
> Michelangelo's *David*
> the movie *Working Girl*

Smaller sections of published works require quotation marks instead of italics.

> The fourth section of *Annual Report 1996* is titled "New Product Research."

Short works require quotation marks.

> "A New Mass Market Emerges" [article]
> "Whistle While You Work" [song]
> "Dover Beach" [poem]

Italics in foreign words

Italicize foreign words not considered part of the English language.

> *quid pro quo*   *carte blanche*   *kanban*

Don't italicize foreign proper names or currency, or foreign words accepted into the English language.

Crédit Lyonnais   yen   pundit   pasta

Scientific names for genera and species are italicized.

Ficus bengalensis   *Penicillium*

Italics in proper names

Use italics for the names of planes (but not the type of plane), ships, aircraft, trains, and the like.

the *Queen Elizabeth*   *Apollo 9*
the *Spirit of St. Louis*   DC 10

Italics for examples of language

If you discuss words as words or letters as letters, you are using them as examples of language. Italicize them to set them apart from other words in the sentence.

Avoid using weak modifiers, such as *very* and *basically*.

Drop the *-y* and add *-ies* to make the plural of most words ending in *-y*.

Putting quotation marks around words as words is also correct, but italics is preferred.

Italics for emphasis

You can use italics to emphasize words, phrases, or whole sentences. Be careful not to overdo this usage—it may create a condescending or abrasive tone.

There is an error in the current meeting schedule. The controllers' meeting on 3/6 is in the *finance conference room*, not the facilities room.

We have consistently kept to our production schedule, *despite layoffs and the elimination of one
shift.* This unprecedented success accounts, in part,
for three new product contracts for next year.

Keep in mind also that overuse of italics for
emphasis may weaken your writing.

Italics in subheadlines

You can italicize subheadlines in a report or document to show they are subordinate to main titles
or section headlines. Italics carries less weight
than boldface, so bold headlines should come first
in your headline level.

Selecting graphic aids

Be sure the graphics you choose have a procedural
function, not just a cosmetic one.

Who is your reader?

Graphics should enhance your readers' understanding of your report or document.

Italics in legal citations and legislative acts

In the titles of court cases, italicizing the names of
the parties is optional. Latin phrases should be italic if the rest of the title is in plain type.

The court has not yet ruled in *Clemson* v. *McIndoe.*

Morrison *et al.* v. Herbert Winter & Co.

The word *Resolved* is always in italics in legislative
acts or resolutions. The word *Provided* should also
be in italics.

Resolved, that the Chairman of the Steering
Committee be . . .

Provided, that . . .

Plain type in italic text

If the entire sentence is printed in italics, any word that would normally be italicized is then set in plain type for contrast.

> To persuade your readers, be confident and precise. Remember this very important point: *avoid using weak modifiers, such as* very *and* basically.

(See also **emphasis, quotation marks**.)

J

jargon

In business and technical writing, **jargon** means
the specialized language of a particular field or
occupation. Members of the same profession
understand their own jargon.

Within a department or industry, jargon that
everyone knows may save time and make communication more streamlined and precise.

> The *drive* on the *PC crashed*.

> We are currently developing a *monolithic dual 16-bit D/A converter*.

> If the topography is rugged, apply the *side-slope construction technique*.

When should you avoid jargon?

If your readers are not members of your profession
or specialty, you should try not to use jargon. If
you can't avoid it completely, be sure to define any
specialized terms so your readers will understand
them. In a long document, consider adding a glossary of terms as an appendix.

(See also **editing your draft**, **gobbledygook**,
word choice.)

justification

Justification refers to the alignment of text along
a margin. Left-justified means text is aligned along
the left margin, right-justified along the right margin. You can center text and have both margins
ragged, as in titles that are several lines long.

In block justification both right and left margins
are aligned.

Most letters and reports are printed with left justification, while books use block text. Block justification requires the use of proportionally spaced fonts that allow your word-processing program to automatically adjust spaces between letters and words, much as typesetters used to do.

To avoid overly wide spaces between words, hyphenate words at the ends of lines when you use block justification.

(See also **font, format, hyphens**.)

K

kerning

Kerning is a printing term that refers to the spacing between characters in text and titles. This spacing can be expanded or contracted to improve readability.

Most word-processing and desktop-publishing programs have the capability to kern, or adjust character spacing.

Use kerning in titles especially to improve readability. Compare the examples that follow.

Marketing Strategies for the 21st Century

Helvetica 12-point boldface font

Marketing Strategies for the 21st Century

Helvetica 12-point boldface font, expanded by 3 points

Marketing Strategies for the 21st Century

Helvetica 12-point boldface font, condensed by 1 point

(See also **font**, **spacing**, **visual design**.)

239

L

leaders

Leaders is the term for the dots, or line of spaced periods, that connect page numbers to entries in a table of contents. Leaders make it easy for readers to follow the connection across the page.

(See also **table of contents**.)

letters: reaching out to your customers and partners

Business **letters** have many purposes: among others, to persuade, call for action, address grievances, and announce decisions. (Memos, or memorandums, are correspondence *inside* a company, while letters are sent *outside*.) Reading your business letters gives your readers an image—both of you and of the organization you represent.

Most businesses want to project a balance between friendliness and propriety.

Your letters should always be clearly written, neatly formatted, and correct in grammar and punctuation. Your choice of language creates a tone and style that will determine how your readers accept what you're saying.

Format styles vary, so consult your company's style guide if you have one. You'll find some general guidelines later in this entry.

Writing to your customers

The opening is the most important part of a customer letter. Your goal in your opening paragraph is to communicate that you

- value your customer
- provide products or services to meet customer needs
- are eager to ensure customer satisfaction.

The body of your letter should include the information your customer needs to know about your products or services. Take advantage of design elements such as headlines and bullets. Bold headlines like "Suggested next steps" show that you are results oriented.

In closing your letter, take a final opportunity to support and thank your reader.

Sales letters

The purpose of a sales letter is to introduce you, your product, or your services. You may be writing as a follow-up to a meeting or request; or you may be writing a "cold" letter, reaching out to potential customers through direct mail.

The purpose of the letter is to influence your readers to take the action you want: buy your product, set up a meeting, attend a preview.

WHAT IS A WINNING SALES LETTER?

Winning sales letters build relationships by creating an atmosphere that puts your readers' interests first. Opening with a question usually gets attention.

Analyze your readers so that your customer-specific question will get a positive response. Avoid questions which may get a negative response from your readers.

If you are looking for real estate customers, for example, "Haven't you always wanted a bigger home?" will send your letter into the trash if the reader wants to move to a condominium. Use the Focus Sheet™ to clearly define your audience and purpose.

IT'S WHAT YOUR READER NEEDS THAT COUNTS

Writers of good sales letters coach their readers through the buying process. Your letter should answer the question, "What's the payoff for my reader?"

Stress the features, benefits, and results that are important to your customer's needs, not yours. Use the "you" attitude more than the "me" attitude.

instead of: *We* can help increase sales productivity.

write: *You* want to increase *your* sales productivity. Here are some strategies *you* can use.

Use questioning as a Start-up Strategy. It is ideal for helping you focus on your customers' needs.

WRITE A SUBJECT LINE WITH IMPACT

Customer-focused sales letters have strong openings. They get your message across right away. Your key, or "bottom line," message should appear at the top of your letter. Use a strategic and specific subject line.

instead of: Sales strategies for XYZ Corporation

write: Increase your sales productivity with our strategic training

USE HEADLINES TO MOVE THE SALE FORWARD

Great sales letters have compelling headlines that make key points obvious and easy to read. Headlines use action words and positive language.

instead of: We do an excellent job

write: How you can increase your sales

SEQUENCE CAREFULLY

Sequence key points so that the reader agrees with them as you present them. This moves the reader through the process in a positive way and lessens resistance. Another sequencing tradition: put fees toward the end of your letter.

BUILD YOUR CREDIBILITY

Include information to show that you have the skills or products to fill your customer's need. Quote happy customers or authorities who endorse you. Let buyers know that others choose and like your company.

USE CLEAR LANGUAGE AND A POSITIVE TONE

Use language that is direct and clear. Avoid words that are inflated, obscure, or archaic. Turn any potential negatives to positives. For example, say *investment* rather than *fees* or *cost*.

Your style should be professional and personable: keep your language direct and your tone positive, and use the active voice.

Do not address your readers by name in the body of your letter. This technique has become so overused in mass-market mailings that your readers will feel as if you have sent them a form letter.

MOVE THE READER TOWARD YOUR GOAL

Sales letters do just that—sell. Don't forget to ask for the meeting or action you want using headlines like "Suggested next steps" or "Action requested." If you don't ask, you certainly won't get.

CLOSE ON A DYNAMIC NOTE

Don't rely on your reader to take the next step. Use a dynamic ending that tells the reader what you plan to do next.

instead of: Please do not hesitate to call if you
have any questions or concerns.

write: I'll call you next Tuesday to schedule a demonstration.

Avoid the "hopeful" close and keep control of the
situation.

instead of: I hope you will like our product.

write: I am sure you will be pleased.

Make it as easy as possible for your reader to
respond to your letter. Include prepaid envelopes
or reply cards, phone and fax numbers, e-mail
addresses, and alternative contact names.
Highlight deadlines if appropriate.

THE FINAL TOUCHES COUNT

Use the standard letter format discussed later in
this entry. Proofread carefully. If you are meticu-
lous about details, customers will feel secure
about choosing you. Ask a colleague to edit your
letter—your professional success may depend on
it.

Getting started

To write the most effective letters, follow the Six
Steps to Reader-Centered Writing™ outlined in the
Introduction. Keep in mind that you're writing for
specific readers, not a faceless audience.

How would you respond if someone sent *you*
your letter? Would you understand it? Would you
be appeased or angered? Would you feel informed
or confused? After reading your letter, your readers
should know

• exactly why you wrote it

• specifically what action they should take.

In general, put your most important information
first in your letter.

instead of:	We are writing to inform you that we have arranged a meeting with our attorneys next month to discuss the Bladesdale merger. Among the topics we will cover is finances. We cannot proceed with the merger until you present your financial report.
write:	Please join us to present your financial report about the Bladesdale merger in a meeting with our attorneys.

- Date: October 7
- Time: 2 p.m.
- Place: Our Galena office

Your first sentence or paragraph must be the strongest of the whole letter. Most people have little time for lengthy introductions or explanations—they want to hear the main point quickly.

If you bury your most important point, your readers may skim your letter looking for it and skip right over other significant information.

Occasionally you might not want to begin with your most important point because it might be controversial and require some preparation. You may need to persuade your reader to be receptive to an idea before you actually describe it.

Begin with an explanation, but keep it brief. Put the most important information under a strong or catchy headline so your readers won't miss it.

Choosing the right style and tone

These general rules should help you find the right language to suit your purpose and readers.

1. Strive for brevity, clarity, and friendliness in your business letters.

instead of:	We have been advised by the responsible personnel that your reimbursement request has been denied.

> This decision is predicated on the
> fact that the repairs were not per-
> formed by an authorized agent of
> our company, as we require in our
> sales agreement.

write: We are sorry to inform you that we
> cannot reimburse you for this repair
> because you did not, as stated in our
> sales agreement, use one of our
> authorized agents.

Stay away from overly friendly, casual, or cute
language, which may not sound genuine.

instead of: We reviewed your request again and
> guess what—we decided to reim-
> burse you after all!

write: We reviewed your request again and
> are happy to inform you that we
> will be reimbursing you for the
> repair.

2. Avoid an overly formal style because it can
   sound wordy, stuffy, and impersonal. It may
   also alienate your readers rather than impress
   them.

   instead of: It has been discovered that, in mak-
   > ing a request for reimbursement, the
   > form was not completely filled out.
   > In consideration of the fact that a
   > complete form is necessary to
   > process a request for reimburse-
   > ment, you are advised to complete
   > the incomplete questions and for-
   > ward the form to our offices.

   write: You omitted several items when you
   > filled out your reimbursement form.
   > We will be happy to process your
   > request as soon as you provide the
   > missing information and return your
   > completed form to us.

3. Make your sentences active rather than passive.

| *instead of:* | Our customer service representative, Farideh Kadivar, *has been requested* to contact you in reference to the request for reimbursement that *was made*. [passive] |
| *write:* | I *have asked* Farideh Kadivar, our customer service representative, to contact you to discuss your reimbursement request. [active] |

4. Your readers are the most important people to consider, so keep them in mind as you write. Use "you" and "your" as often as possible.

| *instead of:* | It is important that all our customers be satisfied. |
| *write:* | *Your* satisfaction is important to us. |

5. Decide whether you are speaking for yourself or your company and use the appropriate pronoun: "I" or "we." Consider two issues:

   • company involvement. If you are writing on behalf of your company, say, "Here at XYZ Co., we . . ."

   • personal involvement. If you have special knowledge or are qualified to deal with a specific issue or question, use "I."

   I have compiled the statistics you requested.

   If you have to apologize for an error, oversight, or poor customer service, make it personal.

| *instead of:* | Thank you for writing to us. *XYZ Co.* apologizes that . . . |
| *write:* | Thank you for writing to us. *I* apologize that. . . |

6. Keep the good will of customers and associates by avoiding terse or provocative language. Be thoughtful and sincere—write the kind of letter you'd like to read.

instead of: Because of the condition of the handle, we can see that you did not install it correctly. Follow the simple instructions in Part 6 to install the replacement handle correctly. We cannot send you another without billing you.

write: We're sorry to hear that you had problems installing the handle. Please accept this replacement and a copy of the instructions. Our designer has also provided additional directions that we hope will be of help. Our policy is to send you only one replacement part for no cost.

The second example is polite, positive, and tactful. As you can see, sometimes longer is better if the tone is more courteous and helpful.

Opening statements

State the main point of your letter right away and quickly focus your readers' attention. The following paragraphs should support your point and give additional information or explanation. Headlines add impact to your message and make your letter easy to read.

REFERENCES

Unless references are the main point of your letter, don't open with them. Instead, refer to other correspondence or meetings after the main subject of the letter.

instead of: This is in reference to our telephone conversation of September 6 in regard to the October 1 order deadline.

write: We appreciate your agreeing to a new order deadline for October 1. As we discussed on the phone on September 6, . . .

ANNOUNCEMENT OF ENCLOSURES

Enclosed are three copies of the parts invoice.

This is a weak beginning that states the obvious. Don't write it. If you have enclosures with your letter, refer to them in the body of the letter, after your opening.

SOCIAL REMARKS

We hope that your new team is progressing well.

Friendly, sociable statements are often useful if you are delivering bad news. If not, it's better to get right to the point. In general, save your chatty sentences for your closing, after you have discussed your business.

Closing statements

In the closing, repeat your main points or suggest next steps for your readers. Avoid cliches. Your closing should be brief, direct, and natural. It could emphasize a main point that you made earlier or give helpful information.

instead of:	Should you need further assistance . . . Thanking you ahead of time . . . Please do not hesitate to write to my attention . . .
write:	If you have any questions, please call me at 222.1111.
or:	We appreciate your business.

Designing your letter for visual emphasis

Center your letter as if it were in a picture frame on the page. If your letter is extremely short, you can lengthen it by widening the margins, double-spacing the body of the letter, and adding extra blank lines between the parts of the letter and before and after headlines.

Put information in short paragraphs, bulleted or numbered lists, and under boldface headlines wherever you can. Use white space to highlight important information. One-sentence paragraphs are acceptable for occasional emphasis.

Letter styles

The block and the modified-block styles are the most common business letter formats.

BLOCK STYLE

Most companies prefer the block style with letterhead stationery. Every line begins at the left margin and the paragraphs aren't indented. See "Letter parts and placement," which follows.

MODIFIED-BLOCK STYLE

In the older-style modified block letter, the heading, any special notations, the complimentary closing, and signature begin just right of center. All the other lines are flush left, with no paragraph indentations. The indenting of elements has lost popularity because it takes longer to input.

You may find variations of these styles. Follow your company's particular style and be consistent. The style you use, as well as the tone of your letter, will create the image that you and your company project.

Parts of a business letter

1. HEADING

DATE

If you are using a company letterhead, write the date at the left margin at least two lines below the letterhead. Leave more space if your letter is short and you need to center it on the page.

Letter Parts and Placement

Date	January 23, 19—
Mailing notation	CERTIFIED MAIL
Address	Mr. Richard McKinney Fogg Warning Systems 773 South Rodeo Drive Los Angeles, CA 90000
Salutation	Dear Mr. McKinney:
Subject line	**Subject: Please approve repairs to smoke alarms**
Body	Thank you for replying quickly to my phone call describing the problems with our Fogg smoke alarms. **Exception to warranty needed** Since your customary repair man, Al S. Besto, is unavailable, we must hire a non-warranteed service firm to repair our system. Although the Fogg policy normally covers expenses only when our dealer does the repairs, I expect that Fogg will relax the policy in our case so we can hire another company. **Location of breakdowns** As you asked, I am sending a list of the rooms where the breakdowns occur most often. I am also enclosing a copy of the hospital floor plan and have noted the areas that have had different types of breakdowns. You'll see that in some rooms (circled in red) the alarms ring at 20-minute intervals, obviously disturbing our patients. **Actions requested and suggested deadline** • Please call me to discuss these problems before Wednesday at 4:30 p.m. • If you OK the exception to your policy, please initial and return this letter to me. Thank you for helping to ensure the safety of the patients and staff of our hospital.
Complimentary closing	Sincerely,
Signature	*Hiram Frost*
Signature line	Hiram Frost, Vice President
Reference line	hf/ao
Enclosure notation	Enc.: breakdown list, floor plan
Postscript	Any questions, please call me.

If you are not using letterhead, then put your full address and the date—but not your name—in the heading.

4775 East Village Road
Cambridge, MA 02139

July 1, 19—

SPECIAL NOTATIONS

If your letter includes a personal or confidential notation, put it at least two lines below the date.

Certified mail   By messenger   Personal
Confidential

2. INSIDE ADDRESS

Begin the inside address at least two lines below the heading at the left margin. The exact placement of the inside address will depend upon the length of your letter.

Use the full name, title, and address of your correspondent. Spell out all the words in the address except the state, which you should abbreviate using the standard U.S. ZIP code abbreviations. Follow this format:

Ms./Mr. Name
Title
Department
Division
Company
P.O. box or street address
City, state, ZIP code

For non-U.S. addresses, add the country on the last line.

If you don't have a specific individual's name, then simply address the business or department.

Sales Manager
Ohio Steel Amalgamated
34 Highland Drive
Cleveland, OH 40000

An *attention line* belongs two lines under the inside address. Use it when you don't have a specific person or department name.

> Ohio Steel Amalgamated
> 34 Highland Drive
> Cleveland, OH 40000
>
> Attention: Sales Manager

If you have a choice between a P.O. box and street address, use the P.O. box for letters and the street address for packages.

SENDING THE SAME LETTER TO SEVERAL PEOPLE

When you need to send the same letter to more than one person in a work group, follow one of two procedures:

- When all the recipients are of equal status, personalize each copy of the letter with a different recipient's name and address. In the copy notation, list everyone else who is receiving the letter.

- When recipients are not of the same status, address the letter to the most influential person. Then list everyone else who receives a copy in the copy notation.

  Never print more than one address at the top of the letter.

3. SALUTATION

If you know the name of a person to address, put it after *Dear* two lines below the inside address, flush with the left margin.

All U.S. business letters should use a colon after the name. However, in some English-speaking countries, such as Bermuda, a comma is acceptable after a salutation in a business letter.

> Dear Ms. Gleason:
>
> *or:*
>
> Dear Patricia:

Spell out titles such as *Lieutenant*, *Professor*, or *President*.

Unless a woman has a preference for *Mrs.* or *Miss*, address her as *Ms.* If you don't know whether your addressee is a man or a woman, use the full name *(Dear Pat Gleason)*.

If you are including both men and women in your salutation, use identifying words that don't express gender. For example, use *Dear Sales Representatives* rather than *Gentlemen*.

Dear Tenant:
Dear Friends:
Dear Members of the Board:
Dear Parts Department:
Dear Human Resource Manager:
Dear Prospective Employer:

When you can't or don't want to be specific, use a general salutation.

instead of:	To Whom It May Concern:
write:	Good Day:
	Hello:
	Dear Prospective Employer:

4. SUBJECT LINE

Always include a *subject line*, usually two lines below the salutation. Some companies prefer to put the subject line between the inside address and salutation.

Dear Pat:

Subject: How are you keeping your name in front of your customers?

A subject line stands out and can replace information you might instead include in the first paragraph of your letter. Well-written subject lines can give marketing letters a vital competitive edge.

5. BODY

Begin the body of your letter two lines below the salutation or subject line. Single-space your paragraphs; double-space only if your letter is very short.

PARAGRAPH FORMAT

Indenting the first word of each paragraph is no longer standard. Double-spacing between paragraphs and before headlines replaces the indent and makes for easier reading.

TWO PAGES OR MORE

Don't crowd too much text on a single page. If your letter is longer than one page, make sure that at least three or four lines of text spill over to the second page. Use plain paper without a letterhead for all pages after the first.

Some companies have special, modified letterheads for second pages.

When your letter is two pages or more, you'll need headings on your continuation pages. Include your correspondent's name, the date, and the page number. Also include any invoice or file numbers that you noted in the subject line on the first page.

Styles vary—follow your company's format.

Ms. Patricia Gleason   -2-   July 1, 19—

---

or:

Ms. Patricia Gleason   July 1, 19—   Page 2
Subject: Invoice #23144-A

---

or:

Ms. Patricia Gleason
July 1, 19—
Page 2

6. COMPLIMENTARY CLOSING AND SIGNATURE

The complimentary closing belongs two lines below the last line of the body of the letter. Capitalize the first word and put a comma at the end.

Use these complimentary closings for most business letters.

Sincerely,   Sincerely yours,   Yours truly,

If your letter is friendly or more informal, you can use these complimentary closings.

Cordially,   Best regards,   Best wishes,

Don't use *Very truly yours* as a complimentary closing—it has become a sentimental cliche.

Type your full name four lines under the complimentary closing. On the next two lines, put your business title and department name, if they're appropriate.

Sincerely,

James D. Aielli
Director of In-Service Training

Sign your name in the space above your typed name. Your signature helps set the tone of your letter. Sign your full name in a letter with legal content or if you want to set a formal tone.

If you're on a first-name basis with your correspondent, sign only your first name to set a warm and friendly tone.

7. REFERENCE LINES

The following information goes at the bottom of the letter, flush with the left-hand margin. You may omit all or some of this information from personal business letters and memos.

REFERENCE INITIALS

Reference initials are the writer's and the word processor's, in that order.

Put the writer's initials in all capital letters and the word processor's in lowercase, separated by either a colon or a slash (no spaces). No initials are necessary if the writer is also the word processor.

KMS:bas   JKR/brr

If the person who signs the letter is not the writer, then put the signer's initials first in capital letters, followed by the writer's and then the word processor's.

BER/KMS/bas

ENCLOSURE NOTATION

Enclosure notations tell readers what other material to expect in the envelope. Put this line right under the reference initials in one of several styles.

Enclosure: Parts list
3 enclosures
Enclosures (3)
Encs.
Encs: Financial report draft
       Finance meeting agenda
       In-service training budget

Remember to mention the enclosures in the body of your letter, but avoid mentioning them in the first sentence if possible.

If you send material in a separate mailing, put a notation below the enclosure line.

Under separate cover:
1. Invoice T3995
2. Price list

COURTESY-COPY OR COPY NOTATION

This information explains who received a copy of your letter. Put this notation below the reference initials, the enclosure line, or the mailing-notation line, whichever is last. Write *cc* or *Copy to* (with or without a colon).

List the people who receive copies either alphabetically or according to rank.

cc: F. Cohen
       P. Najimian
       B. Sato

Copy to: Roxanne Melnitchenko

If you also send enclosures to all the people who receive copies of your letter, use this notation:

cc/encs: F. Cohen
          P. Najimian
          T. Sato

BLIND COURTESY-COPY NOTATION

A blind courtesy-copy notation shows the distribution of a letter without the addressee's knowing about it. Double-space this notation flush left below the enclosure or courtesy-copy notation.

Be sure to put this notation *only* on the blind courtesy copies themselves.

bcc   N.C. Tringh
       B. Cranston

8. POSTSCRIPT

A postscript or P.S. is an afterthought, an addition to a letter after you've finished it. You can begin postscripts with *P.S.*, or you can leave it off. Follow the same paragraph style as the rest of the letter.

You don't need to add another signature after the postscript.

Your postscript should appear two lines below your last reference notation line.

Sincerely,

James D. Aielli
Director of In-Service Training

Enc.

cc   F. Cohen

P.S. Don't forget to bring your tennis racket, and we'll play a game or two after the conference.

or:

> Don't forget to bring your tennis racket, and we'll play a game or two after the conference.

Postscripts can be effective in stating something that you intentionally withhold from the main part of your letter. Placing your idea at the end emphasizes it, so your readers will pay special attention.

However, if you use postscripts to state as an afterthought something that's actually vital to your letter, your writing may seem disorganized or overly hasty.

(See also **Introduction to the Six Steps, Model Documents Appendix, opening letters and memos, subject lines, tone, "you" attitude.**)

line charts

Line charts represent data with points that are connected by straight lines. The data points are placed horizontally across the page, left to right, and show the changes in the data set over time.

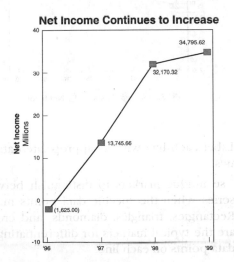

Net Income Continues to Increase

- Use line charts to represent many data points over time. The line is ideal for illustrating a trend.

- Make sure there are no missing data in the line—it must be continuous.

- Consider placing multiple lines on one chart with each line representing a data set. Four series of lines will communicate your message as long as the lines do not cross frequently.

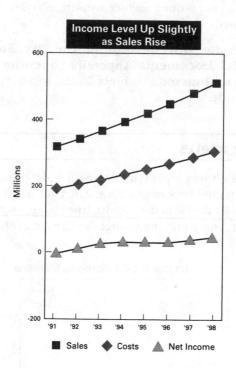

Income Level Up Slightly as Sales Rise

- Label each line with its appropriate data values.

- Use unique markers to distinguish between series when the specific data points matter. Rectangles, triangles, diamonds, and crosses are the typical markers for differentiating the data points on each line.

Cautions

- Multiple lines express individual data trends only, not changes in relation to one another. If lines appear parallel when charted, use individual line charts or multiple bar charts to avoid implying that there is significance to the relationship between the lines.

- Straight lines parallel to the axis do not show trends. Since there is no trend, omit the chart and express the information as text.

- Too many lines cause confusion. They become entangled and are hard to read. For clarity, limit the number of lines displayed on a single graph to four or less, fewer if the lines cross frequently.

- Lines that keep crossing muddle the trend and cloud the message. If lines intersect more than twice, don't use a line chart. Consider using paired columns instead.

- Uneven scaling will cause distortion in the chart. Check to see that the scales are evenly spaced and consistently numbered.

(See also **area charts**, **bar or column charts**, **charts or graphs**, **tables**.)

---

lists: how to present a series

When you group items in **lists**, you help your readers organize what they're reading. Vertical lists emphasize your message far better than lists embedded in sentences, which do not stand out from the rest of the text.

Vertical lists

Vertical lists are usually indented below a paragraph or sentence. Here are some guidelines for creating vertical lists. Also consult the sections that follow on numbered and bulleted lists.

1. If your list is long, or if you want to give it visual emphasis, use a vertical list. You should usually put a colon after the last word that introduces the list.

   Here is a sample of this year's conference topics:

   * Computer Applications for the 21st Century
   * How to Use the World-Wide Web
   * Managing Distributed Environments

   Leave off the colon if the last word is a verb or preposition, or if each item finishes the sentence.

   The options for photo reprints are [verb]

   * 24-hour turnaround
   * discounts for ten reprints or more
   * glossy or matte finish.

   Marketing will present its projections for the next fiscal year in [each item finishes the sentence]

   * hardware
   * software
   * networking
   * application development
   * business.

2. If another sentence comes between the introductory sentence and the list, don't put a colon after the last word before your list. In this case, don't put a period after the last item in your list.

   Here is a sample of conference topics. The variety is much greater this year and should make the conference much more productive.

   * Computer Applications for the 21st Century
   * How to Use the World-Wide Web
   * Managing Distributed Environments

3. If the listed items are sentences, punctuate each as a complete thought, with a capital letter and a period. If the listed items complete the introductory sentence, a period is helpful.

   Marketing will present its projections for the next fiscal year in

- hardware
- software
- networking
- application development
- business.

NUMBERED VERTICAL LISTS

Use a number or letter to identify each item if you want to show steps or sequence, or if you want to refer to the items again.

These are the Six Steps to Reader-Centered Writing™:

1. Analyze your audience and define your purpose.
2. Use a Start-up Strategy.
3. Group information under headlines.
4. Sequence your ideas.
5. Write the first draft.
6. Edit for clarity, conciseness, and accuracy.

BULLETED LISTS

Bullets are a good way to begin each item in a list that doesn't have a specific sequence. Bullets can

- provide variety and "eye relief" from too much prose
- persuade, by clearly emphasizing each point
- frame ideas in white space so they stand out.

Bullets only list points and can't relate them to each other. When you need to show contrast or cause and effect, use paragraphs.

Don't think a paragraph has to be all prose. A short list of bulleted points within a prose discussion

- breaks up a block of text for easier reading
- emphasizes important points.

ALIGNING TEXT UNDER NUMBERS AND BULLETS

Make sure numbers and bullets stand out to the left of the line of text. Use a hanging indent or style setting in your word-processing software for perfect text alignment.

We want a product that can provide

- user-level programs independent of communications protocols

- higher-level protocols independent of lower-level protocols

- systems-based protocols integrated with the OS file system.

A SPECIAL ADVANTAGE OF VERTICAL LISTS

Vertical lists can be effective visual aids for emphasis. They are set apart with indenting and white space above and below. These easy-to-read lists allow readers to skim the page for relevant information.

Your readers will appreciate the special organization and at-a-glance understanding that vertical lists provide.

A CAUTION ABOUT USING VERTICAL LISTS

Don't overuse bullets. Ideas that are only listed, not linked, may sound disjointed, choppy, and illogical. And, just as a page of unbroken prose is tedious to read, so is a blizzard of bullets. Try to balance lists and paragraphs.

Lists within sentences

Since lists within sentences are not set apart from the text, they do not attract attention. Here are some guidelines for creating these lists.

1. If your list is short and you don't need to emphasize it, you can keep it within the sentence.

   The new copier has several useful editing features that should save us time: marker edit, business edit, freehand edit, and creative edit.

2. If the word that introduces the list is a verb or a preposition, omit the colon.

   The editing features on the new copier are marker edit, business edit, freehand edit, and creative edit.

3. If you want to enumerate items, put a number or a letter, enclosed in parentheses, before each item in the list. Don't use any other punctuation after the letter or number.

   We want a product that can provide the following: (1) user-level programs independent of communications protocols; (2) higher-level protocols independent of lower-level protocols; and (3) systems-based protocols integrated with the OS file system.

4. If the list of items is short, use commas between the items. Put the comma before the next number or letter in a numbered list. Use semicolons between items if they are long or if they have internal commas. However, if your list is so long and complex that it needs both commas and semicolons, it will be much easier to read in a vertical format.

   The new copier has several useful editing features that should save us time: marker edit, which highlights a whole area for editing; business edit, which uses a pen to touch an area in a bar chart or other color space; and freehand edit, which traces a random area for editing.

Rules for vertical lists and lists within sentences

1. Capitalize the first word of each item in the list only if the items are complete sentences or begin with proper nouns. When you capitalize one item by this rule, capitalize all items for consistency.

   Here is a sample of this year's conference topics:

   - EPA rules governing wetlands development
   - Managing wetlands development
   - Future development plans

2. Make sure all the items in a list are equally important and of similar length and kind.

The new copier has several useful editing features that should save us time: marker edit, which highlights a whole area for editing; business edit, which uses a pen to touch an area in a bar chart or other color space; and freehand edit, which traces a random area for editing.

instead of: The editing features on the new copier are

- marker edit
- business edit, which uses a pen to touch an area in a bar chart or other color space
- freehand edit.

write: The editing features on the new copier are

- marker edit, which highlights a whole area for editing
- business edit, which uses a pen to touch an area in a bar chart or other color space
- freehand edit, which traces a random area for editing.

3. Use parallel structure for all the items. They should all be words, or all be phrases, or all be similarly constructed sentences. Begin each item with the same kind of word.

instead of: The editing features on the new copier are

- marker edit
- a business edit
- You can edit by freehand.

write: The editing features on the new copier are

- marker edit
- business edit
- freehand edit.

4. Sometimes one list occurs inside another. Use numbers for the outside list and letters for the inside list.

These are the Six Steps to Reader-Centered Writing:

1. Analyze your audience and define your purpose
    a. Complete the Focus Sheet™
    b. Determine your bottom line
2. Generate ideas
    a. The traditional outline
    b. Questioning
    c. The brainstorm outline

(See also **emphasis**, **indenting**, **memorandums**, **parallel structure**.)

M

manuals

When detailed instructions for a product or process are necessary in book form, you may be asked to write a **manual**. Whether a repair, user, job, work instruction, or training manual, it will include a series of procedures that are all part of a process. It may also include checklists and introductory as well as background information.

The difference between a technical and a nontechnical manual is primarily one of content and reader need.

A poor user or assembly manual can sabotage a good product, whereas a good one can become a strong consumer marketing tool.

Understanding your users

Pay the most attention to Step 1 of the Six Steps to Reader-Centered Writing™: analyzing your readers and defining your purpose. Complete the Focus Sheet™ carefully.

If your audience consists of skilled operators or trained technicians, you may not need to include the same amount of detail as you would for a consumer or new employee manual. Remember to define terms that may not be clear to your audience. Consider adding a glossary.

Review carefully the requirements of the governing agencies for the following manual types:

- quality manuals whose purpose is to meet the requirements for ISO 9000 certification

- safety manuals that satisfy OSHA standards

Parts of manuals

Whether your manual is for a computer program or a piece of military aircraft, it can include any of the following sections.

FRONT MATTER

Front matter usually contains:

1. cover
2. title page
3. table of contents
4. list of illustrations
5. overview

BODY

1. The *introduction* explains the purpose and organization of the manual, outlines safety precautions, and provides a list of necessary tools and materials. This section can be either brief or extremely detailed, depending on the complexity of the program or mechanism.

2. The *core instructing section* includes

   - a short description of the program or mechanism

   - numbered step-by-step operating procedures

   - troubleshooting help

   - maintenance advice.

BACK MATTER

The back matter of your manual may include

1. replacement parts information
2. specifications
3. an index.

What makes a good manual?

First of all, a good manual is reader friendly. It must:

USE HEADLINES FOR ACCESSIBILITY

Headlines help readers find their way through a document the same way that a table of contents does. In fact, many word-processing systems allow you to turn the headlines into a table of contents. However, it is necessary to write the manual with the two or three levels of headlines specified in the template.

Before you begin to write, plan your headline-level strategy. You may save hours and guarantee accuracy by this approach.

LEAVE PLENTY OF WHITE SPACE

Too much information crowded on a page makes even the most well-written manual confusing.

BE ADAPTABLE

If you expect frequent updates, consider putting your manual in a ring binder. Plan a document-control strategy to keep track of who has or needs updates.

About safety or warning labels

Safety labels must immediately catch the reader's eye. Be sure the warning appears before the instruction: if not, by the time the reader sees it, it might be too late. Use icons, or small pictures, to make your manual more reader-centered.

danger: hazardous condition exists

warning: potential for injury

caution: damage to
machine or equip-
ment could occur

note: information that
could make opera-
tion more efficient

Boldface, italics, larger fonts, and borders also
attract attention. Another option is to put safety
information in a margin note or separate column.

Most manual writers wisely include their
warning twice: once at the very beginning of the
procedure; a second time just before the actual
step.

Graphics are essential

While some readers will diligently read step-by-
step procedures, others bypass instructions and
jump directly to charts, diagrams, and figures. It is
therefore necessary to make these visuals self-
explanatory.

If a warning appears in the instructions, it
should also appear in the diagram.

Integrate your graphics in the text rather than
grouping them at the end. Label them with one or
two key points. Give all your figures, tables, and
charts clear and specific titles. Use your title to
summarize your message.

instead of: Fig. 8. $V_{\text{ref}}(T)$.

write: Fig. 8. Measured value of $V_{\text{ref}}(T)$ at a
supply voltage of 1 V.

Test your manual

At various stages, test your procedures on a potential user to make sure you explained them clearly.
You'll get valuable feedback this way.

(See also **headline levels**; **organizing informa-tion**; **outlines**; **procedures**; **readers**, **analyzing**; **safety labels**; **visual design**.)

map charts

A **map chart** links a geographic map with a set of numeric data. Use maps to display sales or popula-tion information for states or countries.

Maps show data according to a set of predefined geographic regions, whether it be the United States, Africa, or the world. Each region you choose must have a defined name or representa-tion.

For example, any of the 50 United States is a valid region. You may refer to the state by name, *Colorado*, or postal abbreviation, *CO*, if clearly defined.

(See also **charts or graphs**, **tables**.)

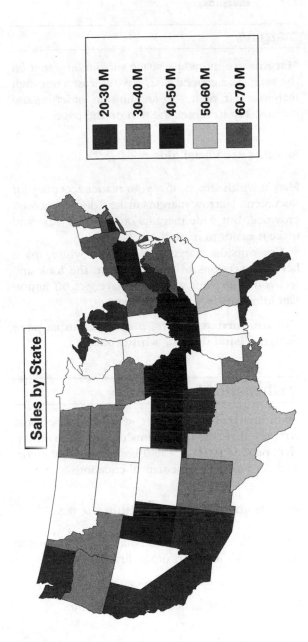

Sales by State

20-30 M
30-40 M
40-50 M
50-60 M
60-70 M

margins

Margins are the white space surrounding text on the page. As a general rule, leave at least a one-inch margin at left, right, top, and bottom for letters and memos. Try to center the text on the page.

Margins are visual aids

Margin width affects how your reader accepts your document. Narrow margins make a document look crowded, but wide margins open up the text and make it easier to read.

Use outside margins as well as white space between sections of text to create the look and feel you want your writing to have. Set off important information with white space.

(See also **format**, **letters**, **memorandums**, **page design**, **visual design**, **white space**.)

mathematical equations

Mathematical equations consist of numbers and symbols that show relationships to each other. Most publications use the following general guidelines for writing mathematical equations.

Include short equations within the text

If you write a short equation that you don't need to highlight, set it as part of the line of text.

In the equation on the handout, $x/a - y/c = 1$.

Never begin a sentence with an equation.

Separate long equations from the text

Long equations can be difficult to read within text, so highlight them by setting them apart.

Print a long equation on a separate line and center it. Double-space above and below the equation.

$$1/(x/y) - 3y + 2(x - x_1) = A + B(x - x_1) + y^2$$

If you have several equations in a sequence, line them up by their equal signs. Break long equations at their equal signs, and carry the equal sign to the next line.

$$1/(x/y) - 3y + 2(x - x_1)$$
$$= A + B(x - x_1) + y^2$$

If you can't break the equation at the equal sign, break it at another operational sign or at parentheses or brackets.

Punctuating equations

Don't use punctuation after the text that introduces a displayed equation or after the equation.

An alternate version of the equation is

$$1/(x/y) - 3y + 2(x - x_1) = A + B(x - x_1) + y^2$$

Numbering equations

Number equations consecutively in a document. Put the number to the right of the equation.

$$1/(x/y) - 3y + 2(x - x_1) = A + B(x - x_1) + y^2 \qquad (7)$$

Grouping expressions

Put grouped expressions in correct mathematical order. Parentheses go inside brackets, brackets go inside braces, and braces go inside parentheses.

$$x = a + b(c\{a - [d + 3(c - 2)]\})$$

(See also **symbols**.)

meetings, announcing

How often have you received a **meeting announcement** that wasted your valuable time making you search for time, date, and location?

Make it easy for your readers to find important information by listing this information in bulleted form or highlighting key words like *When* and *Where*. Always include the meeting's objective; if you can, attach the agenda.

A format like the following should always appear in your announcement:

Who:	Zone 4 Account Managers
	Elena Roznov, Ricardo Sabon, Julian Reese, Jamie Hafford, Ishi Burdett
When:	Tuesday, January 4
	10 a.m.
Where:	Third Floor Conference Room
Decide:	How realistic is it to raise our sales forecast for the fourth quarter?

Why should you follow this format? Meeting announcements are reference, not just information, documents. Readers usually consult them several times, so they must be easy to reread.

Make it a habit to organize your meeting announcements—especially on e-mail—this way and watch how many follow-up calls you *don't* have to answer before the meeting.

(See also **minutes of meetings**.)

memos: action documents at work

Memos or memorandums make things happen in your organization. Whether on paper or e-mail, they keep your business on track by facilitating day-to-day management. Memos document requests, procedures, and agreements. Successful memos stimulate readers to take action.

What are memos best for?

Use memos for communication within your company; use letters for communication outside your company. Exception: e-mail is now breaking down this distinction. Write memos when you need to

- confirm a conversation or an agreement
- persuade others to take action
- describe procedures
- announce policies
- request information
- transmit data.

While document length always depends on purpose and audience, memos should not exceed a page or two. Remember that your readers may receive dozens of interoffice communications every week.

Technical reports and internal proposals in memo form may be longer.

How to write a reader-centered memo

Use the Six Steps to Reader-Centered Writing™ for memos that inspire your readers to act. Next are some essential memo guidelines listed under the step they relate to.

STEP 1: ANALYZE YOUR READERS AND DEFINE YOUR PURPOSE

As you fill out your Focus Sheet™, remember:

1. MATCH YOUR READERS' STYLE AND TONE

Your audience will determine how informal your memo should be. In fact, you are probably acquainted with your readers and interact with them on a daily basis.

This personal knowledge makes it easier to choose the tone of your memo: you'll be more friendly and less formal than in a business letter.

2. HOW MUCH DOES YOUR READER NEED?

People who write more than the reader wants to know lose respect rapidly. Take the time to assess if you're overloading your reader. When in doubt, put possibly extra data toward the end labeled "Background," "History," or "Extra information."

3. ONE TOPIC PER MEMO

Why are you writing this memo? Define your purpose well, and stick to it. If you discuss more than one topic per memo, your readers may not take action—especially if the topic is not in the subject line.

Memos that cover several topics also cause filing problems. If your memo is filed under a minor topic, your reader may never refer to it again for important information on your main message.

STEP 2: USE A START-UP STRATEGY

Questioning is a good Start-up Strategy for memos because it puts you in your readers' shoes. By asking questions your readers will ask, you will give them only the information that they need to know.

This strategy will help you keep your memo brief and to the point—your busy readers will thank you.

STEP 3: GROUP INFORMATION UNDER HEADLINES

Many of your memos will follow a standard format and use the same headlines over and over again. Some examples follow.

1. *Calls to action* or *requests for information* should always have a "Deadline" or "Next steps" headline.

Build these headline categories into an on-line template in your word processing program and call it up when you are ready to organize your memo. Then, as you write, make your headlines as specific as possible.

instead of: Purpose of meeting

write: Meeting purpose: to choose System A, B, or C

2. *Policy and procedure announcements* might include such headlines as
   - Who is affected?
   - What has changed since the last announcement?
   - Step-by-step procedure (with each step in table form)
   - Whom to call for information?

3. *Progress reports* can be organized either by date of steps completed or by topic.

STEP 4: SEQUENCE YOUR IDEAS

As in all good writing, sequencing is a vital step. It is especially important for memo writing because your readers receive so many memos in both paper and electronic form. They won't read yours if you don't put your core message first.

Remember the importance of the subject line, too: if your main point isn't in the subject line, your reader may not even read the memo.

STEP 5: WRITE THE FIRST DRAFT

Don't edit yourself as you write. Just get your thoughts down, following the outline you developed in the first four steps.

STEP 6: EDIT FOR CLARITY, CONCISENESS, AND ACCURACY

Use the "Be Your Own Editor" Checklist. Double-check style and tone. If you are writing to a colleague or a subordinate, you can be less formal than if you are addressing a superior.

An action-oriented memo

The following memo is reader-centered because it

- is short and to the point
- has a specific subject line
- states the important information first
- has clear and specific headlines
- includes headlined action requests.

Date: July 10, 19—
To: Facilities Department staff
From: Joan Ling
Subject: New lab status meeting preview

Meeting purpose: team setup and coordination

At this month's meeting, Barry Matthews, our buildings and grounds consultant, will give us the final plan for the new lab facility. We will then be able to choose team leaders and set up teams to work on

- space layout
- bench organization
- computer system requirements
- remaining equipment needs.

Actions requested

1. Please come prepared to make team member recommendations.

2. Remember to bring your copy of the blueprint to the meeting.

3. Check your e-mail for "July 29 meeting agenda," and bring that, too.

This month's meeting

Date: Friday, July 29
Time: 10:30–11:30
Place: Facilities conference room

See you there!

MEMO FORMAT

Most memos are a variation of a common format. Your organization probably uses preprinted forms or word processing templates for its memos. The following information almost always appears at the top of a memo:

Date:
To:
From:
Subject:

The order and placement of these items may vary. Sometimes, for example, the date may go to the right. Follow your company's format.

DISTRIBUTION LIST

You have the option of putting your distribution list in the "To:" line or, if it is very long, at the end of the memo. List the top-ranking individuals first. For e-mail especially, edit your distribution list frequently, changing it as work teams change.

Sending a memo to too many people may dilute its impact. An overlong distribution list will make your memo look like a form letter; your readers may not even read it.

INITIALS

Since a memo doesn't have a signature line like a letter does, many writers put their initials next to their names on the "From" line. Others sign or initial the bottom of the memo. This is useful in e-mail if a series of forwarded messages starts to cloud who wrote what.

If your company has a preference, observe it.

SUBJECT LINE

The subject line is vital because it highlights content. Readers refer to it first to find out whether it's worth reading the memo. Make your subject line specific so your readers can use it to file the memo and, when they look at it weeks later, to remind themselves of its content.

Specific subject lines are especially important in e-mail writing.

How many times have you scanned your mailbox directory and been confronted with vague and uninformative subject lines? Which one did you open first? Probably the one that caught your attention because it made a specific point.

BODY

The body refers to the actual text of your memo. People often skim memos for the most important information, so put it where it will attract attention. To design your memo for easy readability, use headlines and subheads to help your readers navigate your document.

Your points will stand out if you put them in vertical lists rather than in paragraphs. Use bullets or numbers before each item. Boldface or italics will emphasize important words and phrases.

Be careful not to overdo either headlines or lists—especially in very short memos—or your writing will seem disjointed. Paragraphs are still vital parts of every document.

Consult the **page design** entry for formatting and layout suggestions.

(See also **electronic mail**, **headlines**, **Introduction to the Six Steps**, **lists**, **Model Documents Appendix**, **subject lines**, **tone**.)

memos that solve problems

You need to take action: you've identified a difficult problem, and now you must communicate your ideas in a persuasive memo. But first you must devise and justify an appropriate solution.

Does your company have a problem retaining talented employees? Is manufacturing always complaining about research and development? Perhaps you need to justify getting more temporary help during the tax season.

Use the following approach to present your analysis of a complicated situation and support your strategy for improvement. See the **Model Documents Appendix** for an example of a problem-solving memo.

Apply the Six Steps to problem solving

The problem-solving process that follows encourages you to use the Six Steps to Reader-Centered Writing™. To help you analyze complex problems in your organization, we have added a "Problem-Solving Inventory." It offers a list of questions designed to help you generate ideas during Step 2. You will get the best results if you start with the right questions.

1. ANALYZE YOUR READERS AND DEFINE YOUR PURPOSE

Like all writing projects, begin by filling out a Focus Sheet™. Consult the **readers**, **analyzing** entry.

2. GENERATE IDEAS WITH THE PROBLEM-SOLVING INVENTORY

The Problem-Solving Inventory (P.S.I.) is a Start-up Strategy designed especially for breaking through management problems. The goal of the P.S.I. is to help you

- understand the problem and its cause
- develop realistic solutions.

Avoid this classic mistake: jumping in too quickly to solve a problem before fully understanding what's causing it in the first place.

OTHER START-UP STRATEGIES CAN HELP, TOO

The brainstorm outline, discussed in the **getting started** entry, is another helpful technique for generating ideas. You'll be amazed at the number of ideas you will come up with.

Write them all down—at this point none of them is silly or irrelevant. You'll evaluate them later.

Keep generating ideas until you've fully analyzed the problem and come up with several different solutions. If you're still not satisfied with the solution you've selected, keep brainstorming.

USING THE PROBLEM-SOLVING INVENTORY

Answer the questions under each headline. Some questions may not apply to your particular problem. Use the brainstorm outline for items with an asterisk.

If you are using paper and pencil, use a separate page for each number to simplify later sequencing of the content. If you are working on a computer, you will be able to cut and paste your ideas into their final sequence.

Problem-Solving Inventory

1. Describe the problem

   A. What situation needs to be corrected or changed?

   B. How does the situation deviate from the ideal?

   C. In other words, if the problem did not exist, what would be happening instead?

2. List symptoms: give evidence of the problem

   A. Who is affected by it? To what extent?

   B. What is affected by it? To what extent?

   C. Where is it occurring?

   D. How long has it been going on?

   E. Do others agree that this is a problem?

3. List causes: identify reasons for the problem

   A. What methods or processes are contributing to the problem?

   B. Which materials, equipment, or facilities play a role? How?

   C. Who might be contributing to the situation? How? Lack of information? Lack of skill? Different values, beliefs, or goals?

   D. Why is the problem continuing?

   E. Are there any other possible contributing factors?*

   F. Do we need more data? Input from anyone else?

   G. Of all the causes I've considered, which are the most likely?

4. Generate solutions

   A. What are all the possible ways to change the situation?*

   B. How can I incorporate other people's ideas?

5. Evaluate the benefits and drawbacks of each solution

   A. What are the benefits of each?

   B. What are the drawbacks of each?

   C. Which is the most sensible solution for the least expenditure of resources?

6. Select the best solution(s)

   A. Which solution shall I propose?

   B. Does my solution make sense? Is it realistic?

   C. Are there hidden issues or limitations?

   D. How can I incorporate other people's ideas?

7. Justify your recommendation

   A. Why is my solution best? What are the benefits and costs?*

B. Who would benefit from the change? How?

C. Who is likely to oppose the solution?

D. In summary, what can I do to minimize opposition, maximize support, and gain others' commitment?

8. Plan the implementation

A. What actions can I take?* Short term? Long term?

B. What actions should others take?

C. Whose help do I need?

D. Whose approval do I need? Whose buy-in?

E. What deadlines are appropriate?

F. How will we know we succeeded in solving the problem?

G. How will we measure success? When? For how long?

H. Who will measure success?

ADAPT THE PROCESS TO YOUR OWN NEEDS

After using the P.S.I. several times, you'll probably find ways to abbreviate it while maintaining its effectiveness. With experience, you may find the "short form" sufficient, especially for less complex problems.

Answer the numbered questions and use the lettered subquestions as inspiration or reminders. There are, however, some dangers in glossing over the subquestions. Many are far more relevant than they may appear at first glance.

The P.S.I. is yours; adapt this tool to your own needs. As you internalize the problem-solving process, you will be the best judge of how extensively you need to analyze the challenges you face.

3. GROUP INFORMATION UNDER HEADLINES

You may find that some of the answers you came up with in the P.S.I. were for your own clarification. You won't need to include them in the memo, but use them to determine the right approach.

Create accurate headlines for each section of your memo. Ideas for headlines might come from the questions on the P.S.I. or your responses to them. Here are some examples of headlines that work.

- For a problem statement:

    Problem: lost revenues
    Production is falling behind schedule
    High turnover is increasing costs
    The system is not fulfilling user requirements

- For a recommended solution:

    Recommendations
    How we can improve production
    Ways to reduce turnover
    How we can accommodate users

- For benefits:

    Why this is the best solution
    How we can establish an incentive program
    How will this solution benefit us?

- For background:

    When our requirements began to change
    Who is affected by the situation?
    Why we haven't recognized this problem before

- For alternatives:

    Other solutions considered but rejected
    Benefits and drawbacks of other solutions

- For the implementation plan:

    Implementation plan: June 1-July 31
    Next steps
    Action required now
    Deadlines

4. SEQUENCE YOUR IDEAS

In keeping with the principle of putting your bottom line on top, state your recommendation near the beginning of your memo. Here is one effective sequence of ideas. The numbers in parentheses refer to questions on the P.S.I.

  I.   Description of the problem *(1)*; only a brief mention of symptoms *(2)* and causes *(3)*

 II.   Recommended solution *(6)*

III.   Justification of recommendations *(7)*:

  • why this is the best solution
  • how benefits outweigh costs

 IV.   Background: detailed discussion of

  • symptoms *(2)*
  • causes *(3)*

  V.   Alternative solutions *(5)*:

  • strengths and advantages
  • weaknesses and disadvantages

 VI.   Implementation plan *(8)*

VII.   Summary

The sample problem-solving memo in the **Model Documents Appendix** uses this outline.

There may be times when you should wait to present your recommendation after a background discussion. You may first need to convince your audience that

  • the problem exists
  • the problem is serious
  • the obvious solution isn't the best solution.

5. WRITE THE FIRST DRAFT

With the planning stages behind you, you're ready for Step 5—drafting your memo. Keep in mind that you'll write much more efficiently if you do the first draft as quickly as possible. Resist editing at this stage.

6. Edit for clarity, conciseness, and accuracy

Once you have a draft of the entire memo, follow Step 6. Use the "Be Your Own Editor" checklist in the **editing your draft** entry to edit, revise, and proofread. May all your problems be simple and easy to solve.

(See also **bad news letters and memos**; **editing your draft**; **getting started**; **Introduction to the Six Steps**; **Model Documents Appendix**; **readers, analyzing**.)

metaphors

A figure of speech that compares two things by saying one is the other is called a **metaphor**. We use many metaphors in everyday language.

> That *sales award* is certainly a *giant step* in Gail's career. [The *sales award* is compared to a giant step by saying it *is* a step.]

> Mr. Stafford's *acceptance* of our proposal was a *vote of confidence* in our firm. [The acceptance is compared to a vote of confidence.]

Metaphors can help explain complex concepts in simpler, more accessible terms. For example:

> Communication is a two-way street.

A comparison that uses the words "like" or "as" is called a *simile*.

A caution

If you mix different metaphors in one statement, your writing will sound confused.

> This packaging problem has turned out to be a real *can of worms*, and solving it quickly is a *pipe dream*.

minutes of meetings

After you've left a meeting, it's a serious responsibility to record with accuracy all the decisions made and actions expected. Use a format that makes clear to all involved the

- actions planned
- deliverables
- responsible individuals
- deadlines.

In the **Model Documents Appendix** there are sample minutes in table and narrative form.

(See also **meetings, announcing**; **Model Documents Appendix**.)

misplaced modifiers

Always put modifiers as close as possible to the word or phrase they modify. A **misplaced modifier** is incorrectly placed in a sentence and unintentionally modifies the wrong word or phrase.

instead of: Leah is in charge of these two projects. She must be allowed to give more time to them *both* in planning and following through. [Does *both* belong with *them* or with *planning* and *following through*?]

write: Leah is in charge of these two projects. She must be allowed to give more time to them in *both* planning and following through.

instead of: Ricardo has tried to get a contract to work at Dapple Computer *for two months*. [Does Ricardo want a contract for two months, or has he been trying for two months?]

write:	*For two months*, Ricardo has tried to get a contract to work at Dapple Computer.
instead of:	We found the spare parts in a utility closet, *which Felicia had planned to include in inventory*. [Were the *spare parts* or the *utility closet* planned for inventory?]
write:	We found the spare parts, *which Felicia had planned to include in inventory*, in a utility closet.

Squinting modifiers

A squinting modifier is so positioned that it could modify two elements in the sentence at the same time. Because readers don't know which element the modifier is supposed to modify, the meaning of the sentence is ambiguous.

instead of:	Ginger asked Hal *carefully* to proofread the report. [Was the question *careful*, or should Hal proofread *carefully*?]
write:	Ginger asked Hal to proofread the report *carefully*.

Dangling modifiers

A misplaced modifier is not the same as a dangling modifier. A dangling modifier doesn't refer logically to anything in the sentence, while a misplaced modifier is simply out of its proper place.

instead of:	*Holding down the shift and option keys*, a square or circle can be drawn. [Is a square or circle supposed to hold down the keys?]
write:	Draw a square or circle by holding down the shift and option keys.

(See also **dangling modifiers**, **modifiers**.)

modifiers

Words that describe, limit, or make the meanings of other words in the sentence more exact are called **modifiers**.

> The *new* scheduling system can *efficiently* manage your *most complicated* marketing agenda. [The modifiers are in italics. Read the sentence without the modifiers to see what difference they make.]

We need modifiers to make our meanings precise and clear. The most common kinds of modifiers are adjectives, adverbs, and phrases and clauses that act as adjectives and adverbs.

Adjectives

Adjectives modify nouns and pronouns.

> Ask the *shipping* clerk for an *empty* box to store the *old* manuals.

> Eddie did an *outstanding* job on the poster for *this* fund-raiser. He made it really *beautiful*.

A phrase or clause can act as an adjective.

> The files *in the C drive* can all be deleted. [phrase]

> Her decision *that we move the release date back a week* is a good one. [clause]

Adverbs

Adverbs usually modify verbs.

> The test driver handled the car *carefully* until he got the feel of it. [*Carefully* modifies the verb *handled*.]

> Though sales for the month were down, the manager spoke *encouragingly* at the status meeting. [*Encouragingly* modifies *spoke*.]

A clause can act as an adverb.

> We will upgrade the system *after we move to Atlanta*. [The clause in italics modifies the verb *upgrade*.]

(See also **adjectives**, **adverbs**, **dangling modifiers**, **misplaced modifiers**, **restrictive and nonrestrictive elements**.)

N

nouns

Nouns are words that name people (*engineers*), places (*Wall Street*), things (*computers*), and ideas (*fairness*).

Kinds of nouns

PROPER NOUNS

The names of specific people, places, and things are called proper nouns. They are usually capitalized.

Marie Curie	New Zealand
Ohio River	Pulitzer Prize

COMMON NOUNS

All nouns that are not proper are common nouns. They name general categories. Do not capitalize common nouns unless they begin a sentence.

transmittal	promotion
elevator	committee
portfolio	supervisor

A few nouns can be either proper or common.

China/china	Turkey/turkey

Some common nouns and adjectives are derived from proper nouns but now have common meanings. They begin with lowercase letters.

angstrom	manila folder
oriental	

ABSTRACT AND CONCRETE NOUNS

Abstract nouns—also called noncountable nouns—name things we can't experience with our senses.

nutrition	dedication
democracy	fairness
loyalty	understanding

Concrete nouns name things we know through our senses.

oil	notebook
desk	soup
ladder	file cabinet
pencil sharpener	

COLLECTIVE NOUNS

A collective noun names a group or aggregate.

assembly	committee
staff	herd
crew	community

Collective nouns have plural meanings but singular forms. They usually take singular verbs.

> The finance *team is* working late to finish the figures for the proposal. [the team as one group]

In British usage, collective nouns may take plural verbs.

> The finance *team are* not in agreement over the figures for the proposal. [the team as individual members]

How nouns function in sentences

In general, nouns can be subjects, objects, complements, and appositives. Some nouns also function as adjectives or adverbs.

AS SUBJECTS

Nouns can be subjects of verbs.

> Ricardo's new *office* is conveniently near the computer room.

> The *prototype* will be ready by September.

AS OBJECTS

Nouns can be direct objects, indirect objects, and objects of prepositions.

> The contractor installed *insulation* everywhere, even in the storage room. [direct object]

> The manager gave our *team* a tour of the facilities. [indirect object]

> Put the deliveries of new *equipment* in the *store-room* until we make room on the third *floor*. [objects of prepositions]

AS COMPLEMENTS

A noun used as a *subjective complement* (or predicate nominative) follows a linking verb and completes the meaning of the subject.

> Ira Howitz is our new *sales manager*.

A noun used as an *objective complement* further describes the direct object.

> We repainted the conference room *blue*.

AS APPOSITIVES

Nouns can be appositives, or words that further identify other nouns.

> Use the mouse to select a function from the menu bar, the *line of commands* across the top of your screen.

AS ADJECTIVES OR ADVERBS

Some nouns can also be adjectives or adverbs, depending on their placement and use in the sentence.

> The *downtown* location is convenient for most employees. [adjective]

> The courier had to go *downtown* to pick up the envelope. [adverb]

Forming plurals of nouns

Simply add -*s* to form the plural of most nouns.

> radios   calculators   meals   offices   cars   crowds

Form the plural by adding -*es* if the noun ends in -*s*, -*sh*, -*x*, or -*ch*.

> pass/passes   bush/bushes   tax/taxes
> lunch/lunches

If a noun ends in -*y* preceded by a consonant, change the -*y* to -*ies*.

> delivery/deliveries   laboratory/laboratories
> specialty/specialties

If a noun ends in -*y* preceded by a vowel, add -*s* to form the plural.

> attorney/attorneys   survey/surveys
> holiday/holidays

For proper nouns that end in -*y* preceded by either a consonant or a vowel, just add -*s*.

> the Raffertys   the Baileys

Nouns that end in -*f*, -*ff*, or -*fe* usually add -*s* to form the plural. But some change these letters to -*ves*. You cannot follow a rule here—you must simply memorize the correct plural form.

> roof/roofs   plaintiff/plaintiffs   wife/wives
> half/halves   loaf/loaves

If a noun ends in a vowel, such as -*o*, it forms the plural by adding -*s* or sometimes -*es*. Again, you must memorize the plural form.

> portfolio/portfolios   potato/potatoes
> veto/vetoes

Some nouns change internal vowels to form their plurals.

> foot/feet   tooth/teeth   woman/women
> mouse/mice

Many nouns that come from foreign languages keep their original plurals.

crisis/crises	matrix/matrices
analysis/analyses	phenomenon/phenomena
criterion/criteria	genus/genera

Some foreign nouns have English plurals as well. In the following list, the middle word is the preferred plural:

Noun	Preferred plural	Optional plural
appendix	appendixes	appendices
index	indexes	indices
automaton	automatons	automata
curriculum	curriculums	curricula
memorandum	memorandums	memoranda
formula	formulas	formulae

Many nouns have the same form for both singular and plural. The meaning of the sentence tells you which number is intended.

corps   species   moose   means (method)

Our best *means* for straightening out this mess is to give it all to the graphics department. [singular]

We have limited *means* for straightening out this mess. [plural]

Hyphenated compound nouns add -s to the main word to form the plural.

aides-de-camp   courts-martial   editors-in-chief
sons-in-law

One-word, unhyphenated compound nouns form the plural in the usual way, at the end of the word.

cupfuls   courthouses   letterheads
stockholders   bookcases

Count and mass nouns

Count nouns have both singular or plural forms—you can count them.

disk/disks   wheel/wheels   manual/manuals
letter/letters

Mass nouns, or noncountable nouns, name things we can't count individually. They are usually abstract nouns and are considered collective in their meanings. Mass nouns have the same singular and plural forms.

collateral   profit   time   liquid   integrity

Rather than forming regular plurals, mass nouns usually use comparative words to show more or less.

gasoline/more gasoline   soil/less soil
space/some space

FEWER AND *LESS* WITH COUNT AND MASS NOUNS

To indicate "not as many," count nouns use *fewer* as a modifier.

fewer employees [not *less* employees]   *fewer* tests

To indicate "not as much," *less* modifies mass nouns.

less gasoline [not *fewer* gasoline]
less companionship

AMOUNT AND *NUMBER* WITH COUNT AND MASS NOUNS

Use *number* with count nouns and *amount* with mass nouns.

A small *number* [not *amount*] of employees came to the stress-management seminar.

The *amount* [not *number*] of research will depend on the final proposal.

ARTICLES WITH COUNT AND MASS NOUNS

If you can count a noun, use the articles *a*, *an*, or *the* with the singular form. Use *the* with either singular or plural nouns.

an audience   *a* or *the* nation   *the* companies

You can use *the* with mass nouns (*the* money) but not *a* or *an*.

PUT IT IN CONTEXT

Some nouns can be either count or mass, depending on the context.

> From this office, you can hear the *noise* [noncountable] of the delivery trucks all day.

> The competing *noises* [countable] of the cafeteria and the copy center are distracting.

Forming possessives of nouns

Most singular nouns form the possessive by adding *'s*.

> designer's proposal   employee's car
> computer's files

When a plural noun ends in -*s*, simply add the apostrophe to make the noun possessive.

> designers' proposals   employees' cars
> computers' files

For plural nouns that don't end in -*s*, add *'s*.

> women's   children's   alumni's   people's

Add *'s* to a singular name and an apostrophe alone to a plural name.

> Ted's   Consuelo's   the Hollises'
> Schwartz's *or* Schwartzes'

When a name is followed by Jr., Sr., or a Roman numeral (*I, II*) avoid making this last word possessive and instead rewrite the sentence.

instead of: The city gave *Joseph T. Stone, Jr.'s* family a plaque for community service.

write: The city gave *the family of* Joseph T. Stone, Jr. a plaque for community service.

Add *'s* or an apostrophe alone to the last word in most group and compound words.

someone else's   editor-in-chief's   stockholders'
brother-in-law's

To show joint possession of one thing, put the *'s* after the last name.

Gruber and Simpson's investment
Lucia and Margaret's office

Some expressions that end in *-s* or the sound of *s* use the apostrophe alone to form the possessive.

for old times' sake   for convenience' sake

NOUNS PRECEDING GERUNDS

When a noun precedes a gerund (a verb form that ends in *-ing* and functions as a noun), the noun must always be possessive.

Madeleine's leaving on a business trip means that Bryan will have to finish the report on his own.
[The gerund is *leaving*.]

(See also **possessive case**.)

---

number

Number refers to whether a noun, pronoun, or verb is singular or plural.

Nouns

Most nouns form the plural by adding *-s* or *-es*.

calendar/calendars   elevator/elevators
box/boxes

Pronouns

All pronouns change form in the plural, except *you*.

I/we   he, she, it/they

Verbs

Most verbs add -*s* or -*es* to form the *singular*—not the plural—in the present tense.

> she *finishes*   he *returns*   it *takes*

The only exceptions are outdated and poetic verbs.

> What *hath* God wrought?
> Pride *goeth* before a fall.

The pronouns *I* and *you* (singular and plural) generally *do not* take a verb with -*s* or -*es* added.

> I finish   you finish
> I return   you return

Make number consistent

Be sure the nouns, pronouns, and verbs in a sentence that must agree with each other have the same number.

instead of:	A summary table, not spreadsheets, *are* necessary for clarification.
write:	A summary table, not spreadsheets, *is* necessary for clarification. [*Table*, a singular noun, is the subject of this sentence.]
instead of:	*Head* of households *need* this extra form.
write:	*Heads* of households *need* this extra form. [All *heads* need the form.]

You may use a singular noun with a plural possessive when the noun could belong to each person.

> Seven employees took *their retirement* [not retirements] early.

In formal British usage, collective nouns take either singular or plural verbs or pronouns, depending on meaning. You rarely see this usage in the United States.

We could tell the crowd *was* eager to greet *its* leader. [singular verb and pronoun: crowd as a group]

Now the crowd *are disagreeing* over the judge's decision. [plural verb: crowd as individuals]

(See also **case**, **parallel structure**, **possessive case**.)

---

numbering

We use **numbering** to identify sections of documents or levels of outlines.

Numbering systems

Numbering systems indicate order of importance and levels of subordination in documents. They also serve as easy reference guides in long or very technical documents, and in procedures.

Numbering systems can follow a traditional outline format or use decimals. They are usually combined with headlines.

The numbering system that labels the sections of your document should also appear in the table of contents.

TRADITIONAL OUTLINE

Outlines use a number and letter sequence that shows the relationships of levels of information.

1. uppercase Roman numeral, period   I.
2. capital letter, period   A.
3. Arabic numeral, period   1.
4. lowercase letter, period   a.
5. Arabic numeral in parentheses   (1)
6. lowercase letter in parentheses   (a)
7. lowercase Roman numeral in parentheses   (i)

Use an outline as a system of numbering if your document is not overly long or complex, or if it has only a few subsections.

<small>Decimal system</small>

A decimal system uses successive decimal points and increasing numbers. It is the preferred form for technical documentation and procedure writing.

> 1.0
>   1.1
>   1.2
> 2.0
>   2.1
>   2.1.1
>   2.1.2
>   2.1.2.1

Use a decimal numbering system when your document is long, technical, or has many subsections. Decimals can help readers see the logical structure of your document.

Numbering charts, tables, and illustrations

Number your charts, tables, and illustrations consecutively, from beginning to end of your document. You may refer to them all as *Figures* (abbreviated *Fig.*). Don't begin a new series with each chapter or section unless your document is book length.

In the text, refer to these graphic aids by their numbers, not by the page they appear on.

See Fig. 8 for an example of a redesigned layout.

(See also **headlines**, **lists**, **organizing information**, **outlines**, **procedures**, **table of contents**.)

---

numbers

Style guides offer varying systems for writing out **numbers** or using figures. If your company doesn't have a style guide of its own, choose a format that works best for you and your needs. Apply it consistently.

Here we suggest one set of choices for the key formatting questions you will have to answer.

Numbers over ten

In general write numbers zero through nine as words and numbers over nine as figures.

> three engineers   38 engineers   two parking levels
> 11 parking levels

If a sentence contains more than one number, write all numbers the same way no matter what other rules may apply.

> Last year we supplied area repair shops with 107 alternators, 45 water pumps, and 9 generators.

Never begin a sentence with a figure. Spell out the number or rewrite the sentence.

instead of: 132 acres of this wetland have been destroyed by pollutants.

write: One hundred thirty-two acres of this wetland have been destroyed by pollutants.

better: Pollutants have destroyed 132 acres of this wetland.

Another strategy is to begin the sentence with *Over, More than, Less than, Roughly,* or *Exactly.*

> *Exactly* 132 acres of this wetland have been destroyed by pollutants.

Cardinal and ordinal numbers

Cardinal numbers indicate how many.

> The warehouse delivered *three* boxes of ribbon this morning.

> We were pleased that *23* associates signed up to donate blood.

Ordinal numbers show sequence, rank, or degree. You can spell them out or write them as figures, according to the general rules for numbers.

first	third	forty-sixth	nineteenth	twenty-second
1st	3rd	46th	19th	22nd

When ordinals are spelled out, they are more formal than figures. Use figures for emphasis or brevity.

Help us celebrate our *15th* year in business!

Both cardinal and ordinal numbers are considered adjectives.

Percentages

Always give percentages in figures and write out the word *percent*.

Enrollment is up *12 percent* over last year.

Use the symbol % in tables, charts, business forms, and technical or scientific writing.

Express fractional percents under 1 percent in either words or figures.

one half of 1 percent *or* 0.5 percent

Always put a zero before the decimal point so the number won't be misread (as *5 percent*, for example).

For fractional percents over 1 percent, use figures. In most business or technical applications, decimal fractions are preferred.

6.75 percent *or* 6 3/4 percent

When you write a series of percentages, put the word *percent* after the last figure only. However, if you are using the symbol % in the document, put the symbol after each figure.

We've had increased enrollments of 7, 10, and 11 *percent*, respectively, in the last 3 years.

The margin of error has decreased by 7%, *10%*, and *11%*, respectively, in the last 3 years.

Fractions

Spell out fractions that stand alone without a whole number. If the fraction is a noun, don't hyphenate it. When it's an adjective, use the hyphen.

> one half of the applicants   one-half yard long

If either the numerator or denominator has a hyphen, don't put another hyphen between the two parts of the fraction.

> twenty-five thirty-seconds apart

Write fractions as figures when they follow whole numbers.

> 4 1/2 kilometers [*not* 4 and one-half]

A fraction in figures should not have *-th*, *-ths*, *-nd*, *-nds*, *-rd* or *-rds* after it.

1 1/7	*not*	1 1/7th
3 13/32	*not*	3 13/32nds
8 1/3	*not*	8 1/3rd

You can write *one half* as words in two ways.

> The conference resumes *in a half hour*.

or: The conference resumes *in half an hour*.

Never mix fractions in figures with *of a* or *of an*.

| *instead of:* | The conference resumes in 1/2 (or one-half) *of an* hour. |
| *write:* | The conference resumes *in half an hour*. |

Don't begin a sentence with a fraction in figures.

instead of:	6 1/2 cases of paper are missing from the supply cabinet.
write:	*Six and one-half* cases of paper are missing from the supply cabinet.
better:	We are missing *6 1/2* cases of paper from the supply cabinet.

In all but the most technical writing, you should write fractions as words or decimals wherever possible. Your text will look better.

Decimals

Always write decimals in figures, not words. Don't put commas in the decimal part of a number.

> 9.725   45.6627
> 23,488.776 [no comma in the decimal]

For decimal amounts less than one, put a zero before the decimal point.

> 0.29 inch   0.85 liter   0.010 second

In informal business writing, you can usually eliminate the zero before the decimal point. This is also the rule for quantities that are never more than one.

> Our best company team player is batting *.314* so far this season.

> Don't forget to take into account the consistent probability of *.65.*

Don't begin a sentence with a decimal number.

instead of: *5.5* meters was the depth of the probe.

write: The depth of the probe was *5.5* meters.

Measurements

Use figures for most units of measurement.

> 6 yards   9 kilometers   150 board feet
> 6- by 12-foot carpet

> Our inventory is short *150 board feet* of cedar fencing.

You may spell out measurements that have no important technical meaning.

> Please order *two pounds* of regular coffee, *one pound* of decaf, and *one quart* of milk for next week's seminar.

In technical writing, express dimensions using symbols and abbreviations.

> 10×20 ft (rather than *ten by twenty feet* or *10 by 20 feet*)

Money

In general, write exact or approximate amounts of money in figures.

> $13 $33.12 $20 worth   about $1,200
> a $10 bill

Be consistent about spelling out both the number and the unit of money or putting them in figures with a symbol.

> nine cents *or* $.09 [*not* 9 cents]
> $42 *or* forty-two dollars [*not* 42 dollars]

If your sentence includes both whole numbers and parts of a dollar, write the whole numbers with zeros.

> Those finish nails were *$2.00* a pound last week, but they're on sale now for *$1.69* a pound.

Write large or cumbersome amounts in figures and words, with a dollar sign.

> $5 million $19 billion $1.6 trillion

Write foreign money in much the same way you write U.S. currency. Be consistent about using all words or figures with symbols.

> DM 22 million (Deutsche Marks)
> Fr 193.20 (francs)
> £12.42 (pounds, pence)
> ¥200 (yen)
> Mex$450 (Mexican pesos)

If you use an abbreviation, not a symbol, as in the first two examples in the preceding list, leave one space between the abbreviation and the number. For more information about how to write foreign currency, consult the Government Printing Office *Style Manual*.

Time

If you use a.m. and p.m., write the time in figures. You may indicate time with either lowercase, uppercase, or *small cap* letters. Be consistent about the format you choose.

4:00 p.m.   3:15 A.M.   7:30 P.M.

Don't write *morning, afternoon, evening,* or *o'clock* with a.m. or p.m.

If you don't use a.m. or p.m., write the time in words.

four o'clock   nine o'clock

Use a.m. and p.m. to distinguish between twelve midnight and twelve noon.

12:00 a.m. (midnight)   12:00 p.m. (noon)

Addresses

Spell out street numbers from one to one hundred, unless you need to save space.

South First Avenue   Seventh Street   122nd Street

Write building and house numbers as figures except for the number *one*.

432 Main Street   16 Gibbons Road
One Moseley Plaza

Always write highway numbers in figures.

U.S. 89   I 89   Arizona 16   Interstate 75

Write room numbers in figures.

The lecture on mutual funds will be in room 124.

Pages and chapters

Page numbers and table or chart numbers always appear as figures.

page 8   Figure 3   Table 13   Plate 22

Chapter and volume numbers may be either spelled out or in figures, though figures are usually preferred.

Chapter 7/Chapter Seven   Volume 6/Volume Six

Inclusive and sequential numbers

When you write inclusive or continued numbers, as in a page reference, give only the changed part of the first number for the second number. If the first number ends in zero, use all the digits for the second number.

5-9   200-243   1203-7   611-39   1010-1032

The same rules apply when you connect two year numbers.

the winter of 1992-93   the years 1939-1945
fiscal 1997-98

When the sequence is not continuous, separate the numbers with commas.

Please refer to pages 9, 16, and 18.
We conducted the surveys in 1990, 1992, and 1994.

Hyphenating numbers

Hyphenate compound numbers from 21 to 99.

thirty-second   thirty-two   sixty-one hundred

Don't hyphenate the other words in spelled-out numbers over 100.

five thousand   eight hundred thousand
sixteen hundred   twenty-nine million

Using commas with numbers

Separate figures of one thousand or more with commas after groups of three, beginning from the right.

49,102   7,446   1,002,337   4,221,132,895

Numbers to the right of a decimal point take no punctuation.

3.1417   49,102.0034

Separate two numbers that come together, whether in words or figures, with a comma.

At *1:00, 12* of the attendees have to leave.

The records show that in *1995, 103* houses went to foreclosure.

Don't separate the parts of a measurement with commas.

The overnight envelope weighed *1 pound 2 ounces.*

Writing plural numbers

Write the plural of figures by adding *-s.*

before the 1990s   temperatures in the 50s

Write the plural of spelled-out numbers by adding *-s* or *-es.* Follow the standard rules for forming plurals.

fours   fourths   sixes   eighties   ones
seventy-fives

(See also **apostrophes**, **commas**, **dates**, **hyphens**.)

---

numeric data: presenting quantitative information

You've completed an analysis that required significant research; now you have a large amount of data to convey. How can you make this detailed numeric data easiest to understand?

First ask yourself if the data would best be understood in a chart or a table—you may even need both. A table (or spreadsheet) is often the first step to any chart: with your graphics package you can try displaying the data in different charts to see what looks best.

Charts such as pie or bar charts are best for big-picture messages like trends. They present a straightforward, simple summary of data and, most important, give your reader additional ways of getting a feeling for relationships, size, differences, and anomalous events.

As you keep putting yourself in the readers' shoes, the best choice will become evident. Look back at your Focus Sheet to be sure you're on track.

Is a table the best vehicle?

When many exact values are necessary, the best way to present your data is in a table. Use tables when the readers need the precision of lists of values.

For example, tables are best for offering reference data, such as survey results, when you might want to give the mean response for every survey question you asked. Different readers could scan the results to pick out only those data points of importance to them. You might wish to offer several tables with columns or rows highlighted for easy comparisons.

If you find yourself giving more and more data, be sure you are not overwhelming your readers—perhaps the data should go in an appendix just for those who need it.

Table 1. 1994 and 1995 Bismark Sales

State	Number of Units Sold 1994	1995
Connecticut	2234	2210
Idaho	561	555
Maine	2345	1999
Massachusetts	4456	4070
New Hampshire	1222	1333
New Mexico	1156	1645
Oregon	892	1200
Washington	1567	1600
Wyoming	234	345
Total	**14667**	**14957**

Be sure to put a title on every row or column that contains data. Search for logical subgroups in the columns of data. Provide subtotals for each meaningful subgroup if the subtotal values significantly support your text.

Finally, include a grand total of the numeric column if this value has significance.

Don't give your data twice

In the text itself, your discussion should help the reader make logical connections between the numbers. Mention only the significant numbers that support your argument or results, highlighting values that make a difference or are remarkable in some way.

Don't deliver in sentence form the same information that fills your charts. You chose a table to help your readers visualize. Don't waste their time with prose that does not amplify or explain.

Situations that call for tables

1. To present details of grain production per county for 1999, you could group them by state, including subtotals of grain production per state, and a grand total of the grain produced in 1999.

2. To make a point about average salaries of top managers, you could first provide a table listing average employee salaries for different positions within a company, giving the top managers first.

   You might want to amplify your findings in a second table. You could repeat the first listing in the table, and then include salaries for different types of companies or perhaps companies with different numbers of employees. In other words, group the data by type or by size.

   Your text might also point out the largest differences and unique similarities, suggesting why they exist.

(See also **charts or graphs, figures, tables**.)

O

object

An **object** is the word that receives the action of the verb.

> Writers use *hypertext* to prepare pages for the World-Wide Web. [The object *hypertext* receives the action of the verb *use*.]

Objects are always nouns or noun substitutes, such as pronouns, infinitives, or gerunds.

> Joanne filed the *report*. [noun]
>
> Joanne filed *it*. [pronoun]
>
> Joanne hates *to file*. [infinitive]
>
> Joanne hates *filing*. [gerund, or verb form ending in *-ing*]

There are three kinds of objects: direct, indirect, and object of a preposition.

Direct objects

Direct objects are words or groups of words in the predicate of a sentence that complete the meaning of the verb. Direct objects determine who or what receives the action of the verb.

> He signed the *contract*. [What did he sign?]
>
> She recommended *me* for the job. [Whom did she recommend?]
>
> Customer Service wants *to offer a special incentive for February*. [What does Customer Service want? *To offer a special incentive for February* is an infinitive phrase that acts as a direct object.]

Although the usual word order in a sentence is subject–verb–direct object, the direct object doesn't always have to follow the verb immediately.

> He sent me an *e-mail*. [What did he send?]

She gave him a thorough and detailed *account* of her trip. [What did she give?]

Indirect objects

An indirect object answers *to* or *for whom* or *what* after the verb and before the direct object.

Ben's department bought *him* his own enhanced personal computer. [For whom did the department buy a computer?]

Juanita gave *her administrative assistant* an extra day off. [To whom did Juanita give an extra day off?]

I plan to give *your data transmission problem* my full attention. [To what do I plan to give my full attention?]

Objects of prepositions

An object of a preposition follows a preposition and is part of the prepositional phrase.

Jane stopped at the *office* before she left. [*Office* is the object of the preposition *at*.]

The company bought the site across the *road*. [*Road* is the object of the preposition *across*.]

PRONOUN OBJECTS OF PREPOSITIONS

Pronouns used as objects are always in the objective case.

Give the report to *him* [not *he*] before Friday.

As soon as you send the check to *us* [not *we*], we will ship your order.

Watch out for prepositions that are followed by more than one object. Pronouns that follow prepositions must be in the objective case no matter where they appear.

He brought back samples for Phyllis, Henry, and *us* [not *we*].

The resolution of this grievance is between you and *me* [not *I*].

Understanding objects will help prevent errors in word choice.

(See also **infinitives**, **objective complements**, **predicates**, **prepositions**, **pronouns**, **sentences**, **verbs**.)

objective complements

An **objective complement** is a noun or adjective that follows and modifies a direct object. Such complements complete the meaning of the sentence.

Since the president appointed her *CFO*, her leadership has made the division *profitable*. [*CFO* is a noun objective complement modifying the direct object *her*. *Profitable* is an adjective objective complement modifying the direct object *division*.]

Never separate the objective complement from the direct object with a comma.

instead of: Please make these headers, footers, and headlines, *big* and *bold*.

write: Please make these headers, footers, and headlines *big* and *bold*. [*Big* and *bold* are adjective objective complements modifying the direct objects *headers*, *footers*, and *headlines*.]

(See also **adjectives**, **nouns**, **object**.)

one

One can be a pronoun that designates an indefinite person. It always takes a singular verb.

If *one* works hard and succeeds, *one* will be rewarded.

One is more common in British than American usage.

One can't wait too long, can *one*?

In the U.S., using *one* can make your writing sound too formal or pretentious. It's usually better to write *you*—or avoid the problem altogether by using a noun or rewriting the sentence.

write:	*You* can easily see that this particular solution is not cost effective.
or:	*Management* can easily see that this particular solution is not cost effective.
instead of:	If *one* works hard and succeeds, *one* will be rewarded.
write:	If *you* work hard and succeed, *you* will be rewarded.
or:	Hard work leads to rewards.

Always use pronouns of the same person in a sentence. Don't mix *one* with *you* because *one* is third person and *you* is second person.

instead of:	If *one* finishes a quarterly report ahead of schedule, *you* will receive an efficiency award.
write:	If *you* finish a quarterly report ahead of schedule, *you* will receive an efficiency award.

One can also be a number adjective.

We guarantee shipment within *one* day of receiving your order.

(See also **gender**, **person**, **point of view**, **pronouns**.)

---

only

Always put **only** right before the word or phrase it modifies, or it can change the meaning of the sentence.

Edith *only* gave the first presentation. [Edith only gave it; she didn't write it or summarize it.]

Edith gave *only* the first presentation. [The first was the only presentation Edith gave.]

Only Edith gave the presentation. [Edith was the only one who gave it.]

(See also **misplaced modifiers**.)

open punctuation

An **open punctuation** style consists of minimal punctuation, usually commas. This style omits what some writers consider optional punctuation and includes only what is essential for clarity. It is the opposite of closed punctuation, which requires a strict interpretation of grammatical structure.

Following are a few of the variations in open punctuation style.

COMMAS IN A SERIES

The open style leaves out the comma before *and* and the last item in the series.

Everyone had to attend the meeting, including managers, supervisors, assistants and service staff.

Since leaving out the final comma can cause ambiguity or misreading, we recommend that you always put in the last comma.

instead of:	Chemco decided to divide the proceeds from the sale equally among officers, stockholders and employees.
write:	Chemco decided to divide the proceeds from the sale equally among officers, stockholders, and employees. [In the preceding sentence the added comma actually changes the amounts each party receives.]

COMMAS AFTER DATES

When a date comes mid-sentence, the open punctuation style omits the comma after the year.

> I received my degree on June 2, 1991 from Virginia Polytechnic.

COMMAS BETWEEN INDEPENDENT CLAUSES

Independent clauses can stand alone as complete sentences. If the two clauses are short, the open punctuation style leaves out the comma between them. The key here is the definition of "short." We define it as clauses with no more than five or six words each.

> The proposal is in the mail and I am going home.

Use open punctuation carefully, if at all. Well-placed commas make your meaning clear and correct, and standard punctuation is never wrong.

(See also **commas**.)

---

opening letters and memos

The **opening** is the first part of the letter or memo your readers see, so it should catch their attention. If your letter is short, you probably don't need a formal introduction. The opening should usually be concise and to the point, especially in memos.

Refer to your Focus Sheet™ to find your "bottom line," or most important point. Put that information first. For example:

> Dear Mr. Morales:
>
> Subject: Your loan application
>
> After reviewing your application, we are pleased to grant your loan request for . . .

Dear Ms. Steinberg:

Subject: Testing session planned

The standard testing procedures at the Grotting plant will begin on September 19. The following processes . . .

To: All employees
From: Human Resources
Date: February 28, 19—
Subject: Overtime policy change

Beginning March 15, employees may work a maximum of ten hours overtime per week.

OTHER TYPES OF OPENINGS

If your letter is more conversational, you can use many kinds of openings to capture your readers' interest. Make them feel you are talking to them. Effective openings are businesslike but personable.

instead of: Enclosed please find the . . .

write: Here is the information you requested.

instead of: As per our telephone conversation of November 3 . . .

write: As we discussed on November 3 . . .

instead of: This will acknowledge receipt of your letter . . .

write: Thank you for your letter about *or* interest in . . .

instead of: In reference to your inquiry of November 3 regarding . . .

write: Thank you for your interest in . . .

Your choice of opening will depend on what information you have to communicate and who your readers are. Here are some ideas for attention-getting openers.

DETAIL

You can begin with an interesting detail, fact, idea, or even anecdote about your subject, depending on what would appeal to your readers.

The recipe for the butterscotch sauce we use at Ida's Ice Cream originally belonged to Ida's grandmother, Mrs. Sweethopper. Realizing its value, Mrs. Sweethopper willed the exclusive rights to the recipe to Ida. The current challenge to the rights by Ida's brother Henry has no legal grounds.

BACKGROUND

Giving some background or historical information about your subject can occasionally be a good way to begin.

In the six years that Interstate Movers has been in operation, we have established the best record in the business for delivering goods safely. As we begin our seventh year, . . .

PROJECTION

Projecting a trend or development related to your subject may capture your readers' interest.

By 1999 there should be no unsafe playgrounds left in America. We have been evaluating and successfully rebuilding playgrounds for safety, community by community, since 1990. With our latest expansion, our goal is finally in sight.

QUESTION

Sometimes beginning with a question or questions will keep your audience reading.

How many times have you felt confused and frustrated by the task of finding good day care for your children? How often have you missed a day of work because child care was unavailable? We have the solution to your problems: our own on-site day-care facility, opening on September 7.

(See also **closing a document**, **introductions**, **letters**, **memorandums**, **Model Documents Appendix**, **reports**.)

organizing information: Step 4 to Reader-Centered Writing

Perhaps the most difficult and most important part of writing is **organizing**, or sequencing, **information**. Readers expect all documents, long or short, to be logically organized and easy to follow.

Before you can sequence your document, you must complete Step 3 of the Six Steps to Reader-Centered Writing™: group information under headlines. Otherwise you won't know what you're sequencing.

Develop your main headlines, such as "Recommendations," "Action requested," "Next steps," "Background," and "Conclusions." Only then can you easily organize your document and create the most successful and strategic sequence for presenting your information.

What is the result of successful organization?

After sequencing your information, you should have a list of your topics and subtopics in the order you will be including them.

Whether you draw up a traditional or more casual list outline, it must cover every topic in your document. Without such an organizational plan, you cannot move to Step 5 of Reader-Centered Writing and write your first draft.

Keep your readers in mind

As you choose a method of organization, review your Focus Sheet™. Who are your readers? What do they already know about your topic? What do they need to hear first? Are they already on your side, or do you need to convince them?

If you used questioning as a Start-up Strategy, review your questions. Re-examining your readers' needs will remind you of your purpose for writing—and your purpose will help you organize your document.

You should generally present important information first, but sometimes there are exceptions. If your readers aren't receptive to your ideas, for instance, you may need to lead up to your main point gradually, making strategic points along the way.

If you're writing a long document to an audience unfamiliar with your topic or procedure, you may need to explain your method of organization in the introduction. If, on the other hand, you're writing a memo to colleagues who know about your topic, your organization will be obvious.

How to choose a sequence or method of development

Many companies have prescribed formats standardizing the organization of frequently used or complex documents, such as audit reports, lab reports, performance reviews, and progress or status reports.

Before you invest time in sequencing, check to see if your company has models for your writing task.

Unless you are following fixed company guidelines, you have many options in how you sequence your document. The following are a number of effective organizational strategies or methods of development (M.O.D.'s). The chart entitled "Which Method of Development Should I Use?," at the end of this entry, has sequencing suggestions for many document types.

Let your purpose guide your choice. If you're not sure where to put your key point, focus specifically on what you need to accomplish, who your readers are, and how much time they will spend with your document.

Put yourself in your readers' place by using the questioning Start-up Strategy. What will they look for? What do they want to know first?

M.O.D. #1: ORDER OF IMPORTANCE

MOST IMPORTANT TO LEAST IMPORTANT

This method works best for the majority of writing projects.

Take a trip report, for example. You may think that you should describe in chronological order exactly what you did during an out-of-town conference. But perhaps the final presentation you attended was far more useful to you and your company than the address of the keynote speaker.

It makes sense to begin with your most important information, or your "bottom line."

Another consideration: how much time and interest in your subject does your reader have? In most cases a reader's attention is completely focused on a document only in the first few paragraphs; after that, concentration begins to flag.

Busy readers may be irritated because they can't find your main point right away—or they may file your document for future reading, never to return.

Using the most-important-to-least-important sequence, or "bottom line on top," you will take advantage of your reader's complete attention at the beginning of the document to get across your key points.

THE BAD NEWS SANDWICH

If you have something to say that your reader doesn't particularly want to hear, you'll need to put it between good news sections to make it more palatable.

Some examples of bad news are poor financial results, a recommendation that will require spending more money than expected, or an announcement of layoffs.

If the bad news is the filling, then what's the bread? Well, if possible, some positive news. Maybe your prospects are bright for the next quarter even though the numbers are down this month. Moreover, you have plans for retraining sales people to make them more efficient.

Another way to lead up to a controversial announcement or recommendation is to demonstrate the need for it. Begin by using a specific example to describe a problem—and then show how implementing your idea can prevent the situation from happening again.

However bad the news, always try to end on a positive, action-oriented note.

M.O.D. #2: CHRONOLOGY

Some documents require a chronological method of development, where events are listed in the order in which they happened. Examples are minutes of meetings, descriptions of test procedures, growth statistics, and accident reports.

However, even when using a chronological sequence, remember to emphasize important information. Imagine your reader asking, "What's the bottom line?"

You can highlight important points by stating them first and then giving the details. In an accident report, for example, you might begin by saying:

> On Tuesday, February 9, there was a minor explosion in the third-floor laboratory. No one was hurt, and we have identified the cause of the accident. A detailed description follows.

In meeting minutes, you can highlight important points such as action steps by putting them in boldface type or underlining them. When you describe a scientific procedure, you can summarize the results first and then describe the step-by-step process.

M.O.D. #3: PROCESS

Some documents explain a process that is not chronological but requires a particular order. When you document such a process, you impose your own chronology or sequence: you are not describing an event that already happened, as in an accident report or meeting minutes.

Keep in mind, too, that your process may have parallel subprocesses: several events or steps occurring simultaneously or dependent upon one another, as in a flowchart.

Say, for example, you are writing a manual to install an automatic ice-maker.

There are many steps, ranging from hooking up a water line to screwing in the piece that holds the cubes. If you performed them in the wrong sequence the machine would probably not operate—you might even get a leak or blow a fuse. Proper sequencing is crucial.

It's equally important to be thorough about listing all the steps. Before drafting your instruction manual, try jotting down each step on index cards or Post-it Notes™. You can see all the steps in front of you, make sure you haven't omitted any, and then arrange them in the correct sequence.

If certain steps are particularly vital or require special attention, highlight them.

M.O.D. #4: ORGANIZATION IN SPACE

For some trip reports, descriptions of inventions, sales research reports, and other documents, a spatial organization may be the most logical.

You might lead the reader across the country, for example, by discussing research done in Los Angeles, production carried out in Newark, and sales made in Chicago. On a smaller scale, you might write a technical report about a brand-new machine tool and describe it from top to bottom, left to right, or from the inside out.

You invite your readers to journey with you from Point A to Point B and so on.

Reports organized in this way can be somewhat flat if each section bears equal weight.

Try to engage your reader by highlighting what's new, special, or significant about your research, mechanism, or trip. You can do this by boldfacing the most interesting ideas or placing them at the beginning of each paragraph—or both.

M.O.D. #5: COMPARISON/CONTRAST

In feasibility reports, proposals, and research results, the strongest way to convey information is often to compare or contrast it to something else. When you compare two concepts, you reveal what they have in common; when you contrast, you focus on their differences.

This technique is especially useful if your readers aren't familiar with your topic or product.

For example, if you were describing your company's new toothpaste to your sales force, you could point out how it resembles Crest, Colgate, and Ultrabrite. Then discuss the differences. What does this toothpaste do that the others don't?

By stating succinctly what makes it unique, you're providing an ideal selling handle for the product.

Remember, keep similarities together and differences together. Don't mix them in the same sentence or your readers may find the information difficult to sort out.

If you're introducing a complex subject that is totally new to your readers, like new software, start with a familiar program or service for comparison. Find something that performs a similar function and continue from there.

Comparison/contrast is also a good M.O.D. for discussing the advantages and disadvantages of a given situation. Again, keep the two separate. Start with the most important: whichever one outweighs the other.

Use transition phrases like street signs to warn the reader of shifts in point of view and changes of focus. Some examples:

- in contrast
- in the same way
- in opposition to . . .
- although it is true that . . .
- on one hand
- on the other hand

M.O.D. #6: SPECIFIC TO GENERAL OR GENERAL TO SPECIFIC

In this method of development you

- start with a specific statement and expand it to explain a general idea, *or*
- begin with a general statement and follow with specific examples and supporting statements.

This method is tricky because there are no fixed rules governing which sequence to use. Decide on a case-by-case basis, and be sure to refer to the Focus Sheet you completed to analyze your readers. Their prior knowledge of your topic will be a key factor in your decision.

Here are some examples:

YOUR READER IS UNFAMILIAR WITH YOUR TOPIC

1. You want to discuss how to communicate on the Internet. Your reader doesn't know what the Internet is, but does use a company e-mail system.

    Start with a specific statement about how e-mail works. Expand it to describe external e-mail systems. Then move on to more global applications like Internet e-mail, bulletin boards, and news groups.

2. You want to describe a new gear mechanism in bulldozers to a nontechnical reader.

  Begin with a general statement that bulldozers are easier to drive than they used to be. As you explain why they're more maneuverable, move to specifics about upgraded transmission.

YOUR READER IS FAMILIAR WITH YOUR TOPIC

1. *Lead with a general statement* about the Internet because your reader already knows what it is. Then move to specifics and describe, for example, specific Internet applications that private subscription services provide.

2. Since your reader understands the inner workings of bulldozers, *start with a specific:* your company has vastly improved the gear system by changing its position and design. Since that is your key point, you should say it at the beginning. Then discuss the result of the new design.

  Go on to more general statements about higher efficiency and better maneuverability.

As you can see, choosing an order—general to specific or specific to general—requires you to put yourself in your reader's place and ask, "What do I need to know first?"

M.O.D. #7: ANALYSIS

Analysis means formulating a hypothesis and rigorously testing, through a questioning process, whether it is true or not. Asking questions will lead you to research that will help confirm or disprove your hypothesis.

If you fail to write about every aspect of your hypothesis, your analysis could be discredited or, worse, lead to a bad business decision.

If you analyze material for technical reports, annual reports, economic forecasts, financial reports, or market research, you will need a sharp focus and a logical, detailed, and probably quantitative approach.

You will be analyzing your data for differences, similarities, and logical links as you ask, "How do the pieces all fit together?"

For example, if you're in the healthcare industry, you might need to predict the demand for a certain medical instrument. Formulate a hypothesis that forecasts buying patterns, then do research or market analysis that asks the right questions to determine real trends.

The success of your analysis will rest on the strength and relevance of the questions you ask and your willingness to follow them to their ultimate conclusions, whether expected or not.

Ignore past assumptions, models, and conclusions. If you can divorce yourself from your own point of view and be truly objective, you can better assess your buyer's attitudes and produce the best analysis.

Careful analysis is a complex task, yet you want your document to be easy to read and use. Clarity and logical organization are therefore vital. For advice on sequencing an analytical report, consult the **reports** entry.

Remember these organizing guidelines

Conclude the organization step by finalizing your traditional or list outline. Include every topic in your document. Refer to your outline as you write your draft. Here are a few final reminders:

1. Group similar or related ideas so readers don't have to search for them.

2. In most business and technical writing, put conclusions or decisions first. Then give supporting facts and reasons. Make your details and background subordinate.

3. Remember to put your "bottom line," or most important point, on top. This information should appear first in a short document or in each section of a report. This placement will interest your readers and encourage them to continue reading.

4. If your document is long, put key ideas at the end as well as at the beginning. Your readers will expect a bottom-line statement in your conclusion, especially if it is a separate, headlined section.

5. Let your purpose and type of information determine your method of development. Don't be afraid to combine several M.O.D.'s to achieve the best possible structure for each part of your document.

You are now ready for Step 5 in the writing process: writing the first draft.

(See also **getting started**; **grouping ideas**; **Introduction to the Six Steps**; **organizing information**; **procedures**; **proposals**; **readers, analyzing**; **reports**.)

Which Method of Development Should You Use for Sequencing?

Here are some suggestions for organizing your document, but your best guides are the needs of your reader. You will probably use different methods in various parts of your document.

TYPE OF DOCUMENT	Order of importance	Chronology	Process	Organization in space	Compare/contrast	Specific to general or g. to s.	Analysis
Accident Reports		✓					
Analyses of Trends							✓
Annual Reports	✓						✓
Audits	✓						✓
Customer Service Letters	✓				✓		
Demographic Studies				✓			✓
Descriptions			✓	✓			
Economic Forecasts	✓						✓
Feasibility Studies					✓	✓	✓
Financial Analyses	✓				✓		✓
Findings	✓						
Growth Statistics		✓					✓
Handbooks			✓	✓			
Instructions			✓	✓			
Lab Reports	✓	✓	✓		✓		✓
Minutes	✓	✓					
Problem-solving memos	✓						✓
Procedures/ processes		✓	✓	✓			
Production Reports	✓						
Progress Reports	✓	✓					
Proposals	✓				✓	✓	
Research Results	✓				✓		
Sales Research Reports	✓			✓			
Technical Reports			✓		✓		✓
Test Protocols		✓					
Training		✓	✓		✓	✓	
Trip Reports	✓	✓		✓			
Trouble Reports	✓	✓					✓
User Manuals			✓	✓			
Work Orders		✓			✓		
Yearly Overviews	✓	✓			✓		

outlines

An **outline** is an organized list that shows the structure of your document, highlights important ideas, and subordinates less important details.

When to write an outline

Many people find traditional outlining arduous because they try to formulate key points *before* deciding what they really want to say. To write an outline easily, determine your purpose and audience, generate ideas, group them, and organize them.

In other words, complete the first four steps of the Six Steps to Reader-Centered Writing™ before finalizing your outline.

If, however, you know your topic well and are clear about your organization, you may jot down an accurate outline as part of Step 2, generating ideas. If you can do that, so much the better—you'll save time.

Start-up Strategies

Writers who have a clear vision of their content may begin Step 2 by developing a traditional outline with Roman numerals or decimal numbers that show subordination of ideas. Other writers need a strategy to get them started before they can develop a clearly sequenced outline. They may choose questioning, free writing, index cards, or Post-it Notes™ on a sheet of paper or bulletin board.

Consult the **getting started** entry for an explanation of these Start-up Strategies.

After free writing, for example, check to see if your idea sequence flows smoothly by outlining it. Your outline will show you if your free writing needs to be restructured or at least resequenced—and usually it will.

Traditional outlines

A traditional outline uses letters and Roman and Arabic numerals to indicate levels of information:

1. upper Roman numeral, period   I.

2. capital letter, period   A.

3. Arabic numeral, period   1.

4. lowercase letter, period   a.

5. Arabic numeral in parentheses   (1)

6. lowercase letter in parentheses   (a)

7. lowercase Roman numeral in parentheses   (i)

Decimal outlines

A decimal system uses only decimal points and increasing numbers; you may prefer it to the traditional system because it's easier to remember the progression. You may also add more subsections without fear of running out of numbers and letters.

Use a decimal system for long or technical documents like computer documentation.

```
    1.0
     1.1
     1.2
    2.0
     2.1
         2.1.1
         2.1.2
             2.1.2.1
             2.1.2.2
```

List outlines

A casual list of key ideas often occurs to writers in random sequence. Such a list outline may result from various Start-up Strategies, including questioning, free writing, or simply jotting down your **principal points** on index cards.

Listing your main ideas and seeing them together will make it easier for you to move on to Steps 3 and 4 of the writing process, grouping and sequencing information.

If you used the questioning Start-up Strategy, write down questions your readers would ask, then answer them. From those answers you can extract the key ideas for your document and list them.

If you used free writing to get your thoughts on paper, first read everything you have written, then highlight the most important ideas. Develop a list outline from those ideas. You can decide on sequencing later, in Step 4.

Keep in mind, too, that by outlining on a computer you can easily rearrange the sequence of your document.

Brainstorm outlines

This type of non-linear, free-form outline is a terrific tool for a long, complex document.

Put your purpose for writing in a circle at the center of a blank piece of paper. Think of an idea for your document, draw a line from the circle, and write your idea on the line. Draw other lines as more thoughts occur to you. Place related ideas on branches from the main lines.

Later you can circle groups of related ideas and number them in the best sequence for your document.

Visual outlines

Use the character-formatting functions of your word-processing program to highlight key ideas and create a visual outline. After you gather research or free write, mark ideas on the same level of importance with boldface, italics, or underlining.

This is a way to develop an outline using a headline hierarchy rather than numbers or letters. Themes will emerge as you proceed, and by highlighting significant ideas you'll be able to see the connections between them.

Using this system you tackle 2 of the Six Steps to Reader-Centered Writing at the same time: **getting started** with a Start-up Strategy (Step 2) and **grouping ideas** (Step 3).

If, for example, you are writing about the cause of a computer problem, research your topic and highlight in your notes all the information most relevant to causes.

When you go back and reread, you can decide which causes to discuss. Then, simply write a list of key words or phrases. Since you're not using a numbering system, it's easy to move entries around.

Here is an example of a visual outline in its early stages:

Introduction

Purpose of the project

How this project evolved

Inception

- Identification of need
- Exploratory study

Early alliances

- Venture capital
- Initial public offering

Executive summary

Recommendations

Analysis

Now you are ready to proceed to Step 4 of the writing process, **organizing information**.

The outlining function of your word processor

Most word-processing programs include an outlining feature that will show your entire outline or collapse it to display only the number levels you specify. Viewing only one numbering level at a time is a good way to check if your ideas are correctly subordinated and properly sequenced. You can easily resequence sections and change number levels; the program will automatically renumber them.

These automatic features take the drudgery out of changing your outline and prevent numbering errors.

(See also **getting started**, **Introduction to the Six Steps**, **organizing information**.)

P

page design: adding visual appeal

Writing documents that are reader centered doesn't mean targeting just the text. You must also keep your reader in mind when you consider **page design**. Especially with today's word-processing programs, you are no longer limited to the standard block-text format.

Think about your audience. What kind of visual design would work best for your readers?

Take the time to select the clearest design, and be consistent in applying it. You want to communicate your information while making the words as easy to read as possible.

Which design do you prefer?

How do you want the text on your pages to look? This will determine the page design that you choose. Consider margins and other white space, headlines, fonts, numbered or bulleted lists, and illustrations when you design a page.

Keep visual appeal and emphasis in mind as you place text and illustrations on the page. Don't crowd your pages; try for balance. Remember this key point: the look of a page helps determine how easily your audience will read and understand it.

Here is the same information in a reader-centered format. Notice how much easier this second example is to read.

The text is less dense. The bulleted list pulls essential information out of the paragraph, highlights it, and makes it easy to scan at a glance. The headlines help the reader by organizing related items in separate categories.

How you want the text on your pages to look? This will determine the page design that you choose. Consider these elements when you design a page:

- margins and other white space
- headlines
- fonts
- numbered or bulleted lists
- illustrations

Make the page visually appealing

Keep visual appeal and emphasis in mind as you place text and illustrations on the page. Don't crowd your pages; try for balance.

Bottom line

Remember this key point: the look of a page helps determine how easily your audience will read and understand it.

For more information, refer to the specific entries in the preceding bulleted list. Also consult the **Model Documents Appendix** for examples of page design.

Page layout

Most word-processing programs offer you countless options for every type of document. Consider the different layouts in the following illustration. You may left-justify or center your headlines. To make them stand out, use a different font or type size.

Also consider sidelines, or headlines in a column on the left side of the page. Choose multiple columns, of equal or different widths, to improve reading speed and comprehension.

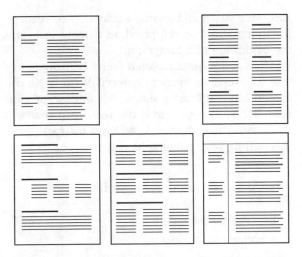

Tables, charts, and graphs are effective tools for displaying complex numerical data. Don't group them all together but intersperse them throughout the text if you can; the variety will hold your reader's interest.

Know your limitations

Page formatting on your own is fine for internal documents and simple letters, proposals, and reports. Complex, high-visibility documents may require a designer's professional touch. Consult the **graphics** entry for tips on dealing with a graphic designer.

(See also **charts or graphs**, **format**, **Model Documents Appendix**, **spacing**, **visual design**, **white space**.)

paragraphs: the building blocks of good writing

Paragraphs are blocks of related sentences that organize your material both logically and visually. Paragraphs mark essential divisions in your writing and offer visual and mental guideposts to readers. An indentation or skipped line usually indicates the beginning of a paragraph.

After you have completed Steps 1 through 4 of the Six Steps to Reader-Centered Writing™, you should have at least a simple list outline of your main ideas. This outline is the road map that will guide you through Step 5, **writing a draft**. From this outline your paragraphs will emerge.

What makes a good paragraph?

Every good paragraph has

- a single idea

- a topic sentence or headline that says what the paragraph is about

- transition words or phrases to connect ideas, both within and between paragraphs

- internal coherence—the paragraph includes only material that relates to the main idea.

If you try to keep all these paragraph guidelines in mind as you begin to write, you may risk losing ideas or interrupting a productive line of thinking.

Put all your thoughts and information on paper first. You can always impose more form and structure on your paragraphs during Step 6 as you edit your draft.

Paragraph preliminaries

Paragraphs organize our thinking and present ideas to readers in easy-to-comprehend pieces. Since ideas and the ways to communicate them are so diverse, no single paragraph style is right for every document.

The following discussion will cover typical paragraphs and offer some general guidelines.

We'll use a few paragraphs from the book *Write to the Top* to illustrate the principles that follow.

How free writing helps

Letting your thoughts range widely on any issues that come to mind—even personal ones—opens the channels for what you are trying to say. This process helps you transfer vague ideas circulating in your mind onto paper before they slip away. Once they are in black and white for you to read, others will soon follow.

Free writing helps you get rid of distracting thoughts that may be interfering with the serious writing you are trying to produce. When your mind keeps returning to last night's yoga class or the fifty dollars Cousin Nelson owes you, it's better to let all those distractions spill onto the paper, too. Soon the bothersome thoughts will be released and your mind will feel clearer, ready for other tasks. If you remember an errand you must do later, such as picking up a loaf of bread on the way home, jot it down on a separate list. This, too, will liberate your mind.

Free writing is, in a way, like meditating. It removes the pressure to create a perfect product: anything you write down is acceptable. The mere act of writing in a nonstop, unfettered way will give you the confidence that more and more thoughts will emerge. Suddenly, you have developed a rhythm. The pen is moving as if propelled across the page. This rhythm will stay with you—it gets you moving the way warm-up exercises help you to jog or dance better.

Paragraphs in the preceding example are longer than recommended in order to preserve the original wide format.

Unity: stick to one idea

Each paragraph should have one controlling idea that unifies it. In general state this idea in a topic sentence that announces what the paragraph is about.

In the third paragraph of the preceding sample, the topic sentence compares free writing to meditating. The rest of the paragraph discusses how they are alike.

All the sentences in a paragraph should support the topic sentence or idea. They should give details, explanations, definitions—whatever is necessary, depending on the method of development you use. Don't introduce new ideas that will distract the reader from the main point.

PLACE YOUR TOPIC SENTENCE CAREFULLY

Topic sentences often appear at the beginning of a paragraph, but they can go anywhere if they will strengthen your message. Even if a paragraph doesn't have an explicit topic sentence, it should have an implied central idea or question.

To see how the placement of a topic sentence affects emphasis, look at the middle paragraph of the free writing example. Put the first sentence— the topic sentence—at the end. Read the paragraph again, beginning with the second sentence.

Putting the topic sentence at the end changes the stress of the paragraph. Although there is no set rule about placement of topic sentences, busy readers prefer key ideas at the beginning of the paragraph, where they can be quickly identified.

USE YOUR TOPIC SENTENCE TO CREATE A PARAGRAPH HEADLINE

The outline topics you developed during Steps 3 and 4 of the writing process may become headlines for paragraphs and sections. After you write a paragraph under a tentative headline, check to make sure it still fits the information. You can always change the headline if your topic expands.

If you write your paragraph first and then want to give it a headline, start by identifying the core message of the paragraph. Pull out key words or a catchy phrase or question. It should tell readers what to expect or where to focus their attention.

The headline "How free writing helps" introduces the paragraphs in our preceding example. Readers expect, and find, information and advice on the technique of free writing.

COHERENCE: ORGANIZE INFORMATION LOGICALLY

Your paragraph is coherent when the information it contains is well organized. Your topic sentence is clear. Supporting sentences guide your reader from one point to the next, each of them explaining and expanding the main point of your topic sentence or headline.

Grammatically, coherence means that the verb tense and sequence as well as the writer's point of view are consistent in the paragraph. Pronouns, repetition, and transition words will help you achieve coherence.

In the third paragraph of the free writing example, notice that *rhythm* appears twice. *Suddenly* provides an unexpected and interesting transition. These techniques help hold the paragraph together.

As you organize your paragraphs, keep in mind the methods of development discussed in the **organizing information** entry. Apply them to your paragraphs as needed.

The method of development you choose should serve the purpose of your writing. Procedures, for example, should be sequenced chronologically in the order of use.

Be sure to consider each paragraph in context. What kinds of paragraphs come before and after? You'll bore your readers if you use the same method of development in each paragraph.

Look at *How free writing helps*: the first and second paragraphs follow a *process* method of development, but the third switches to *comparison/contrast*. Varying your writing this way will maintain your readers' interest.

Linking paragraphs

Though each paragraph should discuss a single topic, all your paragraphs should be related to each other. They should exhibit a logical train of thought.

USE TRANSITIONS BETWEEN PARAGRAPHS

You can connect paragraphs in several ways:

- Repeat a key word. In the preceding example, the second and third paragraphs both begin with the words *free writing*. This repetition helps connect the paragraphs.

- Anticipate the main idea of your next paragraph. For example, the last sentence in the second sample paragraph mentions the mind; the next paragraph compares free writing to meditating.

- Use transition words like *as a result* or *in contrast*.

- Use demonstrative pronouns. *This* and *that* will help you link ideas.

ARE YOU HAVING TROUBLE CONNECTING?

Sometimes your information is disjointed and doesn't lend itself to easy transition between paragraphs. Nevertheless, this is when you need transitions most. Ask yourself:

- Why am I throwing all these facts at the reader?
- What is my point?
- How does this information link together?
- Do I need to elaborate on my ideas?

You may not know the answer until you've written more of your document. After the first draft, check for missing transitions and add them to connect information.

Choosing an appropriate paragraph length

In general, length depends on the kind of writing.

- Paragraphs in business letters and reports should be five or six lines long.

- For technical writing, make paragraphs three or four lines long because the information tends to be more dense.

- Academic journals and books usually have paragraphs longer than five or six lines.

- Newsletters and other documents printed in narrow columns need short paragraphs.

If your paragraph topic needs a longer treatment, break it up into subsections and give each subsection a paragraph.

VARYING PARAGRAPH LENGTH

Your paragraphs should not all be exactly the same length. If they are, your document will have little visual appeal. Short paragraphs attract attention, so you may want to use them to make your most important points.

Paragraphs have different purposes

Paragraphs present different types of information:

- purpose
- recommendations
- study results
- analysis
- supporting data
- procedures
- background
- summary

Your purpose and audience, as analyzed in your Focus Sheet™, will help you decide on paragraph content and organization.

OPENING PARAGRAPHS

The purpose of your opening paragraph is to capture your readers' attention. The opening paragraph of the book *Write to the Top* presents a scenario that we are all familiar with. The present tense helps create a universal situation we can all identify with:

Tom LeBlanc glances at his watch and then back to the empty page in front of him. The ticking of the wall clock grows louder, and a siren outside the window makes him lose his train of thought for the second time. The right words are just beyond his reach.

SINGLE-SENTENCE PARAGRAPHS

Single-sentence paragraphs are acceptable every now and then. Because they stand out from longer paragraphs, they can be quite emphatic and forceful. Use them sparingly, or you will diminish their impact.

Here are two more paragraphs from *Write to the Top*. Notice how forceful and direct the one-sentence paragraph is.

The "Be Your Own Editor" Checklist that follows serves as an outline for this chapter. More important, it will become the checklist you use from now on to make sure your document is reader centered. The Checklist reminds you to refine and polish the draft, then guides you through the remaining steps—right up to your final signature.

Now let's look more closely at each phase in the editing process—beginning with a quick review of Steps 1-4.

TRANSITIONAL PARAGRAPHS

In some long documents or documents with equations, you may need whole paragraphs for transitions. These are usually short bridges from one part of the document to the next. The preceding single-sentence paragraph is a good example of a transitional paragraph.

CLOSING PARAGRAPHS

Your last paragraph may summarize or restate essential information without being redundant. It's the last idea readers take away with them. The closing paragraph of *Write to the Top*, Part 2, provides a brief summary—but also reinforces the core idea of cooperation.

The tips, techniques, and strategies you've read in this section will help you to be more in control of the group dynamics that affect the writing process. We don't write in a vacuum—we write *for* readers and sometimes *with* other writers. As we develop more strategic skill and political savvy, our writing becomes a tool to help us achieve our personal and professional goals. Our strategies should not be used at people's expense, but rather to win their cooperation.

Alternatives to paragraphs

Paragraphs aren't the only way to present information. Vary your presentation to keep your readers' interest alive.

VERTICAL LISTS

If you have a long paragraph with lots of information, consider a bulleted or numbered list. Vertical lists

- stand out from text
- can be read at a glance
- break up the text
- create white space
- are easy on the eyes.

CHARTS, TABLES, AND GRAPHS

Charts and tables can also present information in a visually concise and easy-to-read way. Use them for statistics or other dense information that doesn't lend itself to sentence form.

(See also **clear writing**, **headlines**, **Introduction to the Six Steps**, **lists**, **transitions**, **unity**.)

parallel structure

Present parallel ideas in parallel grammatical form. **Parallel structure** means that sentence elements with identical functions have identical constructions.

Parallel structure has several purposes:

- to help make sentences coherent
- to provide emphasis through a repeated structure
- to organize ideas economically
- to balance equal ideas
- to make writing—and therefore reading— flow smoothly

How to create parallel constructions

In parallel constructions, equal words or phrases must have the same grammatical form or syntax. These forms can be nouns, verbs, prepositional phrases, infinitives, or gerunds.

instead of:	Harold plans to bring the *display easel* and the *manuals* to the seminar, and also *include the work sheets*. [not parallel]
write:	Harold plans to bring *the display easel*, *the manuals*, and *the work sheets* to the seminar. [parallel nouns—*the* may be repeated or not]
instead of:	By next Monday please *complete* the survey, *analyze* the statistics, and *you should hand in* the report. [not parallel]
write:	By next Monday please *complete* the survey, *analyze* the statistics, and *hand in* the report. [parallel verbs]
instead of:	The safety committee voted *for the installation of* more lighting, *to*

	repave the driveway, and *to put* treads on the walkway. [not parallel]
write:	The safety committee voted *to install* more lighting, *to repave* the driveway, and *to put* treads on the walkway. [parallel infinitives—*to* may be repeated or not]
instead of:	The agenda for the meeting includes *the election of* new officers, *discussing* the by-laws, and *setting* a date for the next meeting. [not parallel]
write:	The agenda for the meeting includes *electing* new officers, *discussing* the by-laws, and *setting* a date for the next meeting. [parallel gerunds]
instead of:	Please put some extra space *beneath* the title, *between* the charts, and *the illustrations* on page 3 are too crowded. [not parallel]
write:	Please put some extra space *beneath* the title, *between* the charts, and *around* the illustrations on page 3. [parallel prepositional phrases]

Can you find the one item that isn't parallel to the others in the following list?

Here are some suggestions for streamlining sentences:

- Use as few words as possible.
- Don't repeat yourself.
- Active rather than passive verbs.
- Break long sentences into shorter ones.

The item *Active rather than passive verbs* is not a complete sentence beginning with a verb, like the others. Change this phrase to *Use active rather than passive verbs*, and you have a parallel list.

Coordinating elements

Use the following phrases as a frame for parallel structure.

neither . . . nor
either . . . or
both . . . and
not only . . . but also

These phrases, called coordinating elements, follow the same rules as other parallel constructions. An idea that follows the second element should have the same grammatical form as the idea after the first.

The new contractor will *both* assess the damage *and* recommend repairs.

Their report was *neither* timely *nor* complete.

Their report was *not only* timely, *but also* complete.

Once you start a comparison using a coordinating element, stay with an equal word or phrase to complete the thought.

instead of: The report was not only *timely* but *it was also complete*. [not parallel]

write: The report was not only *timely* but also *complete*. [parallel adjectives]

or: Not only *was the report timely*, but *it was* also *complete*. [parallel clauses]

Faulty parallelism

Parallel constructions are faulty when the ideas are equal, but the grammatical forms are not.

instead of: He liked his new job because of the people, the challenge, and *it was a productive environment to work in*.

write: He liked his new job because of the people, the challenge, and *the productive working environment*.

instead of: Marcia prefers to come in late rather than *leaving* early.

write: Marcia prefers to come in late rather than *to leave* early.

False parallelisms

Parallel constructions are false when ideas that are not equal or balanced are put in parallel grammatical forms.

instead of: This application requires my employment history, my educational background, and *I have to finish it by Friday.*

write: This application requires my employment history and educational background. I have to finish it by Friday.

---

parentheses

Parentheses ( ) are marks of punctuation that enclose words or sentences. Often the material in parentheses isn't as important as the rest of the sentence or paragraph.

> The task force reached no agreement about the recommended level of iron enrichment (see Table 3.1) in enriched flour.

Generally, the material in parentheses is not as closely connected to the rest of the sentence as material set off by commas or dashes. Writers often use parentheses when they want to add information but don't want to distract readers from the main point of the sentence.

Notice the following sentences punctuated three ways.

> We expected the shipment of circuit boards, which we ordered in January, by last Thursday. [commas]

> We expected the shipment of circuit boards—which we ordered in January—by last Thursday. [dashes]

We expected the shipment of circuit boards
(which we ordered in January) by last Thursday.
[parentheses]

The parentheses in the third example indicate
most clearly that the information inside them is
not very closely connected to the rest of the sentence.

Uses of parentheses

1. To enclose explanatory material within a sentence or paragraph.

   The danger of this pesticide can hardly be exaggerated (EPA studies having found it toxic at low
   levels). Furthermore, this study concludes . . .

2. To set off information that breaks the flow of
   thought.

   Ohio (the Buckeye State) has many artificial
   recreational lakes.

3. To express an opinion.

   Ben expects us to complete the R & D phase by
   February (which strikes me as unrealistic).

4. To enclose references or citations outside the
   main thought of a sentence.

   The bandgap cell contains two npn transistors
   (see Fig. 3) which differ in emitter area by 12x.

5. To set off numbers in a list within a sentence.

   We need protocols that are (1) user-level and (2)
   systems-based.

6. To enclose acronyms or abbreviations previously written out.

   At the end of fiscal year (FY) 1989, we showed a
   loss of 1.1 million. By the end of FY 1990, our
   profits were 1.7 million.

   For this year's Christmas charity, we have chosen
   the International Rescue Committee (IRC).

Parentheses with other marks of punctuation

1. PERIODS

If the whole sentence is within parentheses, the period goes inside the parentheses.

> (See Appendix A for a complete listing of conference sites.)

If part of the sentence is in parentheses and that part comes at the end, the period goes outside the parentheses.

> The danger of this pesticide can hardly be exaggerated (see Table 1.1).

As in the preceding example, even if the parenthetical part at the end of a sentence is a complete sentence, the period goes outside the parentheses. Unless the parenthetical sentence is very short, however, avoid adding it to another sentence.

It's often better to let it stand on its own. In that case, remember: the period will go inside the parentheses.

instead of:	The danger of this pesticide can hardly be exaggerated (EPA studies have found it toxic at low levels).
write:	The danger of this pesticide can hardly be exaggerated. (EPA studies have found it toxic at low levels.)

2. COMMAS

If parenthetical material occurs in a part of the sentence that is followed by a comma, put the comma after the parentheses.

> The danger of this pesticide can hardly be exaggerated (see Table 1.1), so we will work to reverse federal approval of it immediately.

3. BRACKETS

Use brackets [. . .] to set off parenthetical material already within parentheses. Since this construction is cumbersome and hard to read, avoid it whenever you can.

instead of: The danger of this pesticide can hardly be exaggerated. (EPA studies [1982, 1985, 1990, 1994] have found it toxic at low levels.)

write: The danger of this pesticide can hardly be exaggerated. EPA studies (1982, 1985, 1990, 1994) have found it toxic at low levels.

A final hint

Although parentheses clearly separate comment from content, use this technique sparingly. Parentheses call attention to themselves as separators and can make you sound uncertain of your own message.

(See also **commas**, **dashes**, **punctuation**, **subordination**.)

participles

Participles are verb forms that commonly end in *-ing* or *-ed* and are used as adjectives.

Participles have properties of both verbs and adjectives. Like a verb, a participle can have an object or complement. And like an adjective, a participle can modify a noun or pronoun.

Hoping to finish the proposal on time, Sally asked her team for help. [*Hoping* modifies *Sally*. *To finish the proposal on time* is the direct object of *hoping*.]

With his schedule *published*, Larry began to plan a series of meetings to organize the project. [*Published* modifies *schedule*.]

Types of participles

A participle can never be the main verb of a sentence because it is incomplete.

instead of:	We all voted to re-elect Samantha to the management committee. Her idea *offering* the best solution. [The second sentence is a fragment.]
write:	We all voted to re-elect Samantha to the management committee, her idea *offering* the best solution.
or:	We all voted to re-elect Samantha to the management committee. Her idea *offered* the best solution.

PRESENT PARTICIPLES

A *present participle* ends in *-ing*.

The workshop was *rewarding* for all the administrators who attended. [*Rewarding* modifies *workshop*.]

Working overtime, we finished the proposal by the deadline. [*Working* modifies *we*.]

Present participle forms can also serve as nouns. When they do, they are called *gerunds*.

Finishing the proposal meant *working overtime*. [*Finishing* is a gerund beginning the noun phrase that is the subject of the sentence. *Working* is a gerund beginning the noun phrase that is the object.]

PAST PARTICIPLES

A *past participle* is a verb form that usually ends in *-ed*. For most verbs, the past participle form looks exactly the same as the simple past tense. For irregular verbs, however, the past participle takes a different form from the simple past, often changing the vowel or ending in *-t, -en, -d,* or *-n*.

The *dropped* charges will not appear on his permanent record. [*Dropped* modifies *charges*.]

This financial report, *written* last month, needs *updated* figures by Friday. [*Written* modifies *report*; *updated* modifies *figures*.]

Participial phrases

A participial phrase consists of

- a participle
- its object or complement
- any modifiers.

Such a phrase acts as an adjective in a sentence, modifying a noun or pronoun.

> *Knowing how close the deadline was*, Katia called a meeting of her team. [The participial phrase *Knowing how close the deadline was* modifies the noun *Katia*.]

> *Confused by the legal jargon*, I called my lawyer. [The participial phrase *Confused by the legal jargon* modifies the pronoun *I*.]

> Ted managed to salvage the contract, *considered a lost cause*. [The participial phrase *considered a lost cause* modifies the noun *contract*.]

Like all modifiers, participial phrases should come as near as possible to the words they modify.

instead of:	*Considered a lost cause*, Ted managed to salvage the contract. [Was Ted a lost cause?]
write:	Ted managed to salvage the contract, *considered a lost cause*. [*Considered a lost cause* logically modifies *contract*.]

(See also **dangling modifiers**, **gerunds**, **misplaced modifiers**, **object**, **verbs**.)

---

parts of speech

To describe how meaning is created, words are grouped into categories called **parts of speech**. There are eight parts of speech that define the roles of all the words in a sentence:

1. verb   5. adverb
2. noun   6. conjunction
3. pronoun   7. preposition
4. adjective   8. interjection

Hooray! [interjection] We [pronoun] won [verb] the federal [adjective] grant [noun], and [conjunction] now [adverb] we must put together our team of [preposition] engineers.

For a description of each part of speech and its use, look under its separate entry.

The same word can become another part of speech if it serves a different purpose in another sentence.

They *update* the report weekly. [update is a verb]

The *update* was late because of the holiday. [update is a noun]

(See also **adjectives**, **adverbs**, **articles**, **conjunctions**, **interjections**, **nouns**, **prepositions**, **pronouns**, **verbs**.)

---

per

Per is a Latin word that means "through," "by means of," or "by the."

per diem   *per* capita   *per* annum

Per is acceptable in these Latin phrases. But in general, you should avoid *per* in business writing because it sounds outdated and awkward. Instead, use *a* or *an* when possible.

instead of: Nordwell pays $15 *per* hour for temporary work in this department.

write: Nordwell pays $15 *an* hour for temporary work in this department.

Per or *as per* meaning "according to" or "in accordance with" is widely used in business writing, but it is imprecise. When you edit, replace *per* with a specific phrase.

instead of:	*Per our conversation* this morning, I will adjust next month's bill.
write:	*As you requested* . . . *As we discussed* . . .
instead of:	*As per your suggestion,* we will leave the vault door unlocked from 12 to 1 p.m.
write:	*As you suggested,* we will leave the vault door unlocked from 12 to 1 p.m.

---

performance reviews

Performance reviews are some of the most difficult documents to write. Use the following guidelines to produce performance reviews that are both supportive and effective.

Bolster self-esteem

An underlying goal of reviewing employee performance is maintaining the reviewee's self-esteem. This is a particular challenge because the review is written instead of given orally, so a reviewee can reread it.

If you need to be critical, focus on the behavior, not the person. An employee who feels competent is more likely to behave competently.

Don't be vague

It's not enough to tell people that they did a good job. You should cite specific examples of behavior so the reviewee isn't left wondering, "Well, what *did* I do?"

Always support any feedback with facts, data, and specific examples. If you don't, your vague statements will not reinforce the desired behavior you so much appreciate.

general:	Your work is improving.
specific:	You met every deadline in the last four months.
general:	I appreciate your support.
specific:	I appreciate your taking the time and effort to cover Dan's day off.
general:	Your work is slipping.
specific:	Last month, nine out of ten of your reports were accurate. This month, however, four out of ten had to be redone because of errors.
	Please start double-checking your typed reports against the computer printouts. Some of your errors may be typos rather than miscalculations.

Do unto others

When writing a review, keep in mind the kind of review you would like to receive—it's probably the same kind you should be writing. Write personably, so readers feels you are speaking to them. Don't reprimand, psychoanalyze, or convey superiority.

Don't mistake actions for attitudes

People are accountable for their actions, not their attitudes. Focusing on actions helps people under-stand where they are going wrong. You will be perceived as more objective and helpful.

On the other hand, if you focus on attitudes, your feedback may be perceived as a personal attack. It may frustrate readers and put them on the defensive.

instead of:	You seemed upset with the customer.

write: When you interrupted the customer
                  and said, "I already told you that,"
                  you sounded upset with her.

Turn negatives into positives

If you sound too negative, you're unlikely to get
the results you're looking for. One way to avoid
sounding negative is to use *and* instead of *but*
whenever you can.

instead of: Your first report was accurate, but
                  your second one didn't measure up
                  to it.

write: Your first report was accurate and
                  your second one had the following
                  errors.

or: Your first report was accurate.
                  Although the second report had the
                  following errors, the rest of the
                  information was correct.

Remember that feedback goes both ways

Relying on your own assessment of someone's job
performance doesn't always give you the complete
picture. Include the employees in your process—
ask them to write their own self-assessments.

Both reviews should also include performance
objectives, development plans, and goals for the
upcoming cycle.

Exchange documents before the scheduled
review. By taking the time to review each other's
expectations and opinions, each is better prepared
to benefit from the review. Also, any negative feelings incited by the written assessments will have
time to settle.

Once together, supervisor and employee—or
fellow team members—can work as partners in
discussing performance objectives, reviewing
accomplishments, and setting goals.

A final note

When writing a performance review, remember to

- maintain self-esteem
- be specific
- solicit feedback.

Approaching all reviews this way will improve performance. You'll promote meaningful communication between supervisors and employees or coaches and team members.

---

periods

The **period** (.) is a mark of punctuation that usually indicates that a sentence has come to an end. The preferred British term for a period is *full stop*.

> If your modem comes without a hardware handshaking cable, you'll have to buy one separately.

In sentences

Use a period at the end of most imperative sentences that make a demand or request.

> Call this number to order your special cable.

Periods are appropriate at the end of polite requests or commands that sound like questions, especially if you expect *yes* as a response.

> May I suggest that you call this number to order your special cable.

If you deliberately write a sentence fragment to serve as a full sentence, put a period after it.

> No discounts after May 31.
> Not including tax and shipping charges.

Use periods after short words or phrases that may answer "yes" or "no" questions or serve as transitions.

Next subject, please.   Of course.   Yes.
No, nothing.   Correct.

With abbreviations and acronyms

Many abbreviations require periods. The trend is to omit them in many acronyms.

Dr.   IBM
Corp.   FDA
etc.   YMCA
Barry J. Roper

In a sentence that ends with an abbreviation, use only one period.

On weekends the business library will be open until 3:30 p.m.

If a sentence ends in an exclamation or question mark after an abbreviation, use both a period and the end mark.

What if you need access to the business library on weekends after 3:30 p.m.?

With numbers

Use a period between a whole number and a decimal fraction.

$4.24   27.33 percent   9.5 gallons

Omit the period after ordinal numbers.

2nd   3rd   4th   36th

Roman numerals do not take periods.

VI   XX   LXVIII

In lists

Put periods after numbers in a vertical list.

These are the Six Steps to Reader-Centered Writing™:

1. Analyze your audience and define your purpose.
2. Use a Start-up Strategy.
3. Group information under headlines.
4. Sequence your ideas.
5. Write the first draft.
6. Edit for clarity, conciseness, and accuracy.

Some lists of items aren't complete sentences themselves, but together they complete a sentence. In this case, put a period after the last item only. It is also acceptable to omit any end punctuation.

Marketing will present its projections for the next fiscal year in

- hardware
- software
- networking
- applications development.

With quotation marks

Periods always go inside quotation marks, whether or not the quotation is a full sentence.

The report states, "Focus groups in Taiwan will help us determine the marketability of our new models."

She told me to mark it "done."

Don't put a period after a quoted sentence that does not end the main sentence. Instead, use a comma.

instead of: "Focus groups in Taiwan will help
                    us determine the marketability of
                    our new models." the report states.

write: "Focus groups in Taiwan will help
                    us determine the marketability of
                    our new models," the report states.

WITH PARENTHESES

If a sentence ends with words in parentheses, put the period outside the parentheses.

The danger of this pesticide can hardly be exaggerated (see Table 1.1).

If a whole sentence appears in parentheses, put the period inside the parentheses.

(See Appendix A for a complete listing of alpha test sites.)

Sometimes a sentence appears in parentheses within another sentence. If the parenthetical material is closely related to the thought in the main sentence, you can omit the capital letter or period.

Please submit the text by Monday (we will proofread it) and the graphics by Friday.

If you enumerate items in a list with numbers in parentheses, don't put a period after the parentheses.

We need protocols that are (1) user-level and (2) systems-based.

As ellipses

Three spaced periods that indicate omitted words are called ellipses. They are usually used in quoted material. If your quote comes at the end of a sentence, insert a fourth period for end punctuation.

The minutes stated that "the new Nickerson package offers many benefits . . . . Overall, it's the one this committee recommends."

As leaders

Leaders are spaced periods that connect one item to another in the same line in Tables of Contents.

(See also **leaders**, **lists**, **numbers**, **parentheses**, **quotation marks**.)

person

Personal pronouns

For personal pronouns, **person** refers to whom or what the pronoun represents.

First person	I, me, my, we, ours, us
Second person	you, your
Third person	he, him, his, she, her, hers, it, its, they, them, their

1. *First person* is the speaker or writer.

   I revised the second chapter of the manual.

2. *Second person* is the person addressed.

   You revised the second chapter of the manual.

3. *Third person* is the person or thing spoken about.

   She (singular) revised the second chapter of the manual.

   They (plural) revised the second chapter of the manual.

Pronouns affect other parts of speech

All nouns are considered third person, but pronouns change form for different persons. Verbs regularly change form in the present tense to show the third person singular.

   I remember. [first person]
   You remember. [second person]
   She *remembers*. [third person singular]
   They remember. [third person plural]

Use person consistently

Be sure all the pronouns in a paragraph reflect the same relationship between the writer and the reader. If you shift persons in the middle of an idea, your writing will be confusing.

instead of: Technical writers must consult the
                  legal department about *your* copy-
                  right issues.

write: Technical writers must consult the
                  legal department about *their* copy-
                  right issues.

or: Consult the legal department for
                  information about *your* copyright
                  issues.

(See also **numbers**, **point of view**, **pronouns**,
verbs.)

---

personal pronouns

Personal pronouns refer to people and things.

As subjects

The subjective personal pronouns are

I, we, you, he, she, it, they.

> *I* can handle the project if *you* will give me a chance.

> *She* signed the contract before *it* was due.

As objects

The objective personal pronouns are

me, you, him, her, us, it, them.

> Send *me* the updates and, after I enter *them*, I'll
> give *you* back the final version.

> The pension plan lets *us* invest an additional per-
> centage every month.

As possessives

There are two types of possessive pronouns: those
that precede a noun and those that stand alone.

Preceding the noun:
my, your, his, her, its, our, their

> *your* terminal   *its* voltage   *their* experiment

Standing alone:
mine, yours, his, hers, its, ours, theirs

> The decision is *hers*.   *Ours* was the best proposal.

Some possessive pronouns sound like contractions. Be careful not to confuse them.

Possessive	*Contraction*
its	it's (it is *or* it has)
their	they're (they are)
theirs	there's (there is *or* there has)
your	you're (you are)

Personal pronoun or reflexive pronoun?

Reflexive pronouns (myself, ourselves) cannot replace personal pronouns.

instead of:	Paul and *myself* planned the sales seminar last year.
write:	Paul and *I* planned the sales seminar last year.
instead of:	You may rely on *ourselves* to implement the new procedures.
write:	You may rely on *us* to implement the new procedures.

Use a reflexive pronoun only to refer back to and intensify the noun or pronoun used earlier. The pronoun must match the noun it refers to in person and number.

> The vice president *himself* gave the address.

> They finished the proposal *themselves*.

> Ask *yourself* if it's worth it. [The subject *you* is understood in this imperative sentence.]

Personal pronouns and tone

Personal pronouns are acceptable in most informal business writing. If you substitute words that create distance from readers, your writing may sound too stiff and formal.

instead of:	*The company* wishes to thank all participants.
write:	*We* wish to thank all participants.
instead of:	*One* can easily apply the formula to *one's* monthly budget as well.
write:	*You* can easily apply the formula to *your* monthly budget as well.

(See also **case**, **person**, **point of view**, **possessive case**, **pronouns**, **reflexive pronouns**, **tone**.)

personal references

In a **personal reference**, you use the name of the person you're writing to. This kind of reference is also called *direct address*.

> Thank you, *Cecily*, for sending me a copy of your article.

> I look forward to our meeting next week, *Julian*.

Always set off the person's name in commas.

If you overuse personal references your letter may sound like a mass-market mailing. Omit them altogether if you don't know your correspondent personally.

(See also **commas**, **emphasis**, **letters**, **tone**.)

phrases

Phrases are groups of words that can't stand alone as complete sentences because they are missing either a subject or a verb.

after the rain   staying late tonight
for many telecommunications providers

Noun, verb, adjective, and adverb phrases are classified by their function in the sentence. Prepositional, participial, infinitive, and gerund phrases are classified by the kind of word that introduces them. As the following examples will show, some of these categories overlap.

Noun phrases

A noun phrase includes a noun and any modifiers. Like nouns, these phrases can be subjects, objects, or complements.

> *The new manager* comes from Chicago. [The noun phrase *the new manager* is the subject of the sentence.]

> Please call *our tax accountant* with these new figures. [The noun phrase *our tax accountant* is the object of the verb *call*.]

> Ernest's expertise is *corporate tax law*. [The noun phrase *corporate tax law* is the complement of the subject *expertise*.]

Verb phrases

A verb phrase includes a verb and any helping or auxiliary verbs. Sometimes a verb phrase includes an adverb.

> Marcia *was supposed* to call this morning.

> The architect *had almost finished* the plans before the takeover. [*Almost* is an adverb.]

Adjective phrases

Adjective phrases act as modifiers of nouns or pronouns. These phrases can consist of adjectives, adverbs, or participial, infinitive, or prepositional phrases.

Working late, we managed to finish the proposal on time. [The participial phrase *working late* modifies *we*.]

We purchased a copier *with color capability*. [The prepositional phrase *with color capability* modifies *copier*.]

Adverb phrases

An adverb phrase acts as a modifier of adjectives, verbs, or other adverbs. These phrases can also be infinitive or prepositional phrases.

Nadia left *on the early bus* to catch a plane to Topeka. [The prepositional phrase *on the early bus* modifies the verb *left*.]

Nadia left early *to catch a plane to Topeka*. [The infinitive phrase *to catch a plane to Topeka* modifies the verb *left*.]

Prepositional phrases

A prepositional phrase includes a preposition, its object, and any modifiers.

After the heavy rain, the foyer *of the main complex* was flooded *for three days*.

Prepositional phrases act as modifiers of nouns or verbs.

We purchased a copier *with color capability*. [The phrase *with color capability* modifies *copier*.]

The parcel came *in the mail*. [The phrase *in the mail* modifies the verb *came*.]

Prepositional phrases can also modify the objects of other prepositional phrases.

The document you need is in Helen's directory *in her projects folder*. [*In her projects folde*r is a prepositional phrase modifying *directory*, which is itself the object of the first preposition *in*.]

Participial phrases

A participial phrase includes a participle, any object, and its modifiers.

This kind of phrase acts as an adjective.

Working late, we managed to finish the proposal on time. [The present participle *working late* modifies *we*.]

Printed on recycled paper, the brochure met with the committee's approval. [The past participle *printed* modifies *brochure*.]

Infinitive phrases

An infinitive phrase includes an infinitive (*to* plus the main form of the verb), its object, and any modifiers. Infinitive phrases can act as nouns or as modifiers.

To open a new branch by December is our goal. [The infinitive phrase *To open a new branch by December* is the subject of the sentence.]

Our need *to meet the loan payment schedule* forced us to postpone the purchase of new test equipment. [*To meet the loan payment schedule* is an infinitive phrase used as an adjective to modify *need*.]

Mary is sorry *to leave Toledo*. [*To leave Toledo* modifies *sorry* and is therefore an adverb phrase.]

Gerund phrases

The *-ing* form of a verb used as a noun is called a gerund. A gerund phrase includes the gerund itself plus an object and any modifiers.

Using keyboard commands is much faster. [*Using keyboard commands* acts as the subject of the verb *is*.]

Hans is worried about *finding good freelancers*. [*Finding good freelancers* acts as the object of the preposition *about*.]

Restrictive and nonrestrictive phrases

A restrictive phrase is necessary to the meaning of the sentence. Don't set it off with commas in almost all cases.

> We've had so many meetings lately. The one *called only yesterday* threw off everyone's schedule. [The participial phrase *called only yesterday* is necessary to the meaning of the sentence; otherwise, you wouldn't know which meeting.]

A nonrestrictive phrase is not necessary to a sentence, and omitting it does not change essential meaning. Set nonrestrictive phrases off with commas.

> This meeting, *called only yesterday*, threw off everyone's schedule. [The participial phrase *called only yesterday* is not necessary to the meaning of the sentence.]

(See also **gerunds**, **infinitive phrases**, **modifiers**, **participles**, **prepositions**, **restrictive and nonrestrictive elements**, **verbs**.)

pictograms

Pictograms, also called pictographs, are diagrams representing statistical data in pictorial form. The most common type of pictogram is a bar chart, with the bar replaced by a series of relevant symbols. The number of symbols reflects the quantity represented.

For example, use cars to represent the number of vehicles produced. Align the cars like a bar in a bar chart. Mark the axis to reflect the scale, and indicate the car production total represented by each symbolic car in the legend.

In order to show a car manufacturer's annual production, you could use cars, trucks, and vans to represent each division's production.

Following is a pictogram presenting data on car color popularity.

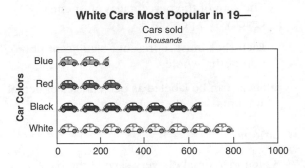

White Cars Most Popular in 19—

Cars sold
Thousands

(See also **bar or column charts**, **charts or graphs**, **tables**.)

pie or circle charts

A **pie chart** is a circular display divided into wedges called *slices*. Each slice represents numerical data as a percentage of the whole. A slice of pie shows the relative proportion of that category.

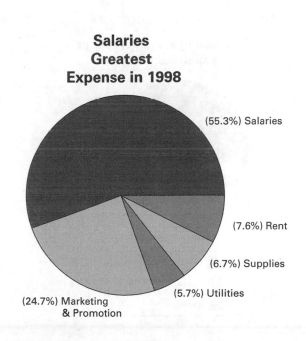

**Salaries
Greatest
Expense in 1998**

(55.3%) Salaries

(7.6%) Rent

(6.7%) Supplies

(5.7%) Utilities

(24.7%) Marketing & Promotion

- The sum of the percentages must equal exactly 100 percent.

- Each slice must represent a significant portion of the whole.

- Slices can be labeled as percentages or actual amounts—or, preferably, both.

Cautions

1. Categorize or label every slice of the pie.
2. Avoid small slices that cannot be distinguished or labeled.
3. Don't display multiple sets of data on one pie. Don't group expenses, costs, and sales into one pie. These items do not add up to form a unity—and they do not add up to 100 percent.

Exploded pie slices

A slice can be moved slightly away from the pie for emphasis.

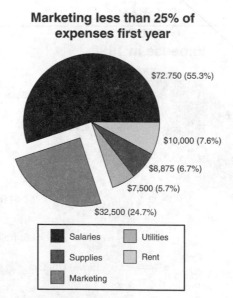

Marketing less than 25% of expenses first year

$72.750 (55.3%)

$10,000 (7.6%)

$8,875 (6.7%)

$7,500 (5.7%)

$32,500 (24.7%)

- Salaries
- Supplies
- Marketing
- Utilities
- Rent

- The exploded slice should convey your key message. It must be significant enough to warrant the special attention.

- A series of pie charts with varying slices removed is an effective technique for presentations. Label the exploded slice and use it to introduce the topic of your paragraph or, in an oral presentation, your slide or transparency.

Three-dimensional pie charts

If the pie has only a few slices, a three-dimensional view may be visually powerful. Personal preference or a need for variety will dictate whether you select a three-dimensional graph.

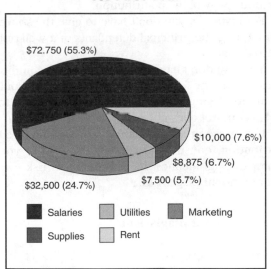

**Salaries Greatest Expense
for First Year**

(See also **charts or graphs**, **tables**.)

plagiarism

Plagiarism means using someone else's words, but passing them off as your own. Plagiarizing published material is illegal. Beware, too, of plagiarizing other kinds of material, such as unpublished works or ideas you hear in a meeting.

Ideas as such are not legally protected under copyright laws that govern published words, music, and images. However, you should still acknowledge your sources when you borrow other people's work.

When you don't give an appropriate attribution for others' words or ideas, you are plagiarizing.

What is the general rule?

Basically, you must acknowledge all outside information. Only if the information is common knowledge, available in many references, can you use it without providing an attribution.

For instance, you don't have to give the source for naming the principal defendants of a well-publicized trial.

You also don't have to give a source for common expressions or for conclusions that anyone could come to. Saying that World War II was a boon for U.S. economy does not require a footnote.

If you aren't sure whether your writing needs attribution, consult an expert in the field or your company's guidelines. Be careful not to risk even unintentional plagiarism.

Ways to avoid plagiarism

USE QUOTATION MARKS

Always put someone's exact words in quotation marks and give the source in a footnote or endnote. Even if the exact words are only a short phrase or figure of speech, put them in quotation marks.

The ruling of the judge was that "no sufficient evidence has been presented to warrant pursuing this matter."

GIVE THE SOURCE FOR IDEAS THAT YOU PARAPHRASE

Paraphrased information does not have to be in quotation marks. However, if you discuss an idea that isn't originally your own, you must state your source. Otherwise, your readers will think the idea is yours.

We want to target new areas in fiscal '95, and, as Team A's study concluded, limited test marketing in several cities simultaneously would be the best approach.

KEEP CAREFUL NOTES

If you're doing research or taking notes at a meeting, be sure you note which ideas or words are directly from someone else.

Develop a system to differentiate, in your notes, your own thoughts from the ones you've copied from other people. Then, when you write your report, you will be able to cite sources and avoid plagiarism.

KNOW THE COPYRIGHT LAWS

Check the relevant copyright laws before you copy or distribute published material. It's almost always a violation to copy an article or document without permission, and sometimes you have to pay for the privilege.

The effects of plagiarism

Plagiarizing is both dishonest and unethical, and often illegal. If your plagiarism is discovered, it will reflect badly on you and your company. Serious legal and personal consequences, including job loss, can result.

(See also **copyright**, **documenting sources**, **quotation marks**, **quotations**, **research**.)

---

point of view (p.o.v.)

Point of view refers to who is speaking, who is spoken to, or who is spoken about. The personal pronouns usually establish the point of view, also know as *person*.

There are three points of view: first, second, and third. Which person you use depends on your audience and the tone you wish to achieve.

First person point of view

In the first person, the writer, or narrator, is the one speaking or observing. The first person personal pronouns are

I, we, us, our, ours, my, mine

> *I* am pleased to inform you that *our* committee has awarded your company the contract.

This point of view is appropriate in most business and in much technical writing. The communication is clearly between two real people, not disembodied entities. The friendly, direct approach sustains readers' interest more than stiff, impersonal writing does.

USE *WE* CAREFULLY

When you write *we*, you speak for more people than yourself.

> *We* are satisfied that your move into research will benefit the company.

Make sure that not only you, but also your colleagues agree with this statement before you use *we*. If the statement reflects your opinion alone, use *I*.

Second person point of view

In the second person, the writer addresses the reader as *you*. The second person personal pronouns are

you, your, yours

> Claim *your* lockers by Friday and sign up for *your* free fitness assessment. [*You* is understood to be the subject of this imperative sentence.]

This point of view is also personal and addresses readers directly.

Third person point of view

In the third person, the writer writes about other people or things. The third person personal pronouns are

she, he, it, her, him, hers, his, they, them, their, theirs

> When Elsa got *her* promotion, *she* celebrated with a big party.

> Dimitri is looking for help on *his* project, and *he* says *he'll* work over the weekend if *he* must.

> *She* installed the new system yesterday, and *it* works perfectly.

THE IMPERSONAL THIRD PERSON POINT OF VIEW

If you don't use any personal pronouns, your writing is in the third person and probably has too impersonal a tone. People most often associate the third person point of view with objective writing about factual information. It is the typical style of formal technical writing.

> The chairman announced that the dividend would rise to $12.40 a share as of January 1.

> The new test can detect impurities down to 1ppm of solution.

> Each experiment must be labeled and the results
> recorded on the daily log sheet.

As in the last example, an impersonal point of view
often uses passive rather than active voice. If you
change this example to second person, the tone
becomes direct, friendly, and more personal. The
voice changes to active.

> Label *your* experiments and record *your* results on
> the daily log sheet.

ONE AS IMPERSONAL THIRD PERSON

Using *one* instead of a personal pronoun is much
more common in British than it is in American
English. In most business and technical writing,
one makes the tone and point of view seem more
distant and formal.

instead of:	If *one* takes a second job, *one* must consider the impact on *one's* family.
write:	If *you* take a second job, *you* must consider the impact on *your* family.

Consistency in point of view

Your letter or document should be consistent in its
point of view. Don't mix first, second, or third person.

instead of:	Managers should turn in *their* budget requests for the next fiscal year before *your* next monthly meeting.
write:	Managers should turn in *their* budget requests for the next fiscal year before *their* next monthly meeting.

If you start with *one* as your point of view, you
must stick with it throughout your paragraph. Do
not switch to *you* in the middle.

(See also **active voice/passive voice**; *one*; **person**;
personal pronouns; **readers, analyzing**; **tone**.)

positive approach

The **positive approach** means writing information in a positive and straightforward way.

instead of: If the wood is *not* properly primed, it will *not* resist weathering.

write: Prime the wood properly to resist weathering.

When you present information in a negative way, you must often use two or more negative words in a sentence. Readers must then sort these words out to decipher what you actually mean.

instead of: In case all the parts are *not* there, do *not* keep the kit.

write: If any parts are missing, send the whole kit back for a replacement.

When you need to write negative information, do it directly and use as few negative words as possible.

> Since the bid did not arrive on time, we refused to accept it.

Sometimes it may be better to imply a negative rather than state it outright.

instead of: Since the bid did not arrive on time, we refused to accept it.

write: If the bid had arrived on time, we would have been happy to accept it.

(See also **concise vs. wordy writing**.)

possessive case

The **possessive case** of nouns and pronouns shows ownership. The usual sign of the possessive is an apostrophe alone or *'s*. Some words embody the possessive without an apostrophe.

The *product's* success is partly dependent on how well *our* marketing people have put it before the public.

Singular and plural possessives

Most singular nouns take an *'s* at the end to form the possessive.

administration's policies   Mr. Chen's case

If the noun ends in an *-s* sound, put an apostrophe alone after the last letter.

James' plans   Hopkins' proposal

Most plural nouns that end in *-s* take an apostrophe following the *-s* to form the possessive.

companies' policies   investors' choices

Compound words

Compound nouns or terms of more than one word form the possessive at the end.

notary public's hours   someone else's idea
brother-in-law's business   Lake District's vote
Sales Department's proposal

Abbreviations

For abbreviations, follow most regular rules to form singular and plural possessives. If the abbreviation ends in a period, put the apostrophe or *'s* after the period.

NASA's projections   U.K.'s roads   FRC's ruling
M.D.s' recommendations

Gerunds and gerund phrases

Always use a possessive noun or pronoun before a gerund (a verb that ends in *-ing* and functions as a noun).

This project depends on *our* having uninterrupted cross-functional communication.

What should we do about *Cynthia's* taking an unpaid leave of absence?

Obvious possession in organization names and titles

Where the understanding of possession is obvious, the apostrophe is often left out.

Peoples Credit Union   teachers college
Builders Savings and Loan

Individual and joint possession

To show individual possession of nouns joined by *and* or *or*, make each noun possessive.

Raymond's and Beth's log-in times were identical. [They each had a separate log-in time.]

To show joint possession of nouns joined by *and* or *or*, make the second or last noun possessive.

Drew and Sunita's first proposal [together]

Grayson and Vogel's law firm [one firm owned by both]

Possession using *of* phrases

Many writers prefer to use the possessive case with people and living things, and an *of* phrase with inanimate things.

dog's collar   architect's drawing
depth of the well [not the well's depth]

management of the portfolio [not the portfolio's management]

When an owner has more than one of the same kind of possession, use an *of* phrase with a personal possessive.

a project of *mine* [not *me*] [If you had only one project, you would say *my project*.]

a business partner of Mr. *Lindstrom's* [if he had only one partner, you would say *Mr. Lindstrom's business partner*]

Possessives standing alone

Sometimes the possessive word modifies a noun that is understood but omitted.

Look for it at your local *pharmacist's* [store].

Today's figures are much better than *yesterday's* [figures].

Indefinite pronouns

Some indefinite pronouns always use an *of* phrase to form the possessive. Others use *'s*.

of *any*   of *each*   of *most*   of *none*   someone*'s*   everybody*'s*

Everybody's predictions were optimistic.

Personal pronouns of possession

Personal pronouns of possession do not use apostrophes. These pronouns are

mine, ours, hers, his, theirs, whose

Kate will be using my computer until *hers* is repaired. [not *her's*]

Pronouns with *'s* are always contractions for a pronoun + *is* or a pronoun + *has*.

contraction: *It's* [*It has*] been only three days since we submitted the proposal.

possession: The committee reached a consensus on *its* goals for the research. [The *goals* belong to the *committee*.]

contraction:	*Who's* next on the list? [Who is next?]
possession:	*Whose* workstation do we upgrade next? [The workstation belonging to whom?]

Possessive adjectives

Possessive adjectives precede nouns. The possessive adjectives are

my, your, her, his, its, our, their

> Kate will be using *my* computer until hers is repaired.

(See also **adjectives**, **case**, **gerunds**, **nouns**, **pronouns**.)

predicates

The **predicate** of a sentence consists of the verb and its objects, complements, or modifiers. The predicate usually follows the subject. The main part of the predicate, or the *simple predicate*, is the verb alone.

> Hannah *will supervise* the distribution and release.

The *complete predicate* is the verb and all its objects, complements, or modifiers.

> Hannah *will supervise the distribution and release*.

A *compound predicate* is two or more predicates in one sentence.

> Hannah *will supervise the distribution and release* and *edit the cover letters*.

Predicate nominative

A *predicate nominative* is the noun complement that follows a linking verb.

> He is *our best troubleshooter*.

(See also **nouns**, **sentences**, **verbs**.)

---

prepositions

Prepositions are connecting words that show the relationship of a noun or pronoun to some other word in the sentence.

> Don't let this issue come *between* Richard and you. [The preposition *between* shows space or location and relates to, or modifies, the verb *come*.]

Following are some of the most common prepositions and the relationship they express.

Location:	in, above, beyond, through, between, across, behind, near
Time:	since, during, after, before, until
Cause:	because of, due to, by means of
Focus:	with regard to, concerning, in spite of, regarding, including
Exclusion:	but, except, except for, excluding, without

Prepositional phrases

A prepositional phrase includes a preposition, its object, and any modifiers.

> Don't let this issue come between *Richard and you*. [*Richard* and *you* are objects of the preposition *between*. The conjunction *and* joins the objects and is part of the prepositional phrase. The prepositional phrase is *between Richard and you*.]

Prepositional phrases act as adjectives when they modify nouns, and as adverbs when they modify verbs.

> We need a new system *with videoconferencing capability*. [The prepositional phrase *with videoconferencing capability* acts as an adjective that modifies *system*.]

We sent our entire sales force *to the Atlanta conference*. [The prepositional phrase *to the Atlanta conference* acts as an adverb that modifies *sent*.]

To avoid ambiguity, always try to put a prepositional phrase as close as possible to the word it modifies.

instead of: The order delivered to the shipping clerk *in the large box* has to be sent back.

write: The order *in the large box* delivered to the shipping clerk has to be sent back.

Prepositions with verbs

Some verbs need a preposition to complete their meaning. Following are some of the frequently used combinations.

agree on (to come to an understanding)

We finally *agreed on* the specifications.

agree to (accept something)

We *agree to* the plan.

apply for (a position)

I think I'll *apply for* the position in finance.

apply to (someone or something)

It's time to *apply* ourselves *to* the task.

correspond to (agree with)

The survey findings don't *correspond to* the focus group conclusions.

correspond with (exchange letters with)

Who *corresponds with* this client on a regular basis?

speak to (tell something to)

I'll *speak to* Gene about the new project.

speak with (discuss)

I *spoke with* Gene yesterday.

Prepositions at the end of a sentence

You may end a sentence with a preposition if it naturally occurs there in informal writing.

Whom should I send the information *to*?

In more formal writing, prepositions usually don't end sentences.

To whom should I send the information?

Many short questions naturally end in prepositions.

Whom did you come *with*? What is this used *for*?

What did you talk *about*? Whom did you give it *to*?

Omissions

Correct omissions

Omit prepositions that don't add to the meaning.

Where did she send the fax [to]?

Take that program off [of] my computer.

Incorrect omissions

In sentences with compound elements, include all prepositions.

She shows respect *for* as well as knowledge *of* these archives.

If one item in a series requires a preposition different from the others, repeat the correct form for each item.

Reta will be conducting product demonstrations in New Delhi, Bombay, and the Pacific Basin.

but:

Reta will be conducting product demonstrations in New Delhi, in Bombay, and at the Pacific Basin conference.

(See also **appositives**, **infinitives**, **parts of speech**, **phrases**.)

---

presentations, oral

If you want to be a great presenter, you must have the will to prepare. Planning ahead will pay you big dividends. Imagine what happens if the material you deliver to your audience does not target their needs or expectations. You risk wasting audience time and possibly your credibility.

Here is a system you can use to analyze your audience's most critical question: "What's in it for me?"

The presenter's Focus Sheet

Instead of using the Focus Sheet™ for documents, use the one that follows. Answering these questions is your first step in preparing for any presentation.

The Presenter's Focus Sheet

1. <u>Purpose or goal</u>

    A. What do I want my audience to think, feel, or do as a result of my presentation?

    B. What is the biggest problem I must confront in preparing and giving this presentation?

    C. How is this an opportunity for me?

    D. Why have I been asked to speak?

2. <u>Audience</u>

    A. Who is attending?

    • size of group

    • age and gender breakdown

    • education level

- language barriers
- cultural differences (values, nonverbal communication)
- formal or informal group
- voluntary or mandatory attendance
- homogeneous or heterogeneous group (technical vs. management)
- titles and organizational levels
- goals of audience's organization

B. How much do they know about my topic?

C. What are their expectations? What do they want to hear?

D. Why should they listen? How does what I say relate to their job or world?

E. What objections might they have? How will I counter these objections?

F. What common ground do we share? Values, goals, experiences, interests, image, concerns, affiliations, expectations, culture? Once I identify common ground, how will I use it to win them over?

G. Who is my *target* audience? Who has the power, influence, resources, money, and affiliations to help or hinder me?

3. <u>Bottom Line</u>

If the audience were to forget everything else, what one key point do I want remembered?

4. <u>Strategy</u>

A. Should I be the presenter? At this time?

B. Would a phone call or one-on-one meeting be more effective?

C. Does the audience have the readiness level to act? If not, should I refine my goal?

D. Do I need to make a series of presentations to achieve my overall goal?

E. Has someone else communicated the same information? Should I check with that person? How did that audience respond?

F. Do I represent a threat to anyone? How so? How can I minimize the threat?

G. What are the possible attitudes

- toward me as a presenter?
- toward my topic?
- toward my department?

H. If this is a team presentation, how can we best complement each other?

Why is the Focus Sheet so important?

Including too much detail—a major barrier to effective presenting—is common when presenters fail to identify a realistic and measurable goal for their presentation. The key to influencing your audience is to identify a goal that meets your purpose and your listeners' expectations.

Your goal is your reason for speaking in the first place: never lose sight of it. Use it to determine which and how much information to include.

Write a specific goal statement by answering in two or three sentences:

What do I want my audience to think, feel, or do as a result of my presentation?

Make sure you begin your goal statement with

To (action verb) . . . .

This is your bottom line. Now answer the following questions to make sure your goal is persuasive and realistic.

Question

Is my presentation goal measurable? How will I know when I achieve it?

Solution

Rewrite your goal in behavioral terms if it's not measurable. How do you want your audience to act?

Question

Is the action verb persuasive in its intent?

Solution

For example, to: accept, agree, attend, buy, contribute, cooperate, excite, help, join, lend, motivate, participate, select, serve, support, sponsor, volunteer, vote.

Question

Can I achieve my goal within the allotted time?

Solution

If not, narrow your objective or negotiate for more time.

Question

Does this audience have the skill, knowledge, or readiness to act?

Solution

If not, you've got the wrong goal. Modify it or strategize ways to influence the audience's readiness.

If necessary, rewrite your goal.

Present with impact: use the Presenter's Blueprint

You are now ready to write your presentation with your goal as a foundation. Use the following simple structure to organize your main ideas.

This Presenter's Blueprint is based on research on how people listen, take in information, and remember it. It has three main parts: introduction, body, and conclusion.

Since organizing a presentation is not the same as organizing a document, stick to this model rather than the sequencing advice in the **organizing information** entry.

A listener is not like a reader who can refer to earlier points in a document—the audience at an oral presentation needs more repetition to get the point.

INTRODUCTION

Whatever effect you wish to have on the audience, this is where it begins. Do not miss this opportunity.

Your first words establish your credibility, sincerity, and spontaneity. They determine the level of attention your audience will give you throughout your talk. Your introduction will consist of five critical components that answer the audience's main questions:

- What's in this presentation for me?

- Why should I listen to you?

1. Grabber

   The unexpected—that's what a grabber is. You have lots of options, but be sure your grabber is directly related to your topic. Here are some examples:

   - A rhetorical question:

     If I could guarantee that any electronic file you sent would print anywhere, would you be interested?

   - A real question:

     How many of you could use client-server software?

   - A quote:

     As Dale Carnegie said, "Visual impressions are like cannonballs; they come with a terrific impact. They imbed themselves. They stick."

   - An anecdote: try a short story, real or imagined.

- A startling statistic:

   By the year 2000 . . .
- A demonstration: product, procedure, or technique.
- Audience participation: for example, ask your listeners to stand up and speak to the person next to them about your topic.
- Humor: a joke or amusing anecdote in good taste.

2. Thesis statement

   This is critical—do not keep your audience in the dark. Tell your listeners what you're going to talk about and how it benefits them specifically. Present your thesis from the audience's point of view. They want to know, "What's in it for me?"

3. Credibility statement

   Mention your experience, any research you've done, an endorsement you've received (keep it brief), or special success related to your topic.

4. Preview

   Your preview orients the audience to the information you'll be covering in the body of your presentation. Make the preview brief. For example:

   Today you'll learn the three techniques for decreasing prespeech anxiety.

5. Question-and-answer format

   Let the audience know your format early. If you want participation and feedback throughout, encourage them to interrupt or signal with questions. Otherwise, ask them to note their questions and hold them until the end of your presentation.

BODY

Spend most of your time here. Provide strong evidence to prove your thesis. Your credibility will be tested by the effectiveness of your reasoning.

1. Main points

   Limit yourself to three to five main ideas.

2. Supporting data

   Support each main point with data or evidence. There are three major types of supporting data:

   - Statistics: cite your source and be ready to defend your data.
   - Testimony: quote experts or peers who support your point of view.
   - Examples: use this powerful tool to hold your audience's attention and persuade them to accept your point of view.

Link each section with clear transitions. They will help you build a logical case and reinforce your message.

CONCLUSION

A strong finish is as important as opening with impact. Your conclusion should consist of three parts:

1. Summary: briefly recap your main points.
2. Thesis restatement: either repeat your original wording or rephrase it for reinforcement.
3. Call to action: tell your audience what you want it to do with the information. Be very specific. Make sure your call to action is appropriate to its readiness level.

How to write your presentation

USING INDEX CARDS

Keep your presentation portable from the beginning. Index cards are one of the most useful ways to track and organize your talk. Use the size you like best and write down your ideas in large and legible print.

Give each idea its own card. Label the top line of the card with the key idea and the section it represents: is it part of the grabber? supporting data? call to action? Use the numbered points from the preceding Presenter's Blueprint.

When you have written down all your ideas, sequence your cards according to the Presenter's Blueprint.

Number and letter your cards according to major sections and subsections in case you drop them. Better yet: attach them with two metal rings.

If you have rehearsed well, you should need to consult your cards only occasionally to keep on track. Don't read from them, but use them as prompts. Their main function is to provide you with a sense of security.

USING A PRESENTATION PROGRAM

The note-page view of your presentation program is also a good way to write your talk. Each note page reproduces a slide or overhead transparency, with half a page of space below for typing or handwriting notes.

Take advantage of the outline view to sort, organize, and re-order your visuals and notes pages according to the Presenter's Blueprint.

Use your note pages as you rehearse, but not during your talk. You don't want to look as if you're reading a speech. If you need notes, write them on index cards or on the frames of your overhead transparencies.

Your visuals should feature the key ideas in your presentation. In some cases they will provide you with all the speaking cues you need. Don't read text in your visuals verbatim; you will bore your audience and appear ineffectual.

The text in your visuals should be no more than six lines long. Limit yourself to six words per line, in a font large enough to see from the back of the room. Plain, or sans-serif, fonts such as Helvetica are easier to read than serif fonts like Times.

Reinforce your message with handouts

Most audiences appreciate a good handout as a reminder of your presentation. Be wary, however, of using your handout as your visual aid. They are very different.

Your handout will often contain too much information to be an effective visual. Keep the following guidelines in mind when designing and using handouts.

DESIGNING HANDOUTS

1. First, question your purpose in using handouts. Do you want them:

   • for people unable to attend the presentation? Be sure that each handout is complete enough to stand alone.

   • to add supplemental data to your presentation? Clearly identify them as such, both on the handouts and during your presentation.

   • to inspire your audience to take needed action? Repeat your request for action.

   • to solicit written information or feedback from your listeners? Make it easy for your audience by providing a form, address, and suggested deadline.

2. Include any picture visuals as handouts. They will reinforce your message.

3. Experiment with colored paper to convey a mood or differentiate ideas, but be judicious. Too much color can be confusing.

4. Make handout copies from clear originals to ensure sharpness.

DISTRIBUTING HANDOUTS

1. During your introduction, tell your audience when you'll distribute handouts and why.

2. If you know that your audience likes to take notes, provide skeleton handouts, such as an agenda, with room for notes. Distribute detailed handouts after your talk.

3. *Never* let your handouts compete with you for the audience's attention. Organize your handouts in separate folders and distribute them only when you're ready to discuss them.

Before distributing, tell your audience what each handout contains. Hold each one up so it can be seen. If you distribute handouts before your talk, you are guaranteed a roomful of heads-down listeners—they'll be reading instead of paying attention to you.

A final tip

The next time you present, ask a colleague in the audience for a supportive critique based on the guidelines in this entry. If your audience is composed of strangers, practice the entire presentation in front of a few people first.

Presenting your products, services, ideas, and recommendations with impact is a key to success in your current position and a prerequisite for career advancement.

As you prepare your next presentation, use the information in this entry to control your behavior, your material, and your audience.

(See also **color**, **font**, **transitions**, **visual aids**.)

---

procedures

Procedures tell your readers how to follow a process—step by step. They should be clear, concise, and as technical or detailed as your purpose and audience require. Procedures can range from how to assemble complex machinery to how to format a report.

The Six Steps to Reader-Centered Writing™ are slightly different for the procedure writing process. Later in this entry you'll see how to tailor the Six Steps to the special requirements of writing work instructions and procedures.

What makes a good procedure?

Most procedures include

1. introduction and purpose
2. scope and audience
3. materials or equipment
4. applicable documents
5. definitions
6. description of an appliance or machine (optional)
7. procedures
8. appendix
9. problem solving or troubleshooting (optional).

INTRODUCTION AND PURPOSE

Here you concisely answer the question, "What does the procedure explain?" Tell your readers what the procedure is for; give the purpose of the process, appliance, or machine.

You might also include its objectives. The principles you state here should preview the procedures described in a later section.

SCOPE AND AUDIENCE

Explain who your audience is and how large it is. Which department, group, division, or individuals will follow the procedure? Will your audience change over time? What is its level of education? familiarity? training? attitude?

MATERIALS OR EQUIPMENT

Describe the items your readers will need to complete the procedures. It may be useful to put the materials in a list or in helpful categories.

APPLICABLE DOCUMENTS

List any documents that you refer to in the procedure. These might include instructions, documents about work standards, or the greater set of procedures to which yours belongs.

DEFINITIONS

Be sure to define any words or acronyms you use that may not be familiar to your audience. That way you'll avoid confusion that could lead to a mishap during the procedure.

DESCRIPTION OF AN APPLIANCE OR MACHINE (OPTIONAL)

This section is necessary if you are detailing the laws of operation and maintenance of a mechanism.

Choose an appropriate method of development: either spatially or chronologically describe the operation of the appliance or machine, part by part, in technical detail. Provide illustrations or photographs to aid understanding.

PROCEDURES

To write your actual procedures, use the Six Steps to Clear Procedures (following). After finishing Step Six, include your final draft here. This section will be the largest, integrating all necessary flow diagrams, tables, logs, and graphs.

Divide the procedures into as many steps and substeps as you need to be clear. Each step should be short and simple, no more than eight or ten words.

Use clear numbering and words that show sequence, such as *first, next,* and *at the same time.* Make sure the sequence is correct. An error here is unacceptable, if not dangerous.

Include as many illustrations, diagrams, or drawings as you need to help your reader understand and follow your text descriptions.

Procedures look best and are easiest to follow when presented in chart or grid form. Put each step on a separate line. Label the left column with a step number. The right columns should list the accompanying action and outcome if appropriate.

CD Renewal Procedure*

Step	Action	
1	Verify caller using existing Telebanking procedures.	
2	Access screen **INQ 202** and determine whether the account is a regular CD or an IRA CD by the type numbers.	
	If	**Then**
	the account is a regular CD	use the white renewal form.
	the account is an IRA CD	use the yellow renewal form.
3	Access screen **INQ 244** and verify the CD will mature during the Summer Drive.	
4	Is today's date past the grace period?	
	• **If yes**, inform the customer that, because the grace period has elapsed, his/her CD has rolled over. Any action now would result in an early withdrawal penalty. • **If no**, take instructions if the request falls in the "what we can do" category above.	

*Reprinted with permission of Bank of Boston, Inc.

Highlight warnings and safety statements in the chart—and ahead of it, too.

Another acceptable but less visually effective way to list procedures uses the decimal outline approach explained in the **outlines** entry in this book.

Each step is assigned a decimal number. Substeps get subnumbers. The reader can easily follow each numbered step because the main subdivisions of each segment stand out clearly.

APPENDIX

In the appendix place information that may be useful to your readers but may not be essential to carrying out the procedure. Sample contents:

1. definitions of items: glossary
2. flow diagrams, forms, tables, and logs
3. other background or related documents
4. user-review page

Consider carefully whether items like the preceding are vital to your reader or truly optional. Misplaced information is often tantamount to omitted information.

PROBLEM SOLVING OR TROUBLESHOOTING (OPTIONAL)

Make a list or chart of possible problems, causes, and solutions your reader may encounter. This is particularly helpful in repair procedures for technicians and operating manuals for consumers.

Following the Six Steps to Clear Procedures

We've tailored the Six Steps to Reader-Centered Writing to procedure writing. This will help you produce the clearest, most accurate instructions possible.

As you use the following chart, note specific suggestions (as in Step 2), which differ from the Six

Steps endorsed at the beginning of this book and in the text body under the various step titles. Following the chart is a brief discussion of each step.

The Six Steps to Clear Procedures

STEP 1.0:   **Analyze your audience and define your purpose with the Focus Sheet™.**

1.1 What is the audience's knowledge? experience?

1.2 What specific tasks(s) will the audience be performing?

1.3 What/how much does the audience need to know to perform the tasks correctly?

STEP 2.0:   **Research or envision your process to generate steps.**

2.1 Use Post-it™ Notes to build a flow diagram as your start-up strategy.

2.2 Restrict content to that necessary to complete tasks.

2.3 Include enough information to be clear. Resist the urge to justify or analyze.

STEP 3.0:   **Group information under headlines.**

3.1 Use categories from your company's templates if you have any.

3.2 Highlight headlines that introduce each step in the procedure.

3.3 List important substeps by responsibility under each headline.

STEP 4.0:   **Sequence your data—as a whole and within sections.**

4.1 Sequence according to the procedure.

4.2 Transfer the information from the Post-it Notes into a flow diagram.

4.3 For long documents, begin with
- a specific title, for example: **How to Access the Internet ... vs. Internet Access**
- a complete table of contents
- a definition and/or overview of the procedure

PLAN

- a glossary (if appropriate for the audience and subject).

STEP 5.0:   **Write the first draft.**

5.1   Explain or complete each step or substep in your flow diagram.

5.2   If possible, use two columns to show who is responsible for each action. Headlines: **RESPONSIBILITY, ACTION**

5.3   Test your draft procedures on a user for clarity and ease of use.

DRAFT

STEP 6.0:   **Edit for clarity, conciseness, and accuracy.**

6.1   Use • headlines for major sections like **INSTALLING YOUR PROGRAM**
   - subheadings or sidelines for subsections like **Cleaning your equipment**.

6.2   Indent steps as needed for visual effect.

6.3   Use numbers (not bullets) to emphasize sequence.

6.4   Be generous with white space— limit amount of text on page.

6.5   Preview safety warnings before introducing each procedure and highlight them again just before related steps.

6.6   Keep paragraphs 3-4 lines long; limit sentences to 8-10 words.

6.7   Use active verbs, parallel structure, and the imperative mode.

6.8   Use visuals (forms, tables, or diagrams) to clarify the process.

6.9   Are visuals clear? labeled? explained in the text? close to the explanation?

6.10 Attach cover pages and user-review pages as needed.

6.11 Proofread for accuracy.

6.12 Ask new reviewers for final user feedback.

EDIT

Step 1: Analyze your audience and define your purpose with the Focus Sheet for Procedure Writing

Just as our Focus Sheet is vital preparation for other documents you write, so the Focus Sheet for Procedure Writing (following) is essential for planning all procedure writing.

Before you begin, you should completely understand the process you plan to describe. Be sure you know the full extent of the purpose and uses of your procedures. An oversight at this planning stage could result in a crucial omission from your document.

Next, consider how much your readers know so that you can adjust your detail and language to their level. Do you have to explain technical terms, or do your readers already know what the terms mean? For example, if you are writing procedures for ISO or QS9000 certification, your audience is likely to consist of knowledgeable users rather than trainees. The level of detail required will dramatically affect your final document.

Before generating and outlining the steps for your instructions, fully complete the Focus Sheet for Procedure Writing. Clearly defining your audience and purpose at the outset will save you time in each of the subsequent steps

Focus Sheet for Procedure Writing

Step 1

Answer these questions as the first step in any procedure-writing task:

1. **Purpose: principles of operation**

   1.1 What will the procedure explain? How to . . . _____

   1.2 Where does the process begin and end? _____

   1.3 How are the instructions organized (if complex)? _____

2. **Audience:**

   2.1 Who is my reader? Do I have more than one? _____

   2.2 What is the reader's role? _____

   2.3 What does the reader know about the subject? _____

   2.4 How will the reader use this document? _____

   2.5 What's in it for the reader? Why should the reader read this or agree with it? ___ _____

3. **Scope:**

   3.1 To whom does this procedure apply? ___ _____

   3.2 To which groups, divisions, or geographic areas does the procedure apply?_____

   3.3 Is the procedure true at all times? If not, clarify. _____

4. **Strategy:**

   4.1 Is someone else communicating the same information? Should I check with that person? _____

   4.2 Is my documentation format the best? Should I talk to the documentation department? _____

Step 2: Research or envision your process to generate steps

Writing a clear procedure is one of the hardest tasks for any writer. Here are a few easy ways to assure success.

1. LAPTOP COMPUTER

Take your portable computer to the place the procedure occurs and list the steps as you watch. Be sure to have the most knowledgeable user or operator there to answer questions.

2. POST-IT™ NOTES

Even professional procedure writers have found breakthroughs using large 3M's Post-It Notes to record every aspect of a process while out on the shop floor or away from their computers. This also works well in conference rooms with teams.

The benefit: omitted steps can easily be inserted and the notes reshuffled as you identify every tiny aspect of each step. There is no need to commit to a sequence until you've gathered all your data.

3. TEAM APPROACH

If you're knowledgeable about your procedure, you can demonstrate it while dictating to a colleague or dictating machine. Technical writers can then collaborate on writing the final draft document.

4. VIDEOTAPING

Videotape the procedure and take it back to the office to write up. If you have multimedia capabilities, include the video in your procedure.

5. PROJECT PLANNING CHART

Consider adding a project planning chart as a way of previewing major steps that operators must follow simultaneously.

Step 3: Group information under headlines

Check with your company to see if it requires a specific format stipulating types of categories and headlines. If not, don't worry: grouping is usually easy when your document is step-by-step. Use the guidelines in the table that follows.

How to group information for procedures	
Step	**Action**
1.	Pinpoint the major steps.
2.	Highlight them with headlines if they're lengthy.
3.	Break them down into substeps as often as possible.
4.	Gather all steps that immediately follow each major step and place under the appropriate major heading.
5.	Use subheads for less important information.

Step 4: Sequence your data—as a whole and within sections

If you understand your procedure completely, proper sequencing should not require much deliberation. It should be evident: sequence according to the steps in the procedure. In some cases your document may be arranged

- chronologically: you list steps in the order in which they should take place, and/or

- spatially: you lead the reader from Point A to Point B on a particular mechanism or from one piece of equipment to another.

Some issues to consider as you sequence the steps:

- Are numerous people involved?
- Who is responsible for which action?
- Will different people carry out different steps simultaneously?
- Do certain individuals need to accomplish a step before others proceed?
- Which steps are most important for success and safety?

If the procedure is complex, requiring many simultaneous steps, use the Post-it Notes start-up strategy (preceding) and build a flow diagram from the notes.

It's an efficient way to see all the steps at once and move them around easily, especially if you are working away from your computer.

Step 5: Writing the first draft

When drafting, be sure to refer frequently to your flow diagram, notes, or video so that you don't omit any steps. Explain each step clearly.

If many people will be involved in carrying out the procedure, use three columns in your document: **Step Number, Responsibility**, and **Action**. That way all readers can see at a glance which actions they are responsible for.

Consider adding a fourth column called **Result** or **Outcome** if you feel this will be helpful. See **Model Documents Appendix** for a sample procedure format.

TEST YOUR PROCEDURE

After you've completed a draft, ask someone who's familiar with the process to go through each step. If you've left anything out, this person should notice it. Such a test will reveal whether or not you've been clear.

Remember, someone's safety may depend on your writing. Take this responsibility seriously.

Step 6: Edit for clarity, conciseness, and accuracy

As you review your document, pay special attention to clarity and accuracy. Both are essential to good procedure writing.

SOME GUIDELINES FOR STYLE

- Use the active voice in writing procedures. Write direct sentences that tell readers exactly what to do.

  instead of: The PILOT knob should be depressed completely and held for one minute.

  write: Depress the PILOT knob completely and hold it for one minute.

- Use as few words as possible—but don't make your sentences so condensed that your readers have to supply crucial omitted words themselves.

  instead of: Clean the brush. Store suspended for aeration.

  write: Clean the brush. Store it suspended to allow it to dry thoroughly.

- Avoid gobbledygook and affected language.

  instead of: *Activate* the motor.

  write: *Start* the motor.

- Watch ambiguous phrases.

  Example: You can't use too much water in mixing.

  Does this mean it's good or bad to use a lot of water?

- Keep paragraphs short. Include only one procedure or a few closely linked ones in each paragraph.

- Use charts, headlines, indenting, and white space to organize your procedures visually.

- Readers always prefer steps that are numbered—not bulleted—and in table format.

(See also **active voice/passive voice**; **flowcharts**; **jargon**; **manuals**; **readers, analyzing**; **technical writing style**; **writing as a team**.)

process control charts

Control charts measure how a process varies during operation. They can be used to monitor process averages and to maintain outputs between upper and lower statistical limits.

Use control charts to determine process capabilities, monitor process outputs, and warn of changing process conditions.

Run charts

A run chart is a specific example of a process control chart that is used to determine if the long-range average is changing. Sample values are placed on a table as the tracking event occurs. These points are then plotted on a chart around the established anticipated average.

A run chart focuses attention on changes in the process with relation to the predetermined, expected average.

On-Time Arrivals: Frozen Serum Shipments

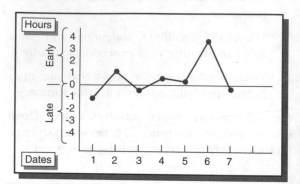

(See also **charts or graphs**, **tables**.)

---

professional articles

Professional articles range from specialized, scholarly articles to general-interest ones. They are published in journals, professional periodicals, trade magazines, and newsletters.

Writing a professional article is one way to make yourself visible in a large corporation and advance your career.

Choosing your topic

Although your idea may not be entirely new, it may be enough of a twist on an established concept to warrant publication. Look around for innovations in methodology, equipment or material—even project management.

Deciding on a publication

Once you have an idea for an article or research, it is essential to consider the range of publications for which it might be suitable and the purpose for publishing. The same set of data might be appropriate for newsletters, trade magazines, and journals.

Research a complete list of publications that pertain to your area of expertise.

Never write an article without focusing on the appropriate publication. Read several issues to get an idea of the kinds of articles it publishes and who its readers are. Find out the following information:

- the publication's reputation
- the professional interests of its readers
- the number of readers or subscribers
- the goals of the publication: will your article fit?

Journals

Journals are the highest level of academic writing, and publication in them carries the most professional prestige. Many journals are severely limited in scope: be sure to check the stated goals to see if your article is appropriate.

Depending on the journal, the readership may be narrow and the lead time for publication as much as several years. It is important, therefore, to consider both the audience you wish to reach and the time constraints you need to meet.

If your material is "hot"—that is, if delay in publication could jeopardize your discovery claim, you might consider preliminary publication in a less prestigious journal or a trade magazine to state publicly what your research has shown to date.

This may be particularly important to establish your rights against a future copyright suit. You may then follow up with an article in your journal of choice.

STYLE GUIDES

Each publication has its own style or signature. This includes the article length, use of graphics, and even a particular set of punctuation rules. Many publications print this information once a year, while others print some requirements in each issue.

Many publications will fax you their guidelines for publication and style. Others still require a self-addressed envelope. Make every effort to obtain a style guide before writing your rough draft.

Study back issues for further information on style. Look for paragraph length, sentence length, use of headlines, and graphics. Concentrate on the liveliest, best-written articles rather than those written by a famous, but perhaps overly formal, expert in the field.

VISUAL DESIGN

Also study the design of the journal articles that catch your attention. You'll notice that, even in the most conservative, visual design plays a key role.

There are often two, three, or even four levels of headlines, bulleted lists, and many graphics. Although you may still see long paragraphs, they are generally shorter than they were a decade ago.

Since graphs and charts generally receive no or little editing, be sure you submit yours exactly as you wish them to appear. Include a caption that sums up the message.

ORGANIZING YOUR ARTICLE

Many journal articles follow this standard academic order:

1. abstract

2. introduction

3. background

4. methodology

5. results

6. conclusion

7. bibliography

Study the journal for which you intend to write to get ideas on the style and content of these sections.

ABSTRACT AND KEY WORDS

With the advent of computer searches, key words have become as important as the abstract. If you do not use the broadest possible list of key words, you will be limiting your audience.

However, never include a key word that you do not include in the abstract. If the connection is not apparent, the harried researcher may think that there was a computer error.

The abstract should always be in the active voice, and should be an example of your liveliest and best writing. If the abstract is dull, none but the most dedicated will request your work, eliminating a number of possible readers.

Be sure to take credit for research: "Our research shows" is far better than "It was shown." First person (*I, we*) is essential to clarify who has done what and to differentiate fact, history, and current research.

Although most authors write the abstract after they have written the article, there are some who prefer to write it first to clarify their key point. You may wish to write a rough draft of the abstract when you complete your Focus Sheet™.

Be sure there is traceability between the abstract and the article: use the same language in each.

THE IMPORTANCE OF A STRONG INTRODUCTION

Along with your purpose and problem definition, this section should include a defense of your approach. It should also discuss alternatives considered but rejected.

This is where readers decide whether the article is worth reading or not, so you must be clear about what is unique in your approach.

AUTHORS: WHOSE NAME GOES FIRST?

Depending on the subject and scope of your article, you might collaborate with one or more colleagues in writing. Often, but not always, the senior researcher is listed first.

If there are three or more authors, only the first is listed in the computerized cross-reference, the others being simply "et al." You should consider this if routinely working with a team, and vary the name listed first.

Varying the author listed first has an advantage other than giving credit to each contributor: the readers are more apt to select articles by a variety of authors, rather than two or three by the same one. As only one name appears on the computer search, variety means more exposure.

Trade magazines

Trade magazines carry advertisements and are often free. For this reason they have a wide circulation and therefore a more varied audience.

Scientists may read them quickly, looking for new advancements because the turnaround or lead time may be just a few weeks—as opposed to years for journal articles. Marketing representatives may study the competition. Managers may look for innovations in products and services.

Many Ph.D.'s scorn trade magazines, preferring the status of journal publications. They may be doing themselves a disservice. Publication in these magazines is much easier. Notifying the world of impending discoveries lays claim to them far in advance of journal publication.

Finally, the broader distribution of these publications may enhance professional reputations.

Keep your company informed

When writing for publication, first obtain clearance from your company. Some matters may be highly sensitive and need legal clearance, others may violate the need for secrecy. Be sure to follow your company's policy.

Maximize the public relations factor

When the journal notifies you that your article has been accepted, you might want to send copies of the letter to management and Human Resources for your file. Do the same when the article is published.

Also compile a distribution list that includes professional associates and colleagues in other companies. A business card attached with a brief note (*FYI; I'd like your feedback*), the date, and your initial is great public relations. Don't waste this opportunity.

Many companies include copies of important articles with their marketing materials. Even a simple list of publications helps establish credibility.

A professional submission

Your manuscript should look professional. No matter how important the content, it will lose its impact if it's filled with typographical errors. Your technical information may arouse doubts if you haven't taken the time to proofread.

Your professional manuscript should follow the publication's style sheet. In general, you should

1. Include a standard title page with

   • your name, address, and social security number in the upper-left-hand corner

   • the type of article and word length in the upper-right-hand corner

   • a centered title, in capital letters, one-third of the way down the page; authors' names as they will appear in the publication.

2. Use one to one-and-a-half inch margins on all four sides.

3. Double-space the text.

4. Use a header with your name on the left and page numbers on the right.

5. Include all graphs, charts, and drawings exactly as you wish them to appear.

6. Use a computer program specifically designed for mathematical and chemical equations.

7. When appropriate, include black-and-white photos or slides. Label them clearly on the reverse side. Use a felt tip pen, and indicate which direction is up.

Include a self-addressed stamped envelope if you want your manuscript back. Some authors today include a self-addressed postcard for a reply, indicating that the manuscript need not be returned.

The review process

Many publications use a committee of referees or reviewers to determine if your technical material is accurate, original, and otherwise worthy of publication. They may like an idea, but require numerous edits. They usually work with an editor who conveys their comments to you.

Since poor editing skills may delay publication, take the extra time to ensure accuracy and correctness before you submit your article.

(See also **abstracts**; **charts or graphs**; **readers, analyzing**; **tables**; **visual design**.)

---

project planning charts

Good project managers never begin without a schedule incorporating the steps and/or resources necessary to complete a complex process.

Depending on the size and duration of the project, different types of schedules, or **project planning charts**, are appropriate. The charts combine the succession of events clearly, showing parallel and independent events.

The Gantt chart

One of the most commonly used planning charts is the Gantt chart. The Gantt chart is a horizontal bar graph displaying time on the x-axis and tasks on the y-axis. It is particularly useful since it can indicate several tasks being performed simultaneously.

Easy-to-read charts like the one following work extremely well for project management. Team members can see their simultaneous and overlapping roles and deadlines with a single glance.

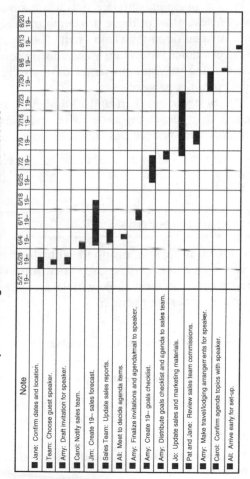

Project Planning Chart for Annual Sales Conference

Choose the chart that works best for your project

Other examples of project-planning charts include

- flowcharts
- Critical Path Method (CPM) charts
- Program Evaluation Review Technique (PERT) charts.

Use CPM and PERT charts to plan complex processes that require sequential events. PERT charts include time schedules for each linking step.

Project planning software is available on a variety of levels. Most of these programs are based on some adaptation of the Gantt chart. They spell out tasks, deadlines, and team roles and responsibilities, helping you stay on target through the very last step of the project.

The best versions can update the entire schedule based on one changed deadline, and almost all can track your budget and tally it for you.

(See also **flowcharts**, **minutes of meetings**, **tables**.)

---

pronoun reference

The relationship of a pronoun with the noun it replaces (its antecedent) is called **pronoun reference**. A pronoun must agree with its antecedent in person, number, and gender.

Agreement in person and number

Jack said *he* would take the chemicals to the lab.

Jack is the antecedent of *he*. *He* agrees with *Jack* in person (third), number (singular), and gender (masculine).

The *economist* brought *her* latest book to the conference.

Economist is the antecedent of *her*. *Economist* agrees with *her* in person (third) and number (singular). We know the gender (feminine) from a previous sentence.

AGREEMENT IN COMPOUND CONSTRUCTIONS

If the antecedent is two or more words joined by *and*, use a plural pronoun.

> *Sid and Priscilla* published *their* collaborative article last month.

If the antecedent is two words joined by *either . . . or* or *neither . . . nor*, the pronoun agrees with the nearest noun.

> *Neither* Paula *nor* the members of her team need *their* laptops today.

> *Either* Chuck *or* Raoul will give *his* approval to the expenditure.

When two people are of different genders, rephrase the sentence to drop the pronoun.

> Either Chuck or Nancy can approve the expenditure.

AGREEMENT WITH INDEFINITE PRONOUN ANTECEDENTS

1. Singular antecedents

The indefinite pronouns, such as *anyone, everybody, someone, none,* and *each,* can cause agreement problems. Most of these words are singular and can refer to both genders.

If both genders are implied in the context, use either *he or she,* or change the construction to the plural. The plural forms are preferred whenever possible because they flow more smoothly. Don't use *he* alone to refer to both men and women.

instead of: Each new *member* should bring *his* ID card to the first meeting.

write:	New *members* should bring *their* ID cards to the first meeting.
instead of:	We want to thank every *participant* in the seminar for *his or her* interest. [It's okay to use *his or her* occasionally.]
write:	We want to thank the *participants* in the seminar for *their* interest.

In the next example, the pronoun *her* is acceptable because we may assume from the context that the antecedent is feminine.

> Every patient in the obstetrician's office has received *her* updated records.

2. Plural antecedents

The pronouns *several, many, others*, and the like are plural. Use plural pronouns with them.

> *Many* come through these doors each day, and *they* all want to invest *their* money wisely.

AGREEMENT WITH COLLECTIVE NOUNS

Determine whether a collective noun is singular (a group as a whole) or plural (individuals in a group). Then make the pronoun agree in number with the noun.

> The company was new, but *it* was profitable. [*Company* is singular.]

> The company said that *they* expected even more success in the next quarter. [*Company* is plural.]

Problem references

VAGUE OR AMBIGUOUS REFERENCES

Avoid confusion when one pronoun could refer to either of two antecedents.

instead of:	Sally finished the report for Juanita, but *she* didn't like it. [Who didn't like it, Sally or Juanita?]
write:	Sally finished the report for Juanita, but *Sally* didn't like it. [Repeat the appropriate noun for clarity.]
or:	Although *Sally* didn't like it, *she* finished the report for Juanita. [Rewrite the sentence to avoid awkward repetition.]

INDEFINITE REFERENCES

Pronouns such as *this*, *they*, or *it* can be confusing if they have no specific antecedent.

instead of:	The tab key advances you to the next field. Shift tab puts you in the previous field. *This* will allow you to add, edit, or delete data. [What will allow you?]
write:	The tab key advances you to the next field. Shift tab puts you in the previous field. Once you are positioned in a field, you may add, edit, or delete data.

SEPARATED REFERENCES

Put a pronoun as close as possible to its antecedent so readers don't have to search for the antecedent.

instead of:	We have to decide whether the *proposal* should include standard maintenance, repair, troubleshooting, and an extended warranty before *it* is complete.
write:	Before the *proposal* is complete, we have to decide whether *it* should include standard maintenance, repair, troubleshooting, and an extended warranty.

(See also **ambiguity**; **gender**; *he, he/she, s/he, (s)he*; **pronouns**.)

---

pronouns

Pronouns are words that stand for nouns or other pronouns.

> Sandra said *she* will bring the prospectus with *her* on Friday.

Pronouns have case, number, person, and gender.

Case

Pronouns can be in the subjective, objective, or possessive case.

Subjective	*Objective*	*Possessive*
I, we	me, us	my, mine, our, ours
you	you	your, yours
he, she, it, they	him, her, it, them	his, hers, its, their, theirs

SUBJECTIVE CASE

Subjective case pronouns are subjects of sentences or clauses.

> *She* finished her part of the proposal yesterday. [*She* is the subject.]

> *He* said that *they* would complete the installation by Friday. [*He* is the subject of the sentence; *they* is the subject of the clause.]

OBJECTIVE CASE

Objective case pronouns are indirect or direct objects of verbs and objects of propositions.

> Stuart gave *him* [indirect] a raise, then asked *him* [direct] to join the team.

> Giving *him* [indirect] a raise was the best thing Stuart could have done for *him* [object of preposition].

POSSESSIVE CASE

Pronouns in the possessive case show ownership.

Carla sent *her* report to *our* client yesterday.

The president was happy about *our* winning the grant. [Always precede a gerund (*winning*) with a possessive noun or pronoun.]

APPOSITIVES

An appositive is a word or phrase next to a noun that further identifies the noun it accompanies. An appositive pronoun should be in the same case as its antecedent.

The new assistants, Jim and *she*, are doing the work of four people. [*Assistants* and *she* are in the subjective case.]

Julio assigned the project to the new assistants, Jim and *her*. [*Assistants* and *her* are in the objective case.]

LINKING VERBS: A SPECIAL CASE

Use subjective case pronouns with linking verbs. A linking verb such as *to be* or *seem* doesn't express action; its purpose is to provide more information about the subject of the sentence.

Linking verbs don't take objects but complements, which should be in the subjective case.

It seems to be *he* in the photo.

The group leaders will be *she* and *I*.

In informal memos and e-mail messages, however, it is becoming more and more common to use the objective case with linking verbs.

It seems to be *him* in the photo.

To avoid sounding either overly pedantic or carelessly ungrammatical, rewrite your sentence.

She and *I* will be the group leaders.

How to determine case

1. In a compound construction, test each pronoun separately.

> We have chosen *you* and *her* to be the project leaders. [objective case]
> We have chosen *you* . . .
> We have chosen *her* [not *she*] . . .

> Bob invited Ling and *me* to the planning meeting.
> Bob invited *me* [not *I*] . . .

2. If a pronoun modifies a noun, use the pronoun alone to determine case.

> Jonathan appealed strongly to (*we/us*) programmers for help on the new project.

> Jonathan appealed strongly to *us* programmers . . . [objective case: *us programmers* is the noun phrase object of the preposition *to*]

> She wasn't aware that (*we/us*) coordinators were waiting for our assignments.

> She wasn't aware that *we* coordinators were waiting. . . [subjective case: *we coordinators* is the noun phrase subject of the clause]

3. When a pronoun follows a comparison, such as *than* or *as*, mentally insert the missing word to determine the case of the pronoun.

> Bruno is more sensitive than *she* on this issue. [more sensitive than *she* is, never *her* is]

4. To determine whether to use *who* or *whom*, substitute *he/she* or *him/her*. For a question or modifying clause, turn the sentence into a statement first.

sentence:	We didn't know (*who/whom*) you gave the check to.
substitute:	We didn't know you gave the check (to *her*). [objective case]
correct pronoun:	We didn't know *whom* you gave the check to.

sentence:	Tanya Szabo is a candidate (*who/whom*) we feel will be responsible.
substitute:	Tanya Szabo is a candidate (we feel *she*) will be responsible. [subjective case]
correct pronoun:	Tanya Szabo is a candidate *who* we feel will be responsible.
sentence:	Do you know (*who/whom*) wrote this report?
substitute:	*He* wrote this report. [subjective case]
correct pronoun:	Do you know *who* wrote this report?

Use the same test for *whoever* and *whomever*.

In American usage, when a question starts with *who* or *whom* as the object of a verb, it is becoming acceptable to use *who* even though grammar dictates the objective case.

instead of:	*Whom* did you see at the conference?
write:	*Who* did you see at the conference?

Except in the most formal documents, *Whom did you see?*—though correct—sounds fussy and overly formal.

5. The phrase *between you and me* is always correct; *between you and I* never is. *Me* is the object of the preposition *between*, so you must use the objective case.

Number

Pronouns can be singular or plural. They must agree in number with their antecedents.

Singular:	I, me, my, mine, you, he, her, it, his, hers, its

Plural: we, us, our, ours, you, your,
                  yours, they, them, their, theirs

Who, whose, and *whom* can be used for both singular and plural.

> *These* are the employees for *whom* we are writing the manual.

> *This* is the employee for *whom* we are purchasing a new computer.

Problems with number can occur with indefinite pronouns such as *none, neither, somebody, anyone,* and *nobody*. These pronouns are singular and take singular verbs and references.

> *Nobody* on the men's volleyball team wants to give up *his* place.

Person

Pronouns can be first, second, or third person. They must agree in person with their antecedents.

First person: I, we, me, my, mine, us, our, ours

Second person: you, your, yours

Third person: he, she, it, him, her, his, hers, its, they, them, their, theirs

> When Gerry goes, *he* will take *his* laptop with *him*.

> When *we* go, *we* will take the laptop with *us*.

Gender

Pronouns can be masculine, feminine, or neuter. Some pronouns are either masculine or feminine, and they must agree in gender with their antecedents.

Masculine: he, him, his
Feminine: she, her, hers
Neuter: it, its

*Masculine or
feminine:*   you, your, yours, they, them, their,
               theirs

> *Barbara* took *her* laptop with *her*.

Use *he or she* or better still, change the construction to the plural to avoid gender bias.

> *Everyone* may stay if *he or she* uses the after-hours door.

> *Employees* may stay if *they* use the after-hours door.

Types of pronouns

PERSONAL PRONOUNS

Personal pronouns name people and things. They are called *personal* because they show the characteristic of *person* in a sentence.

First person: I, we, me, my, mine, us, our, ours

Second person: you, your, yours

Third person: he, she, it, him, her, his, hers, its,
                    they, them, their, theirs

> *You* gave *me his* report before *she* copied *it* for *our* files.

DEMONSTRATIVE PRONOUNS

Demonstrative pronouns—*this, that, these, those*—tell whether something specific is near or far.

> *This* is the prototype design.

> *Those* over there are Katerina's notes.

RELATIVE AND INTERROGATIVE PRONOUNS

The following pronouns are both relative and interrogative:

who, whom, what, which, whose, of which,
whoever, whomever

That is also a relative pronoun.

1. Interrogative pronouns ask questions.

   > *Which* program did Max decide to order?

   > *Whoever* could have used so much paper since Monday?

2. Relative pronouns introduce dependent clauses and serve as their subjects or objects. Relative pronouns also show the relationship of the dependent clause with the main clause of the sentence.

   > The equipment *that we lost in the flood* is covered by insurance. [The dependent clause *that we lost in the flood* modifies *equipment*. Within the dependent clause, *that* is the object of the verb *lost*.]

   > Our accountant wants to know *who will provide the figures*. [The dependent clause *who will provide the figures* is the object of the infinitive *to know*. Within the dependent clause, *who* is the subject of the verb *will provide*.]

When you write about people, use *whose*; when you write about things use *of which*.

> Paula Hartridge, *whose* paper was accepted by the Bioengineering Society, will be the keynote speaker.

> No. 3 widgets, *of which* we have only two cases, are suddenly in demand.

Sometimes *of which* can make a sentence clumsy. When this is the case, use *whose* instead.

instead of:　This computer, the hard drive *of which* keeps crashing, needs to be replaced.

write:　This computer, *whose* hard drive keeps crashing, needs to be replaced.

INDEFINITE PRONOUNS

Indefinite pronouns refer to a large group or category but don't specify particular people or things.
These are some indefinite pronouns.

each	everyone	both	all
someone	another	anybody	any
no one	neither	each other	many
several	others	one another	

So far *no one* has volunteered to cover for Martha when she attends the conference.

Anyone who wants to join the credit union should see Henry in personnel.

You usually need a singular verb with an indefinite pronoun.

Everybody in this department submits a timesheet at the end of each week.

Each of the people who signed the voluntary recycling contract is eligible for a free dinner at Champion House Restaurant.

No one who attended the demonstration was impressed.

Some indefinite pronouns take plural verbs.

Few of the retail giants are immune to today's profit declines.

Some indefinite pronouns can be either singular or plural.

More of the raises this year were for team leaders. [plural]

More of the enthusiasm for this project is needed for the next one. [singular]

RECIPROCAL PRONOUNS

The indefinite pronouns *each other* and *one another* are also *reciprocal pronouns*. They show the relationship or interaction between two or more people or things. Use *each other* for two people or things.

> Claude and Betsy complement *each other* on this project.

Use *one another* for more than two people or things.

> All the auditors in the department get along well with *one another*.

POSSESSIVE PRONOUNS

The possessive pronouns show ownership. Never use an apostrophe with possessive pronouns.

my, mine	our, ours
her, hers, his, its	their, theirs

His record is better than *ours* when it comes to persuasive speaking.

REFLEXIVE AND INTENSIVE PRONOUNS

The reflexive and intensive pronouns are the same:

myself, yourself, himself, herself, itself, oneself
ourselves, yourselves, themselves

1. Reflexive pronouns show that the subject and object of the verb are the same.

   > Many diabetics inject *themselves* with insulin every day.

   > Mohammed said he enjoyed *himself* at the workshop.

   Don't use reflexive pronouns in place of personal pronouns.

   instead of: Give the draft to Eric and *myself* before you revise it.

   write: Give the draft to Eric and *me* before you revise it.

2. Intensive pronouns give added emphasis to the noun or pronoun they follow.

Connie *herself* will inspect the assembly output.

You *yourself* must make sure the cash registers balance when the store closes each night.

EXPLETIVE PRONOUNS

The expletive pronouns *it* and *there* can be subjects when no other subject is suitable. They are, in effect, place holders for the subject, which is explained later in the sentence.

There is no substitute for hard work.

Considering our financial status, *it* makes sense for us to accept the merger proposal.

You can often help your reader get your message sooner by rewriting to eliminate the expletive pronoun.

Considering our financial status, we should accept the merger proposal.

Sometimes, however, popular expressions or the rhythm of the sentence make these expletive pronouns sound natural.

Where *there's* a will, *there's* a way.

It never rains but *it* pours.

When should one use *one*?

One is a formal pronoun. Using *one* frequently makes one's writing sound stuffy and overly formal.

This program makes it easy for *one* to move quickly among folders on *one's* hard disk and find the files *one* needs.

Informal pronoun use

You can use personal pronouns to create an informal style of writing that is more relaxed and familiar than a formal style.

This program makes it easy for *you* to move quickly among folders on *your* hard disk and find the files *you* need.

I have planned *my* research for this project based on the funding *we* received in January.

Informal pronouns are appropriate in most memos and e-mail messages and in some business letters. Create a tone that best suits your audience and purpose.

An informal style sounds most like spoken English, but it might not suit your international readers, who may be used to a more formal style of correspondence.

instead of: *I* have planned *my* research for this project based on the funding *we* received in January. [Fine for a memo or e-mail, but too informal for a proposal.]

write: This project's research plans depend on the funding received in January.

(See also **numbers**, *one*, **person**, **personal pronouns**, **pronoun reference**, *that/which*.)

---

proofreading: your image on paper or screen

Proofreading is the final stage in checking any document for correctness. Your reputation, and possibly your company's, may depend on how error-free and accurate your written materials are. People are definitely judged on these so-called details, so don't be lazy.

After you've made all your editing changes, check every detail. Some proofreading can be done electronically with spellchecking and grammar checking programs, but they are no substitution for reading each word yourself to be sure you catch every error.

Not only should grammar, spelling, and punctuation be correct, but also the alignment of paragraphs and lists. Be sure the appearance of each page is consistent with the graphic style of the whole document.

(See also **capital letters**, **editing your draft**, **lists**, **punctuation**, **sentences**, **spelling**.)

---

proportional spacing

When text is **proportionally spaced**, the space each letter takes up is proportional to the actual width of the letter.

A word processor is not a typewriter

Traditional typewriters can only monospace, which means that each character you type, be it an "i," a capital "M" or a period (.), takes up the same amount of space. For published documents, this didn't used to matter, because typesetters would space the type proportionally when they set it.

```
This is monospacing in Courier font.
Each character takes up the same amount
of space:
```

iii

MMM

. . .

This is proportional spacing in Times font. It's much easier to read:

iii

MMM

. . .

Only one space after sentences

Due to monospacing, typists had always been taught to type two spaces after colons and sentence-ending punctuation like periods and question marks. This convention emphasized the end of the sentence.

Proportional spacing on a word processor, however, has made this rule obsolete. Most word-processing programs have fonts with automatic proportional spacing, which inserts the appropriate amount of blank space when you press the space bar. Therefore, type only one space after sentences.

(See also **font**, **kerning**, **spacing**.)

---

proposals, formal

You write a **formal proposal** to sell your goods or services. The proposal does far more than provide information about the products or services your company offers. Your readers have a problem or need; you must convince them that you have the best solution. The more intently you focus on fixing their problem, the more appealing you will seem in their eyes.

Your proposal should give your readers complete confidence in choosing your company rather than another. Remember, whether you're selling a telecommunications system or a jet aircraft wing actuator, the proposal is your key to winning the contract.

You may be sending your formal proposal in response to a *Request for Proposal* (RFP). In this document, the customer describes a need, lists features and specifications, discusses processes or tooling, and even shows a required proposal format.

Formal proposal or letter proposal: which should you write?

Decide based mostly on the cost and complexity of the project. Write a formal proposal when

- your proposed plan is complex
- your recommendations are costly

- the recipient of your proposal will be discussing it with colleagues before making a decision. You want key decision makers to receive all necessary information in an easily accessible format.

A letter proposal works well when

- your recommendations aren't overly complicated; you can include all relevant information within the scope of a letter

- you are fairly certain you are the only contender for the contract

- you have already addressed many of your readers' questions, possibly in person.

What main points do you need to discuss?

A formal proposal answers three main questions your readers will ask:

1. DOES YOUR COMPANY UNDERSTAND OUR PROBLEM?

   How thoroughly have you studied it? Do you know our needs, piece by piece? How well do you understand our business and technology? Do you have a clear vision of the result we want?

2. HOW WILL YOUR COMPANY SOLVE OUR PROBLEM?

   How will your plan or product work? How will you proceed every step of the way? How long will it take? Will you keep on schedule? How much will it cost? What are your solution's benefits and return on investment?

3. WHY IS YOUR COMPANY THE BEST QUALIFIED?

   Who are your people? What experience and expertise have they had on similar projects? Do you have the facilities, equipment, and management necessary? Can you really deliver what you promise? How will your product or service fill our need better than anyone else's?

The winning proposal will make your readers feel that you understand their needs as well as or better than they do—and that your solution offers the best return on investment.

Your proposal is a blueprint

Your proposal tells your readers how you will proceed, and it does the same for you. By studying the problem and the solution, you're creating a viable blueprint, a project plan.

Your proposal needs to be specific. The more concrete your information, the more real and workable your solution appears—and the more advance work you will have completed.

If you win the bid, the proposal will become a legal document, part of the contract.

Let your readers be collaborators

As you prepare your proposal, try to discuss the main issues with your prospective client. Ask for suggestions; invite discussion. This way you'll learn more about the company's needs.

You'll also make your readers collaborators in the project: they will be your work partners even before signing the contract.

Another critical reason to communicate with your readers: it ensures that they will not be surprised by anything in your final proposal.

What are the main parts of a proposal?

If you're responding to an RFP, your proposal may need to follow the customer's guidelines for topics, content, and layout. But in general, formal proposals include a standard set of sections:

- Title page
- Table of contents
- Executive summary
- Introduction
- Proposed procedures (or Technical plan)
- Implementation plan
- Qualifications
- Cost analysis (or Your investment)
- Statement of agreement
- Appendix

Let's look at each section in more depth.

TITLE PAGE

Your title should convey your bottom line from your Focus Sheet™. It should

- describe your recommendations
- be specific
- emphasize action
- answer your readers' needs.

By delivering the main point, your title will make an impact. Your readers will want to read more.

The title page should also include the customer's and the writer's names, with company logo if appropriate. You can include this information as a subtitle under the main title. For example:

**Reaching 50 More Customers a Day:
TTT Telecommunications Will Improve
Efficiency and Cut Costs**

A Proposal from ABC, Inc.

to

XYZ Corporation

October 1, 19—

If the RFP requires a specific format for the title page, use it. Remember to include the date.

TABLE OF CONTENTS

Your table of contents should reflect a clear and logical design. To achieve it, organize your proposal's contents around your readers' needs.

What will they want to know first? Most likely, they'll want your proposed solution. Then, perhaps they'll wonder if you understand their situation. In any case, choose the most strategic organization.

In your subject headings, use key words—"hot buttons." If appropriate, write with the same dynamic phrasing as you did on your title page. That way, the life and substance of your idea will come through before the reader even turns to the introduction.

Your table of contents should communicate, at a glance, the flow of your thinking. And it should make your proposal easy to use. Because you use specific words, a reader can immediately find any subject.

Finally, keep your page numbering consecutive. Avoid starting again with each new heading.

EXECUTIVE SUMMARY

The executive summary previews the bottom line for busy readers. Some of them may be nontechnical, so write in lay terms—clear, simple, and streamlined.

The summary contains all your main elements: the problem or need, solution, timeline, return on investment, your plan's benefits, your company's experience.

You must clearly develop each element, so you may write the executive summary more easily after you've completed the main proposal.

Keep your bottom line in mind: What one fundamental strength will make your readers award you the contract? You don't have to include every single point in your proposal, but you should follow the proposal sequence.

The summary should be one to two pages long—and never more than one-tenth the total proposal length.

INTRODUCTION

Here you begin formally proposing your ideas.

> ABC, Inc., proposes to develop and install a comprehensive telecommunications system for XYZ Corporation, to be completed by August 31, 19—, at a cost of $000.

Describe your idea in concise, semitechnical terms. Develop key concepts beyond the executive summary. Cite studies and figures to show that you understand the buyer's need and that your product or service specifically addresses that need.

Explain your basic approach and key features. Use a selling strategy: describe the benefits that come from

- solving the problem or filling the need

- choosing your solution over the solutions of others.

Use real evidence to show why your company promises the best return on investment.

If you're responding to an RFP, refer to each specification. If you've done your research, here is where you can make your readers feel that you truly understand their problem.

TECHNICAL PLAN *OR* PROPOSED PROCEDURES

Here begins the body of your proposal. You may, if you prefer, break it into two parts:

1. "Problem" or "Current situation"
2. "Solution" or "Proposed program"

In this section, you describe the nuts and bolts. Let the buyer see exactly what you will be doing, how you will do it, and why your method is best.

Lead your readers through each facet and process. Include personnel, procedures, and methods. Discuss parts and equipment, with specifications. How do they meet the buyer's need?

Present your argument in charts, tables, and statistics. To sell your concept, you must support your technical arguments with hard evidence.

In a longer, more technical proposal, you may include this entire section in a separate binder. Most likely, only technical people will read it. They'll often turn to this part first for an initial impression of your product's viability.

IMPLEMENTATION PLAN

You've covered the problem and your solution. Now demonstrate that you have the ability and the resources needed.

Provide a concise action plan that allocates responsibility. Make it easy for readers to follow by creating a logical sequence and avoiding unnecessary detail. Describe your

- management and organization. Who's in charge? Which departments will you dedicate to this project? Who has what responsibilities? If appropriate, include an organizational chart.

- major tasks. Can you divide them into smaller ones to provide a detailed picture? If complex, use flow charts.

- potential constraints. Are there any foreseeable problems due to personnel or outside factors?

- schedule and deliverables. What are the deadlines by department? By individual? By task? When will you install or implement the components? The completed work?

- accounting and reporting procedures

- financial resources

- plant and equipment

- site preparation

- quality assurance and control.

QUALIFICATIONS

Especially on technical projects, you'll want to include resumes of key personnel to demonstrate their expertise and specialized knowledge.

Begin your resume roster with those team members whose experience best matches the project. Rather than including standard resumes, however, rewrite them to feature the capabilities that would best serve this project. Bring the information up to date.

COST ANALYSIS *OR* YOUR INVESTMENT

Describe the costs only after you have sold your readers on the project. If you've convinced them, they'll be more receptive to your price. Headline the section, "Your investment."

Your best strategy is to cite costs in the context of payoff. If you list the figures in chart form, for instance, add a column that shows return on investment for each item. Or, if your costs are simple, describe them in sentences that highlight the related benefits.

> Our telecommunications system, which will increase customer contact by 50 percent and save you $000 to $000 annually, costs just $000—a one-time investment.

Include your

1. total cost
2. breakdowns

   - labor, both direct and indirect

   - equipment

   - administrative

   - overhead

- miscellaneous

3. methods of cost projection.

In your cost section, make sure that you

1. stay consistent with your technical section—item for item

2. follow RFP requirements.

STATEMENT OF AGREEMENT

Contact your potential customer and review the terms of agreement, especially legal and financial terms. Include a preview of your purchase agreement. The statement of agreement will act as the basis for a future contract and will help eliminate legal problems later on.

APPENDIX

Include in your appendix material that

- may not be crucial to winning the proposal
- most of your readers already know, but some may not
- provides very technical or detailed information that not all readers need to examine.

Assign each appendix a number or letter in the order that you refer to it in the text, and list it in the table of contents.

What makes a sales proposal successful?

Your proposal is part of your sales strategy. To be persuasive, you must

1. BE CUSTOMER FOCUSED

- Use the "you" attitude. Write *you* or the buyer's name more than *I*, *we*, or your company's name.

You wanted a product that can meet *your* need for faster service.

The "you" attitude is especially effective in headlines that reflect, at a glance, that you understand your customer's needs.

• Restate your readers' needs from your Focus Sheet. You will make it clear that you understand their vision of a successful purchase.

For example, if the customer is worried about telecommunications system breakdowns, you should stress your system's reliability.

2. WRITE FROM YOUR READERS' POINT OF VIEW

Think of the questions your reader would ask—and answer them. Use your Focus Sheet carefully.

3. USE FREQUENT, PERSUASIVE HEADLINES

Hold and propel your reader's attention. Specific and persuasive headlines are the most effective.

instead of: Qualifications

write: Why is ABC best equipped to meet your goals?

instead of: This system will increase efficiency by 50 percent.

write: Our system will increase *your* efficiency by 50 percent.

4. SEQUENCE IDEAS STRATEGICALLY

Put the "bottom line" (key message) on top from your readers' point of view. Remember that asking what the benefit will be for them will give you your bottom line. Put costs toward the end.

5. AVOID OVERLOADING YOUR READERS WITH UNNECESSARY INFORMATION

Include pertinent information only. Don't deluge your readers with masses of data in an attempt to impress them. Avoid discussing features or benefits that stress your own goals.

6. EMPHASIZE RELEVANT STRENGTHS

Highlight only the strengths of your product or service that relate to your readers' needs. Try linking your proposal to their corporate goals.

If they're a start-up company, discuss survival and market share. If they're prospering, mention how you can help them retain talented people.

7. DESCRIBE YOUR SOLUTION'S IMPACT ON YOUR CUSTOMER'S BUSINESS

Go beyond features and benefits to impact. For example, discuss why each feature is important to this particular customer. Quantify and prove it.

8. USE A WARM, FRIENDLY, YET PROFESSIONAL TONE

Avoid overly formal language and jargon.

instead of: This will enable rapid calendarization of the product.

write: This system will allow you to meet your product deadlines.

9. USE FACTS

Avoid superlatives and exaggerations. Concrete evidence will sell your product or service.

10. ESTABLISH YOUR CREDIBILITY AND EXPERIENCE

By describing your past experience or success, you establish your expertise. You may want to quote experts or references to enhance your authority.

11. MAKE SURE YOUR PROPOSAL LOOKS PROFESSIONAL AND EASY TO READ

- Follow standard formats.
- Use headlines.
- Balance white space and text.
- Write short words, sentences, and paragraphs.
- Make sure there are no typographical errors or misspellings.

When *not* to write a proposal

Since writing a formal proposal is a major investment of time, energy, and resources, don't undertake one if success seems unlikely.

How can you tell? Perhaps you know your company can't adequately fulfill all the customer's needs. Or maybe you sense that the customer isn't serious yet, just gathering multiple bids. Think carefully before investing in a formal proposal.

(See also **executive summaries**; **headlines**; **lists**; **Model Documents Appendix**; **readers, analyzing**; **request for proposal**; **"you" attitude**.)

---

proposals, letter

A **letter proposal** is an informal proposal that you write mainly to offer a product or service. It often documents oral agreements for your readers to review. Like any proposal, it sets forth a plan of action.

Parts of a letter proposal

Do not confuse these generic parts with the persuasive headlines you will need to insert throughout your proposal.

SUBJECT LINE

Put a subject line that summarizes your topic just after the salutation.

INTRODUCTION

First, thank your readers for inviting your proposal. Then summarize how you plan to meet your readers' needs. Make a point of saying that your solution is based on your company's and your readers' people working together.

Be sure to write "you" when addressing your readers. Mention the readers more than you mention yourself, especially in headlines.

STATEMENT OF NEEDS

Analyze your readers' needs clearly. Restate problems and define them, and acknowledge the buyers' decision criteria. Here are some sample headlines that show you understand your readers' needs.

You asked about . . .

You are facing these obstacles

Your goal is to . . .

You need . . .

Try to avoid "I" or "our"—not because it's incorrect but because it shows you're more interested in selling your product than in meeting your buyers' needs.

SOLUTIONS OR RECOMMENDATIONS

Briefly highlight each of your potential customers' needs, then follow with the features, advantages, and benefits of your service or product. Don't simply provide a list of every wonderful feature and benefit you can think of—make sure they match the needs of your customers.

To build your credibility, you need to show that you listened to the buyers' precise needs. Sample headlines in this section could include:

You need a product with 100% reliability

Your timeframe is very short

You need a team who has succeeded in the toughest situations

You need to demonstrate return on investment in year one

Include an action plan. Be sure to spell out which part of the project your company will do and which part the client will do. Here are some sample headlines.

Recommended approach

What must be in place?

Implementation plan

COSTS

List your costs and justify them. If you relate costs to deliverables, the buyer will see the breakdown. Describe the tangible and intangible benefits of your solutions. Sample headlines:

What productivity results can you expect?

What is your return on investment?

Why choose our firm?

This is the place to explain the unique qualifications of your company to deliver on the proposal. Add a paragraph on key players or experience. Try these headlines:

You have more options with us

What makes ABC Co. different?

APPENDIX PREVIEW

If your proposal is long enough to need an appendix, you have probably written a formal proposal, not a letter proposal. Consider attaching a cover letter instead of making your proposal a letter in itself.

If you are convinced, however, that you should stay with the letter format, then mention the most important appendix documents. Include a bulleted list of appendix contents.

CLOSING STATEMENT

Create a sense of urgency to entice your readers to act quickly. Include an assurance that you'll call soon to go over the proposal with them, answer questions, and talk about the next steps. Sample headline:

Suggested next steps

THANKS

Express your eagerness to work together with a warm, personal tone.

Building on our successful joint ventures in the past, we look forward to working with you again.

APPENDIX

The appendix should include

- an implementation schedule that describes both your and your readers' responsibilities

- background data related to solutions and recommendations

- brochures or biographies that give details about your company's products, people, and services

- copies of your contract or purchase agreement.

In general, the contents of the appendix should give background about you and your company. Attachments should support next steps.

(See also **appendix**; **headlines**; **letters**; **Model Documents Appendix**; **proposals, formal**; **readers, analyzing**; **tone**.)

punctuation

Punctuation marks are symbols that guide readers through your document. They function like highway signs that give directions.

apostrophe	'
brackets	[ ]
colon	:
comma	,
dash	—
ellipses	. . .
exclamation point	!
hyphen	-
parentheses	( )
period	.
question mark	?
quotation marks	" "
semicolon	;
slash	/

The marks of punctuation show structural relationships both within and between sentences and indicate whether ideas are connected, enclosed, separated, or ended.

Punctuation is a substitute for a speaker's gestures, expressions, and voice inflections. If you don't use punctuation correctly, your readers might misunderstand you.

Many rules and conventions govern how you use punctuation. Look up each mark separately for in-depth information.

(See also **open punctuation**.)

Q

---

question marks

An interrogative sentence asks a question and ends with a **question mark (?)**. Following are the common uses of the question mark.

In a direct question

Put a question mark at the end of a direct question.

> How should we implement this policy?

INTRODUCING QUESTIONS WITH STATEMENTS

When you introduce a question with a statement, always put a comma after the statement and don't use quotation marks. In formal writing only, capitalize the first word of the question.

> We should ponder the question, What is the new direction of this company? [formal]

> Before you recommend a change, ask yourself, is it necessary? [informal]

With a series of items

If your interrogative sentence contains a series of items related to a common subject, put a question mark after each item. Do not capitalize each question.

> Where do you want to hold the seminar? set up the displays? put the refreshments?

If you decide to number these questions or put them in a vertical list, use a single question mark at the end.

> Where do you want to (1) hold the seminar, (2) set up the displays, (3) put the refreshments?

Where do you want to

- hold the seminar
- set up the displays
- put the refreshments?

To express doubt

If you want to express doubt or uncertainty about a word or statement, follow it with a question mark in parentheses.

Sales began improving in FY 1995 (?).

In titles that are questions

If a title includes a question mark, always keep it, no matter where in the sentence the title occurs.

Are Your Investments Working? is an excellent book for the experienced investor.

With other punctuation

QUOTATION MARKS

Question marks can be either inside or outside quotation marks, depending on the meaning. If the question mark is part of the quoted material, put it *inside* the quotation marks.

Yesterday Hilda asked, "Can you include the installation and setup documentation in Part I of the manual?"

If the quoted material is not a question, put the question mark *outside* the quotation marks.

Did Jordan say to the engineering department, "We need the specs by Monday"?

PARENTHESES

Put question marks inside parentheses if the parenthetical material is a question.

We found out at the meeting (Weren't you there?) that the deadline has been extended.

COMMAS

If a question within a sentence ends at a place where you need a comma, you may drop the comma and retain the question mark. This is the preferred style.

If the client asks, "How will we penetrate the new market?" Carlos should answer.

An alternative style choice is to drop the question mark and retain the comma.

If the client asks, "How will we penetrate the new market," Carlos should answer.

SEMICOLONS

If a sentence needs a semicolon where a question ends, keep both the question mark and the semi-colon.

These are the main sections of the report: Personal, Partnership, and Corporate Financial Disclosure; Audited Financial Statements; Are Treasury Bonds Still on the Rise?; and Guarantees for Commercial Loans.

Avoid such cumbersome punctuation by rewriting the sentence as a bulleted or numbered list.

When not to use question marks

IN INDIRECT QUESTIONS

Don't put a question mark at the end of an indirect question.

Hilda asked if we could include the installation and setup documentation in Part I of the manual.

How the cash compensation will be calculated is still a question.

IN REQUESTS THAT ARE REALLY COMMANDS

If you write a request that you mean as a polite command, don't use a question mark.

> As you go through the inventory, would you please note the discrepancies between items actually in stock and items on the printout.

If you are actually making a request, especially of a superior or a client, use a question mark.

> Would you please sign the contracts by Friday, March 24?

(See also **commas**, **parentheses**, **semicolons**, **sentences**.)

---

quotation marks

Quotation marks (" ") are most commonly used to enclose exact written or spoken words. Following are some guidelines for using quotation marks.

With exact written or spoken words

Put a comma after the words that introduce the quote if they come first in the sentence. If the attribution comes after the quote, put a comma at the end of the quote.

> According to Benton and Kulik, "Only 40 percent of training programs are followed up afterwards."

> "Illegal memory access," read the error message.

When you repeat a statement but don't quote your source directly, omit the quotation marks.

> The error message said there was an illegal memory access.

For quotations within quotations

When a quotation comes within a quotation, use single quotation marks (an apostrophe) around the inside quote.

Stuart said at the meeting, "Our president believes in the maxim, 'Never complain, never explain.'"

To set off special words

To draw attention to a technical term or to a word's special use in a context, put the word in quotation marks.

"Static," in this context, means that the variable is allocated from static memory.

To define words

Words that define or explain other words should be in quotation marks.

The Latin expression *quid pro quo* means "an exchange of cooperation."

To suggest the opposite meaning of a word

Use quotes to imply that something is untrue or to suggest irony.

The electrical fire destroyed the files in the new "fireproof" cabinet.

After missing his flight, losing his luggage, and canceling his meeting, Antonio said he felt "just great."

Beware of using quotes in labels—they might be interpreted as exaggerated, suspicious, or completely untrue.

"Fresh" every day!   "Homemade"
The "best" on the market

With titles

The titles of articles, documents, reports, and other short pieces should be set off in quotation marks.

The article "Do Women Manage Differently?" in *Fortune* has started some lively discussions around here.

To show repetition

A line of quotation marks underneath text indicates that the words above are to be repeated. Try to avoid this usage, however—it isn't the clearest way to present information and may confuse your readers.

instead of:	Unit A will be shipped on October 10.
	Unit B " " " " November 5.
	Unit C " " " " November 21.
write:	Here are the ship dates for the back-ordered items:

- Unit A: October 10
- Unit B: November 5
- Unit C: November 21

With other marks of punctuation

- Commas and periods always go inside closing quotation marks.
- Colons and semicolons always go outside closing quotation marks.
- Exclamation points and question marks go inside closing quotation marks only if they're part of the quoted material.

(See also **documenting sources, exclamation points, plagiarism, question marks, quotations, titles**.)

quotations

Quotations, or someone's exact written or spoken words, are a powerful writing tool. They can add credibility and strength to your report or proposal.

If you write someone else's words without crediting the author, you are guilty of plagiarism. Always enclose a short quote in quotation marks. If your quote is four lines or longer, indent it.

Direct and indirect quotations

Direct quotations are someone's exact written or spoken words. Always put them in quotation marks.

> The RFP states on page 3 that "key aspects of the development of the system will be low weight, high cooling efficiency, and low cost."

An indirect quotation tells what someone said, but not in exact words.

> The RFP emphasizes that low weight, high cooling efficiency, and low cost are key aspects of system development.

Always document the source of your quotations.

Omitted and added material

The statement you quote must be exact. If you leave out any words, use ellipses (three periods) to show where the omission is. If you add words to an otherwise exact quote, put them in brackets.

> Harold Wodinski told the auditors that "the marketing plan . . . will meet all fiduciary guidelines."

> Harold Wodinski told the auditors that "the marketing plan [which they had questioned] will meet all fiduciary guidelines."

> *Original:* The marketing plan, which includes Asian subsidiaries as well as the home office, will meet all fiduciary guidelines.

Long quotations

If your quoted material is four lines long or more, indent the whole block from the left margin, single-space it, and *omit* the quotation marks.

Here is some useful advice from the book *Write to the Top*:

> Like most skills, writing is improved primarily by practice . . . . You must get involved in order to learn.
>
> No one becomes a faster jogger simply by reading a book about jogging; neither will you improve your writing by reading a book or listening to a lecture . . . . Just as running laps improves your running, every page you actually work on will benefit your writing.

Paraphrasing

A paraphrase is a restatement of a quotation in your own words. Paraphrases don't need quotation marks, but their source does need to be documented.

original:	Due to a lack of centralized planning, there is also the possibility of duplicating efforts and overlapping services.
	For example, the Credit Department has two programs engaged in similar activities. Both the Crown Hill program and "Step up and in" offer advice on budget planning primarily for low-to-moderate income families.
paraphrase:	The Credit Department has two programs—Crown Hill and "Step up and in"—that provide budget planning services for low-to-moderate-income families. A centralized planning strategy would eliminate such overlaps.

(See also **copyright**, **documenting sources**, **plagiarism**, **quotation marks**.)

R

radar charts

A **radar chart** is a line chart wrapped around a central point, with each axis representing a set of data points. Each data point is plotted as the distance from the center point (see below).

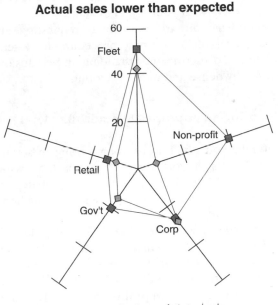

Actual sales lower than expected

■ Expected sales   ◇ Actual sales

Radar charts are useful to show the symmetry of data. For example, they indicate whether each division, such as corporate, government, or individual, has the same pattern of sales. Radar charts can also compare a projected cycle with an actual cycle.

Caution: radar charts are very difficult to read when lines overlap frequently.

(See also **charts or graphs**, **line charts**, **tables**.)

readability: make it easy for your readers

Readability is the degree of ease with which the text of a document can be read. If your readers can't read your words quickly, your document may end up at the bottom of their to-do list.

In any business writing that you do, your over-riding purpose is to communicate—not to dazzle your readers with your literary talents.

Whether you are informing, requesting an action, or explaining a new procedure, it's essential to avoid the misunderstanding and confusion caused by dense and difficult writing.

Choosing an appropriate readability level

Naturally you don't want your writing to sound juvenile. Nor do you want to weigh it down with long words intended to lend it an air of importance. The most sensible approach is somewhere in the middle.

Avoid long words and keep sentence length under 20 words. This will result in a readability level of about 9 on Fry's Readability Graph, a measurement tool explained in the book *Write to the Top*.

The readability level of this book is 9. Here are the scores of some familiar publications:

The Atlantic	12 (difficult)
The New York Times	10
Time Magazine	10
The Boston Globe	10
U.S.A. Today	7
People magazine	6 (easy)

Controlling the readability level

To make your writing easier to read, shorten sentences and use simple, nontechnical terms whenever possible. Think about the expertise of your readers. Are you writing for managers or for clerical trainees?

If you don't know your readers, it's safer to simplify. Perhaps your audience is pressed for time and won't even read your whole document; make your writing accessible so that your main purpose can be quickly understood.

Making technical writing easy to read

One strategy: make comparisons to concrete, everyday things. If you're describing a complex process, try to find some aspect—either appearance or function—that you can compare to a familiar object your readers can visualize.

> The pressure from the anions forces the water into contact with a greater area of fiber, the way pressing an inflated balloon on a tabletop with your hand increases the area of the balloon that touches the table.

Unless you know that your readers are well acquainted with your topic, be sure to define all technical terms and acronyms. If you need to convey technical information to stockholders or clients, translate technical terms or you may lose your audience.

Using software to evaluate readability

Your word processing program may come equipped with a grammar checker that evaluates readability.

If not, Rightwriter, MacProof, FullWrite, and Fogfinder are among the many excellent programs available for readability analysis. They count the syllables per word and words per sentence in a writing sample to compute a readability score.

Most programs also search for grammar errors, analyze sentence structure, and offer editing advice.

(See also **streamlining**, **word choice**.)

Focus Sheet

Step 1

Answer these questions as the first step in any writing task.

☞ Be sure to use these items for short documents.

1. **Purpose:**

☞ A. Why am I writing this? _____

☞ B. What do I want the reader to do? _____

2. **Audience:**

A. Who is my reader? Do I have more than one? _____

B. What is the reader's role? _____

C. What does the reader know about the subject? _____

D. How will the reader react? _____

E. What's in it for the reader? Why should the reader read this or agree with it? _____

F. How will the reader use this document? _____

G. Whom should I include in this mailing? _____

3. **Bottom Line:**

☞ If the reader were to forget everything else, what one key point do I want remembered? _____

4. **Strategy:**

A. Should *I* be writing this? At *this* time? Would a phone call or meeting be more effective?

B. Should I send this at all? Am I too late? Too early?

C. Is someone else communicating the same information? Should I check with that person?

D. Is my method of transmission the best? Should I be using e-mail, fax, or traditional mail?

Completed Focus Sheet™

Focus Sheet
Step 1

Answer these questions as the first step in any writing task:

☞ Be sure to use these items for short documents.

1. Purpose:

☞ A. Why am I writing this? *to propose that we run focus groups to evaluate our new brokerage accounts.*

☞ B. What do I want the reader to do? *organize focus groups, believe that this is a good idea, appropriate a budget for this.*

2. Audience:

A. Who is my reader? Do I have more than one? *Region 11 VP in charge of brokerage accounts and other bank managers.*

B. What is the reader's role? *oversees brokerage accounts for our bank, thought-leader for new ideas and growth respected.*

C. What does the reader know about the subject? *very well informed about brokerage accounts, may not realize its time to evaluate our progress.*

D. How will the reader react? *may be resistant to hiring focus groups because of cost — may be preferring cheaper methods.*

E. What's in it for the reader? Why should the reader read this or agree with it? *because we want to expand our brokerage services and we need to know how to improve our customer service — focus groups are the best way to learn this.*

F. How will the reader use this document? _to evaluate if focus groups are the best approach — to use as a discussion outline with co-workers about the idea of focus groups in general._

G. Whom should I include in this mailing? _all upper-level management involved in brokerage within the bank._

3. Bottom Line:

☞ If the reader were to forget everything else, what one key point do I want remembered? _Focus groups are the way to evaluate customer satisfaction so far. This will help us keep improving and growing._

4. Strategy:

A. Should I be writing this? At *this* time? Would a phone call or meeting be more effective? _Yes, because I'm in charge of customer relations. Proposal is better than phone call because reader can distribute it to other managers._

B. Should I send this at all? Am I too late? Too early? _Yes. Perfect timing for expanding services._

C. Is someone else communicating the same information? Should I check with that person? _Maybe I should coordinate with the focus group consultants we use._

D. Is my method of transmission the best? Should I be using e-mail, fax, or traditional mail? _Memo is most efficient — I'll attach it to e-mail._

readers, analyzing: Step 1 to Reader-Centered Writing

Your **readers** are your customers. Analyzing who they are and what they need is vital for precise and clear communication.

Satisfy your readers' needs

Every day readers' in-boxes and e-mailboxes overflow with countless letters and memos. The first questions every reader asks are, "What's this about?" and "What do I need to do about it?"

In survey after survey, readers complain that even these simple questions are tough to answer in the majority of communications they receive.

By taking the time to analyze their needs, you will avoid irritating your readers and make sure they actually read your document.

When you write a document, you are opening an imaginary dialogue with your readers. You want that dialogue to be clear and efficient, so you need to think carefully about both sides: What information do you need to convey? How are your readers likely to respond?

Even if you don't know your readers personally, use what you know about their positions and roles to anticipate the nature of their response. As you bring your readers into focus, you will also be defining the tone and scope of your writing.

Better Communications™ Inc., has developed a Focus Sheet™ that helps writers pinpoint their purpose and understand their readers' needs. Both a blank and a completed Focus Sheet are found on pages 466–469.

The Focus Sheet™: do you really need it?

The resounding answer is "yes!" Fill one out before writing any document. It will help you sweep aside off-track ideas and concentrate on your main goal.

By analyzing your audience, you'll make effective and persuasive decisions about your content, strategy, and tone. Your readers will thank you for this effort. In return your documents will be read ahead of the competition's, and you will gain

- faster responses
- more cooperation
- greater influence
- increased respect for your clarity of thought.

Our Focus Sheet has four main parts:

1. purpose
2. audience
3. bottom line (or key point)
4. strategy

You need to think creatively about each section and keep all four components in mind as you prepare to write. For instance, if you analyze your readers accurately but ignore your "bottom line," your document may miss its mark.

Purpose: you can't start without it

Your usual purpose in business writing is to inspire action or agreement on a certain issue. Make your purpose active by defining it with a verb. Here are some examples:

to persuade	to analyze	to explain
to request	to motivate	to recommend
to report findings	to respond	to praise
to inform	to propose	to announce

If you always choose "to inform" as your purpose, your memos and letters are probably somewhat bland and ineffectual. Think harder about the final result you are seeking.

It's usually far more than simply providing information. Ask yourself, "*Why* am I informing my readers about this?" Keep searching for a purpose that is action oriented.

Audience: consider all your readers

Your documents often go to more than one reader, which makes your task more complicated. Each reader's role, experience with the subject matter, and anticipated use of your document may vary.

The Focus Sheet helps you create a profile of your readers and consider all their needs before deciding on a strategy.

Your answers to the questions in this part of the Focus Sheet will be the key to your approach.

Ask yourself, "Will my readers be receptive, indifferent, or resistant?" The response will tell you whether you should be exceptionally tactful in making the request or use a politely assertive tone and sequence.

Foresee your readers' use of the document and you'll have a clearer idea of the form it should take.

WATCH TECHNICAL LANGUAGE

Don't overwhelm even a technical audience with too much technical detail in too short a space. If the writing is too dense, it will be difficult to get through.

Ask yourself what knowledge and experience your readers are likely to have of the subject. Then adjust your technical language accordingly.

CHOOSE A FRIENDLY OR A FORMAL TONE

In most business and even some technical writing, a friendly tone is perfectly acceptable. Visualize your readers and write as if you were speaking to them.

In some long documents or formal reports, however, a more formal tone is appropriate. If you don't know your readers directly, you will want to be more formal than with people you have met.

Bottom line: the core of your message

Your writing will be clearer and more effective if you can formulate your main idea concisely. Sometimes that's difficult to do.

The Focus Sheet asks you, "If my readers were to forget everything else, what one key point would I want them to remember?" This is probably the best way to get at your "bottom line" because it forces you to summarize your message.

Keep in mind that the "bottom line" may not always be the most obvious approach.

For example, if you're proposing a new strategy, your bottom line may not be, "Here's my great new idea," but, "This strategy will give us a big lead on the competition." Before you write, determine the key idea that will stick with your reader.

Remember, too, that most of your readers are already drowning in information. They usually skim a document, whether e-mail or paper, to decide if it's worth their immediate attention.

If they can't figure out the writer's bottom line in the subject or re line, they may postpone a more careful reading—and you've lost a valuable opportunity to capture their interest.

Strategy: generating action

No matter how brilliant a proposal you write, it could fail completely if your timing is off. Be sure to take into account the schedules and needs of your readers. Don't, for example, send a document that requests an action the day before a reader leaves for vacation.

The form of your communication can also be strategic. Ask yourself, "Would it be most effective to e-mail, write, fax, phone, send a videotape, or call a meeting?" Do you need one document or two?

Should you include a cover letter separate from your main document? Decide according to your readers. Think, too, about whether you are the best person to communicate this information at this time.

Your strategy may include some accountability, such as "Please correct the figures in the Ishikawa proposal by May 12." Be sure that your request for action or response is clear and well timed.

The scope of your document

When you decide what information to include in your document and what to leave out, you are determining its scope. Scope depends on the knowledge and expertise of your readers.

Use your Focus Sheet to help you decide how deeply—or with what limitations—to cover your subject. Determining the scope of your document at this stage will help you plan your research and organize information later.

Where do you go from here?

Now that you've used the Focus Sheet to analyze your audience and define your purpose, it's time to generate ideas. Step 2 in the Six Steps to Reader-Centered Writing™, getting started with a Start-up Strategy, is designed to help you pull your thoughts together.

Some of the strategies are new; others have been used by writers for decades. At least one of the strategies in the **getting started** entry will increase your productivity and see you safely toward your deadline.

(See also **format**, **Introduction to the Six Steps**, **jargon**, **organizing information**, **point of view**, **reports**, **tone**.)

redundancy

Redundancy means needless repetition.

> The new complex is much more convenient because the lab and the plant are finally in *close proximity* to each other.

Close proximity is redundant because the word *proximity* alone means "close" or "nearby." Rewrite the sentence:

> The new complex is much more convenient because the lab is finally located close to the plant.

You can use either word of a redundant pair, but not both. Here are some common redundant phrases. The redundant word in each group is in italics.

absolutely complete	connect *together*
seems apparent	*still* continue
mutual cooperation	*past* experience
assembled *together*	*final* conclusion
grateful thanks	*true* facts
barracks *buildings*	*young* juveniles
skirt *around*	shuttle *back and forth*
descend *down*	depreciated *in value*
classified *into groups*	filled *to capacity*

Do not use repetition unless you want to establish a contrast or emphasize a point.

> I need a memory upgrade; mine *fills to capacity* much too quickly with this new program.

> The 386 may have *depreciated in value*, but it was still a good investment.

> The president said, "We extend our *grateful thanks* especially to the architects of the merger."

(See also **concise vs. wordy writing**.)

reflexive pronouns: the *self* words

Reflexive pronouns refer to a subject or object that is the same as the pronoun. The reflexive pronouns are

myself   ourselves
yourself   yourselves
himself, herself, itself, oneself   themselves.

George sent *himself* an e-mail as a reminder.
[*Himself* refers back to the subject, *George*.]

Reflexive pronouns are also used to emphasize the
noun or pronoun they refer to.

Simon wrote the program *himself*.

For a faster response, you can bring the form to personnel *yourself*.

The tape *itself* should be cleaned, as well as the
tape drive.

Reflexive or personal pronoun?

Don't use reflexive pronouns in place of personal
pronouns like *me*, *him*, *her*, or *you*.

instead of: As for *myself*, I don't think it's a
                   good idea.

write: As for *me*, I don't think it's a good idea.

(See also **personal pronouns**, **pronoun reference**, **pronouns**.)

---

relative pronouns

Relative pronouns are the first words in dependent clauses and can also be subjects or objects in
such clauses. The relative pronouns are

who, whom, what, which, whose, whoever,
whomever, that.

These pronouns indicate the relationship of the
dependent clause with the main clause.

The shipment *that we ordered last month* will
arrive tomorrow. [The dependent clause *that we
ordered last month* modifies *shipment*. Within the
dependent clause, *that* is the object of the verb
ordered.]

Tomorrow we will hear *who won the award*. [The dependent clause *who won the award* is the object of the verb *will hear*. Within the dependent clause, *who* is the subject of the verb *won*.]

Sometimes you can omit *that*. If you aren't sure, or if you're afraid your sentence might be unclear, leave it in.

Beth finished the article [*that*] Gunther requested for the newsletter.

The shipment [*that*] we ordered last month will arrive tomorrow.

The relative pronouns, except for *that*, are also the interrogative pronouns.

Who won the award?

Whose project won the award?

Which system do you think is best for our needs?

That and *which*

Writers often use *which* instead of *that*. *That* is correct when the clause that follows contains essential information.

The valve *that controls this series of drains* is in the pipe to your left.

Use *which* if the clause that follows contains nonessential information. Such a clause is preceded by a comma.

The program has a graphical user interface, *which means that the program will be easy to use*.

(See also **pronouns**, **restrictive and nonrestrictive elements**, *that/which*.)

---

reports

A **report** can inform readers about the status of a project, recommend solutions to a problem, evaluate a situation, or provide a comprehensive study of all work done in a certain area.

There are hundreds of different kinds of reports; your style, tone, and approach will vary according to your purpose in writing.

Formal vs. informal: what's the difference?

A formal report is at least six double-spaced pages long—or it could occupy six volumes. It usually requires extensive research and planning.

For example, it may fulfill a contractual agreement between companies or present data collected over years of study. A formal report is intended to have lasting value, often for a wide audience of readers.

There are distinct guidelines governing the structure of a formal report, although company standards do vary. Pay particular attention to the appearance of the report to convey the best possible image of you and your company.

An informal report is usually shorter, less complex, and less comprehensive than a formal one.

Its purpose is to present information concisely without unnecessary detail. It may be as simple as a memorandum to a co-worker, or it may be a 50-page progress report outlining all work done on a project to date.

Some kinds of reports, such as feasibility reports, can be formal or informal, depending on their purpose and your audience. Others, like letter reports, are nearly always informal.

What type of report are you writing?

At the outset define why you need to write a report. The reason will dictate the format. In all cases, use your Focus Sheet™ to analyze your readers, decide how technical to be, and determine how much background to provide.

Before writing, try to find out how much detail your readers expect. Then follow the Six Steps to

Reader-Centered Writing™ explained in the Introduction to the Six Steps.

LETTER REPORT

A letter report, whether informal or dignified in tone, usually conveys information from one company to another. It can make recommendations, request an action, or evaluate an idea.

It looks very much like a typical business letter, with letterhead, date, inside address, salutation, subject line, complimentary closing, and signature.

The subject line is the title of your report. Keep it between 6 and 12 words long.

Letter reports usually include the following sections:

1. introduction: purpose in writing; background information vital to the reader's understanding of the report
2. summary: the key message of the report
3. discussion: supporting facts and details
4. conclusion: results and effects

Think hard before putting even a brief report in letter form. It is usually better to separate a report—even a four-page one—from the cover letter.

Reports go to a lot of people; some of them may be readers you didn't anticipate. Do you want all of them to read the individual, relationship-building, and even personal parts of your letter? Save such comments for a separate cover letter to a limited audience you know well.

When in doubt, write a separate transmittal letter to give your letter report a more formal look. Put the title either on a separate cover page or at the top of your first page.

Separating the letter also allows you to present complex material in more sections you can easily format, with clear headline levels to show the subordination of ideas.

FEASIBILITY REPORT

A feasibility study presents a concept and analyzes whether it is economically or technically feasible. This type of analysis often takes place between different companies at the management level.

For example, a small real-estate company might not have employees with sufficient technical expertise to decide on the purchase of a new computer system.

The company might require a feasibility study from a computer consulting firm. A brief feasibility report can take the form of a letter; anything over five pages would require a formal report.

INVESTIGATIVE REPORT

You can organize the results of your research on a particular topic in an investigative report. This type of report analyzes a subject, such as choosing a voice-mail system for your company. The report presents comparative facts, conclusions, and recommendations.

PROGRESS REPORT

As the name implies, a progress report describes the status of a project in progress. It summarizes what has been accomplished so far, pinpoints problems, and offers a schedule for the remainder of the project.

A progress report usually focuses on a single project, such as the development of a specific product.

If the project is small, a single progress report in letter or memo form two weeks into the work may suffice. Larger undertakings might require formal progress reports at regular intervals over a long period of time.

Supervisors and sponsors read progress reports. They want to know:

- **What work has your company completed?**

- Have you encountered any difficulties?
- Will you be able to keep to the schedule?
- Will you be able to deliver according to specifications?
- Are you sticking to the budget?

A progress report contains basically the same components as a letter report:

1. The introduction describes the relevant background and states your objectives. If you're writing a second, third, or fourth progress report, make sure you refer to the immediately preceding report.

2. A summary provides an overview of the project.

3. A discussion section describes past work and tells what lies ahead, usually in the form of a chronological narrative or list.

4. The conclusion evaluates the project to date and makes a realistic projection about the schedule and deliverables ahead.

COMPLETION REPORT

This is a comprehensive record of a completed project. It may be a formal or informal report, depending on the length and complexity of the project discussed.

Why write a completion report? In the following situations a complete record of past work is essential.

1. Change of personnel: an employee who is the only one familiar with a particular function may be leaving the company. Replacement staff will need a full and clear completion report to understand and perform the function.

2. Problem resolution: if problems arise after a project has been completed, managers and technical experts will want to review the entire project to pinpoint errors.

A completion report summarizes all aspects of a project, thus facilitating review of the whole process.

3. New projects: a background review is always worthwhile before forging ahead. Analyze past methods to increase efficiency. Examine how a project affected existing conditions—or left them unchanged.

Parts of a formal report

Companies differ in their guidelines for writing formal reports. Some are exacting to the smallest detail, while others are considerably freer.

Your company may demand over a dozen distinct parts to a report; elsewhere six main sections are the norm. In addition to the main sections, there are always subsidiary parts of a report, some of which are optional.

COVER LETTER

A letter or memo identifying the report and conveying thanks or other relationship-building messages is often clipped to the cover.

TRANSMITTAL LETTER

More formal than a cover letter, an optional transmittal letter states the purpose of the report and summarizes findings. It is in the form of a standard business letter and may be attached to the outside cover or bound inside.

COVER

The outside jacket protects the report and identifies it; it states the title and the name of the company that researched and wrote the report.

TITLE PAGE

The title page lists the title, author, name of the author's company, date, and sometimes the client's name and location.

TABLE OF CONTENTS

The table of contents lists report sections and the page number on which each section starts. It shows readers how the report is organized. Omit it only if your report is very short. Include a list of illustrations, figures, tables, and appendixes with their page numbers.

ACKNOWLEDGMENTS

An optional page, this is the place to thank all who contributed to the project or helped write the report

EXECUTIVE SUMMARY

This essential section summarizes the key issues of the entire report. It describes the purpose of writing and makes recommendations.

Concise and clear, your executive summary must convey the essence of your report to the senior executive who has little time to read any further.

Write your executive summary last, after your report is organized and complete. If you write it first, you might end up rewriting it. Include all your key points in the order you present them in the body of the report.

The executive summary is not, however, an exact miniature of your report—it may not contain all the same sections. Concentrate on a succinct presentation of your purpose and recommendations.

Keep the executive summary short and informative—no more than two pages. It should never exceed 1/10 of your report in length.

Include an executive summary with any report that is four pages or longer. Your readers will absorb your main message in the executive summary, then skim the rest of the report and concentrate on the information that they need.

INTRODUCTION OR PURPOSE OF REPORT

The introduction describes the purpose, background, and scope of the report. In not-too-technical terms, it tells the reasons for the study or project and sets it in context.

Make the background explanation brief, however. Writers often include too much background at the beginning and irritate their knowledgeable readers. Don't lose sight of the reader analysis you did on your Focus Sheet.

RECOMMENDATIONS

State in a strong, active voice the actions and procedures that you recommend. Use the first person point of view unless your company objects.

> I recommend that you test the new system for one month.

Some companies prefer the plural "we" to indicate that the report represents the views of the whole company.

Number your recommendations for easy discussion and to create a checklist for action.

BODY

The body can include many sections, depending on your field and the subject of the report. Here are some typical sections:

- procedure or methodology
- implementation plan
- analysis

- discussion
- supporting data
- background

In the body of your report, describe in full your study and how you conducted it. This is the place to be highly technical. Cover one point per paragraph and move logically from results to analysis. Use charts and tables to convey complex information quickly and clearly.

Don't bury critical supporting data too deeply. Many managers admit that they read only the first few pages of a report. Bear this in mind and state your most convincing points early.

Background describes what led to your study and how your report is related to others in the field. Only towards the end of the body do you expand on background. Does this surprise you?

All too often writers include background material simply because they've done the research. Your readers, however, may not need to know as much about your subject as you do.

Ask yourself whether a piece of background information is necessary for your readers' understanding of your report. If it isn't, think about eliminating it, moving it toward the end, or putting it in an appendix.

CONCLUSION AND FINAL SUMMARY

The key ideas of the entire report should come to a logical conclusion here.

Don't surprise your readers with new ideas— the main points of your conclusion should arise logically from the body of the report.

If you are including a final summary, be as brief as possible.

Many readers, pressed for time, read only the beginning and end of a report. Simply stated, they want to know what the project or study is about and how it turned out. Describe your main idea clearly and emphatically.

Here's your last chance to convince your readers. Use it well by stating your conclusions and recommendations persuasively. Don't present a tired—and boring—recapitulation.

The content of your conclusion will depend on your readers and on the type of report you are writing.

PROGRESS REPORT

Your conclusion may be transitional since a completion report will probably follow. You should simply state how the project is going. If it's going well, say so; but avoid overstatement.

> Construction of the new apartment building is on schedule. We feel confident that the building will be completed by August 31, as promised.

FEASIBILITY REPORT

Your conclusion will state whether or not you recommend a certain course of action, based on data in the body of the report.

> Given the high cost of the new machine and its limited testing in the marketplace, we advise XYZ Co. not to purchase it.

LETTER REPORT

The conclusion often includes a brief summary of the letter, along with future plans.

> In conclusion, the surveys have revealed a need for product improvement. I'll call your office next Tuesday to arrange a meeting to discuss your next steps.

FORMAL REPORT OR COMPLETION REPORT

Your conclusions should emphasize the most important points in the body of the report. If you have one or two conclusions, state them in narrative form. For more than two, you may want to use a numbered list or table to add impact.

State your main conclusion first, followed by others in decreasing order of importance. Be sure to close with a statement about the overall effectiveness of the project.

> The committee concludes that the planned manufacturing expansion is both advisable and necessary for the continued good health of the company.

BIBLIOGRAPHY OR REFERENCES

Each is a list of sources used in preparing your document. A bibliography is arranged alphabetically by the author's last name; a reference list, also called endnotes, is numbered sequentially to correspond with a raised number located in the body of the text.

You must include a bibliography or reference list if you quote or paraphrase written material, whether books, journal articles, or other in-house reports.

DISTRIBUTION LIST

This list of report recipients may also be included in an appendix.

APPENDIXES

Put in an appendix material that

- may not be crucial to the understanding of the document
- most of your readers already know, but some may not.

Number or letter each appendix in the order that you refer to it in the text. List all appendixes in the table of contents. An appendix may contain a sim-

ple photograph or a complex table—there are few
restrictions.

Sequencing your report

After you've decided which sections you require
in your report, you need to determine their most
effective sequence. Perhaps you find one element fascinating and want to put it first when, in
fact, it distracts the reader from your main purpose.

Refer to your Focus Sheet again. Who are your
readers? What is your purpose in writing the
report? Use the Focus Sheet as an organization
guide.

Here is one way to sequence a formal report.

1. Title page

2. Table of contents

3. Preface and Acknowledgments

4. List of figures

5. List of tables

6. Executive summary

7. Introduction and purpose of report

8. Recommendations

9. Analysis and supporting data

10. Implementation plan

11. Background

12. Conclusion and final summary

13. Appendixes

One last step

Significant work went into your report. To make it
pay off, be sure your report is well organized,
clearly presented, and responds to your readers'
needs. You also need to double-check for accura-

cy, especially if your report contains legal or technical material.

It is therefore essential to have someone review your report before you submit it. Ask your customer, colleagues, legal department, or technical staff—anyone who has a stake in the project, possesses specialized knowledge, or whose opinion you trust.

(See also **appendix**; **documenting sources**; **executive summaries**; **headlines**; **readers, analyzing**; **research**.)

---

request for proposal (RFP)

When a government agency or private company needs an external supplier to provide a customized product or service, that organization issues a **Request for Proposal** (RFP). An RFP

- describes the need for a product or service
- lists required features and specifications
- details a time line and deliverable dates
- sometimes shows a required proposal format.

A potential supplier uses the information in the RFP to submit a detailed and well-researched proposal

Your RFP must be well-thought-out, comprehensive, and specific. You, or others on your team, must have a complete knowledge of the need involved; otherwise you risk leaving an important component out of your RFP.

If you accept a bid and find out after your vendor has begun work that you omitted a crucial deliverable, you may have to renegotiate the contract. Vendors have the legal right not to fulfill additional requests—they are obligated to supply only what's in the RFP.

(See also **proposals, formal**.)

research

If you write reports, especially on technical topics, a major part of your task will be to perform thorough and accurate **research**. You'll need to make decisions about the most efficient ways to gather information.

Without foresight and experience, you may waste a lot of your—and your company's—time.

Before undertaking a large project, therefore, get acquainted with resources available to you, such as the Internet, computerized data banks, libraries, government agencies, educational institutions, and technical societies.

Primary research

This is information that you gather first hand, through interviews, experiments, and observations. It may prove to be the most exciting and noteworthy part of your report because it will be original and new.

If you are conducting interviews, compile a list of questions ahead of time. Even if you don't follow it rigidly, your notes will help remind you about the material you need to cover.

If possible, outline your report before interviewing—you'll be able to gather information that feeds directly into your main points. As you take notes, develop your own abbreviations to speed up the process.

If you tape an interview, you must by law ask the person's permission to do so. Even if you use a tape recorder, take notes too, in case the tape breaks or is unclear.

Secondary research

You may not know where to do primary research until you've done some secondary research; that is, culled information from others who have written about your topic.

Use Internet news groups and bulletin boards, on-line or CD-ROM literature search services, libraries, government agencies, and universities.

Benefit from the work others have done—it will contribute valuable information on your topic and provide a context for it. If you refer to the studies and findings of others, be sure to give them credit.

Libraries

Local libraries may be limited. Seek out business or university libraries if you can. They usually have a better selection of periodicals and technical references.

If you're unsure of how to locate information, ask a reference librarian for help. It's a good idea to check with the librarians even if you think you've found all relevant material—they may know about a resource that you didn't find.

A CHECKLIST OF REFERENCE MATERIALS

- Books about your topic

- Encyclopedias and almanacs, including:

  1 Encarta (a CD-ROM multimedia encyclopedia)

  2. Bookshelf (a CD-ROM dictionary and almanac)

- Technical journals: see the *Standard Rate and Data*

- Directories of engineering and technical societies

- *Thomas Register of American Manufacturers*

- *Moody's Industrials*

- Indexes:

  1. *Reader's Guide to Periodical Literature*

  2. *Vertical File Index*

3. *Industrial Arts Index*

4. *Engineering Index*

5. *Science Abstracts*

6. *Electronics Abstracts*

7. *Annual Index of Inventors* (for patents)

- On-line data sources:

   1. CompuServe (over 2,000 different databases)

   2. America Online (fewer databases than CompuServe, but thousands of Internet news groups)

   3. Prodigy (less comprehensive than the first two)

   4. Dow Jones (general business database)

   5. Standard & Poor's (general business database)

   6. Lexus/Nexus (legal database)

Permissions

If you use information from another book, journal, or report, always give credit in the text, footnotes or endnotes, or acknowledgments. If you take copyrighted material directly from another source and insert it in your document, you may nccd to obtain permission to use it.

Limits on fair usage vary tremendously from one author to another and one publisher to another. The safest strategy is to check in all cases.

Commercial publishers are the most restrictive because they fear infringement of profits. An author or publisher in the academic world is likely to be far more generous, especially toward other academics. You may use government material freely, without special permission.

Be aware that electronic use is very restricted since on-line sources are available to millions of people.

To obtain permission to use material, write to the copyright owner. You will need to provide information about the nature of your report, including date of issue, number of copies to be published, and distribution. Include a permission form to be signed by the copyright owner.

Allow time for a response—it probably won't happen overnight.

Good research takes good planning

Allow plenty of time for research, especially if it requires writing away for government publications.

Although you should do background research before conducting interviews so you can ask informed questions, do set up your interviews when you begin your project. Your interviewees probably have schedules as hectic as yours.

Finally, whether on paper or electronically, store your research so it is easy to access, add to, and reorganize.

(See also **bibliography**, **copyright**, **documenting sources**, **plagiarism**, **professional articles**, **reports**.)

restrictive and nonrestrictive elements

Restrictive elements

Restrictive elements are phrases or clauses that restrict, or limit, the meaning of the noun or pronoun they modify. They are essential because if you omit them, you lose the meaning of the sentence.

Restrictive elements are never set off with commas.

We are interested in Hong Kong businesses *that participate in the international market*.

The clause *that participate in the international market* is necessary to the meaning of the sentence. It identifies which businesses the writer means.

Nonrestrictive elements

Nonrestrictive elements add extra information about the nouns they refer to. They are not essential to the sentence because if you remove them, the sentence still has its intended meaning.

Nonrestrictive elements are usually set off with commas because the information they provide is parenthetical. Think of commas as "handles" that allow you to "lift" the element or clause out of the sentence.

> Hong Kong, *which plays an important role in the international market*, is an ideal entry point into the Chinese market.

If you were to lift the clause *which plays an important role in the international market* out of the sentence, the sentence would still have its intended meaning. This extra clause gives the reader additional information.

You may also use dashes or parentheses in place of commas to set off nonrestrictive elements.

In general, use *that* to introduce a restrictive and *which* to introduce a nonrestrictive element.

A note of caution

You can change the entire meaning of your sentence by not distinguishing between restrictive and nonrestrictive elements. Consider the following sentence:

> The customer service manager *who works on the fifth floor* will be able to help Mr. Kent.

This means that out of all the customer service managers, only the one who works on the fifth floor can help Mr. Kent.

If the writer is referring to the *only* customer service manager, the fact that he happens to work on the fifth floor is additional information that can be left out of the sentence without affecting its meaning.

In this case, the nonrestrictive information must be set off with commas or dashes.

> The customer service manager, *who works on the fifth floor*, will be able to help Mr. Kent.

(See also **commas**, **phrases**, **pronouns**, **relative pronouns**, *that/which*.)

---

run-on sentences

When two or more sentences are strung together without correct punctuation separating them, the result is a **run-on sentence**. Run-on sentences are confusing. They make readers stop and reread as they try to understand.

> We voted to give up our floating holiday rather than decrease sick days some people dissented.

In this example, the word *some* begins a new sentence. Without end punctuation after *sick days,* readers "run on" with the sentence and realize too late that another sentence has begun.

Correcting run-on sentences

Run-on sentences are easy to fix. They consist of two or more independent clauses that you should consider separately as you add or correct the punctuation.

1. The easiest correction is often to insert a period to separate the two sentences.

   > We voted to give up our floating holiday rather than decrease sick days. Some people dissented.

2. Make a compound sentence in one of two ways:

- If the two ideas are closely related, put a semicolon between the sentences.

  We voted to give up our floating holiday rather than decrease sick days; some people dissented.

- Put a coordinating conjunction and either a comma or a semicolon at the end of the first sentence. If you use a conjunction such as *however*, use a semicolon before and a comma after.

  We voted to give up our floating holiday rather than decrease sick days, *but* some people dissented.

  We voted to give up our floating holiday rather than decrease sick days; *however*, some people dissented.

3. Make one sentence subordinate to the other.

   After we voted to give up our floating holiday rather than decrease sick days, some people dissented. [The first clause is subordinate to the second.]

(See also **commas**, **conjunctions**, **periods**, **semicolons**, **sentences**.)

S

safety labels

Safety labels are essential in many kinds of manuals. Emphasize labels like *Danger*, *Warning*, and *Caution* so users can easily see them.

Icons are essential

Icons—stylized graphic figures or images—work well for emphasizing important safety measures.

Think of the impact of the classic skull-and-crossbones symbol. But don't limit yourself. Take advantage of your word-processing or graphics program to flag important safety precautions with icons like these:

CAUTION

RADIATION
AREA

Place safety labels correctly

Your manual may be organized according to a chronological sequence or according to a particular process. First be sure your organization is appropriate for the procedure described; then place safety labels clearly and correctly.

The U.S. government publishes proper standards for the placement of safety labels on products and manuals. It's worth checking to see if they apply to your publication.

The safest approach: put safety and warning labels in the document twice—once in the overview of instructions, and once before the actual step that requires the safety measure.

(See also **manuals**, **procedures**, **technical writers' responsibilities**.)

scatter charts

Use a **scatter chart** to present the possible relationships between two variables. Scatter charts are formed by plotting numerical data against the x- and y-axes.

They are also called *dot charts* because each data point is a dot on the chart. (Some computer programs present the dots as tiny boxes.)

The purpose of the chart is to help find a pattern among the dots if there is one, or to help show the pattern you are demonstrating. Here's an overview:

- The dots show individual pairs of data, and the trend can be highlighted with a line or highlighted swath.

- Two or more variables can be displayed on a scatter chart by using symbols in place of dots. Thus, Rio de Janeiro data can be represented by an *R* and Buenos Aires data by a *B*.

- Multiple scatter charts, all with the same scale, can be joined in a rectangle to form a scatterplot matrix. This will allow you to compare four variables.

- When viewing the points, you can determine only the relationship between the x and y values, not cause and effect: that is, x does not determine y.

- If the pattern is embedded in a lot of *noise* (multiple close data points), it will be difficult to see. Improve the clarity of the chart by turning it into a box chart. This means highlighting with a box significant clusters of dots that show trends.

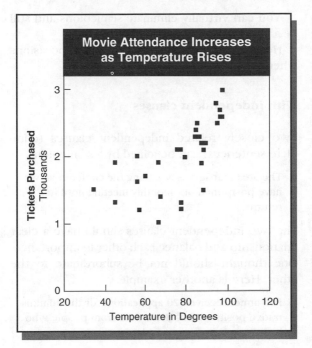

Movie Attendance Increases as Temperature Rises

Tickets Purchased (Thousands) vs. Temperature in Degrees

(See also **box charts**, **charts or graphs**, **tables**.)

semicolons

A **semicolon** (;) separates sentence elements of equal importance. Such elements are usually independent clauses or a list of items in phrase form. A semicolon says "stop" more emphatically than a comma, but not as forcefully as a period.

As readers require information in segments that are shorter and easier to read, semicolons are becoming a less desirable form of punctuation. They encourage overlong sentences that slow down both reader and writer.

You can virtually eliminate semicolons and still be a fine writer.

Here are some rules for those few occasions when you decide to use a semicolon.

With independent clauses

Two closely related independent clauses (complete sentences) can be joined by a semicolon.

> The area manager is attending the conference; we have postponed our monthly meeting until he returns.

The two independent clauses should have a clear relationship and balance each other in importance. One thought should not be subordinate to the other. Here is another example.

> Personnel received 20 applications for the administrative position; 8 of them were from people who had worked here previously.

With conjunctive adverbs

A conjunctive adverb is an introductory word that joins two independent clauses and also modifies the clause it introduces. The most common conjunctive adverbs are

also	consequently
then	however
thus	moreover
therefore	nevertheless
furthermore	

Conjunctive adverbs require a semicolon before and a comma after when they introduce an independent clause in a compound sentence.

> We ordered too many tester kits; *therefore,* we'll have to sell them at a discount.

With connecting words other than conjunctions

Many transitional words and phrases function like conjunctive adverbs. In compound sentences, put a semicolon before and a comma after such transitions as

for example	accordingly
that is	in other words
on the other hand	namely

The clause following the transition word or phrase should be a complete sentence that contains an explanation of or example relating to the first clause.

> Our literature provides an in-depth technical overview of the newest advances; *for example*, teleportation developments are covered on pages 6–7.

With phrases in a list

Your first choice should always be to write lists vertically, in bulleted or numbered form. If you must present your list in sentence form, use semicolons to separate lengthy items that contain commas. Be sure to introduce the list with a colon.

> Seminar topics for the first day include the following: using inter-application information transfers; assessing the need for design with internalization; and creating, testing, and redesigning prototypes.

With quotation marks and parentheses

Always place semicolons after closing quotation marks.

> Everyone has read Morgen's "Sales on the Line"; we can start the role play.

Also put semicolons outside parentheses.

> The new director took the smallest office (traditionally, directors used the large corner office); we wondered what surprises were next.

Semicolon or comma?

A semicolon slows the pace of a sentence because it signals a stronger pause than a comma. If two connected ideas are long or complicated, a semicolon gives the reader a chance to take in the first idea before moving on to the next.

> The takeover of the company was inevitable after last year's fiscal crisis; now we have a chance to revitalize and turn a profit.

If you want to hurry the reader on to the second idea, use a comma and a conjunction, such as *and* or *but*, between the clauses.

> The takeover of the company was inevitable after last year's fiscal crisis, *but* now we have a chance to revitalize and turn a profit.

Semicolons are not, however, always slower than conjunctions.

consider:	We can get it for you tomorrow; I promise you that.
vs.:	We can get it for you tomorrow, and I promise you that.

Incorrect use of semicolons

TO INTRODUCE A LIST

Never use a semicolon to introduce a list. Colons introduce lists.

instead of:	Roger's research shows three critical design problems;
write:	Roger's research shows three critical design problems:

To introduce a direct quote

Never use a semicolon to introduce a direct quote. Use a comma or a colon.

instead of: I quote from the president's speech; "Our work will change the course of telecommunications technology."

write: I quote from the president's speech: "Our work will change the course of telecommunications technology."

or: The president said, "Our work will change the course of telecommunications technology."

A final tip

Because semicolons slow the flow of ideas and lengthen your sentences unnecessarily, use them sparingly. Instead of using a semicolon in a series of words or phrases, for example, consider putting the information in a bulleted list.

(See also **colons**, **commas**, **conjunctions**, **run-on sentences**.)

---

sentences

Sentences are self-contained units of words that present a complete idea. Carefully structured sentences can mean the difference between coherent and muddled communication.

Your goal should always be to streamline your sentences: eliminate wordiness to make them concise and to the point.

Sentence elements

Generally sentences have two parts: a subject and a predicate.

Subject

The subject performs the action of a sentence—it is what the sentence is about. It can be a noun, noun phrase, or clause. In the passive voice, the subject is acted upon.

Predicate

The simple predicate is the verb alone. A complete predicate is the verb with its objects, complements, and modifiers—which may themselves be words, phrases, or clauses. These elements appear in different orders and create sentence patterns.

Sentence patterns

Understanding the common positions of words and their relationships to each other will help you write clearly. The order in which words appear—the syntax of the sentence—conveys meaning. If you change the word order, you may change the meaning.

compare: The machine runs the program.

with: The program runs the machine.

The basic sentence patterns are:

1. Subject—verb

   The computer crashed.

2. Subject—verb—direct object

   Directories contain files.

3. Subject—verb—indirect object—direct object

   I told Lucas the news.
   I told Lucas the computer crashed.

4. Subject—verb—direct object—objective complement

   We consider a scanner a necessity.

5. SUBJECT—LINKING VERB—SUBJECTIVE COMPLEMENT

The survey is too complicated.

6. VERB—SUBJECT—VERB—OBJECT (SENTENCES THAT ASK A QUESTION)

Has the lab received the shipment?

Sentence types

There are four basic sentence types.

1. SIMPLE

Simple sentences have one independent clause that contains at least a subject and a verb.

Productivity increased.

Productivity increased last quarter.

Productivity increased 24 percent last quarter.

2. COMPOUND

A compound sentence has two or more independent clauses. They can be joined by a comma and a coordinating conjunction or joining word, a semicolon, a colon, or a dash.

We've made progress, *and* we expect a positive response from our partners.

We've made progress; we expect a positive response from our partners.

We've made progress: we expect a positive response from our partners.

We've made progress—we expect a positive response from our partners.

3. COMPLEX

A complex sentence has at least one independent and one dependent or subordinate clause. The subordinate clause, which cannot stand alone as a sentence, can come either before or after the main clause.

> *When you turn this dial clockwise*, the pressure inside the tank increases. [comma after introductory clause]

> The pressure inside the tank increases *when you turn this dial clockwise*. [no comma necessary]

4. COMPOUND-COMPLEX

A compound-complex sentence has at least two independent clauses and one dependent clause.

> When you turn this dial clockwise [subordinate], the pressure inside the tank increases [indepen-dent], and a buzzer will sound. [independent]

A SPECIAL TYPE: THE ONE-WORD SENTENCE

Some sentences contain only one or two words and imply what's missing. They often answer a question.

> You asked when we can fill your order. *Tomorrow*. [*We can fill it* tomorrow.]

> Jenna wants to know if I can meet Mr. Williams at the airport. *Of course*. [*Of course I can meet him.*]

Sentence functions

Sentences can make statements, give commands, ask questions, or make exclamations.

1. DECLARATIVE

A declarative sentence states information.

> This program demonstrates simple string processing.

> Geophysics includes the disciplines of meteorology and oceanography, among others.

> We finally hired a new sales rep yesterday.

2. IMPERATIVE

An imperative sentence gives a command or order. It begins with a verb. "You," the implied subject, is understood.

> [You] Multiply the fractions and add the exponents. [You] Then normalize the result.

3. INTERROGATIVE

An interrogative sentence asks a question and has a question mark for final punctuation.

> After you installed the ink cartridge, did you remember to clear it?

4. EXCLAMATORY

An exclamatory sentence is a declarative sentence stated with strong feeling. It has an exclamation point at the end.

> Great news—Thibault Ltd. accepted our proposal!

Sentence length

Keep sentences short. Otherwise, your readers may have to read long and complex sentences more than once to understand them. Follow these guidelines for average sentence length:

- general business and technical writing: 15 to 20 words
- business and technical writing for international readers: 8 to 12 words
- procedures: 8 to 10 words.

Do, however, vary your sentence length to avoid sounding choppy or monotonous. Simple concepts and uncomplicated statements of fact can occasionally be expressed in a longer sentence.

Writing dynamic sentences

BEGINNING YOUR SENTENCE

Make the beginning words of a sentence count. In general, start with a strong subject and an action verb that will catch your readers' attention. Avoid "placeholder" words like *there* and *this*.

instead of: There were four contractors who sent proposals.

write: Four contractors submitted proposals.

In informal writing, it is acceptable to start a sentence with a coordinating conjunction (*and, but, or, for, nor, yet,* and *so*). A beginning conjunction can provide a smooth transition, add emphasis, or break up long thoughts.

> We would like to set up more work stations and hire temps to help with this project. *But* the budget won't accommodate either more terminals or more people.

Avoid overusing this technique—your writing will sound choppy and ungrammatical. Don't begin sentences with conjunctions in formal documents.

Your writing will also sound repetitive if you begin all your sentences the same way.

instead of: *The new lot* will hold 300 cars . . . *The cars* should be parked facing in . . . *The employees* will receive a monthly pass. . . *The attendant* will keep track of . . .

write: *The new lot* will hold 300 cars . . . *To maximize space*, please park your car facing in . . . *Obtain* a monthly pass . . . *The attendant* will keep track of . . .

ENDING YOUR SENTENCE

The ending of a sentence often contains less important information than the beginning.

The drop in investment is a direct result of the current low interest rates.

You probably often put your important idea first and subordinate other ideas to it. For particular emphasis, however, you may want to lead up to your main point by putting it towards the end of your sentence.

After we installed an 800 number, *we received dozens of calls* about our graphics services. [Placing *we received dozens of calls* after an introductory clause creates interest: what was the result of installing an 800 number?]

ACTIVATING VERBS

Turn passive verbs into active ones.

instead of:	It *is believed* by management that the Acme account *should be given* to Jill.
write:	Management *believes* that Jill *deserves* the Acme account.

USING PARALLEL STRUCTURE

Parallel structure means that sentence elements with the same function have the same construction.

instead of:	We offer a full range of consulting services as you plan your meeting: site *location, choosing* audiovisual equipment, *ordering* supplies, *food*, and even travel *arrangements*.
write:	We offer a full range of consulting services as you plan your meeting: *locating* a site, *choosing* audiovisual equipment, *ordering* supplies, *catering* the food, and even *making* travel arrangements.

In the first example, the italicized words are not parallel: they are a mixture of nouns and gerunds, or verbs ending in *-ing* used as nouns.

In the rewrite, the list items are all introduced by gerunds. Because the structure of the rewrite is parallel, the sentence, although long, is easier to understand.

POSITIONING MODIFIERS

Add interest by varying the position of modifiers. You don't have to use the same word order all the time—but you should place modifiers near the words they modify. Here are three different ways to position the same modifier.

> *To save time*, two clerks are working *around the clock* on entering specifications and index locations.

> Two clerks are working *around the clock* on entering specifications and index locations *to save time*.

> *Around-the-clock* entry of specifications and index locations should *save time*. [modifying phrase changed to a verb and object]

INSERTING A PHRASE OR CLAUSE

Inserting phrases and clauses changes the flow of a sentence, adds variety, and keeps readers alert. Use commas or dashes to set off the inserted material.

> Our mission, *as first stated by E. F. Hamm*, has not changed in over 50 years.

> Terminal availability and machine downtime—*two problems that MIS is working on*—will affect how well you meet deadlines.

STREAMLINING

Get to the point. Edit out unnecessary words or ideas that clutter the main thought.

instead of:	The purpose of this e-mail is to inform you that soon the new bonus policy will be sent to all current employees.
write:	All employees will shortly receive the new bonus policy.

SOME FINAL TIPS

- As you edit, put the main point of your sentence where it will catch your reader's attention.
- Use conjunctions and transition words to provide smooth connections between sentences.
- Check that subjects are near their verbs and modifiers are near the words they modify.

(See also **active voice/passive voice**, **object**, **parallel structure**.)

sentences: fragments

Sentence fragments are incomplete ideas capitalized and punctuated like complete sentences. Sometimes fragments are intentional, and sometimes they are errors.

No more waiting six months for the next edition. Order your copy now! [The first sentence is an intentional fragment.]

I need to talk to Vincente tomorrow about the modifications. The engineer who submitted the specs. [The second sentence is an error.]

Intentional fragments

Save intentional fragments for very informal documents—and use them sparingly.

A sentence fragment can be stylistically effective as an answer to a rhetorical question or as an exclamation.

What did Benson accomplish when he worked overtime? *Absolutely nothing.*

Fragments can also be effective in descriptive passages.

We are sure you will enjoy our latest product line. *The expanded color selection. The improvements in style. The convenience of ordering by phone.*

In business and technical writing, however, intentional fragments occur mostly in e-mail messages, memos, and lists.

Meeting Thursday at 1 p.m.?   OK for now.

Unintentional fragments

You are most likely to create an unintentional fragment when you add an idea to an already complete sentence. Relative pronouns (*who, which, that*) often lead to sentence fragments, as in the example that follows.

instead of:	I heard Dana Hansen speak at the conference. *Who just happens to be my hero.* [sentence fragment]
write:	I heard Dana Hansen speak at the conference. He just happens to be my hero.
or:	I heard Dana Hansen, who just happens to be my hero, speak at the conference.

Also watch out for subordinating conjunctions, such as *after, before, although, because, since,* and *if.*

instead of:	Although the files on the disk you gave me were corrupted.

write:	Although the files on the disk you gave me were corrupted, we managed to recover all the data.
instead of:	If only we upgrade our system.
write:	If only we upgrade our system, we will be able to exchange data files with the Singapore office daily.

Such as, for example, and *that is* usually introduce explanations. Attach them to the main sentence to eliminate the fragment.

instead of:	To ensure speedier delivery, we could buy directly from a distributor. *For example, Moskowitz Rubber.*
write:	To ensure speedier deliver, we could buy directly from a distributor, *for example, Moskowitz Rubber.*

HOW TO CORRECT UNINTENTIONAL FRAGMENTS

When you edit, correct unintentional sentence fragments by joining them to either the previous or the following sentence:

instead of:	The financial managers decided to expand their group by one person. *Pending budget approval.*
write:	The financial managers decided to expand their group by one person, pending budget approval.
instead of:	*Since she's receiving too much new information too quickly.* The new administrator seems a bit overwhelmed.
write:	*Since she's receiving too much new information too quickly,* the new administrator seems a bit overwhelmed.

A FINAL TIP

Reading your draft aloud helps catch sentence fragments.

(See also **conjunctions**, **relative pronouns**.)

---

sentences: problems

Concentrate on correcting **sentence problems** during Step 6 to Reader-Centered Writing, **editing your draft**.

Ambiguity

Many sentences are ambiguous because the modifier is in the wrong place.

instead of:	*As a valued member of the board*, I hope you will speak at the stockholders' meeting. [Who is the valued member, *you* or *I?*]
write:	I hope that, *as a valued member of the board*, you will speak at the stockholders' meeting.
instead of:	She *just* completed her first year of business school. [She completed her first year and plans to continue.]
write:	She completed *just* her first year of business school. [She completed just one year before she left school.]

Dangling modifiers

This kind of modifier doesn't logically refer to any word in the sentence.

instead of:	Unless automated by month's end, the team will not keep up with the demand. [The goal isn't to automate the team.]

write:	*Unless the fulfillment procedures are automated by month's end, the team will not keep up with the demand.*
instead of:	Using market research, dog food was packaged in pouches rather than cans.
write:	*Using market research, the company* packaged dog food in pouches rather than cans.

Awkward word order

Put related ideas next to each other in a sentence.

instead of:	Budgets using the new system will help if they are turned in by June 1 so the managers can plan hiring.
write:	If they are turned in by June 1, budgets using the new system will help managers plan hiring.

Clauses with no logical relationship

Do not join two unconnected items of information in a single sentence.

instead of:	The standoff boundary surrounds the graphic, and you can change standoff size using the Text Wrap dialog box.
write:	The standoff boundary surrounds the graphic. Change standoff size using the Text Wrap dialog box.

Overlong sentences

Long sentences slow down and confuse readers. Streamline: keep your sentences to 15–20 words maximum.

instead of: Our survey results agree with research data that indicate a clear relationship between family leave time and employee morale and suggest that a generous family leave policy encourages positive attitudes about work and the workplace, as confirmed by most of the employees we surveyed.

write: Our research data indicate a clear relationship between family leave time and employee morale. According to the employee survey, a generous family leave policy encourages positive attitudes about work and the workplace.

(See also **ambiguity**, **concise vs. wordy writing**, **modifiers**, **sentences**, **streamlining**.)

---

sexist language: how to avoid it

Language isn't static. Although much of it remains constant over the decades, some words and usage shift to reflect changing lifestyles and values.

Society's perceptions of and attitudes towards women and women's rights have changed radically over the past several decades. An evolving awareness of gender equality has triggered a reconsideration of even well-accepted terms like "mankind."

We avoid words that assume maleness largely because they refer to roles traditionally held by men. In business correspondence, we no longer use outdated forms of salutation.

Don't distinguish gender unless you have to

In most situations gender isn't relevant, so there is no reason to reveal it. Avoid the following terms.

instead of:	*write:*
actress	actor
authoress	author
directress	director
hostess	host
millionairess	millionaire
poetess	poet
stewardess	flight attendant
workman	employee

The *-person* dilemma

To change the assumption that it's a male world out there, society has amended many words that once ended with *-man*. The new form of these words ends with *-person*. This form disregards the gender of the individual in question.

Such *-person* words may, however, sound self-conscious or contrived. If you're faced with this dilemma, try substituting another word. In most cases there is one, and it's often stronger and less awkward than the *-person* ending. For example:

instead of:	*write:*	*or:*
chairman	chairperson	chair
layman	layperson	lay reader, lay audience
spokesman	spokesperson	representative

Avoid sexist language and stereotypes

By now it's well known that women should not be called "girls" because they are adults. You may do so only in an informal, nonbusiness setting, where you might also refer to men as "boys."

Beware, too, of broad statements that stereotype women or men. Examples:

Women can talk about their feelings better than men.

Women are less ambitious than men.

First, even if a stereotype contains a bit of truth, there are always exceptions. Second, such statements imply a narrow-minded attitude that you definitely want to avoid in any writing you do.

Salutations

Before writing a letter to a woman, try to find out how she likes to be addressed. Does she use *Mrs.*? *Miss*? or the more widely accepted *Ms.*?

If you don't know, don't use a title at all. This may surprise you, but recent U.S. surveys show that more women prefer to be addressed by their full name than by Ms. followed by the last name.

> Dear Angela Rossi:

Be consistent: if you omit *Ms.* in the salutation, do the same in the inside address.

For your international correspondents or very formal situations like job application letters, stick to *Ms.* Your readers will be used to this form of address and might be surprised or offended if you address them by their first and last names.

If you are writing to a company and don't have a specific name, don't assume your letter will be read by men.

Avoid "Dear Sirs" or "Gentlemen." "Dear Sir or Madam" or "Ladies and Gentlemen," while acceptable, are very old-fashioned. Try simply "Good day" or "Greetings" instead.

If you are writing to someone whose position you know, use "Dear Director" or "Dear Human Resources Manager." But again, "Greetings" may be your preference.

Indefinite pronouns: problems and solutions

When you use an indefinite pronoun like *everyone* followed by a pronoun that refers to it, don't assume that the indefinite pronoun represents only men.

> *Everyone* must present *his* report at the meeting tomorrow.

Correct the problem with one of the following solutions:

1. Make the subject of the sentence plural.

   All employees must present *their* reports at the meeting tomorrow.

2. Use both male and female pronouns. This is the least desirable solution: although it's correct, it's also awkward and wordy.

   Everyone must present *his or her* report at the meeting tomorrow.

3. Delete the personal pronoun unless it's necessary to identify the noun that follows it. If you say,

   Everyone must present *a* [instead of *his*] report at the meeting tomorrow.

   Be sure everyone knows which report you have in mind.

He as the subject of the sentence

Finally, don't use *he* as the subject of your sentence unless you are referring to a specific male. Rewrite the sentence and use *you*, or make it plural: *they*. Again, avoid the clumsy *he or she* construction.

instead of:	If a respondent doesn't complete the survey, he will not receive a thank-you gift.
write:	If you don't complete the survey, you will not receive a thank-you gift.
or:	If respondents don't complete the survey, they will not receive thank-you gifts.

(See also **gender**; *he, he/she, s/he, (s)he*.)

---

signs and symbols

Common **symbols** are an appropriate way to communicate a message. Use an equation like $E = mc^2$, or a sign or symbol such as the ones that follow to enhance text. If there is any possibility that your readers are not familiar with a symbol or sign, include an explanation the first time you use a symbol.

Map symbol   *Highway sign*   *Professional symbol*

Some signs and symbols are available through standard computer fonts. But many word processing applications take graphics support a step further by providing

- basic drawing tools through a graphics editor
- graphics-import features.

Many word processors are even packaged with their own clip-art files. To find out if any clip-art files were packaged with your word processor, look through your word processor's documentation.

spacing: how to enhance readability

When you make **spacing** decisions, you choose the visual arrangement of your letter or document.

Margins, headlines, white space, illustrations, and text should all enhance readability. If your text is dense with narrow margins and few visual breaks, readers will have difficulty plowing through it.

Using spacing to enhance readability will make your important points stand out and help readers skim your letter or document quickly. Here are a few guidelines.

- Margins should be at least one inch on each side. If you must put a lot of information on one page, don't reduce your margins to less than 3/4 inch.

- Leave enough white space around your most important information to make it stand out.

- Tables, figures, lists, and illustrations break up long blocks of text. Frame them in white space, too.

- Headlines organize and divide text while highlighting key items or sections.

Single vs. double spacing

For most business and technical letters and documents, use single spacing. Leave a blank line between paragraphs. You may double-space the text of very short letters to help fill out the page.

Space between lines of type

Leading, or spacing, between lines of type is usually keyed to the maximum height and width of letters for each font size. With sans serif typefaces especially, too much space between lines and between letters actually reduces legibility.

In most cases you can trust your word processing program to automatically set leading for you.

Here are some examples of how leading can affect readability.

crowded (Times 10 pt.):

> Leading, or spacing, between lines of type is usually keyed to the maximum height and depth of the letters for each font size. With sans serif typefaces especially, too much space between lines and between letters actually reduces legibility.

preferred (Times 10 pt.):

> Leading, or spacing, between lines
> of type is usually keyed to the
> maximum height and depth of the
> letters for each font size. With sans
> serif typefaces especially, too
> much space between lines and
> between letters actually reduces
> legibility.

excessive (Helvetica 10 pt):

> Helvetica is a sans
> serif typeface.
> Unlike Times, a
> serif typeface,
> Helvetica has no
> extra strokes at the
> tops and bottoms of
> characters.

(See also **font**, **format**, **headlines**, **kerning**, **page design**, **visual design**, **white space**.)

spelling

Correct **spelling** is a mark of professionalism. Spelling errors will cause your readers to mistrust what you say—or at least wonder about your attention to detail.

Some common spelling mistakes

One problem area for many writers: *ie* vs. *ei*. The rule is *i* before *e* except after *c*, or when sounded like *a* as in *neighbor* and *weigh*.

Exceptions to this rule are in the sentence: *Neither* Sheila's *height* nor the *leisured foreign sheik seized their weird heifer* when they *forfeited protein*.

Exceptions to the "after *c*" rule are *science*, *financier*, and *species*.

Some other common problems with spelling often occur with such errors as:

- plurals (monkies instead of monkeys)

- suffixes (collectable instead of collectible)

- possessives (it's instead of its)

- compound words (a merchandise sell out instead of sellout)

The limitations of your spellchecker

Always use the spellchecker in your word processing program before you print a final version of a letter or report. But spellchecking isn't enough—you must also proofread with care. Your spellchecker won't catch errors like transposed letters (*sue* for *use*; *unclear* for *nuclear*) or incorrect word use (*principal* for *principle*). Keep a good dictionary handy when you edit.

(See also **contractions**, **possessive case**.)

---

streamlining: make every word count

Eliminating unnecessary words from your sentences is a courtesy to your readers. **Streamline** your sentences when you edit your draft, Step 6 to Reader-Centered Writing.

Check your sentences for any words that don't add meaning. They are deadwood. Pruning them strengthens your writing.

Streamlining strategies

1. Use as few words as possible.

   instead of: I would like to ask that . . .
   write: Please . . .

2. Avoid redundancy, or needless repetition.

   instead of: filled to capacity
   write: filled

3. Use an active verb wherever you can.

   instead of: The objection was made by the marketing rep.
   write: The marketing rep objected.

4. Use the shorter, clearer word.

   instead of: utilize
   write: use

   instead of: commence
   write: start

5. Change or eliminate the phrases *is where* and *is when*.

   instead of: After Jess returns *is when* the beta testing begins.
   write: The beta testing begins after Jess returns.

6. Change prepositional phrases to adjectives.

   instead of: a locker without identification
   write: an unidentified locker

Rearranging or dividing sentences is also part of streamlining. Keep your sentences to 15 or 20 words. Don't put more than one or two ideas in a sentence.

instead of: Managers who are effective give praise to their employees who are outstanding workers and endeavor to implement motivational strategies with subordinates working under them who do not perform well.

write: Effective managers praise outstanding employees and try to motivate poor performers.

E-mail subject lines

Streamlining is vital for e-mail subject lines. Short, clear, and uncluttered subject lines are read first.

instead of: We are having problems locating the missing combination

write: Missing combination—help needed

A caution about streamlining

The purpose of streamlining is to convey your message to the reader as simply as possible. Be sure you don't prune your sentences so much that you leave out vital information.

Especially in technical writing, keep your readers in mind. Ask yourself if they have enough information to understand what you mean.

(See also **active voice/passive voice**, **clear writing**, **concise vs. wordy writing**, **redundancy**.)

---

style: match yours to your readers'

Style refers to the choices a writer makes about how a document will sound and look. In short, style is the *appeal* of a piece of writing.

As you write, be aware of the characteristics of style, including tone, language, sentence structure, and visual design. Make your final style choices during Step 6 to Reader-Centered Writing: **editing your draft**.

Characteristics of style

TONE

The effect or impression that writing has on the reader is its tone. Your tone can be formal, informal, amusing, persuasive, conversational, condescending, friendly, inspirational, angry, or encouraging. Obviously, you want to avoid some of these tone choices.

formal: Systems personnel will no longer be assisting during peak times.

friendly: We're sorry that systems personnel won't be able to help you at peak times after March 1.

angry: Don't expect systems personnel to help out any more at peak times.

encouraging: Although systems personnel won't be able to help out at peak times, we will do our best to support you by hiring temporary staff.

LANGUAGE

Word choice helps create style. In the examples in the previous section, the tone—and, consequently, the style—is formal, friendly, angry, or encouraging because of the words. For example:

friendly: *We're sorry* that systems personnel won't be able to help *you* at peak times after March 1.

The italicized words sound almost conversational and make a friendly appeal to the reader.

encouraging: *Although* systems personnel won't be able to help out at peak times, *we will do our best to support you* by hiring temporary staff.

The italicized words show concern for people who might otherwise feel overworked at peak times.

SENTENCE STRUCTURE

The way a sentence is constructed—its clauses, subordination, verb phrases, sequence of ideas, and punctuation—affects style. Long sentences with many clauses and phrases can be difficult to decipher.

instead of: Small retailers should realize that the customer is the one who really signs their paychecks and should therefore treat customers like friends coming to visit: this is the best way for the small retailer to build a loyal customer base while the big chains are fighting it out.

write: Small retailers should treat their customers like friends. After all, it is the customer who really signs the paychecks. In the face of stiff competition from the big chains, small retailers need to build a loyal customer base to survive.

VISUAL DESIGN

The way your page looks is part of its style. Visually appealing pages have

- margins of at least an inch on all four sides: otherwise, your page will look crowded and difficult to read

- headlines and short paragraphs to add white space and improve readability

- graphs, tables, and illustrations to create visual interest and highlight important information.

Formal or informal?

Most writers speak generally of two kinds of style: *formal* and *informal*. Their audiences and purposes differ, as do the choices writers make in creating each style.

INFORMAL STYLE

An informal style is relaxed, personal, and friendly—much like the way you would speak. When you write in this style, you are making some assumptions:

- You know your reader, or want to project that feeling that you do.

- Your reader will appreciate being addressed directly, often as *you*.

- Friendliness will help achieve your purpose.

Here are some characteristics of informal style.

- The tone is usually positive and warm.

- The language is direct, familiar, and accessible. Active verbs help make the style direct and personable.

- Sentence structure is often simple: most sentences do not exceed 20 words in length and have little or no complicated subordination. Readers won't have to slow down their reading to understand what you're saying.

An informal style is appropriate for personal letters, memos, e-mail, invitations, and some customer letters (usually good-news letters).

You can make a difference in Global Bank's future

Recently, Jesse Hernandez and Kay Johnston wrote to all of us at Global Bank asking for help and participation in our quality program for the 21st century.

The challenge before us, they said, is to make continuous quality improvement everyone's most important job. Why? Because quality—in every aspect of our work—is essential for Global Bank's future.

FORMAL STYLE

A formal style is restrained, impersonal, objective, and factual. You probably don't know your readers, who are looking for unbiased data. Formal documents may have legal implications because they represent the viewpoint of the company, not of the individual writer.

In general, the writer's personality shouldn't intrude in formal style.

These are some typical characteristics of formal style.

- The tone is polite, but impersonal. The pronoun *you* isn't usually appropriate in formal writing.

- The language of formal writing doesn't include contractions, slang, or humor. It is often technical. In an attempt to avoid pronouns like *I, you*, and *me*, some writers overuse the passive voice, which makes their writing stuffy and indirect.

  On using the active voice without personal pronouns, consult the **active voice/passive voice** and **tone** entries.

- Sentence structure includes lengthy sentences with complex subordination, long verb phrases, and expletives for subjects.

  Since the information content of formal, technical, or legal documents is high, both readers and writers expect the reading pace to be slower than in informal writing.

Formal style is appropriate for official documents, computer documentation, scholarly articles and books, technical reports, or letters with a negative message.

Conrad Adler, our customer service representative, has carefully considered your request. We are confident that he has explored every avenue in an effort to restore your satisfaction. His decision represents our company's position. Unfortunately, we cannot offer you an additional discount on your equipment repair.

We regret that a more favorable response is not possible. We are, of course, prepared to resolve any concerns you may have in the future.

Another meaning of style

Style also means the standards which a particular document must observe. Rules about punctuation, capitalization, abbreviations, numbers, references, and so on are handled differently, for example, by the *New York Times* and the U.S. Government Printing Office.

Your organization probably has its own style guide that explains preferred or even required standards.

(See also **active voice/passive voice**, **point of view**, **sentences**, **subordination**, **tone**, **word choice**.)

---

style guides

A **style guide** explains rules and guidelines for document formats, titles and headlines, bulleted lists, fonts, and even word choice.

Professional associations often publish style guides for their discipline. To maintain corporate identity and consistency, companies often develop their own manuals or adopt a published style guide.

Published style guides

Find out what style guide your company uses for the documents you write. Here is a small sampling of some general guides available to you:

The Chicago Manual of Style. 14th ed. Chicago: University of Chicago Press, 1993.

Dodd, Janet S., ed. *The ACS Style Guide: A Manual for Authors and Editors.* Washington, DC: American Chemical Society, 1986.

Gibaldi, Joseph, and Walter S. Achtert. *MLA Handbook for Writers of Research Papers.* 3rd ed. New York: Modern Language Association of America, 1988.

U.S. Government Printing Office. *A Manual of Style.* New York: Gramercy, 1986.

(See also **headline levels**, **lists**, **numbers**, **punctuation**, **style**, **visual design**.)

---

style sheets for word processors

Most word-processing programs allow you to save paragraph formats, including font style, font size, and indentations, as individual commands called *styles*. These styles are stored in one or more **style sheets** that you attach to your on-line documents.

Once you have a style sheet, you can automatically format paragraphs without interrupting the flow of your writing and editing.

The procedure for creating a style is simple: select a paragraph that has the combination of formats you want to reuse, and name it. You can now apply the style to any paragraph in your document.

What are the advantages of style sheets?

Style sheets have many benefits over manual formatting. They

- are faster to use. You won't have to set margins, indentations, tabs, and fonts separately for each paragraph; nor will you be forced to copy and paste paragraphs to repeat formats.

- are easy to change. If you should need to reformat the layout of your document, a style sheet will vastly simplify your task.

- guarantee a consistent format. Styles are especially valuable in team writing projects—everyone uses the same style commands.

What should you include in *your* style sheet?

Style sheets work particularly well for

1. headline levels. For each headline, choose
   - font style and size
   - character format: uppercase, boldface, underlined, or italics
   - amount of white space before and after the headline.

2. bulleted and numbered lists. Choose
   - paragraph margins: flush left or indented
   - hanging indent (vertical text alignment)
   - amount of white space between list items.

3. table formats. Choose
   - number of columns
   - column widths.

4. headers and footers. Choose
   - font style and size
   - page number placement.

5. borders and shading. Choose
   - type of paragraph border: line, box, or shadow box
   - shading pattern.

A final note

Styles copy and apply paragraph *formats*, not actual text. If you want to repeat blocks of text, use a glossary or autotext command. Consult your word-processing manual or the **templates** entry in this book.

(See also **font**, **headline levels**, **indenting**, **templates for word processors**.)

subject lines

Subject lines may well be one of the most important parts of today's short business documents. They are the first words your reader sees. Whether in an e-mail message or a sales letter, the subject line may determine whether your reader actually reads the document you wrote.

Subject lines are also called "re" lines, but this old notation is less suitable in an international context. In letters the subject line follows the salutation; in memos it follows the date, to, and from lines.

How to write an attention-getting subject line

USE AS FEW WORDS AS POSSIBLE

The famous adage, "My report would have been shorter, but I didn't have the time," is particularly applicable to subject lines.

Writing your document took time—don't waste that effort by shortchanging your subject line. Take the time to write a specific and streamlined statement that sums up your message in action-oriented terms.

In e-mail, where only the first few words of your subject line may be visible, drop words and phrases that don't add meaning, such as *the*, *a*, *there is*, and *we are about to*.

instead of: Don's new computer is in need of repairs tonight—it's vital

write: Tonight: Vital to fix Don's computer—thanks

Also abbreviate long words like management (*mgt.*) to fit as much as possible into the subject field.

SUMMARIZE CAREFULLY TO HIGHLIGHT CORE ISSUES

Be sure to put the true message of your document in the subject line. You may be explaining a problem you solved, but also need the reader to approve your solution before you can implement it. If so, your subject line should focus on the action you want from your reader.

instead of: Problem with line 20 solved

write: Your okay needed to repair line 20

In sales documents especially, beware of thinking too much about your needs, rather than those of your readers.

instead of: Why you should buy wiper blades
from Liebling

write: A breakthrough in Liebling wiper
blades

How do you make sure that your subject line is on target? Use your Focus Sheet™. It will help you pinpoint the one thing that you want your reader to remember: the "bottom line" of your message.

USE KEY WORDS

Key words clarify your topic and make it easy for readers to file your document for future use. Obscure or humorous lines may pique interest, but weeks later the reader may forget what your document was about and never refer to it again.

(See also **electronic mail, getting started**, **letters, memorandums, streamlining**.)

subordination

Subordination makes less important or restrictive ideas secondary to main ideas. A subordinate clause, also called a dependent clause, cannot stand alone as a sentence. The following clauses depend on another clause to form a complete sentence:

Because the air filter was damaged, . . .

When the error is obvious and might otherwise seem inappropriate, . . .

How to subordinate

The following sentences illustrate the process of subordination.

Consumers do not always increase their buying in response to a promotional campaign. Retailers may then lose interest in the product.

The second sentence contains the main idea, but the two sentences are closely related and equal in importance. Use *if* to subordinate the first sentence and connect it to the second.

If consumers do not increase their buying in response to a promotional campaign, retailers may lose interest in the product.

Now the sentence has a main or independent clause and an introductory clause that is subordinate. This sentence structure makes the main clause sound more important than the introductory clause. Notice that a comma follows the introductory subordinate clause.

CHANGING THE FOCUS

To change the focus of the sentence, put the second idea in the subordinate clause.

If retailers lose interest in a product, it may be because consumers do not increase their buying in response to a promotional campaign.

Now the main idea is that consumers aren't buying.

Subordinating words

Some words that commonly subordinate ideas fall into the following categories.

1. Place: *where*

   Look for the geological maps *where* Liesel keeps her research.

2. Cause or purpose: *because, since, that, so*

   Since we convene only three times a year, we must coordinate our agendas carefully.

3. Concession: *even if, although, though*

   They bought the new tire line *though* it hasn't been adequately market tested.

4. Time: *before, after, while, until*

   Before the automated inventory system, we used to spend days in the warehouse counting every item.

Benefits of subordination

- It controls emphasis.
- It streamlines your writing.
- It adds variety and adds to your document.
- It organizes your ideas by giving them balance and clarifying relationships.

A final note

Coordinating conjunctions link ideas of equal importance. They do not create subordination. The coordinating conjunctions are

    and   but   or   nor   for   so   yet.

(See also **commas**, **conjunctions**, **emphasis**, **phrases**, **sentences**.)

T

table of contents

A table of contents lists section headlines or chapter titles and the page where each begins. It outlines the entire contents of a document, with section levels and sublevels indicated by indentation or a numbering system.

A report or other document ten or more pages in length needs a table of contents.

The table of contents gives readers an overview of the scope and organization of your document. It should list all the sections of a formal report or proposal, from the preface to the appendixes and glossary.

The table of contents comes right after the cover page. To help readers locate page numbers, use leaders, or a row of periods across the page.

To simplify an often laborious task, use the table of contents function of your word processing program. It will automatically generate a table of contents, including page numbers and a list of figures.

If you rearrange sections at the last minute, the table of contents will automatically repaginate itself.

(See also **leaders, reports**.)

tables

A **table** (or a spreadsheet) is a rectangular array of numeric data. The raw numeric data you collect to support your document can be organized into rows and columns.

A *cell* is the intersection of a row and column where a single data value is placed. A table contains many cells, enabling you to present a large quantity of exact data.

Tables are an effective way of comparing product or service features and advantages. They allow you to compare large amounts of data quickly, for example, the popularity of different products.

You can present many products and their features on one page the way magazines evaluate and compare products.

Because tables present precise numeric data in a row and column format, tables are more concise than text and more accurate and detailed than charts. Tables can accompany charts, with the tables providing the exact data.

Table 1. Sales Increasing on the East Coast

State	Number of Units Sold 1994	1995
Alabama	2234	2210
Arizona	2345	1999
California	4456	4070
• Connecticut	1222	1333
• Delaware	1156	1345
• Florida	1567	1800
• Georgia	234	345
Iowa	892	892
Idaho	561	543

• denotes states in the East Coast region

Table 2. Sales Decreasing on the West Coast

| State | Number of Units Sold | |
	1994	1995
Alabama	2234	2307
Arizona	2345	2300
Connecticut	4456	4678
California	1222	1205
Delaware	1156	1170
Florida	1567	1800
Georgia	234	297
Oregon	998	990
Washington	2360	2349

Shading   denotes states in the West Coast region

Draw attention to important trends, relationships, or anomalies in a table by highlighting it in some way as shown in the preceding samples. If you choose to emphasize data by shading it, as in Table 2, be careful: shaded text can be difficult to read on reproduced copies.

Table guidelines

- Use tables instead of text to present more than two or three different numeric values.
- Since reading across rows on a table is as important as reading up and down the columns, pay careful attention to spacing and font size.
- Check that column headings define the content of the column precisely.
- Include data terms (for example, percent, pounds, miles) in the table's title or in each row or column heading if the terms change from column to column or row to row.
- Give totals wherever meaningful, using the following styles.

On a computer:	In a hand-drawn table:
italicize *subtotals*	single underline <u>subtotals</u>
boldface **totals**	double underline <u>totals</u>

avoid ALL CAPS
and <u>underlining</u>

- Provide subtotals to make long columns or rows digestible to your readers, or any time if they are an item of discussion.

- If tables are several pages long, give subtotals and grand totals on *all* pages.

- Consider offering totals for rows as well as columns if this would help your reader.

- If items add up to 100% show this. If they don't, explain why: did you round off the numbers?

- Always give the scale of your numbers, unless the data values are exact.

- Left-justify text descriptors, right-justify numbers, and center column headings.

- Always title, source, and date your data.

Should you use a chart or table?

A table is often the first step to any chart. Should you stop at a table or keep going to a chart?

Charts such as pie or bar charts are best for big-picture messages like trends. They present a straightforward, simple summary of data and, most important, give your reader additional ways of getting a feeling for relationships, size, differences, and anomalous events.

With your graphics package you can easily try displaying the data in different charts to see what looks best.

Tables are best when you need to convey the precision of many exact values. When your data are numerous and your readers need the details, prefer a table. Or perhaps you need both. Let your analysis in your Focus Sheet be your guide.

Numbering tables

Assign table numbers sequentially and print the number at the top of the table, before the title. For example, number and title your first table, "Table 1. Population Continues to Grow in Western States." In the text, refer to a table by its table number, "Table 3," rather than the title or "the above table."

Number tables independently from figures. You may use letters or Roman numerals to identify tables and distinguish them from figures. Include a list of tables in your table of contents.

Cautions

- Although a table lists numerical data, do not assume readers will see the trend. A chart shows trends and distributions more readily.

- Maintain the same number of decimal places and significant numbers unless you mark the changes clearly.

- Beware of efforts to add substance to biased data and nonrandom samples by presenting the data in tables.

- You don't always need a table to show data in tabular form. If you have two or three numeric data items and want to represent them as a two-column table, use an informal table.

    Indent the text and type the two columns in tabular format. Include column headings and contents that exactly define the contents of the column. You do not need a title or table number in this case.

- After you align the data in each column, look at the column titles.

    Do they vary in length or greatly exceed the width of the column? If so, avoid a messy or disorganized look by condensing the heading text, using abbreviated headings that are explained in a table footnote, or reducing the heading font sizes and bolding them.

The "Be Your Own Table Editor" Checklist

Use the following checklist to be sure your table is useful and accurate.

❑ Do the data in the table deliver a clear and concise message?

❑ Have you placed the table for easy reference on the same or facing page?

❑ Have you referenced all your tables in the text?

❑ Have you rounded values where appropriate?

❑ If totals are needed, have you displayed them?

❑ Have you provided the necessary subtotals? .

❑ Have you noted that column/row addition may not be accurate due to rounding?

❑ If the data are not central to the discussion, is the table in an appendix?

❑ Have you performed all calculations twice and compared your final text to first drafts to be certain that <u>all</u> the data in your tables are accurate?

(See also **charts or graphs**, **numeric data**.)

---

technical writers' responsibilities

Although most other types of writing allow you great freedom to make choices, technical writing comes with serious responsibilities to your reader.

When you're writing a technical document that outlines a process, making the words clear and easy to read is not enough. The thoroughness and clarity of your writing are vital.

Someone else's safety or job performance could easily depend on your ability to explain processes correctly and understandably.

Choice of content is key

In Step 1 of the Six Steps to Reader-Centered Writing™, you used the Focus Sheet ™ to analyze your readers and define your purpose. During Steps 5 and 6, as you write and edit your document, refer often to your Focus Sheet. Ask yourself:

- Have I included absolutely *everything* my audience needs?
- Have I included too much?
- Am I writing in a style that my audience will easily understand?

Readers of technical documents should never have to draw their own conclusions. To increase comprehension, you may need to include background information about the process you're describing.

Safety first

If you're writing a document that involves, for example, operation of heavy machinery, someone's safety is in your hands. List steps clearly using numbers. Whenever possible, put safety information and instructions in chart or grid form.

Always place safety warnings in prominent positions and label them clearly—government guidelines are available for that very purpose.

Leave no chance for misinterpretation

If you're writing a user manual for a software program, you're helping people do their jobs. Don't take this responsibility lightly. Reread and proof carefully to avoid any chance of unclear phrasing or a downright mistake. Have a nontechnical user read it, too.

Your reputation and career, let alone the safety of your readers, may well rest on the excellence of your technical documentation.

(See also **editing your draft**; **manuals**; **procedures**; **readers, analyzing**; **safety labels**.)

technical writing style

Technical writing is the most specialized form of business writing. The goal: your reader should understand every word you write and have a clear picture of what you are saying.

The more complicated your information, the simpler your language must be. Use short and simple words, sentences, and paragraphs for long or complex ideas.

Following are some general rules for lucid and precise technical writing. Within this framework, your own style still has a chance to emerge through your choice of examples and the way you combine and interpret these guidelines.

Tone: don't condescend

Isn't it obvious that all intelligent technical and scientific writers should know how to avoid condescension? Shouldn't it be clear that everyone can figure this out without being told? If it isn't obvious at first, does it make you feel inadequate?

Be careful not to sound like this in your writing.

Sentence structure

SENTENCE VARIETY

Most sentences begin with a subject and a verb. You will probably want to vary this structure every fifth or sixth sentence to add interest to your writing.

Vary your sentences in the editing stage, however, not the writing stage. But be careful: too much variety will make your writing sound stilted or contrived.

SENTENCE LENGTH

Long sentences slow the reader down and make your writing seem unnecessarily difficult. Short crisp sentences—of varying lengths—pick up the pace, while too many sentences of the same length make your writing sound sing-song or choppy. Follow these guidelines:

- general technical writing: 15 to 20 words
- technical writing for international readers: 8 to 12 words
- procedures: 8 to 10 words

When using figures, acronyms, or many multisyllabic words, keep your sentences on the short side. Remember, a sentence is too long if your reader needs to read it twice to understand it.

Word choice

FIRST PERSON

Using the first person is acceptable when it helps clarify your meaning.

> When Smith and Jackson demonstrated their new technique, *we* found that . . .

ONE

Using *one* too often makes you sound stuffy, pretentious, or academic. Worse, *one* puts a wall between oneself and one's readers as they begin to distance themselves from the anonymous One.

SLANG

Few technical writers include slang in their documents. Slang sets a casual, offhand tone which is at odds with a more professional, scientific approach. Also, it may not be easy for your readers, especially international ones, to look up slang words in a dictionary.

It is also difficult to look up meanings for acronyms and jargon. *WYSIWYG* (what you see is what you get) or *SCSI* (small computer system interface, often pronounced *scuzzy*) are probably perfectly understandable to you and your colleagues. These acronyms may, however, be incomprehensible to your audience.

Be sure to define acronyms in parentheses the first time that you use them in each document. In long documents with several acronyms, repeat the full word with the acronym in parentheses after three to four pages. If you think you might need an acronym and initialism glossary at the end of your document, you're probably right.

Although acronyms and jargon can be a valuable shorthand approach to communication within your immediate area, use them sparingly outside your department or company.

CONCRETE LANGUAGE

Back up general statements with examples. If, for example, you are describing X-ray technology, you should illustrate your statement in concrete terms.

> X-ray technology allows us to see inside the human body. An X-ray camera fires electrons at a plate covered with silver halide crystals, which are sensitive to light.
>
> When an electron reaches the plate unimpeded, it turns a halide crystal black. The crystals that receive no electrons fall away when the plate is developed and leave that area transparent, or white under the light.
>
> Most X-ray particles pass right through flesh, which is primarily water, leaving only a vague image on the film where a few of them were stopped.

Bones, on the other hand, are very densely packed and contain large amounts of calcium and other heavy elements. They stop the X rays by absorbing them. The crack in your tibia shows up black on the plate because the X rays can slip through the crack.

Your choice of examples will add interest and variety to your technical writing style.

ANTIQUATED AND OVERLY FORMAL LANGUAGE

Avoid words like *deem*, *henceforth*, *heretofore*, *prior to*, *pursuant to*, and *endeavor to* in technical and scientific writing.

Unnecessarily formal writing just adds to the level of difficulty and limits the audience you can reach. When your material is difficult, your language should be simple. "If you wouldn't say it, don't write it" is the best test for a readable style.

LATIN EXPRESSIONS

The abbreviations *i.e.* and *e.g.*, though still prevalent in scientific and technical journals, are frequently misused and misunderstood. Since perfectly good English alternatives exist, avoid using Latin expressions even when writing to a scientific audience

That is, *for example*, and *such as* work just as well.

Verb choice

STRONG AND SPECIFIC VERBS

Strong verbs make for powerful prose. When possible avoid forms of *to be* and verbs like *appears* or *seems*—such hedging words weaken your writing.

Also use the most specific verb possible. For instance, should you be specific with verbs like *enter*, *list*, *catalog*, *record*, or *register*—or do they all mean the same for your particular purpose?

ACTIVE AND PASSIVE VOICE

Use the active voice whenever possible—it is more straightforward, less ambiguous, and less wordy than the passive voice. Learn how to use the active voice without using *I*, *me*, or *you*.

instead of: These studies will continue during the next reporting period and the results *will be reported*.

write: The next reporting period *will include* results of these continuing studies.

Use the passive voice to report scientific procedures when the actor is unknown or unimportant.

    The figures *were entered* and *run*.

VERB TENSE (OR TIME)

Be careful in your use of verb tenses. Use the simple past tense to discuss your procedures and the present, perfect, or future tenses to discuss what is still true.

    Faraday, who investigated magnetoelectric generation, *discovered* that magnetism *can generate* electricity.

    We *have been working* on an exciting project which we *expect* to complete in two months.

Paragraph length

The paragraph length for technical material should generally be no more than three or four lines; for nontechnical material such as introductions, no more than five to six lines if the page is 8 1/2″ × 11″.

You must consider your audience. If you are submitting an article to a scientific journal, vary your paragraph length. Even for the most formal journal, try to avoid many long paragraphs—intersperse short ones to provide visual interest, pick up the pace, and aid understanding.

Before you submit material to a journal, study the most readable articles it has published and use them as a guide.

Document length

Remember: all things being equal, the shorter document is read first.

Document appeal: make a good first impression

Readers typically skim through a document quickly to get a feel for how easy—or how difficult—it will be to read. Your document's appearance will influence this judgment. Here are some tips to keep your document visually appealing.

- Maximize white space by experimenting with wide margins, multiple columns, and other page formatting techniques—such as headlines, sidelines, and bulleted or numbered lists

- Include a list of document conventions when appropriate—for example, when a specific font has a specific meaning. But be careful. readers are quickly overwhelmed by more than just a few conventions.

- Use headlines to help users navigate through the document.

- Present procedures in chart or grid form as described in the **procedures** entry of this book.

- Include illustrations wherever they will convey complex information clearly.

- Use icons, sidelines, and borders to draw attention to safety issues and time-saving tips.

(See also **active voice/passive voice**, **headline levels**, **jargon**, **safety labels**, **visual design**, **word choice**.)

templates for word processors

A **template** is a computer file that serves as a starting point for routine documents in which only content, but not format, changes. Templates, called *stationery* in some word-processing programs, have preformatted font styles, margins, indentations, headlines, headers, and footers.

What does a template contain?

FREQUENTLY USED TEXT AND GRAPHICS

A template stores often-used text and graphics, called *boilerplate*, as glossaries or autotext. You can insert a glossary item, be it a word, phrase, sentence, paragraph, or series of paragraphs, into your document by using a simple command. Use glossaries for:

- names: your own name, your company name, names and addresses of your frequent correspondents
- sentences you write often, such as

If you have any questions, please call me at 1.800.888.8888, ext. 888.

- paragraphs or groups of paragraphs, such as standard disclaimers, product warnings, and contract clauses.

STYLES

Individual commands or styles store formatting for headlines, paragraphs, tables, headers, and footers.

All your styles stored together in a template are called a *style sheet*. Consult the **style sheets** entry in this book for more information.

When should you use a template?

Use a template whenever you want to save time and ensure consistency. Then you won't have to format every document you write: just apply a template.

LETTERS

A letter template ensures consistent placement and formatting of all parts of a letter, from inside address to courtesy copy notations.

MEMOS

A memo template comes equipped with *to*, *from*, *date*, and *subject* headings and distribution list notations.

REPORTS

Report templates standardize formatting throughout a long document. They are especially valuable for team writing projects.

When the time comes to assemble the final draft, standardizing the format of individual contributions is quick and easy. Simply apply the report template. Of course, you must still edit to ensure consistency of style among the various team members.

Cover page, table of contents, appendix, and bibliography templates are invaluable time savers as you hurry to meet your deadline.

How do you use a template?

Save formatting, text, and graphics that you use repeatedly as a template file or glossary entries.

Consult your word-processing manual for a full explanation.

Then, when you are ready to write your draft, open a template and type in the text that is specific to your particular document.

Why must you proofread?

Boilerplate text saves time and ensures standardization. You may think that it's unnecessary to proofread glossary insertions—after all, they've already been corrected. However, you must check carefully to make sure that

- you haven't strung together a series of paragraphs without regard to organization, transition, or overall unity.

- your glossary passage exactly fits the situation you are writing about. Sometimes boilerplate text is vague because it's generic. Insert a specific word or phrase if necessary.

(See also **format**, **headlines**, **letters**, **style sheets**.)

---

tense

Tense indicates whether the action of the verb takes place in the past, present, or future. Compound tenses tell you whether the action is completed or continuing. Following are the basic tenses of English verbs, as illustrated by the verb *to improve*.

SIMPLE TENSES

1. *present*	I improve
2. *past*	I improved
3. *future*	I will improve

PERFECT TENSES (COMPLETED ACTION)

1. *present perfect* I have improved
2. *past perfect* I had improved
3. *future perfect* I will have improved

PROGRESSIVE OR CONTINUOUS TENSES

1. *present progressive* I am improving
2. *past progressive* I was improving
3. *future progressive* I will be improving

PERFECT PROGRESSIVE TENSES

1. *present perfect progressive* I have been improving
2. *past perfect progressive* I had been improving
3. *future perfect progressive* I will have been improving

The simple tenses

The three simple tenses use the base form of the verb without forms of the verb *to be*. The future tense adds *will* to the main verb.

PRESENT: AN ACTION HAPPENING NOW OR HABITUALLY.

This animal *responds* differently to the same stimulus.

I *write* the monthly newsletter for our department.

PAST: AN ACTION THAT HAPPENED AND IS FINISHED.

Winthrop's speech to the board members *lasted* thirteen minutes.

Joe *ordered* the components yesterday.

<u>FUTURE</u>: AN ACTION THAT WILL HAPPEN.

> Joyce *will send* a duplicate of the transmittal to accounting.

> Tomorrow I *will enter* the engineers' changes in the specifications appendix of the proposal.

The perfect tenses (completed action)

The perfect tenses use the past participle with a form of the verb *to have*. The action of the verb in the perfect tense must be completed before the action of a second verb. This second verb is either stated, or its action is understood.

<u>PRESENT PERFECT</u>: AN ACTION THAT BEGAN IN THE PAST AND AFFECTS THE PRESENT.

> This animal *has responded* differently to the same stimulus. [In the past, this animal has responded differently to the same stimulus than it responds today. *Than it responds today* does not appear in the sentence but is understood.]

> I *have written* the monthly newsletter for our department. [Although I no longer write it, I have written the monthly newsletter before.]

<u>PAST PERFECT</u>: AN ACTION FINISHED IN THE PAST BEFORE ANOTHER PAST ACTION.

> Winthrop's speech to the board members *had lasted* thirteen minutes when the fire alarm sounded.

> Joe *had ordered* the components before the factory closed.

<u>FUTURE PERFECT</u>: AN ACTION THAT IS ACCOMPLISHED BEFORE SOMETHING ELSE HAPPENS IN THE FUTURE.

> Joyce *will have sent* a duplicate of the transmittal to accounting by the time the books are balanced.

The proposal is scheduled to go to the print shop tomorrow. By then I *will have entered* the engineers' changes in the specifications appendix.

The progressive or continuous tenses

The progressive tenses use the present participle with a form of the verb *to be*.

PRESENT PROGRESSIVE: AN ACTION CURRENTLY IN PROGRESS.

I *am designing* a new template for the manual.

Our attorneys *are considering* the offer.

PAST PROGRESSIVE: AN ACTION THAT CONTINUED FOR A PERIOD OF TIME IN THE PAST.

Art *was working* on the tax returns when the auditors called. [*When the auditors called* is a completed action that occurred while Art was working on the tax returns.]

Plumbers *were* constantly *repairing* frozen pipes last winter. [The pipes froze so often that repairing them was an ongoing process.]

FUTURE PROGRESSIVE: AN ACTION THAT WILL BE CONTINUING FOR A PERIOD OF TIME IN THE FUTURE.

We *will be remodeling* the customer service center in April.

I *will be organizing* a goodbye party for Fiona next week.

The perfect progressive tenses

The perfect progressive tenses use the past participle of the verb *to be* with the present participle of the main verb. These tenses indicate a continuing action completed before another action, either stated or understood.

<u>PRESENT PERFECT PROGRESSIVE</u>: AN ACTION THAT BEGAN IN THE PAST AND CONTINUES INTO THE PRESENT.

MIS *has been adding* system enhancements that increase our productivity.

<u>PAST PERFECT PROGRESSIVE</u>: AN ACTION IN PROGRESS IN THE PAST WHILE ANOTHER PAST ACTION OCCURRED. BOTH ACTIONS ARE NOW COMPLETED.

Our networking problems *had been increasing* before the codes were changed.

<u>FUTURE PERFECT PROGRESSIVE</u>: AN ACTION THAT WILL BE IN PROGRESS BEFORE SOMETHING ELSE HAPPENS IN THE FUTURE.

I *will have been planning* the conference agenda for a week before Hector even sees any session titles.

Tense consistency

Sentences and paragraphs should generally be consistent in tense. When you do shift tense, be sure that you intend to show a change in time.

We *have* authorization to use the research lab after hours, so we *will run* the last test tonight. [intentional time shift from present to future]

Before they *wrote* the report, they *do* the research. [unintentional—and incorrect—time shift from past to present]

(See also **predicates**, **verbs**.)

that/which

The relative pronouns ***that*** and ***which*** are used to start two different kinds of modifying clauses: restrictive and nonrestrictive. These types of clauses are also called essential and nonessential.

Which introduces a nonrestrictive clause. A nonrestrictive clause

- can be omitted without changing the meaning of the sentence

- is always set off by commas.

That introduces a restrictive clause. A restrictive clause

- cannot be omitted without changing the meaning of the sentence

- is never set off by commas.

> She sent her supervisor e-mail, *which* was the best way to reach him under the circumstances. It was the only means of communication *that* would get his attention before the meeting.

The clause *which was the best way . . .* is nonrestrictive because it could be taken out and the first sentence would still have its intended meaning.

However, *that would get his attention . . .* is essential for the second sentence to make sense. If you took it out, you would leave your reader with the impression that e-mail was the only means of communication in the universe.

When a nonrestrictive clause occurs in the middle of a sentence, be sure to put a comma both before and after the clause.

> Send e-mail, *which is the best way to communicate with me,* to the address above.

The parentheses test

Think of commas that set off clauses as a weaker form of parentheses. Only nonessential clauses can be put into parentheses.

She sent her supervisor e-mail *(which was the best way to reach him under the circumstances)*. It was the only means of communication *that* would get his attention before the meeting.

When in doubt, ask yourself if the clause could go in parentheses. If not, you're probably safe with *that*.

(See also **relative pronouns**, **restrictive and nonrestrictive elements**.)

---

thesaurus

A **thesaurus** is a book or computer program of synonyms and antonyms. To avoid overusing a word, look it up in your thesaurus to find an alternative.

Don't use a thesaurus simply to find a fancier or more obscure word to impress your readers. Your writing is most effective when you stick to simple, direct communication.

Most word-processing programs have an on-line thesaurus that is quicker to use than a book. Take advantage of this feature—but be aware that a computer thesaurus is probably not as complete as a book version, such as *Roget's Thesaurus*.

An on-line version won't give you guidance in choosing the precise word that fits your meaning. Nor will it offer definitions or shades of meaning that expand your choice.

(See also **word choice**.)

---

titles: capturing your readers' interest

Strategies for effective titles

The **title** of your document is the first thing readers see. Design it to catch their attention. Follow these guidelines:

1. The title should summarize the content of your document. It should be specific enough so the reader can decide—based on what it says—whether to read the document.

   instead of: *Mechanized Harvesting* [too general]

   write: *Mechanized Harvesting for Thinning Sawtimber Red Pine* [more specific]

2. You may include a second level of specificity in a title, with the first level announcing a general topic. Put a colon between the levels.

   System Upgrades: Install Tomorrow's System on Today's Computer

   The second level of specificity should go beyond summary and make your reader *want* to read your document.

3. Unless your readers are specialists who will understand abbreviations and acronyms, leave them out of titles. If they can't understand the title, your readers will read no further.

Formatting titles

Capitalization

In the title of an article, report, document, or book, each word begins with a capital letter, except prepositions of four or fewer letters. Articles and prepositions that begin titles are always capitalized.

The Bentley Short Course in Word Processing

Learning About the Internet

Investment Advice from a Pro

Italics, underlining, or quotation marks?

Italicize the titles of long works, such as books, newspapers, reports, and films. Before word processing and the ability to italicize, the rule was to underline such titles.

Put quotation marks around the titles of short works, such as articles, book chapters, report sections, and encyclopedia entries.

(See also **acronyms and initialisms**, **bibliography**, **capital letters**, **italics**, **quotation marks**, **underlining**.)

---

tone: what's your attitude?

The attitude writers take toward their subject, purpose, and readers is called **tone**. Your choice of language and sentence structure creates tone.

Pronouns and names

If you use the second person—*you*—your tone is friendly.

> As our customer, *you* are our top priority.

> Mike Applebaum invites *you* to the awards dinner on Friday.

> If *you* would like to review *your* retirement stock options, please call Marvin at ext. 772.

Be careful not to create a false friendliness that sounds like a computer-generated letter selling swampland to the unwary.

> Remember, Ms. Jones, that no vacation would be complete without your personal guided tour of . . .

Using the third person instead of the second, including the pronoun *one*, creates distance between you and your reader.

> *All employees* are invited to the awards dinner on Friday. [*All employees* is third person. Compare with the second example in this entry.]

> *Those employees* wanting to review retirement stock options should call Marvin at ext. 772. [*Those*

employees is third person. Compare with the third example in this entry.]

instead of:	*One* may bring a recording device.
write:	*You* may bring a recording device.
or:	Feel free to bring a recording device. ["You" is understood.]

Many companies do not, however, use personal pronouns—I, me, you—in formal technical writing. Check your company's style guide or editing department for guidance.

Contractions

Contractions make your tone more conversational.

instead of:	If you *cannot* finish the beta testing, *do not* sign off on your section of the project at the end of the month.
write:	If you *can't* finish the beta testing, *don't* sign off on your section of the project at the end of the month.

Don't use contractions in formal business and technical writing.

Sentence structure

Although simple, direct sentences are easy to read, a string of short sentences is choppy and can sound abrupt, if not impolite.

> Activities are grouped under Customer Service. This category includes Collections. The activities all have similar aims. Choose one activity per session.

In comparison, a long sentence with subordinate clauses and phrases sounds friendlier, almost conversational.

> Although the details vary, the activities grouped under Customer Service, including Collections, have similar aims. Choose one activity per session.

Active voice

IN BUSINESS WRITING

The active voice is more friendly and direct than the passive voice. In the active voice, the subject performs the action of the sentence. In the passive voice, the subject is acted upon.

instead of: Both good and bad interface design *is shown* in this example.

write: This example *shows* both good and bad interface design.

IN TECHNICAL WRITING

Learn to use the active voice without personal pronouns. Your writing will be livelier, but no less appropriate for technical situations.

instead of: It was concluded that . . .

or: We concluded that . . .

write: The study concludes that . . .

Directions

Giving directions can sometimes sound too authoritarian and even confrontational. Choose your words carefully.

instead of: Surrender your key to the guard as you leave each night.

write: Regulations require that you turn your key in to the guard as you leave each night. [The tone is still formal, but not as harsh.]

Sometimes a direction is appropriate and the clearest way to communicate necessary information.

Do not use rubber stripping on storm doors.

Visual design and tone

Just as language and sentence structure create tone, so does visual format. A page with an open look created with white space and headlines looks friendlier and more inviting than dense text with few breaks.

The typeface you choose can be straight and stark or softer and less formal looking. Consider how you want your letter or document to look and what impression you want it to give. This is all part of establishing tone.

Choosing an appropriate tone

Choose a tone that suits your readers as well as your purpose in writing.

A letter of congratulations to a colleague should be friendly and personal. A letter asking for an overdue payment should sound more formal and official. A quarterly financial report will probably be still more formal and authoritative and avoid a personal tone altogether.

Remember that an appropriate tone is part of effective writing. Some writers like to read their drafts aloud to hear whether their tone is right.

The importance of a final proof

What does proofreading your document have to do with tone? Carelessness and typographical errors send a message to your readers, too. You don't want them to think that they're not important enough to merit a polished document.

Proofread carefully, therefore, for tone and style as well as content.

(See also **active voice/passive voice**, **letters**, **memorandums**, **point of view**, **style**, **word choice**, **"you" attitude**.)

topic sentence: the key to each paragraph

In business and technical writing, the **topic sentence** that states the main idea should usually come first in the paragraph. Often the topic sentence becomes a headline.

Some paragraphs have a topic sentence last, or even in the middle. Journal articles and longer reports should vary their placement.

topic sentence first:	Don't worry about perfection. Avoid editing or censoring the words you dictate—just as you would avoid editing if you were *writing* the draft for Step 5. For now, you just want to get the draft on tape; you can correct your grammar and sentence structure when the draft comes back on paper. [from the book *Write to the Top* by Deborah Dumaine, p. 62]
topic sentence last:	Avoid editing or censoring the words you dictate—just as you would avoid editing if you were *writing* the draft for Step 5. For now, you just want to get the draft on tape; you can correct your grammar and sentence structure when the draft comes back on paper. Don't worry about perfection.

Putting the topic sentence last in the second example gives it a different emphasis—a final punch at the end for readers to remember. Neither example is more correct. Your placement of the topic sentence depends on the effect you want to achieve.

(See also **emphasis**, **headlines**, **paragraphs**.)

---

transitions: smoothing the flow of ideas

To smooth the flow between sentences, paragraphs, and sections of a document, writers use **transitions**. Transitions connect ideas and help readers navigate a document. A lack of transition makes writing sound choppy and disconnected.

Common transitional devices

1. Pronouns that refer to nouns help connect ideas.

   By September International Motors had three electric vehicles in service in Detroit. *They* [the vehicles] were able to fulfill all the functions of the regular fleet.

2. Repeating a word or using a synonym keeps readers focused on your topic. The repeated and related words in the following passage are in italics.

   To dig the foundations and sink the towers of the bridge, workers used a pneumatic *caisson*. *This* huge *cylinder* has a lower cutting edge, closed at the top and filled with compressed air to prevent soil and water from pouring in. The *caisson* contains an internal, airtight deck, with pressurized chambers below the *vessel*.

3. Parallel structure creates transition, especially if the same word or phrase is repeated in the same structural location.

   We shall fight on the beaches, we shall fight on the landing grounds, we shall fight in the fields and in the streets, we shall fight in the hills; we shall never surrender. [Winston Churchill, Speech on Dunkirk, House of Commons, June 4, 1940]

4. Transition words carry ideas from one sentence or paragraph to the next. Here are some common transitional words and phrases.

therefore	consequently	for example
likewise	still	on the other hand
furthermore	in addition	later
since	second	as an illustration

> A simple text editor uses a single font style and size. A word processor, *on the other hand*, is a complex text editor. *Therefore*, it can handle many different font sizes and shapes. *For example* . . .

Since transition words interrupt the sentence, they should be set off, usually with commas.

> Consolidating the supplier and retailer base, *therefore*, will likely continue into the next fiscal year.

Don't confuse an interruption, like the one in the preceding example, with a sentence containing two independent clauses.

In the next example, the transition phrase introduces an independent clause; it does not interrupt it. Put a semicolon before the transition and a comma after it.

> The Olde Village Conference Centre would accommodate us best; *on the other hand,* the Great Pines Complex is cheaper and closer.

5. Previewing or announcing what comes next provides an effective transition to information that follows.

> The following section defines four ready sources of revenue for building additional warehouses.
>
> 1. <u>Venture capital</u>
>
>   The most available source of funding is . . .

6. Ending a paragraph with a question that you answer at the beginning of the next paragraph is a transitional device designed to arouse your reader's interest.

. . . What additional work would go to the business area managers if we adopt this reorganization plan?

Of the three managers, only Kim would have increased responsibilities . . .

Transitions and the writing process

Watch for opportunities to use transitions during Steps 5 and 6 to Reader-Centered Writing, as you write and edit your draft. Transitions are the connective tissue of your document. They make all the difference between smooth and choppy writing.

(See also **clear writing, conjunctions, draft writing, editing your draft, paragraphs, parallel structure, unity**.)

U

underlining

Underlining, like boldface and italics, is one way to emphasize information. Before word processing, when it wasn't possible to italicize on a typewriter, underlining was used instead of italics. Today underlining is used chiefly for emphasis or in headlines, but as a last choice after bold and italics. In long documents underlining might be your lowest-level subheading.

Most word processors can underline both continuously and word by word. Continuous underlining is the preferred style, though either method is acceptable.

(See also **emphasis**, **headline levels**, **headlines**, **italics**.)

units of measurement

Units of measurement are either English (customary U.S. measures) or metric (the International System of Units, or SI). Most countries besides the U.S. use metric measurements. Even in the U.S., the scientific and engineering communities use the metric system. Here are the English-to-metric equivalents for some common measures.

English	metric
1 inch	2.54 centimeters
1 foot	0.30 meter
1 yard	0.91 meter
1 mile	1.61 kilometers
1 acre	0.40 hectare
1 ounce	28.3 grams
1 pound	0.45 kilogram
1 English ton	0.91 metric ton
1 quart	0.95 liter

| 32° Fahrenheit | 0° centigrade |
| 212° Fahrenheit | 100° centigrade |

Be aware that your international correspondents may not be familiar with customary U.S. measures. Convert to metric as a courtesy to your readers.

(See also **International System of Units**.)

---

unity

A document has **unity** when it is a cohesive whole, complete in itself. No information is missing; none is extraneous. You achieve unity in writing when your main message is evident in every part of your document. Its different sections are clearly and logically related to your principal idea like branches to the trunk of a tree.

Unity is the result of a well-thought-out plan. Without a logical pattern, your readers will not be able to follow your thought process. However, once clear thinking and careful organization impose a structure, your readers will understand what they are reading. It will be evident to them how the different parts of your document relate to its main idea and to one another.

Use the Six Steps to Reader-Centered Writing™

You will achieve unity by planning your entire document before you begin to write your first draft. Follow the Six Steps to Reader-Centered Writing.

1. <u>Analyze your readers and define your purpose</u>. Filling out the Focus Sheet™ will provide you with a unifying idea that will match your readers' needs.

2. <u>Use a Start-up Strategy</u>. Generate ideas with a brainstorm outline, questioning, a traditional outline, or another Start-up Strategy that works for you.

3. <u>Group information under headlines</u>. Concentrate on moving related ideas and backup data together. Don't worry about sequencing them until Step 4. Make sure you have all the information you need to support your main ideas.

4. <u>Sequence your ideas</u>. Now make sure that your plan is clear and well sequenced. Refer to your Focus Sheet once again. An organizational scheme based on your readers' point of view will help unify your document. The result should be an organized list of topics and subtopics—a traditional or list outline.

5. <u>Write the first draft</u>. Put your sequenced outline before you and start to draft. Concentrate on filling in the details that support your main idea. Remember your Focus Sheet: don't give your readers information they don't need.

6. <u>Edit for clarity, conciseness, and accuracy</u>. To improve unity, pay particular attention to these aspects of the editing process:

   • <u>Transitions</u>. Make smooth transitions between sentences and between paragraphs. The simple addition of words like *on the other hand*, *therefore*, and *after that* indicate how your sentences are linked. Your readers will easily follow you from one thought to the next.

   • <u>Point of view</u>. Don't make sudden shifts in your point of view; for example, from *our company's strategy* to *their success*. You will startle and confuse your readers. Maintain your argument throughout. If you offer an opposing one, make it clear that it is not yours. Relate it to your own.

Finish with an editorial review using the "Be Your Own Editor" Checklist—standard process for any document.

(See also **clear writing**, **concise vs. wordy writing**, **Introduction to the Six Steps**, **paragraphs**, **point of view**, **sentences**, **transitions**.)

V

verbs

Verbs express an action, an occurrence, or a state of being. They define what the subject is or does and indicate when the action takes place.

Classes of verbs

There are four classes of verbs: transitive, intransitive, linking, and helping.

1. TRANSITIVE VERBS

Transitive verbs need a direct object to complete their meaning.

> Solana *will develop* [verb] *guidelines* [direct object] for using classified material.

Transitive verbs may also have indirect objects or object complements.

> The manufacturer *provides* [verb] *customers* [indirect object] a *guarantee* [direct object] on all its products.

> Kurt painted his office *blue*. [object complement]

2. INTRANSITIVE VERBS

Verbs that do not need an object to complete their meaning are called intransitive.

> The package *arrived*.

> After I gave blood this morning, I had to *lie down*.

3. LINKING VERBS

Linking verbs are followed by a complement because they require more information to be

571

complete. Some common linking verbs are *be*, *become*, *seem*, *appear*, *taste*, *feel*, and *look*.

> Their international office *appears* successful. [The complement *successful* completes the meaning of the verb *appears*.]

> Our supervising chef makes sure each dish *tastes* first class before he's satisfied. [The complement *first class* completes the meaning of the verb *tastes*. But in the sentence *The chef tastes each dish*, *tastes* is a transitive verb followed by the direct object *dish*.]

The most common linking verb is *to be* when it stands by itself without another verb. It establishes a relationship or defines a quality of the subject.

> Francine *is* never late. [The complement *late* completes the meaning of the verb *is*; *never* modifies *late*.]

> The CEO *is* a retired air force test pilot.

> The new network *will be* a success.

Because they don't take direct objects, linking verbs are also intransitive.

4. Helping verbs

Helping verbs (also called auxiliary verbs) are parts of compound tenses. The main helping verbs are forms of *to be*, *to have*, and *to do*.

> The owners *were* traveling to the annual conference when the factory fire started. [helping verb *were* + present participle *traveling* = past progressive tense]

> The driver *had* blocked the loading dock before the shipment arrived. [helping verb *had* + past participle *blocked* = past perfect tense]

> She assured me that she *does* report to the vice president daily. [helping verb *do* + base form *report* = present perfect tense]

Regular and irregular verbs

REGULAR VERBS

Regular verbs have predictable endings when they change form. They add an *-s* or *-es* in the third person singular present tense.

improve/improves   catch/catches

Regular verbs form the past tense and the past participle by adding *-ed*, and the progressive tenses by adding *-ing*.

install/installed/installing
remark/remarked/remarking

Some regular verbs also have alternative irregular forms.

shine/shined *or* shone

IRREGULAR VERBS

Irregular verbs form the past tense and the past participle in nonstandard ways. They may add *-t* instead of *-ed*, change a vowel, or remain the same for different forms.

think/thought   cut/cut   sell/sold   freeze/froze
see/saw

See the irregular verb list in the **irregular verbs** entry.

Characteristics of verbs

Verbs change form in different ways to show person, number, tense, voice, and mood.

PERSON

Person refers to who or what is doing the action of the verb. There are three persons: first, second, and third. They may be singular or plural:

First person singular	I improve
Second person singular	you improve
Third person singular	he, she, it improves
First person plural	we improve
Second person plural	you improve
Third person plural	they improve

To determine person, look at the subject of the sentence. The pronouns *I* and *we* are first person. *You* is second person. Like the pronouns *he*, *she*, *it*, and *they*, all nouns are third person:

> Johanna improves   The managers improve

The verb *to be* is irregular. Different persons require different verb forms.

First person singular	I am
Second person singular	you are
Third person singular	he, she, it is
First person plural	we are
Second person plural	you are
Third person plural	they are

A modifying word or phrase that follows the subject does not affect the person of the verb.

> You, *the leading contractor*, stand a good chance of winning. [Third person modifier follows second person subject.]

> I, *your president*, am pleased to announce a new program. [Third person modifier follows first person subject.]

NUMBER

Number refers to whether the subject of the sentence is singular or plural. The verb form must agree with that number. Verb endings change to indicate number in the third person singular of the present tense only. Most verbs add an *-s* or *-es*:

> he improves   she teaches   Pat does
> *but* it has [irregular verb]

The only verb to show a difference between singular and plural in any other person is *to be*. The first person singular and plural are different.

I am	we are
you are	you are
he, she, it is	they are

TENSE

Time is one characteristic of tense. Aspect—completeness vs. continuity of action—is another. The main English verb tenses follow.

SIMPLE TENSES

1. *present*	I give
2. *past*	I gave
3. *future*	I will give

PERFECT TENSES (COMPLETED ACTION)

1. *present perfect*	I have given
2. *past perfect*	I had given
3. *future perfect*	I will have given

PROGRESSIVE OR CONTINUOUS TENSES

1. *present progressive*	I am giving
2. *past progressive*	I was giving
3. *future progressive*	I will be giving

PERFECT PROGRESSIVE TENSES

1. *present perfect progressive*	I have been giving
2. *past perfect progressive*	I had been giving
3. *future perfect progressive*	I will have been giving

See the **tense** entry for a complete description of these tenses.

VOICE

Voice determines whether the subject acts or is acted upon. In the preceding list of tenses, all the verbs are in the active voice. The subject—*I*—is performing the action of giving.

The following list shows verbs in the passive voice, where the subject is acted upon. The passive voice uses a form of the verb *to be* with the past participle of the main verb.

SIMPLE TENSES

1. *present*	I am given
2. *past*	I was given
3. *future*	I will be given

PERFECT TENSES (COMPLETED ACTION)

1. *present perfect*	I have been given
2. *past perfect*	I had been given
3. *future perfect*	I will have been given

PROGRESSIVE OR CONTINUOUS TENSES

1. *present progressive*	I am being given
2. *past progressive*	I was being given
3. *future progressive*	*no passive forms exist*

PERFECT PROGRESSIVE TENSES   *NO PASSIVE FORMS EXIST*

Consult the **active voice/passive voice** entry for a discussion on avoiding cumbersome and indirect passive constructions.

Mood

The mood of a verb refers to the manner of action that the verb expresses and the consequent form of the verb. The most common categories of mood are: indicative, imperative, and subjunctive.

<u>Indicative</u>: a declarative or interrogative sentence

The shareholders *met* on June 12.

Will our company *pursue* this project?

<u>Imperative</u>: a command

In the following examples the subject of the verbs is "you" understood (see entry).

Fax this memo immediately!

Edit the final copy and *send* it to all managers.

<u>Subjunctive</u>: an improbable condition, wish, command

The president suggested *that she go to the meeting*.

The consultant recommended *that we reduce spending*.

He insisted *that the meeting be rescheduled*.

The verbs in the *that* clauses are in the subjunctive mood. Notice that they use the base form of the verb, even after the third person singular. In the first example, we say *she go*, whereas we would normally say *she goes*.

Use the subjunctive in a condition contrary to fact:

If this mechanism *were not used*, the entire procedure would take twice as long.

Overuse or incorrect use of the subjunctive can result in stilted writing. Be especially careful of *if* clauses that do not introduce a condition contrary to fact; in those clauses use the indicative mood.

She checked to see if the fax *was* in. (not *were*)

Clauses following *as if* or *as though* usually describe a condition that doesn't exist. They require the past subjunctive form of the verb.

> He spoke as if he *were* the President of the United States.

Agreement of verbs

Verbs must agree with their subjects in number.

> A double-linked *list contains* two links. [A singular subject takes a singular verb.]

> Double-linked *lists contain* two links. [A plural subject takes a plural verb.]

> The forward *link* and the backward *link need* to be adjusted. [Two singular nouns joined by *and* form a plural subject and take a plural verb.]

Be sure you identify the subject correctly. Sometimes several words intervene between subject and verb.

instead of: The *results* of the second test *indicates* that we can't use this check to monitor the operation.

write: The *results* of the second test *indicate* that we can't use this check to monitor the operation. [The plural verb *indicate* agrees with the plural subject *results*, not with the nearest noun, *test*.]

Verb phrases

A group of words that expresses the action of the subject is called a *verb phrase*. It normally consists of the main verb and any helping verbs and acts as a single verb.

> Gerri *will have completed* the report by the time she leaves for vacation on March 30.

> I *had planned* to hire a grant writer, but my budget *has been cut*.

(See also **active voice/passive voice**, **irregular verbs**, **person**, **tense**, **"you" understood**.)

---

visual aids: improving your presentation skills

In today's business climate you must learn to communicate effectively, both orally and in writing. Both management and increasing numbers of non-management staff are called upon to make presentations.

Your capabilities and contributions to the organization are often assessed in direct proportion to your presentation skills. It is imperative for you to be able to stand and deliver.

This entry focuses on the preparation and delivery of **visual aids** with an emphasis on overhead transparencies, also called view foils or vu-graphs. You will learn how to

- determine when a visual aid is necessary
- choose what to put on your transparency
- use proper techniques when preparing transparencies
- deliver the information on your transparency with impact
- apply correct techniques for using different visual aids
- distribute handouts.

How to make your point

Your audience will understand and remember your core message in three possible ways. Listeners absorb information when they

- hear you speak (auditory)
- see a visual aid (visual)
- touch or examine a prop (kinesthetic).

Consider which of these methods can work for you and how each can help you to reach your audience.

Why use visual aids?

An hour after a presentation, most people will retain only about 10 percent of the information they heard. The proper use of visual aids will significantly increase the odds that your audience will remember what you had to say. Use visual aids to

- capture your audience's attention

- make your presentation come to life

- help your audience remember the "bottom line" or core message of your presentation

- illustrate key points

- explain complicated ideas.

Visual aids can be as simple as a few words on a white board or as complex as a sophisticated video presentation. You have many options to choose from.

Transparencies

At a Fortune 500 aerospace company, over 600 supervisors and managers were asked, "What's wrong with this company's presentations?" An overwhelming majority of the responses referred to improper preparation and use of overhead transparencies.

Pay attention to each transparency's readability. Follow these general guidelines:

1. "6 × 6": limit yourself to

   - six lines of text

   - six words per line.

2. Use an 18-point or larger font size.

3. Include only one message per chart. Leave complex information for handouts.

4. Limit the number of charts. Consider carefully how many are really necessary to deliver your message.

WHAT TO PUT ON YOUR TRANSPARENCIES

Simply stated—and as a minimum—display the following information:

- the purpose and point of your presentation
- arguments for and examples of your main point
- a call to action: what you want your audience to do as a result of your presentation.

TIPS FOR A PROFESSIONAL PRESENTATION

1. Mount your transparencies in frames. Frames will help you center each transparency on the projector.

2. Make sure that everyone can read the projection screen, especially detailed illustrations. Don't block the screen.

3. Shut off the projector when you're not discussing the transparency. Never leave the screen blank. Make quick and smooth transitions from one transparency to the next.

4. Number your transparencies in case you drop them.

5. Use symbols, drawings, and pictures. Drawings of familiar objects will reduce audience resistance to your ideas. Pictures that reflect written content will help your audience remember the point you want to make.

As the following example illustrates, abstract concepts, in particular, benefit from concrete illustrations.

Which Side of the Brain Do You Use Most?

$$L[y] = a_0 y^{(n)} + a_1 y^{(n-1)}$$
$$+ \cdots + a_{n-1} y' + a_n y = g(x)$$

Right Brain Hemisphere

Imagination
Creativity
Art
Insight
Intuition
Planning

Left Brain Hemisphere

Reasoning
Logic
Science
Language
Grammar
Spelling

6. Know how to work the projector. Make sure a spare bulb is available and be able to switch to it if your existing bulb burns out.

A FEW DON'TS

1. Don't read from the projection screen. If you need a memory aid, you may

   • refer to—but don't read—the text on the overhead projector

   • jot down a few notes on your transparency frames

   • use 3-by-5-inch cards.

   It's better to glance down occasionally than to turn your back on your audience.

2. Don't use a pointer for word transparencies. Save it for more complex graphs and charts.

3. Don't use transparencies as a crutch or you will lose credibility with your audience. It's better to leave a point unillustrated than to use a poor visual aid.

4. Don't play with the pointer or swing it. It's distracting, and you risk hitting yourself or an audience member.

Movies, videos, and slides[*]

Audiences enjoy films, yet you still need to maintain your presence as the key to your presentation's effectiveness. Do not hand over the job of presenting to your visual aid.

You should never be in the dark, even when showing movies or slides. A small light should still be on you. Your authority is diminished if you are invisible.

Follow these guidelines:

1. Check all your equipment, including the screen and projector. Find out in advance if you will need an extension cord and make sure one is available. Bring tape and use it to anchor the cord—you don't want anyone to trip over it.

2. Decide ahead of time if you or someone else will operate the equipment. Arrange for an assistant if necessary.

3. Place the slide projector at the back of the room, where it won't block anyone's view.

4. A laser pointer is better than a regular pointer for slides.

5. Even before designing your presentation, make sure the room can be made dark enough for slides or a movie. If not, use different visual aids.

Easel charts and graphs

There is no firm rule regarding where you stand when presenting a chart or graph on an easel. Position yourself where you are comfortable, but make sure you don't block the audience's view.

---

[*]Adapted from *How to Be a Good Speaker*, The Research Institute of America, Inc., New York, 1985.

White boards and easels

These aids allow you to create a visual during your talk—an effective technique in capturing your audience's interest. Follow these guidelines:

1. Print legibly.

2. Make sure your writing is large enough to be read from the back of the room.

3. Use a variety of colors to emphasize different points.

4. Draw simple stick figures where appropriate: you do not need to be an artist to be convincing.

Maintain eye contact when speaking—never talk to the board. If your visuals are complicated, prepare them ahead of time so you can focus on your audience.

Props

Props are greatly underutilized, but they can do wonders for your presentation. Explaining what a computer chip looks like takes three times as long as showing it, so bring one in and pass it around.

Handouts

Should you distribute your handouts before or after your presentation? If you hand them out before, your audience might be on page 10 while you're on page 3. Handing them out after may frustrate those audience members who like to make notes as they follow along with you.

Consider these issues before you decide:

1. Why do you have handouts? If they're for an audience who couldn't attend, distribute them at the end. Don't duplicate your transparencies in this case—only with difficulty will those who were absent be able to piece together your message from transparencies alone.

2. If the handouts duplicate your transparencies, distribute them before so the audience can make notes on them. Remember, however, that rarely do even excellent transparencies substitute for more detailed handouts.

Consult the **presentations**, **oral** entry for advice on preparing handouts.

Some final questions to consider

1. Do you have a backup method if—in spite of your efforts—your visual aids fail right before or during a presentation?
2. Would a variety of visual aids reinforce your purpose and key message?
3. Do you know precisely when in your presentation to use each visual aid?
4. Will your visual aids become more important than the point they are intended to make?

Prepare carefully. The quality of your visual aids directly affects the success of your presentation.

(See also **graphics**; **presentations, oral**.)

---

visual design: make your reader want to read

Visual design refers to how your document looks on the page. Take a few minutes to examine some documents and magazine articles. Which pages capture your attention? Which ones can you read quickly? Which are dense and uninviting?

Readers develop attitudes toward a piece of writing—and the writer—from the appearance of the writing alone. They make judgments about how difficult it is to read or how organized it may be.

Readers notice and appreciate a writer's effort when a document is visually appealing. Carefully designed documents tell your readers that you care not only about your message but about them. Make your format work for you—not against you.

Use techniques like headlines, white space, and bulleted lists to enhance the appearance of your document. Your goal is to entice the reader by making the page attractive and easy to read. The following table provides an overview of strategies for designing your document.

How to Design for Visual Impact	
What to use?	**When to use it?**
Headlines	• to introduce most paragraphs • to focus your reader on your major ideas
Sidelines	• for extra emphasis • for persuasion
Text font	• to assure readability • to unify style
Short paragraphs	• to avoid overwhelming your reader • to attract speed readers
Two columns	• to convey two kinds of information simultaneously • to encourage faster reading
Bulleted lists	• to replace lists within sentences
Numbered lists	• when sequence is important • when listing steps in a procedure • for easy reference to the list later • when items are quantified
White space and indentation	• to frame your ideas • to improve readability
Graphs, charts, and tables	• to present numbers, dollar amounts, and technical data
Color (use judiciously)	• to highlight information (limit to two colors) • for aesthetic appeal
You can emphasize	**by using**
• deadlines • action items	underlining *italics* **bold typeface** different fonts ALL CAPITALS different type sizes

Headlines

Informative headlines immediately draw your reader into your document. At a glance your reader can find key topics, whereas scanning many paragraphs of equal importance without headlines can be time consuming and uninformative.

Use headlines to break up a solid page of text. Don't write more than three paragraphs without inserting a headline. Short documents may require a headline for each paragraph.

Choose a few words that illustrate the message of the paragraph; use boldface type or a different font to highlight them.

FONT SIZE AND STYLE FOR HEADLINES

Headlines make your ideas virtually jump off the page, so choose an easy-to-read font to reinforce this effect. Don't try to be decorative by selecting too many different fonts; keep to one or two per document.

Font size may be the same or slightly larger than that of the text body. To emphasize headlines, use boldface type, underlining, or all capitals.

POSITION

Place headlines flush left. You may center headlines to create major divisions in long documents.

BE CREATIVE—CATCH YOUR READERS' ATTENTION

Strong, original headlines will kindle your readers' interest far more than dull, generic ones. Remember to

- be specific
- include your point
- emphasize action by using verbs
- be positive
- use questions as headlines.

Also be sure that your headlines flow in a logical sequence. You want to lead your reader through the document strategically, not haphazardly.

Sidelines

Placed to the side of the text, sidelines—like headlines—are one- or two-line phrases that summarize the core message of a paragraph. Just like headlines they emphasize the content of the text. They are particularly useful for persuasion: by stating your message in a sideline *and* in the text you double your opportunity to emphasize your point.

Another benefit is purely visual. By using sidelines you create the effect of two columns rather than one: the resulting text column is narrower than it otherwise would be.

Studies reveal that the narrower the column, the faster people can read. Busy executives may well read more of your document if the text is narrower.

Sometimes it is useful to present just a few key paragraphs with sidelines. It's not necessary to use the sideline format throughout the document. This allows you to combine headlines and sidelines in one document.

Two columns

Business documents often go to two types of readers: technical and nontechnical. A two-column headlined format can address both groups by allowing you to present two versions of your document.

One side is more technical and detailed for your technical readers; the other, summarizing key issues and defining technical points, is directed towards managers and other nontechnical readers.

Text font

Use a font size that's large enough for easy readability. Eleven and twelve point are the standard sizes.

Use fonts smaller than 10 point very rarely and for less important information—footnotes, for example. People with less than perfect vision always complain about 10 point and below.

Your organization probably has font standards. If you have a choice, select a style that's accessible and appropriate for the kind of document you're writing. A font used for a newsletter article may not be suitable for a proposal.

Remember, a serif typeface such as Times Roman—our favorite font—is easier to read than a sans serif typeface like Helvetica.

Limit your document to two or three fonts: one or two for headlines, perhaps; and one for text. In the following example, too many fonts in one document are dizzying.

An Example of Poor Visual Design

Don't let the sun go down on you!

May 14-17
Interactive Conference & Expo
Softbank Institute
Anaheim, CA

May 22-24
49th Annual Quality Congress
American Society for
Quality Control
Cincinnati, OH

June 4-6
ASTD International
Conference & Exposition
American Society for Training
and Development
Dallas, TX

July 10-14
Strategic Human Resource Planning
University of Michigan Business School
Ann Arbor, MI

July 13-14
Introduction to Multimedia
USDA Graduate School
Washington, D.C.

July 17-19
Advanced Facilitator Development
Association for Quality and Participation
Cincinnati, OH

Using all uppercase letters

Reading all uppercase letters is like having someone shout at you: you listen at first, then turn a deaf ear. It is particularly important not to use all capitals in e-mail writing—they convey an impolite or angry tone. Since all-capital letters have been proven to be hard to read for anything longer than a title, use them for occasional emphasis only.

Short paragraphs

Readers bog down in long, dense paragraphs. The eye tends to skim over or even shy away from weighty blocks of text. If your page is 8 1/2″ × 11″, keep paragraphs to five or six typed lines—not sentences. In technical documents make paragraphs even shorter—about three to four lines.

It's usually appropriate to single-space the lines within a paragraph. If the document will be pencil edited, it's better to double-space. Leave a double-space between paragraphs in single-spaced documents.

Bulleted lists

Lists embedded in the text body are usually hard to grasp and difficult to remember. You can help your reader absorb larger amounts of information by making it more accessible visually: place key points in a bulleted list. This technique also adds emphasis to that information.

It's best to introduce bulleted lists with a sentence or a paragraph in addition to a headline. Skip a line between groups of bulleted items when

- there are four or more items
- space allows
- the items are longer than one line.

Caution: don't overuse bullets. If your document is one string of bullets after another, it will look like an outline. Your reader will lose your argument or train of thought, and the information in the bulleted lists will seem disjointed.

If your goal is to persuade, there's no substitute for the well-crafted paragraph.

Numbered lists

When you want to show that the items in your list have a certain priority or order, use numbers instead of bullets or hyphens. Numbers are vital when you are explaining how to carry out a procedure. Numbers emphasize the importance of doing a particular step before another.

Many step-by-step instructions, if carried out in the wrong sequence, could produce disastrous results.

Numbering is also useful if you need to refer to a particular item in a list, either later in the document or orally to colleagues. You may indent bulleted and numbered lists or line them up flush left. Generally indent following an introductory phrase or sentence for easy reading.

White space and indentation

White space gives the reader a visual break. It offers relief from a dense page of text. Create white space by establishing margins of at least one inch on both sides and at the top and bottom of your page.

You can increase white space by keeping your paragraphs short and double-spacing between paragraphs. White space can showcase important information.

By contrast, indenting sub-ideas within a paragraph will call your reader's attention to the introductory statement.

Indent to send a visual signal to your reader that you are supporting a key idea with data that explains or expands it. The white space created by the indentation draws the reader's eye to the list or quote and makes for easy reference later.

Charts, graphs, and tables

Like white space, charts offer a welcome contrast to a solid block of text. Leave white space around your figures and illustrations to make them stand out. Too much white space, however, will look like poor planning. Balance tables, charts, and illustrations with text.

Explore software possibilities for visually appealing graphics. However, never use charts and tables for decorative effect—sending your message clearly and concisely is the goal.

Color

Many computers today can produce graphics and text in a range of colors. Once you have a color printer, it's easy to get carried away and create lavish, multi-colored documents. Overuse may distract your reader from your key ideas.

As always, consider who your audience is and what image you wish to convey. Use color to highlight information but limit yourself to two.

Techniques for adding emphasis

Certain information requires special emphasis— your readers must see it. Examples: deadlines, requests for action, or next steps. You may highlight this information by placing it in boldface type, italics, a different font, all capitals, or by underlining it.

As with your use of color, be judicious and don't overuse these techniques or they will lose their impact. Never underline full blocks of text or put them in all capitals, boldface, or italics.

How do the experts use visual design?

Learn from professionals. As you look at magazines and newspapers, note how each medium uses white space. Compare, for example, *USA Today* to a more traditionally designed publication like *The New York Times* or the *Wall Street Journal*.

Choose the design that matches your document and your readers' needs.

(See also **color**, **format**, **charts or graphs**, **headlines**, **lists**, **page design**.)

white space: give your readers a break

The space around text is often just as important as the text itself. Newspapers have known about this for years and use their **white space** wisely.

The visual impact of strategically placed white space can lend a whole new design element to your document. It can make it far easier to read—and the more readable your text is, the clearer your message will be.

To take advantage of the benefits of using white space, organize your document visually.

- Write short paragraphs, no more than six lines in length if the page is 8 1/2″ × 11″.

- Use headlines, sidelines, and numbered or bulleted lists.

- Break out important passages and isolate them using borders or indenting.

- Experiment with wider margins, columns, and other page formatting techniques.

(See also **format**, **page design**, **visual design**.)

word choice: say what you mean

Word choice is critical to precise meaning. It also affects style and tone.

Connotation and denotation

The **connotation** of a word refers to its emotional and suggested meanings, often different from a word's **denotation**, or its literal, dictionary meanings.

Compare these two sentences:

Old people make up 24 percent of the population of this community.

Senior citizens make up 24 percent of the population of this community.

The difference between the terms *old people* and *senior citizens* is significant. Though they both mean people over 65, we often think of *old people* as frail, helpless, poor, or unimportant. *Senior citizens*, on the other hand, are respected and considered capable participants in society.

Connotative language is often used in advertising and politics as a form of hidden persuasion to influence the unwary reader's opinion. Both these phrases could describe the same person:

the distinguished representative from the fifth Congressional District

the little lady from Abilene

Whom would you trust with the affairs of state?

In most business and technical writing, you need to be impartial. Avoid stirring emotions or suggesting inappropriate connotations. Consider the connotations associated with your words so readers don't misinterpret you.

Vague language

Vague words have no specific meaning. Common words, such as *soon, important, basically, good,* and *really*, make writing too general. These and other similar words have so many meanings that they've become weak and ineffective.

instead of:	The test group responded *really* well to the new soft drink.
write:	The test group preferred the new soft drink six to one.
instead of:	Please respond to this message *soon*.

write: Please respond to this message by
                  Friday.

Vaguely phrased and unspecific language will
diminish your message. Always be as precise as
possible. In a performance review, for example:

instead of: Chris is slow in answering customer
                  correspondence.

write: Chris answered only 12 out of the
                  expected 20 letters assigned.

When you edit your document, make sure your
message is as specific as possible. Learn to spot the
vague language that takes the power out of your
writing.

Affectation

To make their documents sound important, some
writers try to adopt a serious or weighty tone. But
adding unnecessary words and phrases can make
your writing sound affected, verbose, and insin-
cere. Keep your prose simple and unembellished.

instead of: Prior notice of vacation schedules
                  will assist us in planning our calen-
                  dar for the forthcoming year.

write: Informing us of your vacation sched-
                  ule now will help us plan next year's
                  calendar.

Instead of *prior notice*, *assist*, and *forthcoming
year*, say *informing*, *help*, and *next year*. Your
readers will thank you.

   Also eliminate from your vocabulary phrases
like *it may be said that*, *apropos of*, *in point of
fact*, and *as it were*.

instead of: *In point of fact*, the new financial
                  manager has saved this company
                  from bankruptcy.

write: The new financial manager has saved
                  this company from bankruptcy.

Functional shifts

A functional shift occurs when you convert one part of speech to another. The most common functional shift is using a noun as a verb. For example:

to liaise   to impact   to interface   to critique
memo me   copy me

To critique has become standard usage. Inelegant as they may sound, *to impact* and *to interface* are also gaining acceptance. Try using *to affect*, and *to meet* instead. *Memo me* and *copy me* are fine in informal, usually internal, correspondence.

As always, consider your readers. If they are highly sophisticated and language-oriented people, they will consider a functional shift, like *to liaise*, to be a grammatical error. Err on the side of caution and change these words during the editing step.

Malapropisms

The humorous confusion of two similar words is called a *malapropism*. Usually the words sound similar.

instead of:	He was white as a *sheep*. [barnyard animal]
write:	He was white as a *sheet*. [bed-clothes]
instead of:	This proposal is like an *albacore* [tuna fish] around my neck.
write:	This proposal is like an *albatross* around my neck. [The metaphorical meaning of *albatross* is "burden" or "handicap."]

The importance of word choice

Remember that your vocabulary says a lot about you and the organization you represent. Using vague language or inappropriate words will make your readers look unfavorably upon both you and your document. Using affected language to try to impress readers usually has the opposite effect. Always be as accurate in meaning as possible.

Refine word choice when you edit your draft, during Step 6 to Reader-Centered Writing.

(See also **abstract and concrete words, editing your draft, tone**.)

---

word processing

Word processing makes every step of the writing process easier, more efficient, and more productive. Your document will be more powerful conceptually because you can organize ideas so easily.

- Cut, copy, paste, and insert file commands simplify both organization and editing.

- Formatting options give your document a professional look.

- Spellcheckers and grammar checkers scan your work for errors and suggest alternatives.

The Six Steps to Reader-Centered Writing™ on a word processor

1. ANALYZE YOUR READERS AND DEFINE YOUR PURPOSE

Create a blank Focus Sheet™ as a template and fill it out on-line. If you've filled out your Focus Sheet by hand, you can still do the rest of the job at your computer screen.

2. USE A START-UP STRATEGY

- If you use questioning as a Start-up Strategy, enter your questions, answer them, and use them to begin your outline.

- Free write or free screen at your keyboard.

- Transfer a brainstorming outline to a traditional or list outline on the screen.

- Create separate data files for different research topics that you can merge later.

3. GROUP INFORMATION UNDER HEADLINES

- Move related information together as you create categories with headlines.

- Use outlining features to turn outline topics into preliminary headlines.

4. SEQUENCE YOUR IDEAS

It's easy to resequence blocks of text. You can even try more than one method of development to see which works best.

5. WRITE THE FIRST DRAFT

- Write paragraphs under the headlines you've generated in any order; you don't have to begin at the beginning.

- If necessary, insert new headlines and paragraphs as you write.

6. EDIT FOR CLARITY, CONCISENESS, AND ACCURACY

Editing and proofreading changes are clean and easy with a word processor. You can read your changed sentences without wading through crossed-out words, arrows, and marginal notations.

- Use style sheets to assure absolute consistency of format.

- Always proof a paper copy. Double-check formatting and page breaks.

(See also **Introduction to the Six Steps**; **style sheets**; **templates**; **writing, software for**.)

---

writing as a team

In businesses today people are increasingly taking on projects in **teams** rather than as individuals. Among these projects is writing—be it a procedure, audit report, proposal, or position paper.

Team writing takes place whenever more than one person participates in developing a document. Whether two people are involved or ten, the same issues arise and the same problems need solutions.

Team writing can be successful and rewarding if it capitalizes on different skills and maximizes individual strong points. Without proper planning and role assignment, a team effort can be chaotic, counterproductive, and unsuccessful. The result is wounded egos and a document without unity.

Everyone involved in team writing—even those who don't actually write—needs to understand the entire process. Perhaps you are the manager assigning the project or a peer who will review a first draft. You need to be aware of all stages of writing and editing so that you can successfully complete your task.

Furthermore, your responsibilities might change in the middle of the project, and you'll need to know how to stay afloat.

Clarify roles and coordinate tasks

Save everyone time and make clear assignments at the outset of the project. Every member of the team, no matter how peripheral, must know who will

- assign work (delegator)
- draft (writers)
- edit (peer writer or delegator)
- sign off (delegator or manager).

Those who write, edit, and sign off should know for which document sections they are responsible. Coordinating activities at the outset will provide an overview and allow team members to set realistic deadlines.

The following table illustrates the roles in team writing. Use it to full advantage: write the name of the person who is performing the role in the role column next to each activity.

Writing as a Team—Suggested Roles

Step	Activity		Roles		
			Delegator/ Editor Who:	Writer Who:	Entire Team Who:
1	Fill out the Focus Sheet	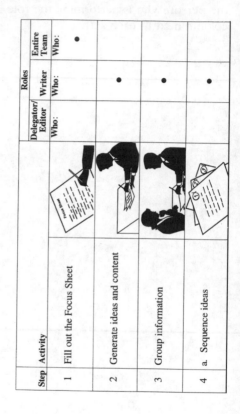			•
2	Generate ideas and content			•	
3	Group information			•	
4	a. Sequence ideas			•	

602

•				b. Deliver idea draft for approval: categories and sequence okay?	
	•			Write the draft	5
	•	•		a. Edit using the "Be Your Own Editor" (BYOE) Checklist	6
		•		b. Delegator applies the BYOE Checklist then gives writer the final draft	
	•			c. Writer returns revised draft to delegator/editor	
		•		d. Delegator returns document with praise and final comments, if any	

Team Writing
Project Planning Chart

Step	Who's responsible?	Date to check in/submit	Submit to	In what form?*	Meeting date
☞ Step 1: Analyze your audience and define your purpose. Use overheads or flip chart to share key points/bottom line.	*Team:*				
Step 2: Use a Start-up Strategy. Revise overheads.					
Brainstorm together.					
Step 3: Group information under headlines.					
Step 4: Sequence your ideas.					
☞ Get feedback on Idea Draft.					

Step 5: Write the first draft.				
Step 6: Edit for clarity, conciseness, and accuracy.				
☞ Writer submits edited draft with Focus Sheet and "Blank "Be Your Own Editor" Checklist to editor.				
Editor applies BYOE Checklist to final draft.				
☞ Writer returns revised draft to editor.				
☞ Editor polishes and returns document with praise and final comments, if any.				

• Times to check in.
*Overheads? Disk? Paper?

Delegator: communicate from start to finish

It's your responsibility to communicate your expectations to the team. Present your vision of the project as specifically as possible. Facilitate communication: make sure that all team members interact openly with one another from start to finish.

If you, as delegator or writer, are dissatisfied with someone's contribution, explain your concerns tactfully rather than harboring resentment which will only undermine the process.

Writer(s): strategy is in, ego is out

Avoid this common mistake: falling in love with your own words, digging in your heels, and refusing to change a syllable. Such intractability is divisive to the team.

Never lose sight of the overall purpose of the document. Remain flexible and open to the best interests of your company, not your ego.

Your common language: The Six Steps to Reader-Centered Writing™

Working systematically through the Six Steps to Reader-Centered Writing will help team members define roles, coordinate functions, and solve or avoid problems.

The Team Writing Project Planning Chart (pages 604 and 605) provides an overview of the Six Steps as well as ways to document progress in each area.

Step 1: [as a team:] Analyze your readers

Team writing flounders if initial goals are unclear. It's critical that delegators, editors, and writers *together* define why they are writing and for whom. Optimally all team members should be present at the first meeting to complete the Focus Sheet™ (see **readers**, **analyzing**).

Even if the entire team can't be present, key players should hold a planning meeting to analyze their readers and define their purpose. Absentee team members other than the delegator can fill out their own Focus Sheets, send them to the meeting, and compare and finalize later.

Careful advance preparation will guide you through the project and save many hours of misguided work.

Keep in mind that the Focus Sheet not only helps you determine the content of your document. It also guides you in choosing an appropriate style and tone—a particularly tricky aspect of team writing.

To achieve uniformity of style and approach, team members should review their readers' style needs and their likely attitudes toward the document.

Step 2: [as a team:] Generate ideas

It's especially important for delegators to be involved in the first part of this step, apart from actual research. They should present their plans for the project, highlight key issues, and request input from every member of the team.

The team as a whole should participate in different Start-up Strategies like questioning and free writing to generate ideas.

Step 3: Group information (one or two team members)

At this point, one or two team members should attack the task of developing an outline. The purpose of this step is to establish categories and working headlines for the issues discussed during the planning meeting. Organizing information occurs during the next step.

STEP 4: SEQUENCE IDEAS AS A TEAM

The entire team should review the outline and decide on headlines and sequence. The delegator, or editor if there is one, should approve the outline before the writers take over.

THE IDEA DRAFT—AN OPTION IN TEAM WRITING

How many times have you seen writers spend days writing the perfect proposal, only to have the delegator send it back because it's not what she had in mind? The idea draft prevents this problem. It is an outline or list of ideas that presents the plan for your document. It outlines the relevant facts in a strategic sequence.

Writers focus on content and sequence only, not on grammar and style. They use the idea draft as a preview, to show the delegator the key concepts of the work in progress before writing the first draft.

The delegator approves content only—a grammar and style critique will come later.

Delegators and writers should have a mutual understanding—in effect an agreement—about the purpose of the idea draft. It is to get approval of the overall outline/plan for a document.

The idea draft prevents writers from wasting time writing a detailed document when the main ideas and strategy still may be off course and in need of revision.

You won't need an idea draft every time you write, but in the following situations it will be especially useful:

- you are new on the job and just learning
- you need to speed up the process

- you have a complex or high-stakes writing project, such as a proposal

With the delegator's comments on concepts and strategy in the idea draft, writers can go on to draft the document.

STEP 5: DRAFT AS A TEAM

By now writers should know their assignments and go to work on their designated sections. If there is still disagreement about who does what, the delegator or editor(s) should take charge and make assignments clear. To ensure consistency of tone and approach in the different sections, the delegator may present a writing sample.

If there is a separate editor for the project, he or she may play this role. A model is always clearer, more specific, and easier to follow than a general description of style, tone, and format. This is also a good time to remind writers that "strategy is in, ego is out."

If the document is not extremely long, another solution to the style consistency issue is to select one writer to do an entire first draft. The team will then review the draft.

The writer and delegator should communicate as needed throughout the drafting process. Writers, remember: refer frequently to your Focus Sheet and outline. The purpose of all that planning is to speed you along.

STEP 6: EDIT YOUR TEAM MEMBERS

Follow this team editing process for maximum efficiency and optimal use of individual skills:

a. Writers edit themselves using the "Be Your Own Editor" (BYOE) Checklist™ (see **editing your draft**).

b. Writers submit their draft along with the BYOE Checklist and Focus Sheet to the delegator or the editor(s).

c. The delegator or the editor(s) reviews drafts and returns them to writers with BYOE Checklist.

d. Writers revise and submit final draft to the delegator/editor(s).

e. Delegator or editor(s) polishes.

f. Delegator approves and signs off with praise.

How to critique supportively

First, always find at least one aspect of the document to praise. That way writers will feel encouraged and will not begin their meeting on the defensive. Even in a report with many errors, you should be able to say, "You're off to a good start," or "Your opener is catchy."

Create a bond with the writer and communicate that you want to work together for the best possible results.

Second, when time allows, act as a mentor rather than a critical rescuer. It's in everyone's best interest.

If you make all the revisions yourself, your writers will not learn how to solve problems. Writers will also be tempted to turn in documents full of problems because they know you will fix them.

By commenting on errors rather than correcting them, you encourage independence, which will save you time in the long run. Often the best comments are questions, which demand that writers think for themselves:

Is your main point clear in the first paragraph?

Could you end with more optimism?

What is your most important message here?

In the case of a grammar error, define the problem generally: "dangling modifier" or "subject/verb agreement." Then writers can look up the topic in this book and learn how to correct themselves.

Editing is a complex task. The "Constructive Editing Comments Guide" will help you point out writing problems in a positive way. (See pages 612–615.)

Finally, some general reminders about team editing:

1. <u>Consider timing and be considerate</u>. If your writer is experiencing problems at home or at work, be diplomatic when you deliver a challenging critique.

2. <u>Critique the writing, not the writer</u>. Writing is a point of vulnerability for many people. Don't phrase your comments personally. The writer may lose confidence and become paralyzed in the face of the next assignment.

3. <u>Praise a job well done</u>. Without positive feedback writers may find the completion of the task anticlimactic, and they may not approach the next project with much enthusiasm. If writers have contributed their share, they deserve to bask in some glory.

D<small>ELEGATOR</small>—<small>TIME TO SIGN OFF</small>

At the end of any team writing project, the delegator or an editor (if there is one) should review the document for consistency of style and content.

He or she should delete unnecessary repetition of information, be sure all text coordinates with graphics, and be alert for anything contradictory. After that the delegator reviews the document, gives final approval, and signs off.

(See also **editing your draft; Introduction to the Six Steps; readers, analyzing**.)

Constructive Editing

How to edit constructively

The Approach

1. Make no style changes yourself; only suggest revisions. Then have the writer make them. (Of course, you should correct content errors.)

The Process

2. First, critique the larger issues of
   - content
   - design
   - sequence
   - paragraph length and structure.

   If these edits are substantial, return the document for rework now.

3. If the document does not need a major overhaul, continue on to critique
   - sentence clarity and conciseness
   - tone and style
   - grammar, spelling, and punctuation.

4. Give the writer specific directions or ask questions at each stage. See the *Constructive Editing Comments Guide* next.

5. Clearly highlight the area your comments address. For example, use brackets, parentheses, or underlining.

6. Limit the number of comments so you won't overwhelm or discourage the writer. If necessary, give general directions:
   • "Deflate the tone of the introduction."
   • "Limit all paragraphs to six lines each."
   • "Add transitions."

7. Make at least one positive comment at the top!

Why edit constructively?

When you use the techniques suggested, you teach writers to fish instead of just giving them a fish. Editing others constructively

   • saves you time
   • prevents a "turn in anything" attitude from your writers
   • teaches good writing
   • reinforces good writing.

Constructive Editing Comments Guide

Design
Is the document visually appealing?

- Good headlines!
- Please add headlines to help the reader.
- What headlines would help?
- Great headlines; add more!

Sequence
Are ideas presented in the best sequence?

- Good opener!
- Highlight conclusions by putting them first.
- Is this your point? Should it be earlier?
- Please put B.L.O.T. (Bottom line on top)!
- Where is purpose? Rearrange documents to highlight it!

Paragraphs
Are they well-sequenced and coherent?

- Readable paragraphs!
- Please add a topic sentence.
- Please add a transition between paragraphs.
- Add transitions (or linkage words) between these sentences.
- Information overload!
- Divide this paragraph for easier reading.

Sentences
Are they clear and concise?

- Clear, straightforward style!
- One (phrase) is out of place here. Which?
- Make this sentence active.
- How could you simplify this sentence for directness?
- Limit sentences to 15-20 words.
- Please simplify or divide for clarity.
- What else could you remove?
- Please try deleting this phrase.
- Be more concrete.

Tone
Is it personable?

- Is there a smoother way to say this?
- Reader-friendly enough?
- Please phrase this more positively.
- Make this opener/closer more personable.
- Reword for variety.

Proofreading
Are details correct?

- Please clarify with (punctuation).
- Will your reader understand this?
- Please add punctuation.
- Proofread!

writing, software for

Computers offer more help than just programming and word processing—a whole array of writing and editing tools awaits today's writers.

Software exists to help you prepare presentations, newsletters, financial reports, medical charts, resumes, and even screenplays.

Programs like Inspiration® get you started with such strategies as brainstorm outlines and traditional outlines—and even convert a brainstorm into a traditional outline.

Grammar-checking programs come already installed in your word-processing software or as separate packages. These programs search for errors, analyze sentence structure and length, and offer editing advice.

The newest software allows you to control the kind of editing feedback you get. If too much detailed editing slows you down, you can turn off various functions and focus on the key issues of your choice.

Some programs include three grammar-checking levels: formal, business, and casual.

(See also **getting started**, **readability**, **word processing**.)

Y, Z

"you" attitude

Involve your reader with a **"you" attitude**. *You* are important. This document is for *you*. Will *you* advise me?

Statements like these draw the reader into your document. When you send a letter or memo, either electronically or traditionally, your opening must capture your readers and make them want to read more.

The product, service, or information you offer your readers should be designed to meet their needs. So should your language. The following phrases reveal self-focus, not reader focus:

I thought you'd like to know . . .

I'm writing to inform you . . .

Our products are excellent because . . .

I need some of your time . . .

One sales representative explained that he used to write in great detail about all the features of the products he sold. Today he is ten times more successful because he writes about how his products will meet *your* needs, ensure *your* productivity, and make *you* a success in your organization.

Follow his example: analyze your readers, define your purpose in writing, and use the "you" attitude.

(See also **letters**; **readers**, **analyzing**.)

"you" understood

In a command, request, or suggestion, the verb is usually at or near the beginning of the sentence. The subject **"you"** is **understood**. This construction is called the *imperative mood*.

command:	Fix the network immediately! Resize the columns using the Table Cells command.
request:	Please come to the briefing.
suggestion:	Try resizing the columns using the table feature.

(See also **verbs**.)

ZIP codes

The most valuable piece of information you'll ever put in an address is the **ZIP code**. Use ZIP codes in both the inside address of a letter and on the accompanying envelope. Put it on the last line of the address, a space or two after the two-letter state abbreviation.

> Better Communications Inc.
> 1666 Massachusetts Avenue
> Lexington, MA 02173-5313

Mail is sorted by the ZIP code, so if you are addressing an envelope by hand, make sure the ZIP code is legible. If it isn't, your recipients may wait longer than necessary to get your letter.

If you know the four-digit ZIP code extension, use it. Your letter will reach its destination even faster.

(See also **envelopes**, **letters**.)

Appendix:
Model Documents

Description: Technical

Technical Devices, Inc.

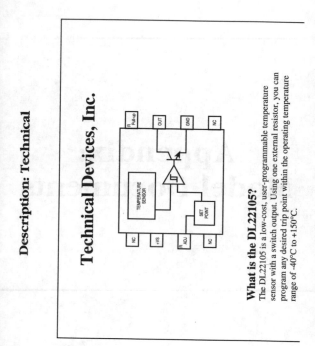

What is the DL22105?

The DL22105 is a low-cost, user-programmable temperature sensor with a switch output. Using one external resistor, you can program any desired trip point within the operating temperature range of -40°C to +150°C.

For example, once the temperature crosses a "hot" setpoint, the open-collector output switches from high to low, activating the user's overheat protection function.

How can you use the DL22105?

Due to its wide supply range (2.7V to 7.0V), the DL22105 will work equally well in 3.3V and 5.0V applications. This monolithic device also features

- low power dissipation of 250μW (typical @ 3.3V)
- 4°C factory-programmed hysteresis
- 2.0°C setpoint accuracy.

Because of its accuracy, you can apply the DL22105 to a variety of uses. You can obtain it in SO-8 and SOT-23 surface-mount packages, as well as in die form.

Diagram

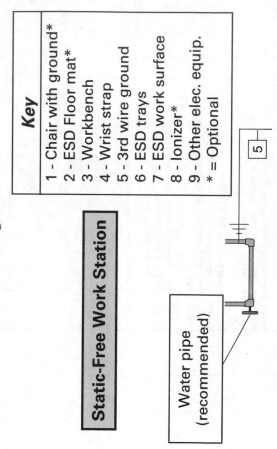

Static-Free Work Station

Key

1 - Chair with ground*
2 - ESD Floor mat*
3 - Workbench
4 - Wrist strap
5 - 3rd wire ground
6 - ESD trays
7 - ESD work surface
8 - Ionizer*
9 - Other elec. equip.
* = Optional

Water pipe (recommended)

5

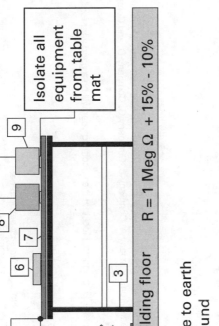

Isolate all equipment from table mat

$R = 1$ Meg Ω $+ 15\% - 10\%$

Building floor

Pipe to earth ground

Drag chain

Executive Summary: 19— -19— Business Plan

This 19— -19— Business Plan features the following topics:

- 19— -19—business recap
- 19—projections
- top five accounts—percentage
- top five accounts—individual.

19— -19— business recap

The past year has been very difficult with the war and recession, but I was able to come out ahead of last year. My entire sales territory was up 6 percent with major increases from Company A, Company B, Company C, Company D, and Company E.

19—projections

With the introduction of DST and the addition of new ES* products, I feel that the upcoming year will be a good year for ES sales:

- 19—actual: $6.132 million
- 19—forecast: $7.223 million

I anticipate growth from Company A, Company D, and Company F.

Top five accounts-percentage

Out of 21 ES dealers, the following accounts are my top 5 accounts by percentage:

- Company D 28%
- Company C 13%
- Company M 5%
- Company A 24%
- Company G 6%
- Other 24%

Top five accounts—individual

Company D   The SuperStereo store will close May 1, and its 57th Street store will be renovated. It will concentrate on promoting our new logo in its ads, and we will schedule "Vendor Day" sometime in June.

Company A   Company A will add MHC products to its SKU mix, create a Home Theater System in two stores, and advertise the VV88ES in *N.Y. Magazine*. We will participate in this year's Mozart Festival, and DST/ES training will follow in July.

Company C   Company C needs to follow up on credit issues and track Club Stereo's budget this year. The company also plans to set up Car Stereo Department training for the summer, followed by a car show.

Company G   Company G will feature "Stereo Week" in the fall, including a DST seminar in New York City. Training will be in-store with incentives and prizes.

Company M   We will continue to promote ES on rock radio. In addition, we will focus on getting in more crossover models and developing DAT campaigns. Training will be in-store after June CES.

*Always define acronyms if unknown to your readers.

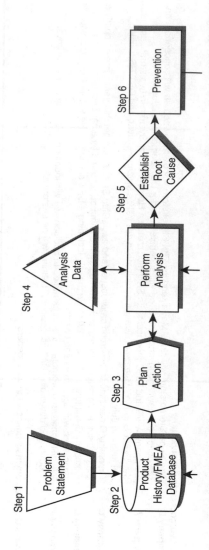

Flowchart

Failure Analysis Procedure

Step 1 — Problem Statement

Step 2 — Product History/FMEA Database

Step 3 — Plan Action

Step 4 — Analysis Data

Step 5 — Establish Root Cause

Step 6 — Prevention

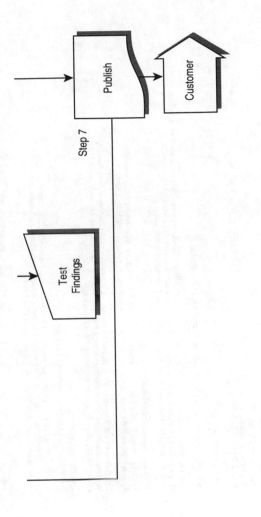

Step 7

Publish

Customer

Test
Findings

Letter: Complaint

April 11, 19——

Ms. Jeannine Jameson
The DuBarry Hotel
939 Grand Avenue
Grand Rapids, MI 49503

Dear Jeannine:

Subject: Lowering of charges for our March 13, 19——, meeting

The Blythe Corporation has often enjoyed the service of DuBarry Hotels, and we'd like to continue to do so. Before we do that, however, we need to tell you what happened at our March 13 meeting in your Washington Suite. And we'd like you to adjust your charges for that meeting.

Problem: unacceptably late setup

For this event, we needed at least six hours to construct our displays and to arrange our materials. Because we wanted to start our agenda at 7 p.m., we needed the room available by 1 p.m.

I explained this to you—both by letter and by phone—at least two weeks in advance. Nonetheless, your staff failed to complete room setup until 6:43 p.m.—*two minutes* before the doors opened. As even you admitted, the service that night was inexcusable.

Specific complaints

The Washington Suite was empty at 11 a.m. But your staff

1. took until 2 p.m. to drop the staging—three hours after it arrived in the room
2. delayed until 4 p.m. to bring in my equipment—three hours later than I requested
3. waited until 5:30 p.m. to set up the registration tables

4. failed to install the stage skirting until 6:43 p.m.

Consequences we lost credibility

Because you were late,

- we started 25 minutes late and appeared disorganized to our clients (they told us so)
- we failed to finish our agenda
- our product sales were well below average.

On a personal note, our senior vice president arrived early and asked why I was unprepared. In his eyes, I lost credibility.

How you can remedy the situation

We agreed to rent the Washington Suite from 1–10 p.m. (9 hours) for $1500. Because we had the room for only 6 hours, we'd feel better if you deducted one-third—$500—from our bill.

Action requested

Jeannine, I'm sorry that we had this problem. I want to continue to work with you and with DuBarry. Please let me know by April 22, 19—, whether you accept our solution, which we feel is fair. Let us know if you have further thoughts.

Sincerely,

Barbara Jones

Barbara Jones
Travel and Incentive Coordinator

cc: D. Gillespie, Blythe Corporation
    K. Wrighthouse, DuBarry Hotels

Letter: Confirmation

Dana Rainville, M.D.
Department of Medicine
University Medical School
Osceola, IA 50213

Subject: Patient Serum Sample Shipment Plan and Procedures

Dear Dr. Rainville:

As you requested, here is a summary of our discussions of the past few weeks. Your laboratory will serve as the core lab for hormone and lipid determination analysis for our Acuba Drug Sure and Fixed Dose Study. We will use the following system to provide you with patient serum samples.

1. Serum sample collection procedures
    The collection centers will collect blood samples of approximately 3 ml at specified times during the patient's participation in the study. The center will then spin down the blood sample, separate out the serum, and freeze the serum sample at −30°.

2. Serum sample labeling and storage procedures
    The center will attach one pre-numbered label to the specimen tube and then place a second label with the same number on the shipment summary sheet. The center will then specify on the shipment summary sheet when the sample was taken and which tests your lab should perform.

3. Serum sample shipping procedures
   Frozen patient-serum samples will be shipped by overnight delivery to your lab for analysis. The samples will be sent at ambient temperature without dry ice or cold packs.

4. Turnaround time for data generation
   We agreed on a two-week turnaround time for returning data to the centers. Please send me a backup copy of the patient data sheet whenever you send the sheet to the center.

Testing fees
We will reimburse you on a per-test basis according to the following fee schedule:

1. Hormone 1 $70
2. Hormone 2 $30
3. Lipid 1 $35
4. Lipid 2 $23

Suggested deadline for your response: October 25
I hope this is an accurate summary of our discussions. Please let me know by October 25 if you agree with this plan. If so, we will prepare formal procedures for you. I look forward to working with you.

Sincerely,

Marquita Buckman

Marquita Buckman
Clinical Operations

Letter: Customer Service—Alert

June 27, 19—

Mr. Franklin O'Shea, CPA
54321 San Vincente Blvd.
Los Angeles, CA 90049

Dear Mr. O'Shea:

Subject: Your quarterly installment appears to be overdue
Signal CPA Liability Policy No. **CL04731**
Covering the period **January 1, 19— to December 31, 19—**
Cancellation date: **July 6, 19—, 12:01 a.m.**

Are you aware that our records show your quarterly installment on your Signal Accountants' Professional Liability policy is overdue? If you have already sent us your payment, please disregard this notice and accept our apologies.

Your payment was due on June 21, 19—, but as of June 26, 19—, we have not received your check.

Policy cancellation date: July 6, 19—, 12:01 a.m.

We regret that, due to nonpayment of premium, your insurance will be canceled pro rata as of this hour and date. This cancellation procedure is in accordance with the terms and conditions of your policy.

Avoid policy cancellation

Just send us your quarterly installment payment before the cancellation date.

How can we help you?

If you have any questions regarding your policy or this quarterly installment, please call or fax me at the numbers below.

Sincerely,

 *Janet M. Brown*

Janet M. Brown
Accountants' Professional Liability Administrator
Telephone: 508.555.6789
FAX: 508.555.9981

Letter: Customer Service

October 22, 19—

Mr. Bill Doe
Mr. John Jones
RAINSTORM PRODUCTIONS
P.O. Box 5555
Visalia, CA 99999

Dear Bill and John:

Subject: We are processing your year-end film order

Thanks for meeting with me last week to discuss your original order for 1,100 cases of film. We are scrutinizing all large film orders to assure that no one comes up short.

Here is what we have allocated for you so far:

	Cases Requested	Cases Allocated	% Allocated of Original Request
Bingo Card Shows	310	170	55%
Mall Photos	180	153	85%
Other	610	610	100%
Total	1,100	933*	85%

*only 15 cases were placed on "will call" last Friday; we will ship the balance of your order this week.

Why did we modify your order?

- Some June Center locations are receiving shipments from other Quick Service Companies. You may have lost those contracts.
- Over 8,000-picture/store estimates seem too high for Acme's.

We need more details

Before we can release any more film, we need more information from you by return mail or fax. Please take time to

1. separate 19— film needs from your projected 1st quarter 19— film needs
2. provide confirmed shipping addresses and dates for all June Center and Acme locations
3. verify film estimates for Acme.

Call me when you return from your bingo card show

I will see that your film arrives on time. We want to make sure that you and Filmax make the most of this profitable season.

Sincerely,

Dick Smith

Dick Smith
Customer Service Manager

Letter: Resume Cover

January 9, 19—

Ms. Sally Grove
Pathway Computers, Inc.
1234 Madison Avenue
New York, NY 10011

Dear Ms. Grove:

Subject: Using my technical writing services

Thanks for talking with me about your current documentation project. I'd love to work for Pathway, and I would do an excellent job for you.

How I can contribute to Pathway

As a technical writer, I specialize in user guides and on-line help for computer hardware and software products. I can write about highly technical subjects in words that anyone can understand.

On page two of the enclosed resumé, you'll find a listing of my contract projects and of the software I've used. And on the three enclosed samples, you'll get a feel for my ability.

Suggested next steps

I'll call you the week of January 23 so we can talk further. I'm eager to hear your thoughts. In the meantime, please write or call me whenever you'd like. You can also reach me on e-mail at the address listed below.

Thanks again for your consideration.

Sincerely yours,

Daniel M. Moore

Daniel M. Moore
212.555.8377
DanielM15@aol.com

Letter: Sales

July 10, 19—

Kenneth Vascomb
247 Marvin Street
Norwood, MA 02062

Dear Mr. Vascomb:

Subject: Protecting your account from overdrafts

If you have ever accidentally overdrawn your checking account, you know how inconvenient and costly that can be. Why not protect yourself from that possibility with our First Draft revolving line of credit?

How First Draft works

Once you qualify, First Draft can cover checking account overdrafts up to your maximum approved credit line. What does this mean? As long as you stay within your credit limit, you will have

 • **NO service charges** for overdrawing your account

- NO unpaid checks returned to you.

Use First Draft as an automatic loan

Sometimes you have unexpected expenses or want to make a special purchase. Having First Draft is like having a pre-approved loan—just write a check up to your approved maximum credit limit, and your check will automatically activate your overdraft protection.

Applying is easy

Please take a moment to complete the enclosed application and return it to us in the postage-paid envelope provided. You can expect to hear from us within two weeks regarding approval.

Questions?

If you have questions about First Draft or any of the services we offer, please visit a Personal Banker at your nearest First National Bank office, or call 1-800-FIRST NA. We're here to help.

Sincerely,

Susanna Blakely

Susanna Blakely
Customer Service Representative

Letter: Sales Follow-up

April 19, 19—

Mr. Andrew Carter
Spring Hill Manufacturing Company
1880 Industrial Road
Littleton, IA 50300

Dear Andrew:

Subject: Finding a financial partner who's right for you

I enjoyed talking with you yesterday and appreciate your calling Fintron. Thanks for sending your annual report—I found it fascinating.

Here is the information you requested

I'm enclosing fact sheets on asset-based loans. You'll also find information on other areas of interest to you, namely:

- security through accounts receivable, inventory, and equipment
- merger and acquisition financing
- growth and income equity results.

Helping you reach your goals

Working with you, we can support Spring Hill in any or all of the above areas. We offer loans ranging between $1 million and $15 million, so we meet your needs specifically. In addition, you can get

- quick loan approval
- attractively structured, secured lines.

Why go with Fintron?

The enclosed information shows why Fintron can serve you expertly, dependably, and reasonably. It includes

- a history of Fintron, its current ownership, and its management
- an outline of our financial services
- resumés of Fintron staff who may work with you
- a breakdown of our fees.

Suggested next steps

Once you and your committee have reviewed our materials, I'd like to meet with you. After May 1, I'll call to hear your thoughts and to schedule a meeting.

If you have questions in the meantime, please call me at ext. 2345. Thank you again for considering Fintron.

Sincerely yours,

C. D. Hernandez
Vice President

Letter: Transmittal

April 25, 19—

Mr. Alan Stone
National Customer Relations Manager
Worldwide Automobile Corporation
Ten Oak Street
Newark, NJ 07658

Dear Alan:

Subject: Deliverable for Automatic Letter System Phase II: Document Model 14

We are happy to send you Document Model 14, General Response.

A brief overview of our edits
1. Where we have added paragraphs, we have numbered them 74a, 74b, 74c, etc. This system makes it easier for you to compare Model 14 with Letter System Draft 2.

2. As a result of the information you have supplied, we have developed 14 basic models. Many of the paragraphs in Letter System Draft 2 have also been expanded into models.

Two disks enclosed for different users
1. The one labeled "Worldwide Letter System Templates and Glossaries" is for your MIS department. They will use it to enter the system into Worldwide's computer system. We are also enclosing a list of template names for them.

2. The disk labeled "Draft 3" is for you. It is the contents of the enclosed binder labeled "Worldwide Letter System Draft 3."

Action requested by June 14 about Legal's edits

We are enclosing the questionable edits, highlighted in yellow, from the Legal Department. As I mentioned in my fax of May 23, we recommend keeping some of our original language unless you have objections. We did not make some of Legal's edits because we felt they were unnecessary or unclear.

Please let us know with your June 14 feedback if we are to enter these edits after all. We will assume you approve our recommendation to omit them until we hear otherwise.

Your upcoming deadlines

According to the Project Plan, we can anticipate receiving your feedback on this Draft 3 of the System on June 15. By that time you will have tested the system and given us your final edits, comments, and suggestions for improvement. This should include your final instructions about Legal's edits.

Our deadlines

Our deliverable date for the final product is June 30. We will be able to meet this deadline only if we receive your edits and comments by June 15. We appreciate how promptly you have worked with us to date to meet your June 30 deadline. With this level of team work, the rest should be smooth sailing.

Best regards,

Claire Matthews
Vice President

Enc.:   Worldwide Letter System Draft 3, two copies
Diskette for Alan Stone containing Draft 3
Diskette for MIS Dept.
Template list for MIS Dept.
Questionable edits from Legal Dept.

Memo: e-mail message

Date: Wed, 18 May 19— 10:36
Via: 2
To: rgordon
To: diane
To: fgreen
To: lburrows
To: rbrightwood
Subject: Need OK to repair switch

You'll be happy to know that I've nipped a routing problem in the bud. I just need your approval to finalize the repair.

THE PROBLEM: faulty switch at Ogallala, Nebraska

This morning the switch supervisor from Ogallala telephoned to say that our operators are unable to reach the correct positions for Ogallala's operator services.

I identified the problem and confirmed that, instead of sending only digits 09, our switch is also outpulsing the city code 84.

THE SOLUTION: add a routing case to our database

I suggest we install a new routing case for handling calls to Ogallala operator services. Specifically, we should

1. add to table 67: C=19-409, R=74, PC=XXX, T=4
2. change the sending program in the routing case as follows: CR=XXXX, PS=NP9.

ACTIONS TAKEN

To confirm the workability of these database changes, I

- tested them
- placed several calls to verify them
- confirmed that the Ogallala operator was getting the correct data. We then deleted the changes and left the tables as they were.

When I get your OK, I'll make the changes final.

SUGGESTED DEADLINE

Can you please let me know by COB 20 May 19— whether you approve this solution? Thanks.

Best regards,

Miguel

Note: While boldface headlines work best, type-style choices are often limited in e-mail systems. Instead of boldface type, use all capitals—as shown above—or an "arrow" (two hyphens followed by a greater-than symbol) to draw attention to a headline. If you use an arrow, capitalize only the first word of the headline: for example, -->
Suggested deadline.

Memo: Internal Change Announcement

Date: October 24, 19—

To: Accounting Department

From: Ellen

Subject: **Automated Ticket System Conversion Deadline 11/19/—**

On Friday, 11/9/19—, we will fully convert to the Automated Ticket System. After that date, the Team Managers will not allow their teams to produce tickets manually.

Rationale behind full conversion

Consistency of information
Using the manual and automated systems concurrently causes consistency problems, as the manually produced tickets are not recorded on the automated system. The conversion will create a uniform ticket system.

Improved controls
By moving to the automated system, we will have a departmental accounting system for tickets. This system will improve controls and conform with audit guidelines.

Increase in accuracy
The automated system will increase the accuracy of ticket dates and of the management reports.

Why you can trust the system

Easily accessible information
Once the information is input into the system, it will always be there: no more flipping through folders and files.

Helpful consultants
Jim and Donna will continue to act as project consultants and will be available to answer any questions you have.

The system can prorate the percentage faster than your Excel spreadsheets. Also, using the system eliminates many keystroke errors, since you don't have to input every calculation amount when the system prorates the percentages for you.

Enormous time savings

Accurate calculations	
Enormous time savings	
600 hours a year!	Mike timed himself during quarter-end. He saved four hours using the automated system versus writing the tickets manually. On a large scale, this will save the department 600 hours a year. We reached this figure by multiplying the savings in time (2 minutes per ticket) by the number of tickets the department produces yearly (approximately 20,000).
1049 tickets so far	Thus far, we have input 320 customers on the ticket system—and produced 1,049 tickets! Lucia is in the lead for the department—she has input 52 customers into the system and has produced 363 tickets. Great job!

Next steps before deadline

Sign up for training	Jerome and Ellen will provide one-on-one training for all interested. Sign up during your team meetings next week (the week of 10/29).
Read the manual	Ellen gave each team a ticket manual outlining the system. Everyone should read it before the training session to learn how to use the system correctly.
Deadline / or last - minute revisions	Submit any revision suggestions to Jerome by **Friday, 10/26/19—**. Remember, this is your system, so we need to know what works and what we need to change.

Thank you!

If you have any further questions, let me know. Wish us luck!

Memo: Problem Follow-up

From: jarcher
To: tholden
Date: May 17, 19—
Subject: Frit problem solved and fixed

Tom,

LIFE IN THE BIOTECH FAST LANE!
We have replaced the BS-II frit. Here are the events leading to the malfunction.

HETP RESULTS OK BEFORE COLUMN PROBLEMS
Original lab test showed

* HETP at 0.05 cm/plate
* 198 plates.

This amount was acceptable.

SUBSEQUENT TESTS FAILED: WE DETECTED TRAPPED AIR
Between regeneration and WFI rinse, air was accidentally pumped into the headspace. This area is between the top frit and the resin bed. An HETP test revealed unacceptable results: fewer than 100 plates.

We tried to displace the air by pumping WFI up through the column. Most of the air was pushed through the top column tube. We repacked the column with WFI. HETP tests were again unacceptable so we tried the procedure again.

DISCOVERY OF KEY PROBLEM
While pumping WFI through the column a second time I detected

  * resin flowing into tubing at column inlet
  * top frit mesh torn away from support piece

Because of the break resin was passing by the top frit. Refer to the frit diagram I placed in your mailbox.

ACTIONS TAKEN
I took the following steps:

  * replaced the top frit
  * reslurried the resin
  * repacked the column
  * ran an HETP test.

The results of the test were good: HETP=0.043 and 230 plates.

CURRENT STATUS
The bottom frit is intact and no resin has been lost. The column has been regenerated and stored; it is ready for use in the next batch.

Memo: Problem solving

Date: May 25, 19—

To: Paul Mangone, Publisher

From: Phyllis Mayberry, Circulation Manager

Subject: **Poor service from our subscriber fulfillment company**

Problem: Tortuga, Inc., is not fulfilling its contract

The number of customer complaints about our subscription service has risen sharply in the past few months. Subscription cancellations have dramatically increased because our customers are so dissatisfied.

A recent survey shows that customer complaints fall into the following categories:

- payment not credited   37%
- change of address or status not processed 26%
- complaints unanswered   24%
- magazine delivered late   13%.

Tortuga's contract promises a one-month processing time, but the company is taking two to three months to respond to customers.

Recommended solution: switch to Levrier, Inc.

Since we can trace all problems except late delivery of the magazine directly to Tortuga's service, I recommend a switch to the Levrier Company at the start of the next audit period.

Why go with Levrier?

Levrier has an excellent reputation for customer service and reliability. It is a small, family-run subscriber fulfillment company with a corporate plan of slow and natural growth. By switching to Levrier, we can

- shorten turnaround time for all subscription-related processing
- pay fees comparable to what we now pay Tortuga
- enjoy the position of being Levrier's largest client—one they've tried to attract for years. They'll be eager to give us
- excellent service.

Background: causes of Tortuga's poor service

- Tortuga has taken on five large companies recently. They are pursuing an aggressive policy of fast growth with two direct effects on service:

  —Tortuga's workforce hasn't grown enough to meet increased demand.
  —We have become one of their less important clients.

- Tortuga has had a high turnover rate as employees are hired away by new high-tech firms in the area. Though new employees are continually being hired, it takes four to six months' training to get a new processor up to speed.

We have considered other solutions but rejected them

We could stay with Tortuga under a written agreement that they fix these problems immediately and promise to stay up to speed on our account. However, I don't think this would work. Given the speed with which Tortuga has been growing in recent months, I don't think they can guarantee us better service until they develop solutions to more profound management problems.

Next steps

I'll be calling soon to get your reaction and to discuss a plan for switching over to Levrier.

Minutes: Meeting —Table Format

"The Winner's Circle": Hardware Build and Repair

Meeting topic: Bringing the RAMAR system on-line

Meeting Date: March 21, 19—

Desired outcome(s): to enhance the process for bringing the new RAMAR system on-line

Participants: Lawrence Belosian, Jeannie Clark, Alan Davis, Frank Jameson, Carmen Ortega, Manuel Ramos, Benny Smith, James Wu

Facilitator: Benny Smith

Recorder: Carmen Ortega

Agenda topic	Discussion/decisions/who spoke?	Action steps	Who's responsible?	Deliverables/ outcome?	Deadline
1. Review the GR-4 system and RAMAR	Jeannie Clark gave an overview of the GR-4 and RAMAR systems	Follow-up at next meeting? Yes			
		1. Compile equipment and materials list	James	Distribute at meeting	4/4
2. Continue developing the specifications for RAMAR X-Y process	• Lawrence Belosian demonstrated how GR-4's X-Y coordinates parallel those of RAMAR	Follow-up at next meeting? Yes			

• Benny Smith answered questions about software specifications and whom to contact
 	
  a. Alan: Can we get an Ethernet spot?
 	
  b. Frank: What SPC chart will work best? Alternatives?
 	
Decision: The specifications are ready to finalize.
	1. Write up new procedures
	
	2. Benny and Alan to set up Ethernet spot
	
	3. Get all info and charts from Harold Green
		Carmen
		
		Benny
		
		Jeannie
			Draft completed for first review
			
			Ethernet O.K.d or new plan made
			
			Present all chart options at next meeting
				3/28
				
				3/24
				
				4/4

3. Next meeting	Tuesday, April 4 2–4 PM Fourth floor conference room		Carmen	**Agenda:** Completing the specifications for X-Y coordinates	3/31

Minutes: Meeting—Text Format

"The Winner's Circle": Hardware Build and Repair

Date of meeting	March 21, 19—
Desired outcome(s)	To enhance the process for bringing the new RAMAR system on-line
Facilitator	Benny Smith
Recorder	Carmen Ortega
Attendees	Frank Jameson — Vice President, MIS
	Manuel Ramos — Plant Supervisor
	Lawrence Belosian — Supervisor for Technical Services
	Jeannie Clark — Software Development Specialist
	Alan Davis — Software Development Specialist
	Benny Smith — Software Development Specialist
	James Wu — Computer Analyst
	Carmen Ortega — Office Manager
Topics	1. Review the GR-4 system and RAMAR
	2. Continue developing the specifications for RAMAR X-Y process
Discussion/decisions	1. Jeannie Clark gave an overview of the GR-4 and RAMAR systems.
	2. Lawrence Belosian demonstrated how GR-4's X-Y coordinates parallel those of RAMAR.

3. Benny Smith answered questions about software specifications and whom to contact next.

<u>Decision</u>: The specifications are ready to finalize.

Action steps & deadlines

- **Carmen**— Write up new procedures for specification documents.

  <u>Deadline: March 28</u> — Draft completed for first review

- **Benny**— Work with Alan to see if we can get an Ethernet spot on the system.

  <u>Deadline: March 24</u>

- **Jeannie**— Ask Harold Green what SPC chart will work best. Report to us and show us chart options.

  <u>Deadline: April 4</u> — Our next meeting

- **James**— a. Compile an equipment and materials list.
  b. Distribute list to all.

  <u>Deadline: April 4</u> — Our next meeting

Next meeting   Tuesday, April 4, 19—

2–4 PM

Fourth floor conference room

Agenda: Completing the specifications for X-Y coordinates

Procedure: Medicine dispenser

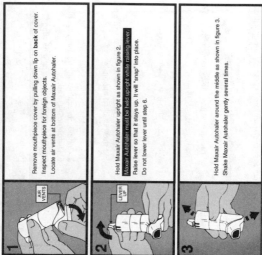

1. Remove mouthpiece cover by pulling down lip on **back** of cover.
Inspect mouthpiece for foreign objects.
Locate air vents at bottom of Maxair Autohaler.

2. Hold Maxair Autohaler upright as shown in figure 2.
Maxair Autohaler must be held upright while raising lever
Raise lever so that it stays up. It will "snap" into place.
Do not lower lever until step 6.

3. Hold Maxair Autohaler around the middle as shown in figure 3.
Shake Maxair Autohaler gently several times.

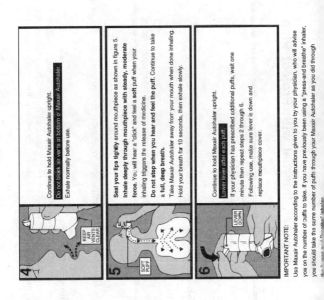

4 KEEP AIR VENTS CLEAR

Continue to hold Maxair Autohaler upright.
Do not block air vents at bottom of Maxair Autohaler.
Exhale normally before use.

5 SOFT PUFF

Seal your lips tightly around mouthpiece as shown in figure 5. Inhale deeply through mouthpiece with steady, moderate force. You will hear a 'click' and feel a soft puff when your inhaling triggers the release of medicine.
Do not stop when you hear and feel the puff. Continue to take a full, deep breath.
Take Maxair Autohaler away from your mouth when done inhaling.
Hold your breath for 10 seconds, then exhale slowly.

6 LEVER DOWN

Continue to hold Maxair Autohaler upright.
Lower lever after each puff.
If your physician has prescribed additional puffs, wait one minute then repeat steps 2 through 6.
Following use, make sure lever is down and replace mouthpiece cover.

IMPORTANT NOTE:

Use Maxair Autohaler according to the instructions given to you by your physician, who will advise you on the number of puffs to take. If you have previously been using a "press-and-breathe" inhaler, you should take the same number of puffs through your Maxair Autohaler as you did through

Proposal: Internal with Project Plan

To: Georgia Nolan, HR Director, Beaucrest Books
           Ken White, Systems Specialist, Beaucrest Books

           cc: John Haley

From: Kimberly Smith, HR Systems Specialist

Date: May 5, 19—

Subject: **Suggest immediate installation of the HR1 Standalone Site System**

Thanks for our conversation last week about the HR Standalone Site System. I'm excited about it. With this data base, we can streamline our operation and better serve our people. Here are my thoughts:

We must act now

There is just one site license available at this time; I don't know when I'll get more, and we need this system now. With the HR1, we can update our insurance reports, catalogue our record keeping, and do much more. We should move on this opportunity immediately.

What will it cost?

Our three-year contract will cost an annual maintenance support fee of only $_____. According to the HR1 rep, that price will go up next year. So if we move now, we'll stay at the lower fee until 19—.

How will the system benefit us?

Once we've installed the system, we'll be able to run our own reports and have quick access to current employee data including

- demographics
- compensation
- insurance coverage
- dependent information.

How do you get your data?

The initial database comes with the system when we install it. After that, we will receive bi-weekly update diskettes and instructions for installation. The updates will follow our payroll cycle. *You must install and return them immediately.*

Actions required and deadlines

I suggest we follow this schedule:

Action	Date Due	Who's responsible?
Purchase and set up PC according to these specifications:	8/1	Georgia Nolan
• Pentium microprocessor		Ken White
• 810 MB HD (minimum)		
• 16 MB RAM (minimum)		
• configured for expanded memory.		
Install dial-in software (Carbon Copy)	8/30	Ken White
Review, customize, and create site system	8/30	Kimberly Smith
Install system at site	9/15	Kimberly Smith
Train users at site	9/15	Kimberly Smith
Review special requests	9/15	Georgia Nolan
		Kimberly Smith

Training

I will provide training once the system is in place. Training components will include

- documentation, quick card, and security
- security and setup
- screen review and moving through the system
- fields and descriptions
- menus
- report writing.

Suggested next steps—goal: by July 29

This is a rough summary of the project plan. If there is anything you'd like to include or change, please call me by July 29 at 508.555.3124, or send an e-mail to my BB/Shoptalk address: KSmith3.

Thanks for your help—I hope we can move on this soon.

Proposal: Sales

The following are abbreviated excerpts from a sales proposal. They are designed to give you the flavor, style, and format of a finished product. Please read the text entry under *P* for detailed advice on proposals.

Title Page

Foster-Miller

Designing an Aircrew Personnel
Environmental Control System
(APECS)

Submitted to
U.S. Air Force

July 1, 19—

Attention: Judy Monroe
123 First Avenue
The Air Force Base, USA 12345

Submitted by: Foster-Miller
350 Second Avenue
Waltham, MA 02154

Table of Contents

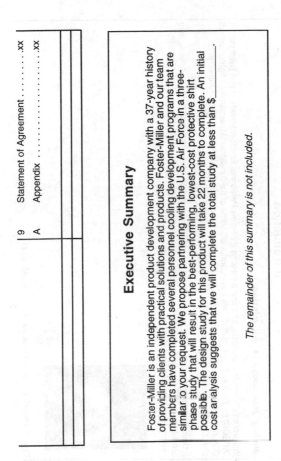

Executive Summary

Foster-Miller is an independent product development company with a 37-year history of providing clients with practical solutions and products. Foster-Miller and our team members have completed several personnel cooling development programs that are similar to your request. We propose partnering with the U.S. Air Force in a three-phase study that will result in the best-performing, lowest-cost protective shirt possible. The design study for this product will take 22 months to complete. An initial cost analysis suggests that we will complete the total study at less than $_____.

The remainder of this summary is not included.

Introduction

Meeting your needs is our mission

We propose to design, fabricate, and test a prototype Aircrew Personnel Environmental Control System (APECS) for F-15 and F-16 aircraft. We have conducted some of the fundamental research on fighter aircraft ECS humidity control and mist separation. You need a solution to your problem: a simple-to-implement, direct cooling device for your aircrew.

Solutions are our business. The answer to your need is a system that will cool aircrew, particularly while they are wearing NBC (nuclear, biological, and chemical) protective gear and an anti-G pressure suit. The shirt system is shown in figure 1-1.

The highest performance at the lowest cost

Microclimate cooling will cool each crew member with a garment that provides direct or close contact of cooling air or water to the torso. The APECS will remove 200W from each wearer. To minimize the life-cycle cost of providing this additional capability, we will design the APECS to interface with the existing aircraft Environmental Control System (ECS). We can do this without affecting the performance or operation of the ECS

Proposed Procedures

A Team: Foster-Miller and the U.S. Air Force

Foster-Miller has assembled an experienced and broadly competent team for this program. We consider you, the U.S. Air Force, a part of this team. We will work closely with you to understand the background, constraints, and human factors that are vital to success.

Foster-Miller's Responsibilities

As the prime contractor, Foster-Miller will be responsible for

- overall strategy
- integration
- technical solutions and management
- program budget and schedule
- performing most of the program effort.

Implementation Plan

Summary of Design Study: Three phases

Phase I

Our six-month design study will examine alternative concepts and technologies to define one or more good approaches. The Air Force Contracting Officer will approve one concept for more critical examination and definition in Phase II.

Phase II

Phase II will be an eight-month effort. The team will develop a detailed design for the prototype APECS. After the Air Force Contracting Officer approves the prototype design, we will undertake Phase III.

Phase III

In seven months we will develop and test a realistic prototype APECS. We suggest a follow-up project to verify the product in a live thermal stress environment at DCIEM or a similar environmental test facility.

Qualifications

Three uniquely qualified organizations will assist us as subcontractors or consultants.

Carleton Technologies Inc., Florida

Responsibility: Flight suit integration and cooling garments. Carleton Technologies Inc. will be responsible for the cooling garment, including the physiology of microclimate cooling liquid and air cooling garments. Their successful combat experience in three conflicts makes them well-suited for this design challenge.

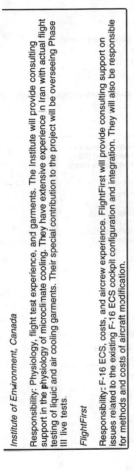

Institute of Environment, Canada

Responsibility: Physiology, flight test experience, and garments. The Institute will provide consulting support in the physiology of microclimate cooling. They have extensive experience in Iran with actual flight testing of liquid and air cooling garments. Their special contribution to the project will be overseeing Phase III live tests.

FlightFirst

Responsibility: F-16 ECS, costs, and aircrew experience. FlightFirst will provide consulting support on issues related to the existing F-16 ECS cockpit configuration and integration. They will also be responsible for methods and costs of aircraft modification.

Additional sections not included in excerpt.

Report: Formal

Since it is impossible to reproduce a full-length report in this book we offer an excerpt from a typical report, including
- title page
- abbreviated table of contents
- executive summary
- two pages from the body of the report—section 5—to show organization and layout.

Note especially the
- headline level format
- combination of paragraphs with bulleted and numbered passages.

Remember to number every page.

Consult the **reports** and **executive summaries** entries for advice on writing reports.

Title Page

**Assessment of New System Prototypes:
The Supply Distribution Project (SDP)
The Automated Manifest System (AMS)**

Prepared for:
Research, Inc.

Prepared by:
*Michael Wolfe, Chief
Intermodal and Logistics Systems Division
Volpe Center*

March, 19—

**Abbreviated Table of Contents
(selected subsections only)**

Table of Contents

Section 1: Executive Summary

Objective of the study (section 2)

This report presents Volpe Center's performance assessment of two system demonstrations for Research, Inc.:
1. the Supply Distribution Project (SDP)
2. the Automated Manifest System (AMS).

Recommendations: deploy SDP and AMS to supply depots (section 3)

Both systems generated significant benefits at Research, Inc. Their implementation–or variations tailored to individual sites–would yield major improvements in depot operating efficiency.

Results: SDP and AMS performance (section 4)

Reduced processing time

Both SDP and AMS generated meaningful reductions in pipeline processing time compared to the baseline business process:
- SDP's depot implementation for Research, Inc., saved an average of 2.0 working days.
- AMS's installation level implementation saved half a day.

Labor savings

SDP and AMS also streamlined processes. Using these systems, it is possible to reduce labor input while speeding up process time.

Implementation plan: provide complete system support (section 6)

Volpe Center recommends providing
1. limited full-time on-site support for new users
2. dedicated user support
3. detailed, user-friendly documentation.

Only with such support will it be possible to duplicate the field implementation successes of SDP and AMS. A detailed implementation plan is presented in section 6.

Assessment methodology (section 5)

This study included qualitative and quantitative assessments, tempered by constraints of cost and feasibility. The Volpe Center team studied processing time and labor requirements, qualitatively. Quantitative methods were applied to manifest accuracy, automatic reconciliation, receipt confirmation, and in-transit visibility.

The assessment team also devoted considerable effort to testing and evaluation.

Although abridged, this summary highlights the information a good summary will contain.

Section 5: Assessment Methodology

Section 5 explains the analytical framework and assessment methodology:
1. Section 5.1 describes the *quantitative* methods.
2. Section 5.2 summarizes the *quantitative* methodology.
3. Sections 5.3–5.7 discuss the *quantitative* analyses in detail.

A comprehensive study of the impact of new technologies on logistics processes requires both qualitative and quantitative assessments. Our assessment team used qualitative methods to study
• processing time
• labor requirements.

We applied quantitative methods to
• manifest accuracy
• automatic reconciliation
• receipt confirmation
• in-transit visibility.

5.1. Qualitative methodology

5.1.1. Test observations

(Section not included in excerpt.)

5.1.2. Participant survey

(Section not included in excerpt.)

5.2. Overview of quantitative methodology

Our three-part quantitative methodology is illustrated in Figure 5-1 and explained in depth in sections 5.3 through 5.7. *(Section not included in excerpt.)*

5.2.1: Business process analysis.
A detailed review of the business processes at the depot and both installations.
5.2.2: Data collection.
The project required systematic information to be gathered both before and after the implementation of both SDP and AMS.
5.2.3: Modeling and analysis.
Using complex probability-based tools, the team was able to draw conclusions based upon the field measurements.

Figure 5-1
Quantitative Methodology

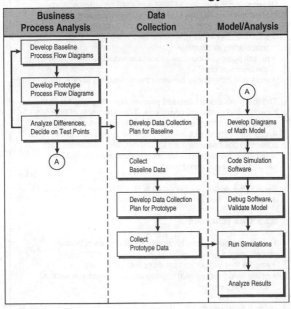

5.2.1. Business process analysis

Determining the impact of SDP and AMS on order-delivery processing time required the assessment team to thoroughly understand
- baseline operation: how processes were performed before introducing automation
- prototype operation: how processes would be performed using the new systems
- essential differences between the two modes of operation.

The team developed detailed process flow diagrams for both baseline and prototype operations. These two sets of flow diagrams were then analyzed to identify process differences. Areas with differences were highlighted as potential data collection points for field measurement. We considered cost, feasibility, and statistical impact and evaluated alternatives before finalizing the test points.

Section 5.3 discusses the process flow diagrams. Section 5.4 describes the test point selection process.

5.2.2. Data collection

The assessment team developed detailed data collection procedures to
- ensure that proper sample sizes were collected
- guide field personnel in making accurate measurements at each test point.

Section 5.5 describes the data collection process in detail. Here is a summary:

1. Data were collected during the baseline and prototype phases.
2. On a daily basis, field personnel entered data into a specially developed computer program for transfer to the Volpe Center.
3. At the Center, data were "scrubbed" for reasonableness and filed for analysis.

5.2.3. Modeling and analysis

The assessment team developed a simulation model to aid in impact analysis. Using this model, we were able to avoid the prohibitive cost and operational disruption required for universal measurement of field operations. Data gathering was not permitted to change "business-as-usual" routines, nor were goods specially marked to trace the same item through multiple test points.

Simulation also allowed us to filter out the impact of many variables that were not affected by either SDP or AMS. For example, the model eliminated transportation delays.

We combined the baseline and prototype results of the model with a statistical package to generate the improvement or difference data. This methodology allowed us to determine the impact of SDP and AMS on processing time and required labor points.

Report: Trip

Date: July 16, 19—

To: John Payne

From: Joe Truller

Subject: Following up on our time together

Thank you for a productive visit. I enjoyed seeing you again and working with you.

We accomplished our objectives

I appreciated the opportunity to meet prominent physicians from the Medical Hospital. These included an important heart transplant cardiologist and a key ophthalmologist.

We also had time to discuss

- your progress toward sales objectives
- your suggestions for the upcoming District Meeting
- your role in programs for your territory in early 19—.

Your product discussions were well done

Throughout the day, your product discussions were succinct, hard hitting, and results oriented. Responding to your sense of urgency, those you visited gave you the time needed for your calls. You tactfully convinced both paramedical staff and physicians to prescribe your products.

You are getting results

With this approach, you are progressing toward objectives. Your performance on your activity reports reflects this progress.

We discussed your plans for PharmaE and PharmaD

PharmaE   During our conference time, we also discussed your plans for special programs on PharmaE for the rest of 19— and early 19—. I agreed that your plans for PharmaE in early 19— will continue the momentum you established this year.

PharmaD   You also gave me your ideas for the promotional overview of PharmaD at the coming district meeting. I was pleased to see your more proactive approach as district product coordinator for PharmaD.

Action requested: replace tires on fleet vehicle

Our inspection of your fleet vehicle showed everything to be in order except for the tires. As soon as possible, please get approval from Fleet to replace them.

Next steps

As we agreed, I look forward to receiving several brief memos from you by February 1 following up on these issues:

- your suggestions for the upcoming District Meeting
- ideas for your role in programs for your territory in early 19—
- the minor adjustments in your PharmaB and/or PharmaC sequencing
- increased product discussions on PharmaD for the rest of this quarter
- your special program plans for PharmaE in early 19—.

Luck is what happens when planning meets opportunity

You're showing fine progress. Thank you again for a most productive visit.

Index

Deborah Dumaine

Deborah has been changing the way corporations write since 1978. She is

- the founder of Better Communications Inc.—a national management-training and consulting firm specializing in reader-centered writing

- the author of the best-selling book *Write to the Top™: Writing for Corporate Success* (Random House)—also available in Chinese

- an acknowledged pioneer in diagnostic writing skill development

- a contributor to the World Book Encyclopedia

- a member of the Instructional Systems Association and the American Society for Training and Development.

Deborah holds graduate and undergraduate degrees from Smith College and studied at the University of Iowa.